Exposing the Third Reich

American Warriors

Throughout the nation's history, numerous men and women of all ranks and branches of the U.S. military have served their country with honor and distinction. During times of war and peace, there are individuals whose exemplary achievements embody the highest standards of the U.S. armed forces. The aim of the American Warriors series is to examine the unique historical contributions of these individuals, whose legacies serve as enduring examples for soldiers and citizens alike. The series will promote a deeper and more comprehensive understanding of the U.S. armed forces.

Series editor: Roger Cirillo

An AUSA Book

EXPOSING THE THIRD REICH

Colonel Truman Smith in Hitler's Germany

Henry G. Gole

University Press of Kentucky

Scholarly publisher for the Commonwealth,
serving Bellarmine University, Berea College, Centre College of Kentucky, Eastern Kentucky University, The Filson Historical Society, Georgetown College, Kentucky Historical Society, Kentucky State University, Morehead State University, Murray State University, Northern Kentucky University, Transylvania University, University of Kentucky, University of Louisville, and Western Kentucky University.

Editorial and Sales Offices: The University Press of Kentucky
663 South Limestone Street, Lexington, Kentucky 40508-4008
www.kentuckypress.com

17 16 15 14 13   5 4 3 2 1

Maps by Dick Gilbreath, University of Kentucky Cartography Lab.

Library of Congress Cataloging-in-Publication Data

Gole, Henry G., 1933-
Exposing the Third Reich : Colonel Truman Smith in Hitler's Germany / Henry G. Gole.
p. cm. — (American warriors)
Includes bibliographical references and index.
ISBN 978-0-8131-4176-3 (hardcover : alk. paper) – ISBN 978-0-8131-4177-0 (epub) – ISBN 978-0-8131-4178-7 (pdf)
1. Germany—History—1933-1945. 2. Smith, Truman, 1893-1970. 3. Military attaches—United States—Biography. 4. United States. Army—Officers—Biography. I. Title.
DD256.5.G5944 2013
943.086—dc23   2013008901

This book is printed on acid-free paper meeting the requirements of the American National Standard for Permanence in Paper for Printed Library Materials.

Manufactured in the United States of America.

Member of the Association of
American University Presses

To Irene and Henry Gole,
who paid my high school tuition
when the cupboard was bare

Contents

Foreword

During World War I, Truman Smith acquired a distinguished record as an infantry officer commanding a company and later a battalion in combat. After the war he served in the occupation troops stationed in Coblenz. Then, in the twenty years between the world wars, he spent two four-year tours in Germany as an assistant military attaché and, then, as the military attaché. During the first tour in the 1920s, he became good friends with several of the German officers and was able to maintain those friendships after Hitler became dictator. Between these tours, he attended several of the army schools in the United States, and, at Fort Benning, he became one of the select group known as the Marshall Men. He also spent two years as a battalion commander in Hawaii. Although he developed diabetes, which in the army requires retirement, General George C. Marshall returned him to active duty. The chief of staff knew that he was the best American expert on the German army and, throughout the war, relied on him for his knowledge.

After the war, the Smiths traveled extensively and kept up with friends, including Charles Lindbergh and Herbert Hoover. Truman Smith also stayed in touch with his German army friends, including Hans Speidel, a World War II general who became a NATO commander. Both of the Smiths wrote memoirs. Kay's complemented Truman's, since she offered accounts of several situations in his career that he merely mentioned. She outlived him by twenty-two years and was active until the last days of her life.

Henry Gole is well qualified to write a biography of Truman Smith. In addition to the invaluable memoirs of Truman and Kay Smith, he had access to their correspondence and conducted extensive research of relevant books and articles. His experience as a soldier has helped him understand Smith's military career. He left college to fight in Korea as an infantryman and then finished college, earned two graduate degrees, and taught high school. When he heard President Kennedy's inaugural speech encouraging Americans to ask what they could do for their country, he volunteered and took a sizable cut in his salary to become a second lieutenant.

Then he attended the Basic Infantry Officer Course at Fort Benning, Ranger training, and jump school and eventually joined Special Forces. He saw combat in Vietnam with that elite organization.

Henry studied at Stanford under the noted historian Gordon Craig and spent a year in Germany. Later, he served there four years as the assistant military attaché. With this background, he was an excellent teacher at West Point and the Army War College. It was my good fortune to meet and become a good friend of Henry's when we both arrived at West Point in the summer of 1977. Later, in another visiting professor year, we became reacquainted at the Army War College. After he retired, Henry continued to teach at the War College. He earned his doctorate under the distinguished historian Russell Weigley. This is the fourth book he has published since he retired from the army, and it is my hope that he will write more in the future.

Edward M. Coffman

Preface and Acknowledgments

This book began with several straws blowing in the wind that landed on my desk. One was awareness of rich sources conveniently located. Another was readiness for a new project. Yet another was appreciation of the personal story of Truman Smith's dedicated service to this country, which parallels the general decline of the patrician class, sometimes called "the northeastern establishment," in American political leadership.

Friends at the U.S. Army Military History Institute (MHI) in Carlisle, Pennsylvania, who had supported me in earlier work, among them Marty Andreson, David Keogh, Louise Arnold-Friend, Rich Baker, and Rick Eiserman, had years ago made me aware that Truman Smith's memoir, "Facts of Life," and his wife Katharine's memoir, "My Life," were in the MHI archives, crying for attention. After my biography of General William E. DuPuy was published in 2008, I was considering a novel as my next project. Richard Sommers encouraged me instead to tell the Truman Smith story. I thank him for that and the entire MHI staff for support and professionalism.

I knew that Rick Eiserman had planned to write his dissertation on Smith and had done extensive research. However, he had put his project aside for personal and professional reasons. When he became aware of my interest in Smith, he sent me five banker's boxes of research materials he had gathered from several archives and interviews he had conducted. That generosity was crowned with his best wishes for my success in telling this story.

Roger Cirillo, editor of American Warriors, a series sponsored by the Association of the United States Army, encouraged me to write this book as an entry in the series. Roger had been enormously supportive in placing my three earlier books with their eventual publishers.

At that point Steve Wrinn, Director of the University Press of Kentucky, entered the picture. Having recently published my Du-

Puy biography, he joined Roger in encouraging me to write this book.

Scanning the MHI holdings and the materials Rick had sent me, I became increasingly enthusiastic as I learned more about Smith from those sources and from reading letters and diaries I had uncovered.

Truman Smith was born at West Point in 1893. His father, a U.S. Army captain, one of the last of the Indian fighters and an instructor at the United States Military Academy, was killed in action in 1900 in the Philippines. An old Yankee family, the Smiths had been in New England since the seventeenth century. Smith's grandfather and namesake (Yale, 1815) had been a U.S. senator from Connecticut. Like his grandfather, Smith too was a Yale graduate (1915).

He did graduate work in history at Columbia University, volunteered for the New York National Guard, served on the Mexican border, and became an officer of the Regular Army. He distinguished himself as a commander in intense close combat in France in 1918, for which he was recommended for the Distinguished Service Cross and awarded the Silver Star for heroism.

He served in the occupation of Germany from 1918 to 1920 in Coblenz where, among other accomplishments, he was editor and principal author of the "Report on Civil Government of the Army," commonly known as the Hunt Report, later used as a reference for the occupation of Germany in the waning years of World War II. He served in Berlin from 1920 to 1924 during the early period of the Weimar Republic, first as "observer," then as Assistant Military Attaché. In 1922 he interviewed Hitler in Munich and reported his impressions of Hitler and the "Fascisti" in Germany and Italy.

He attended professional courses at the Infantry School and at Fort Leavenworth before becoming one of "Marshall's men" at Fort Benning from 1928 to 1932. He and George Marshall maintained direct contact and correspondence until Marshall's death in 1959.

Upon completing the Army War College course, Smith commanded a battalion of the 27th Infantry in Hawaii from 1933 to 1935. I served in the same Wolfhound Regiment during the Korean War as well as in the 4th Infantry Regiment in Germany, Smith's outfit in France in 1918. Also like Smith, I was assistant army attaché from 1973 to 1977, but in Bonn, Germany, not Berlin.

Smith was military attaché in Hitler's Germany from 1935 to

1939. His close friendship with Charles A. Lindbergh allowed him to penetrate the Luftwaffe and provide valuable insights into the bare-knuckle fight of the interventionists and isolationists in the period just before American entry into World War II.

Smith's published and unpublished "Strategicus" articles of the early 1940s were masterful analyses of the geopolitical situation, American national interests, and possible American military courses of action in World War II. Marshall held Smith in very high regard as a strategist and German specialist and retained him on active duty despite Army regulations that would have required him to be medically retired when Smith was diagnosed with diabetes in 1939. During World War II, Smith, then a colonel, served in G-2, General Staff, in Washington. He enjoyed considerable freedom of action as he tracked current events, briefed Marshall and other senior officials, and wrote estimates and manuals.

Upon retirement from the army, Smith ran for Congress in 1946, but was defeated in the Republican primary election. Due to his personal and professional contacts with influential Germans and Americans, he played a major part in German rearmament and selection of Bundeswehr leaders in the 1950s.

During my preliminary research, I came upon Truman Smith holdings in several archives and discovered that Smith's daughter, Katchen (b. 1924), was alive and willing to talk to me. She and her two daughters, Lissy and Kitty, exchanged emails with me and also provided photos for the book.

Lieutenant General A. C. Wedemeyer said of Smith, "Had this illness [diabetes] not intervened, I have little doubt that Smith would have risen to high rank and might have played a role equal in influence to Eisenhower's during World War II." He reminds us that the study of less well-known figures—compared to Omar N. Bradley, George S. Patton, and Henry H. Arnold, for example—contributes to the historiography of the U.S. Army in World War II, twentieth-century Germany, and aspects of the Cold War. Smith was a close observer of the kaiser's army in World War I, von Seekt's Reichswehr of the Weimer Republic, and Hitler's Wehrmacht—and he was with his friend Hans Speidel at the creation of the Bundeswehr.

Truman Smith was both a friend of Germany and an American patriot. His lucid writing sheds light on the world he observed until his death in 1970. For the reasons summarized here—and others—

Truman Smith should be more than a footnote to history. That's why I wrote this book.

I thank Gary Johnson and Jim McNally for their generous assistance with photography. Donna Bouvier, expert copyeditor, has once again saved me from myself in grilling me; then she hid my sins. She forced me to answer questions as she represented the general reader. I also appreciate David Cobb's patience and thoroughness in producing the book in your hands. Finally, brother Bill Gole and longtime colleague Dave Keough read early drafts and provided sage advice and encouragement. These good people deserve credit for their support; shortcomings and errors are mine alone.

1

Patrician Heritage

> I come from old New England stock, the ninth Smith since old John and his thirteen-year-old son Richard left Sudbury in Suffolk to try to better their lot in the New World.
>
> —Truman Smith, "The Facts of Life"

Truman Smith, born to a prominent family at West Point in 1893, was well educated, confident, and responsible, and, while he never used these words to describe himself or his class, he was an American aristocrat. Like European gentry, his Yankee patrician class knew without saying that the price of economic well-being and high social status is responsibility to society at large, a sense of noblesse oblige.

The Smith family history exemplifies the evolution of the American patrician class and illustrates how attaining that status and its attendant sense of responsibility shaped its members' worldview and personal behavior. Smith's family knew good times and bad, but Richard Smith (1621–1680) enjoyed what a modern person would call a meteoric career. He arrived in Massachusetts as an apprenticed servant to a rich Puritan. He rose to prosperity and social prominence, played a part in the founding of Lancaster and Groton in Massachusetts and Lyme in Connecticut, and represented his hometown in the colonial legislature in Hartford. His landholdings included a pasture on Smith's Neck near the mouth of the Connecticut River that was still in Smith family hands in 1964, when Truman wrote his memoir, "The Facts of Life," at the urging of his wife and William L. Shirer, author of *The Rise and Fall of the Third Reich.*[1]

After three generations in New England, during which the Smiths grew poorer, Richard's great-great-grandson Phineas Smith (1759–1839) restored the family's wealth, served in the 8th Connecticut Regiment of the Continental Army, and achieved local prominence by representing Roxbury in the Hartford legislature. His two brothers rose to national eminence. Nathaniel, the second brother,

Senator Truman Smith, 1792–1884 (Yale, 1815), father of Captain Edmund Dickinson Smith (USMA, 1879), who was killed in combat in the Philippines in 1900, and grandfather of Colonel Truman Smith, 1893–1970 (Yale, 1915). (Box 4, Photo albums, Truman Smith Papers, U.S. Army Military History Institute, Carlisle Barracks, Pa.)

became a leader of the Connecticut Federalist party, a Washington congressman, and an associate justice in Connecticut, and he played a leading role in the Hartford Convention of 1814. Nathan, the youngest brother, helped found Trinity College at Hartford, was prominent in the Episcopal Church, and died a U.S. senator.

Truman Smith's grandfather, also named Truman Smith (1792–1884), graduated from Yale in 1815, exactly one century before his grandson. He studied law and entered politics, serving three years in the Hartford legislature and nine years in the House of Representatives in Washington. He became one of the leaders of the Whig party and, according to his grandson, directed Zachary Taylor's successful nomination and election to the presidency. He declined the president's offer to become the first secretary of the interior and was elected a U.S. senator by the Hartford legislature.

When the senator's grandson and namesake had retired from the army in 1946 and was living in Fairfield, Connecticut, he gathered documents pertaining to his father, Edmund Dickenson Smith (1858–1900) and wrote a narrative of his life and military career. Truman's training as a historian is evident in this unpublished document and enclosures.[2]

Edmund, the second son of the elder Truman, was born in Stamford, Connecticut, in 1858 and graduated from the U.S. Military Academy at West Point in 1879, thirteenth in a class of forty-nine, whereupon he was commissioned into the infantry. Except for two tours teaching mathematics at West Point (1884–1888 and 1891–1895), the 19th Infantry was his home until he was killed while leading his troops in action in the Philippines in 1900. His son observes that "the regiments of the 'Old Army' were clubs in a very real sense, as the British regiments are to this day." (Truman is referring here to the British Army he knew. Later reductions in force and "amalgamation" changed the character of the British regimental system, to the chagrin of British soldiers. Prior to that amalgamation, the permanence of officers and enlisted personnel brought about powerful regimental pride.) Edmund's sentiments regarding the infantry and his regiment were clear. Truman recalls his father uttering these words to a family member. "The Army is composed of three sorts of people: Asses, those tooting their own horns, and the 19th Infantry."

In the army of this era, promotions were slow. Edmund was a second lieutenant from 13 June 1879 until his promotion to first lieutenant on 3 December 1889. He would remain in that grade for another six years before promotion to captain on 3 January 1895. During these years his duties took him to Kansas, Indian Territory, Texas, Louisiana, Michigan, and the United States Military Academy at West Point. Immediately following graduation, he served in the Ute War, entitling him to wear the Indian Wars Medal. For a while he commanded the Seminole Scouts at Neville Springs, Texas, regarded as a good assignment for a promising young infantry officer. During his second tour of duty at the Military Academy, Edmund courted and married Truman's mother, Mary Dewing Smith (1862–1929), on 29 June 1892 in Stamford. She was the daughter of another prosperous Connecticut family whose wealth derived from her father's success as a merchant in South Carolina and then as a New York stockbroker residing in Stamford. Her father, Hiram Dewing, was in business in Charleston, South Carolina, when the Civil War broke out. Being Connecticut Yankees, Hiram and his wife were interned in Somerville, South Carolina, where Truman's mother was born on 15 October 1862. After the war, the family was repatriated.

Truman writes that his mother received "an excellent education

Mary Dewing Smith, Smith's mother. She and Edmund were married on 29 June 1892 in Stamford, Connecticut, during Edmund's second teaching tour at West Point. Her parents were in Charleston, South Carolina, when the Civil War broke out. The Connecticut Yankees were interned in Somerville, South Carolina, where Mary was born in 1862. (Box 4, Photo albums, Truman Smith Papers, U.S. Army Military History Institute, Carlisle Barracks, Pa.)

for the age" at the Katherine Aiken School in Stamford. She also studied for about a year in Berlin, Germany, and, he reports, "She was the last person to shake hands with Bismarck after the Kaiser Wilhelm II cashiered him." American ladies of a certain class did the

Annie Corliss, Truman's nurse, with two-year-old Truman. Little boys were dressed in this manner, indistinguishable from little girls, into the twentieth century. (Box 4, Photo albums, Truman Smith Papers, U.S. Army Military History Institute, Carlisle Barracks, Pa.)

Sister Charlotte and Truman with their parents before the family was separated. The 19th Infantry was in Puerto Rico in August 1898 with Edmund commanding Company G. The regiment returned, reorganized, and recruited in Middletown, Pennsylvania, from May to July 1899 before deploying to the Philippines. Mother and children went to Stamford. (Box 4, Photo albums, Truman Smith Papers, U.S. Army Military History Institute, Carlisle Barracks, Pa.)

Grand Tour of Europe after finishing school, presumably to put the icing on the cake. French was the first foreign language and France the nation of great attraction among the elite of the Northeast, whose young men attended the Ivy League colleges while the young ladies attended finishing schools. But German universities also enjoyed a great and growing reputation in the United States and around the world in the late nineteenth century. Considering her son's later career, Mary's choice of Berlin over Paris is worth noting in passing.

Truman's earliest memory went back to 1896 and his father's assignment in the 2d Battalion, 19th Infantry in Detroit and in Sault Ste. Marie, before war was declared against Spain on 15 April 1898. The family was separated when his father departed with his unit for Puerto Rico via Mobile and Tampa. His mother took Truman and his younger sister and only sibling, Charlotte, to Stamford, her old home, to be near family. The 19th Infantry landed at Ponce in Puerto Rico on 2–3 August. The officers of the 19th had been eager to join the Manila expedition, then the Cuban expedition. But they were frustrated by a seemingly endless series of delays and counter-orders, not uncommon as the American frontier army was clumsily being transformed into an expeditionary force. Other regiments joined in the fighting on the island—and the glory of infantry and cavalry combat—but Captain Edmund Smith's regiment was ordered to remain in the relatively tranquil city of Ponce to secure that place and its environs.

However, on 8 August, Smith's G Company was assigned to a composite force to launch an attack on San Juan, the capital and center of Spanish military power. A forced march across rugged mountains in tropical downpours made for rough going, and Smith's company failed to make contact with the enemy before the end of hostilities on 13 August.

Sickness took its toll. In two weeks of operations and garrison duty in Puerto Rico, disease, especially typhoid fever, struck hard at U.S. forces. On 6 September, 81 men from three companies of the 19th were reported sick. Other units were even more seriously affected. For example, the 11th Infantry Regiment reported over 600 men on the sick list.

The 19th remained a part of the garrison on the island until 4 May 1899. Captain Smith was detached to act first as president of the Board of Health, Ponce, and then collector of customs at the port. U.S. Army officers were frequently jacks-of-all trades outside of the

United States, then and later. Smith could have remained in Puerto Rico, but he was eager to rejoin his regiment, which was preparing to go to the Far East, and requested permission to do so.

Company G reached Camp Meade at Middletown, near Harrisburg, Pennsylvania, on 15 May 1899, where the regiment reorganized and recruited to regain its strength until July 1899. It entrained on 17 July and arrived a week later in San Francisco. On 21 August the 19th Infantry reached Manila. After two months of inactivity the regiment was moved from the city, then to the island of Panay by ship. In November and the first half of December the 19th was involved in a series of skirmishes with insurgents, some of them small battles.

On 17 December the entire regiment went by ship to the island of Cebu, where the terrain was rugged and the enemy merciless. In one of a series of fights in January 1900, eight soldiers, five from G Company, were captured by insurgents. "All eight men were later discovered to have been murdered after they had surrendered." G Company was successful in a fight at Mount Mandagooc, during which Smith's men captured an 8-inch smooth-bore cannon. After Smith's death, the 19th shipped the cannon to West Point to be erected as a memorial to Edmund D. Smith, but it never arrived. It was presumed that it was thrown overboard from the steamship carrying it to avoid foundering during a typhoon. Truman Smith reconstructed the following account of the wounding and death of his father.[3]

In late January and into February, Edmund Smith took two companies on a reconnaissance, during which they made several contacts with insurgents. An hour before dark on 4 February 1900, after marching all day, Smith saw huts on a ridge that would provide shelter for his troops for the night. He halted the company as it began to rain and took three men with him to inspect the huts. As they neared the huts they received a volley of rifle fire. Smith was hit twice in the abdomen but continued to advance under his own power before he realized the seriousness of his wounds and said, "I am badly hit." Private Louis Gideon told the other two soldiers to get their captain back to the company while he engaged the enemy. The citation for the Medal of Honor awarded Gideon on 10 March 1902 said in part that he "single handed[ly] defended his mortally wounded Captain from an overwhelming force of the enemy."

Corporal Benjamin Foulois of G Company observed the action,

engaged the enemy, and later gave the following account to Truman's mother. The company started up the hill when they heard the shooting and came upon their commander, who directed them to "go up and get Gideon." Gideon had by then held off the insurgents for twenty minutes, firing over ninety shots from his rifle. Foulois was part of the skirmish line that swept over the huts, killing some of the enemy, driving the others off, freeing an American prisoner, and capturing weapons. He praised the captain for his stoic behavior while in great pain: "I never saw such grit in all my life."

Foulois was also in the detail that marched to the camp for a doctor. "I'll never forget that tramp back to the camp, fourteen miles over mountain trails. It rained all night long and was so dark that we had to get down on our knees part of the time to find the trail." They arrived at the camp at about 0400 hours and started back with the doctor. Halfway back they met the company carrying the captain. Suffering great pain and subject to the most primitive medical care during the long, hard trek, he succumbed before he could be evacuated by sea. Foulois said, "Almost the last words the Captain said was that Private Gideon should be recommended for a medal of honor, and he deserves it too."

Foulois re-entered Truman's life after the Great War, when both men were in Berlin. He enjoyed a remarkable and successful military career. Commissioned in 1901, he became America's first military pilot. Taught to fly by Wilbur and Orville Wright in 1910, he flew in 1916 for the American army during Pershing's expedition into Mexico. Later, for his work in the Great War as Pershing's chief of air service, he received the Distinguished Service Medal. Truman Smith cites Foulois's description of "the events surrounding the mortal wounding of my father, [that] clearly indicates what a fine soldier young Foulois was in his youth in early 1900."[4]

Truman distinctly remembered his mother taking him to Camp Meade, Pennsyvania, where he had the last sight of his father before Edmund deployed for the Far East. His sister, Charlotte, was born at Stamford on 16 October 1899, after their father departed. She and her father were fated never to see each other.

Stamford became Truman's hometown. He describes his boyhood and youth from 1900 to 1912 as "happy and uneventful." About once a year, his mother took him and his sister to Washington to visit his father's half-sister Jenny, the wife of Senator Orville Platt of Connecticut and the daughter of Senator Truman Smith. Young

This is the last known photo of Truman's father, Captain Edmund Dickinson Smith. He died on 5 February 1900 from gunshot wounds in combat action on 4 February on the island of Cebu in the Philippines. (Box 4, Photo albums, Truman Smith Papers, U.S. Army Military History Institute, Carlisle Barracks, Pa.)

Truman attended the King School, a private day school, where, in his words, he "received a moderately adequate education"; and, beginning in 1909, for two months each summer he attended a boys' camp in New Hampshire. Truman's 1897 Christmas wish list was imperfectly drafted, but he was only four years and four months old. Nevertheless, according to his adult recollection, "Shant Claus" responded generously.

Fort Brady Mich. Dec. 7th 1897

Dear Shant Claus,

Please jib me Ihave a wee-wee sister and please jive her sometings Please jive me a chariot and some books and toy Bring Baby a ball and me a hole lot of nice things Just as nice things as Chant Claus chan make An a chircus and some tent that belong to a chircus Bring Mama a nice chape and bring Annie a nice choat fur-lined and bring Papa a nice new blouse.

Jood bye
TTRUMAN SMITH

A copy of this photo of Smith's father was displayed in Kay and Truman's Fairfield, Connecticut, retirement home. Edmund was teaching at West Point when Truman was born in 1893. His father said, "The Army is composed of three sorts of people: Asses, those tooting their own horns, and the 19th Infantry." (Box 4, Photo albums, Truman Smith Papers, U.S. Army Military History Institute, Carlisle Barracks, Pa.)

At the age of seven and a half, Truman produced "Winter," a handwritten poem that should have made Robert Frost grateful that Truman chose soldiering as a career.

Winter
A little peek
at the animals
a little peep
at the run.
winter has come.
the animals
are all asleep
the birds do not sing.
winter has come
the snow falls
fast up on the grass
the ice looks white
winter has come
the boys slide down
the hill the boys do not
care if that winter
has come
the pretty flowers
are not there now
the ground looks
white the roses and [unreadable] are under
the ground winter has come.
—Truman Smith
Feb 8th 1901[5]

In the autumn of 1912 Smith entered Yale as a freshman. He regretted not having attended boarding school, believing that his Yale classmates who had attended boarding school were more mature and generally better prepared, both socially and academically. He did well in history, but his other marks were "rather poor." In extracurricular activities, he did well in swimming and less well in dramatics.[6]

While at Yale he made lifelong friends, one of whom was Brad Coley, whose elder son later married Smith's daughter and only surviving child. Also in his Yale class were poet Archibald MacLeish and Dean Acheson, later secretary of state. Throughout his lifetime,

Smith would mingle with luminaries and high achievers on both sides of the Atlantic. His social status provided entrée into influential circles; his personal qualities would make him an esteemed colleague and friend.

Undecided as to what he would do with his life and stimulated at Yale by his study of history, Smith continued those studies at Columbia University in the autumn of 1915 in pursuit of a graduate degree. He roomed with a young man he had known at Yale, Alonzo Elliot, composer of the best-known ballad of World War I, "The Long, Long Trail." During this period, he also saw much of Katharine Hollister, his future wife.

The Great War had begun during his junior year at Yale. In his words, "It both interested and excited me. I suppose the army was in my blood. After all I was my father's son." After his Yale graduation in 1915, he had attended the Plattsburg, New York, military camp and enjoyed it. In April 1916, he accepted an invitation to join the 12th Infantry Regiment of the New York National Guard as a second lieutenant. Smith called his regiment "an anachronism in the twentieth century, a strange sort of military unit indeed." He said the officers constituted a club into which admission was by invitation, a residue of the eighteenth century in Britain and America. "Almost all of the officers of the 12th belonged to well known New York clubs." Wellington's and Washington's officers would have been at home in the clubby atmosphere of the 12th New York Infantry. In contrast, the enlisted soldiers were the London street toughs of Charles Dickens transported to New York City. They were members of the city's West Side gangs, and "not a few had criminal records."

Disturbances on the border with Mexico in the spring of 1916, most notoriously Pancho Villa's raid on Columbus, New Mexico, were countered by President Woodrow Wilson. Lacking sufficient regular army troops, he federalized the National Guard. On 19 June 1916, the 12th New York was activated. Smith later remarked, "This day was more fateful than I thought at the time. I was not to take off the uniform of the United States Army for thirty years. Also it destroyed my chance of obtaining a master's degree in history and perhaps in so doing altered the course of my life."

Fortunately, the regiment's tasks were rather routine border patrolling. Smith found "utter confusion prevailing." The 12th Infantry was unprepared for field service, unprepared for the tropical heat of southern Texas, undisciplined, untrained, and lacking essential equipment. "We officers knew little." Nevertheless, Smith looked back at those hot and dusty months on the Rio Grande as memorable and pleasant. Conditions improved under the leadership of a regular army colonel, and he made friends, most notably Thomas H. Barber, a lifelong friend who became godfather to his daughter.

And war was in the air!

Smith and his comrades believed that America would soon enter the Great War on the side of the Allies. The army was expanding and seeking recent college graduates to augment the small number of officers graduated by West Point. His respected regimental commander suggested that Smith seek a regular commission. The offer appealed to Smith, who found military life to his liking. He assented and was sent to the 26th U.S. Infantry at Harlingen, Texas, near Brownsville, where he was examined and appeared before a board of officers in September. He was accepted as a provisional lieutenant, largely on the strength of his Yale education.

He was sent to a company of the 26th in Kingsville, Texas, until his commission and War Department orders were received. While there his company and another guarded the huge King Ranch from Mexican marauders. Smith's duties were "anything but arduous," but he was pleased to be subjected to a course of instruction in the duties of a lieutenant conducted by the noncommissioned officers, many of whom were veterans of the Philippine insurrection. On 28 November 1916 his commission as a provisional lieutenant of the U.S. Army reached him, along with orders to report on 2 January 1917 to a course for provisional officers at Fort Leavenworth, Kansas. He took a short leave to his home in Stamford, during which he became engaged to Katharine Alling Hollister of New York City, whom he had known since 1913.

Katharine, known as Kay to friends, saved a dozen letters from Truman that describe his adventures in Texas between 7 July 1916 and 26 December 1916. She gets to their essence in her own words: "Disorder, unpreparedness and downright ignorance of the task of the New York National Guard . . . need no amplification from me." She says of her future husband, "He was rather inclined to spend his future life as a Professor of History. His mother urged him to study law. There was also a pull to follow in his father's steps and take up the profession of the soldier . . . events decided for him." He went off with his regiment "just a few weeks before [Columbia] graduation" and did not graduate.[7]

Truman's letter of 7 July 1916 provides the basis for Katharine's comments regarding disorder: "Tents had been forgotten." The troops were hopelessly exposed to the "dirty, hot, dusty place." And: "Our battalion was forgotten by the powers that be for the last two days of the trip down." The officers "had to buy our men food from our own pockets." Later in this letter he says that Regular Army exams were to be held in a month. Despite the bad show by his regiment, he also says, "I'm praying for war."

His 2 August 1916 letter reports that he got an offer of promotion in the National Guard, "but [I] shall go to regulars immediately instead." In this letter he is extremely critical of the Texas Rangers, "the most lawless, bloodthirsty bunch of ruffians which ever lives. . . . A great many people who know, said that they are more at fault than the Mexicans."

On the personal level, references to their engagement and to Yale, Harvard, and Princeton friends are expressed in a sweet and naive manner recalling the language of Booth Tarkington in *Seventeen* or the banter in *The Music Man.* Words like "molly coddle" and "cad" bring a smile to a modern reader. But both Truman and Kay were much more than ordinary correspondents. They were very good writers, she tending a bit to hyperbole and interesting asides.

His 11 August 1916 letter begins, "What a change! Comfortable quarters—good food and soldiers that know their business." He is describing the profound difference between the regular 26th Infantry Regiment he joined and the National Guard regiment he left. It is interesting to note that he wanted assignment to the 24th Infantry (Colored), "a better outfit than the 26th," in his own words. But the Yale man in a letter to his cultivated fiancé unblinkingly refers to the 24th as "the Niggers."

He reports in a letter of 20 October 1916, "I hear from Washington I passed the [Regular Army test]—despite a failure in German," an interesting fact. His professional reputation later rested on his expert knowledge of things German, including the language. A Regular Army commission was a great prize at the time, even for an Ivy Leaguer. A number of his college friends and acquaintances were "turned down," even as the possibility of joining the big war in Europe was in the air. Smith's class sensibilities are further revealed in this observation regarding his enlisted soldiers from Hell's Kitchen. "This camp would be ideal if the men could be stricken dumb—their talk is 10th Avenue and nothing else. Disgusting!"

He found the Leavenworth course, which lasted until 3 April 1917, rigorous and rewarding, remarking that that he attained there a degree of self-assurance never felt before. But he was modest in remarking that he was not yet a mature man nor a capable officer. At the conclusion of the Leavenworth course he reported to the 4th Infantry at Brownsville, Texas, the regiment to which he was assigned by the War Department. On 7 April the United States declared war on Germany. As a part of the great expansion of the army the 4th Infantry, like most regular regiments, was ordered to divide its trained troops into three equal parts, each to be the nucleus of newly formed regiments. To execute the plan, the 4th was ordered to a new army camp at Gettysburg in early May. There the 4th organized the 58th and 59th Infantry. After a month, Smith took leave to visit his mother and to begin a new chapter in his life by marrying Kay at Greenport, Long Island, on 14 July 1917.

2

Over There

> My head will be very high after the war, when I say, "I've been in the Infantry."
>
> —Truman Smith, letter to Kay, 9 June 1918

The war years of 1917–1918 were a formative time for Truman. His marriage to Kay began a long and loving relationship that was also a professional partnership. Her charm, wit, and high intelligence enabled her to keep pace with her talented husband as he matured and became first a good soldier and later a skilled reporter and analyst. His personal qualities, sound education, social connctions, and diligence enabled him to perform well and brought him to the attention of superiors. The brutal combat of 1918 was life-altering. Recognition as a brave leader resulted in a staff job in Coblenz and later assignment to the American Embassy in Berlin that put him on the path to expertise in matters German.

Kay adjusted to life in the army and matured rapidly. She accompanied him in frequent moves early in their marriage, did volunteer work for soldiers in transit to France, and rejoiced when she joined him in Germany after a long separation to remain at his side for over fifty years.

Katharine Alling Hollister was born in Rutherford, New Jersey, on 1 January 1898, but living in the big city in her formative years and going to school there made her the quintessential New Yorker of a certain class—a type admired and envied by some and disliked, even despised, by others. Truman wrote that his wife had a first-rate education at Miss Spence's school in New York City. She was gifted at languages and knew a great deal about art, music, literature, and botany. Her parents had been to Europe on at least two extended trips before the Great War and were cultivated people. Close reading of her writings and attention to her life reveal that Kay was certainly privileged, but she was also an intelligent observer and insightful

On 14 July 1917, Katharine Alling Hollister married Truman at her father's summer house in Greenport, New York. Truman was promoted to captain, after two years of service, on the same day. It had taken his father sixteen years to make captain. The married couple was whisked from Orient Point to New London, Connecticut, in a mahogany powerboat provided by the Fish family. (Courtesy of Katharine Smith Coley and family.)

reporter. She was a good listener, attentive to national and international issues, and adept at polite conversation even as a child.

The Smiths' was a marriage of equals. In addition to the affection they had for each other, Kay admired and respected Truman's analytical skills and his ability to articulate complex arguments in speech and in writing. She supported him in his work, tended to his personal well-being, and protected his reputation. He found in her a loving wife and devoted mother of their treasured daughter as well as a reliable sounding board for his ideas and opinions.

Kay's father, George Trowbridge Hollister, moved to New York City from New Jersey and purchased a summer retreat at Greenport, on the northern fork of Long Island that ends at nearby Orient Point. Despite some setbacks in 1907 and 1914, Hollister had a successful career on Wall Street. Katharine and Truman were married at the Hollister retreat in Greenport on 14 July 1917. The Fishes, a distinguished New York family that produced, among others, Hamilton, the sixteenth governor of New York, a U.S. senator, and secretary of state under President Grant, provided a mahogany powerboat to whisk bride and groom away from Greenport, around Orient Point, and on to New London, Connecticut, to begin a honeymoon and life as an army couple.

Smith observed, "It was a strange coincidence that I was promoted to captain on the very day I was married." That was two years after his graduation from Yale, when he had been just about a year in uniform. In contrast, it had taken his father sixteen years from his graduation from West Point to his promotion to captain, the rank he held when he was killed in combat in 1900 with twenty-one years of army service, not counting four years at the Military Academy as a cadet. The Great War saw a vast expansion of the U.S. Army in 1917 and 1918, as it was reconfigured from a scattered prewar frontier force of fewer than 100,000 men to an expeditionary force of millions.

The general turmoil that accompanied wartime expansion directly affected the newlyweds. Truman refers to the "nomadic existence" they led from their wedding day to mid-April 1918, when he shipped out for France. He commanded Company B of the 4th Infantry in Gettysburg, Pennsylvania; at Camp Greene near Charlotte, North Carolina; and finally at Camp Stuart at Newport News, Virginia, where at Christmastime the regiment was assigned to the newly organized 3rd Division. In February 1918 Truman was transferred from command of B Company to command of A Company. He remembered the particularly cold winter of 1917–1918, with the salt water of Hampton Roads frozen over and the "shabby room in the local Hotel Warwick." It was one of the "dreariest and most uncomfortable periods of our married life."[1]

Truman credits his bride with adapting well to the vagaries of army life. But as she moved about with her new officer-husband in Pennsylvania, Maryland, Virginia, and North Carolina before he deployed to France and the Great War, she confided to her diary that she had never been west of 6th Avenue in New York [City], except to go to New Jersey once or twice. That she had been nurtured almost exclusively in the gilded circle of her peers is evident in her confession that she had never met an educated person in her life who was Catholic, since in New York, at that time, only Irish maids were Catholics.

An anecdote illustrates the effect of Kay's formerly cloistered life, as well as her sense of humor. Early in her married life and new to the army, she informed a duty soldier that something was wrong with the basement stove in the quarters the government provided the young couple. It was cold. The soldier fixed the problem. She thanked him. The next day, however, the problem recurred: the stove was cold. She informed the same duty soldier of her problem. Again, he somehow fixed the stove. It was at this point that the soldier told her that the problem was that there was no coal in the stove, so the fire went out. That fires need fuel was a reality that never before required her attention. In her father's houses, domestic help attended to such matters. Kay had the good humor to confess her ignorance.[2]

She made herself useful in Camp Stuart, Newport News, with volunteer work before Truman shipped out. While Truman was in France, she returned to New York, where she volunteered for the Emergency Canteen, pouring coffee for soldiers preparing to deploy, seeing them off to rail and sea transportation, and chatting with the lonely young men, many of them away from home for the first time. Later, she assisted in receiving wounded as they returned from overseas, noting at one point that there was also "lots of tuberculosis." In 1918, concentrations of people, such as those in close contact in military units and those living in big cities, were particularly susceptible to what Kay called "Spanish Flu," the pandemic that killed more than 20 million people around the world.

Truman's battalion sailed for France in mid-April on the "slow, dirty, and uncomfortable" *Madawaska,* a cattle ship. The voyage, in a large convoy escorted by destroyers, required two weeks to make the crossing from Virginia to Saint-Nazaire. Then he and his soldiers entrained and moved across France to the 3d Division training area in the vicinity of Toul.

Smith's description of A Company of the 4th Infantry before its first combat is matter-of-fact and revealing. As a result of the expansion of the army, he recalled that he had three or four noncommissioned officers (NCOs) and a single cook from the seventy regular soldiers who had belonged to the company when he joined it a year earlier at Brownsville. Regulars became the core of forming organizations that were filled with citizen soldiers, volunteers, and conscripts, all new to the army.

While at Gettysburg, Smith got "a good-sized" contingent of volunteers from rural Pennsylvania, men he called "reliable and intelligent." By the time the company arrived in France, the Pennsylvanians comprised the bulk of its NCOs. Two other groups of recruits, unlike the Pennsylvanians, were composed exclusively of conscripts. About forty came from rural Louisiana. They were Cajuns who spoke a French patois and turned out to be good soldiers. A larger group were "cast-offs" of the New York City 77th Division, "partly Jews, partly Italian." While among them were some good men, as a whole they became A Company's "problem children." Smith said that in the fighting to come, "these New Yorkers disappeared in droves during every move towards the front, turning up at the company kitchen, days or weeks later, when A Company had been relieved from front-line duty."

At Camp Stuart the company received yet another contingent, this one Kansas and Nebraska farm boys Smith called "stolid, loyal, ever reliable." He noted that while they seemed to lack the ambition to become NCOs, they were the solid base of the company by the time of the "fierce fighting" at the Meuse-Argonne, where Smith would distinguish himself. They were unflinching under German machine-gun fire and shelling, he said, adding that he had several American Indians always ready to volunteer for night patrols. "I could count on every one of these Indian doughboys coming forward."

Smith said the company was a cross section of the American population, all in all an average sort of company like many regular regiments "stripped of their veteran soldiers to form the nucleus of new regiments."[3]

Training near Toul was curtailed by an emergency in June: German tactical success in the vicinity of the Marne River. That success was part of the great German offensive begun in the spring of 1918, whose purpose was to win the war before the Americans arrived and achieved the state of combat effectiveness required for war on the grand scale new to the Americans. General Erich von Ludendorff's strategic concept in execution was characterized by exemplary small-unit effectiveness that won numerous tactical victories while failing to achieve the strategic purpose of the offensive. Skilled and brave German assault teams penetrated friendly front lines in many places, to the great concern of Allied leadership, but local successes could not be exploited to produce the victory Ludendorff sought in his roll of the dice. The failure of the German offensive was followed by an Allied counteroffensive, which ended the war in November.[4]

The not-yet-prepared 3d Division was employed to prevent German expansion of a penetration that threatened to cross the Marne and advance to Paris. The division was successful and was henceforth called "the Rock of the Marne." Smith was engaged briefly as an infantry commander in June for the division's baptism of fire, but it was his successful command during the bloody fighting from late September through late October 1918 that marked him for life.

Considering the glowing official praise from his superiors, citations for a valor award (the Distinguished Service Cross, later downgraded to a Silver Star), and recommendations for battlefield promotion to major (delayed for bureaucratic reasons), Smith's 1964 recollection of what happened in 1918 is low key and modest. His letters to Kay at the time of the action are also self-effacing. They express love and yearning for his bride and pride in being an American infantryman, and they reported front-line accounts of close combat. He wrote at least 124 letters and sent several telegrams from France and Germany to Kay before she joined him in Germany.[5]

The 43 letters from 2 May to early November 1918 focus on Smith's first combat experience in June, detached duty at an officer school from July to September, and the month of constant close combat he experienced from late September to late October 1918. His letters from mid-November 1918 until Kay joined him in Coblenz in the late summer of 1919 record an odyssey. Smith wended his way through the confusion in immediate post-Armistice France in search of the 4th Infantry after a stay in hospital and some convalescence leave. Then he reported his impressions of the French and Germans, the Allied occupation, and peacemaking efforts. His necessarily myopic observations of battle are put in context and confirmed by official histories of the events he describes.[6]

Smith wrote that on 27 May the Germans broke through the French defensive system along the Aisne River, "creating a deep though narrow salient towards the heart of France. The French army was once again in desperate straits." He does not mention the widespread mutinies in the French army that were brought under control the previous year. It is probable that he did not know of their magnitude, nor of the great accomplishment of Marshal Henri Philippe Petain in preserving and restoring the French army until the fresh Americans arrived. He probably had Verdun and other bloody battles in mind with his "once again." In any event, although the 3d Division "was quite unprepared to enter the battle, the crisis on the Marne was so great that we were ordered to the front."

Smith's battalion "received its baptism of fire" on 28 June while attached to a French division northwest of Chateau Thierry. The prominent terrain feature was Hill 204. He and his troops were subjected to shell and gas bombardment by German artillery, but there were no infantry attacks by either side. His A Company suffered four or five wounded in the several days before the battalion returned to a reserve position.

In Smith's detached and objective memoir we hear the voice of a seventy-year-old professional. In his letters to his young wife we hear the voice of the engaged and idealistic twenty-five-year-old as he describes his impression before and after first combat. "I'm glad, Dear, I'm an infantryman. In France a member of the S.O.S. [Service of Supply] is despised by every division soldier" (6 June 1918). This comment has been echoed over the ages by those who engage in close combat with the enemy as they consider their brethren "in the rear." The rear is relative. To the rifleman on an outpost or "on line," the rest of the army is in the rear.

"My head will be very high after the war, when I say, 'I've been in the Infantry,' he writes on 9 June (note the capitalization of "Infantry"). "Oh, Kay, our boys are wonderful . . . the spirit of Pickett and

Round Top is ours" (24 June). He begins by telling Kay the names of the killed and wounded, many known to her, in his 25 June letter. They include men from the 4th Infantry and other regiments and divisions. And he has intimations of his own mortality: "Kay, if I fall, you must be absolutely free to lead your own life again. You have done more, you've given me yours" (28 June, the date of his first personal experience on line). He expresses pride in what he and his men accomplished at Hill 204 (4 July) and in his wife for the volunteer work Kay is doing back in Newport News (11 July).

In his letter of 17 July Smith reports that he is no longer at the front. He has been ordered to duty as an instructor at an officer candidate school in a safe place. His letters while he was an instructor, from late July until early September 1918, express remorse and guilt that he is not with his company and the 4th Infantry Regiment as they take heavy casualties in extremely hard summer fighting, as indicated in these end-of-month strength figures for the 4th Infantry: 31 May, 3,597; 30 June, 3,490; and 31 July, 2,499.[7] He could not know it as he wrote, but he would return for the bloodiest combat his regiment experienced.

Kay's letters to him came in batches, in sixes and sevens, often after as much as three weeks without one. A letter Kay sent on 27 June, for example, arrived on 9 August.

Among the staff and the officer candidates were friends and acquaintances of Smith's from Yale and New York, and old comrades with whom he served in various places. His 22 August letter to Kay sends "xxxxxxx, Many on my [25th] birthday." His 26 August letter reflects on friends killed, "so gloriously young and eager for battle," and, for the first time he opines that Germany "after her four years struggle may well quail."

In a postscript to his 4 September letter he wrote, "Why not come over, dear." At this point he had been married for thirteen months, the last five separated from Kay. They could afford her transportation and residence in a safe part of France. But nothing came of this suggestion—despite his mention of it in several other letters—for another year, when she joined him on occupation duty on the Rhine with official approval. His 5 September letter mentions six of her letters arriving at once, thanks her for 600 cigarettes, and reports that Joe Patch, a comrade from Texas days on the Mexican border who would later command a corps in World War II, is not dead. Truman had seen Patch's name on a casualty list and had written Kay earlier that Patch was dead.

In a letter dated 6 September he reports, "All well, but not in a situation to write as I have been the last few days. No longer exactly where we were." He was always careful to avoid giving specific current or future locations, as one would expect. After an action, however, he would usually say where it took place. In this case it is unclear why he was within enemy artillery range when he wrote, "Also had a nickel's worth of gas, and dearest mine, it isn't nice. This was mustard." It could be that staff and students went near the front for training purposes. In the way that personal letters produce non sequiturs in a kind of stream of consciousness, he adds, "as I see what chances we run over here, I'm happier than ever we didn't have a baby. It would have been horrible. After the war will be time enough."

On 7 September, twenty-six letters from Kay arrived! His letter of 9 September notes: "Our poor friends are getting cut to pieces pretty quickly. Nine officers from the 4th are on the casualty lists as killed. I have already seen their names. Poor Tarr . . . Cut down by a machine gun . . . Had nine bullets in him when found."

At this point, letters from Truman stop until 23 September, but he did send a telegram to Kay on 16 September care of Mrs. G. T. Hollister, his mother-in-law, at 930 Park Avenue in New York City: "Cable from France All well Much love, Truman." Good news, but it must have caused a fright! A telegram from France would be opened in New York with trembling fingers as one anticipated bad news about the recipient's doughboy "over there."

Apparently Smith had some free time between leaving his school assignment and his return to the 4th Infantry. His 23 September letter indicates that he is back with his regiment, though it took him six days to find the regiment. In that letter, he brings Kay up to date regarding soldiers she knows. He was located where he could hear the sound of the guns and indicated that he was "to move to the very front soon." On 25 September he wrote, "Notice the date. Tonight we start out somewhere. Compare this with the newspapers and you'll see what we are doing." This was his way of getting around the censor by giving Kay enough information to get the outline of his part in the events that were being reported openly in the newspapers available to her in New York.

Soldiers inclined to capture their adventures in writing have usually found ways to circumvent army rules regarding letters and diaries in time of war. Carefully formulated letters from the front continue to be the best way to beat the bureaucratic barriers between a combat reporter and an intended audience. A soldier's own letters are the best mnemonic device years later, good for memoirs, histories—or nightmares.

After she received this 25 September letter, Kay heard not one word from her husband until November as she read about the intense combat in October 1918, knowing that he was in the middle of it.

In his 1964 memoir, Truman says he returned to the 3d Division around 22 September, his two months of teaching at the Infantry School having ended a few days earlier. He had missed being with his regiment in the counteroffensive north of the Marne in June–July and the reduction of the St. Mihiel salient in September, but he was about to fight in one of the bloodiest sustained campaigns in which American troops participated. He resumed command of A Company on 24 September. The next day the American First Army launched the second large-scale American attack of the war, the Meuse-Argonne offensive. The combination of his letters to Kay immediately after the events, his 1964 recollections, and official accounts provide a detailed picture of his part in the offensive.[8]

"It's been over a month since I've written, a long hard month, and I haven't had the heart to write, as it couldn't be a happy letter and as I could give you no assurances for even a minute in advance." That is the first sentence of Smith's 3 November 1918 letter written from Base Hospital 25. A seven-page narrative follows. "I love you lots and as it's warm and bright, I can give you a bit of the experiences of thirty-five days. But dear it just can be a little bit."

He joined the regiment on 20 September in the mud. The company was much the same; most of the Chateau Thierry wounded were back. On 25 September the division commander "told us we were about to participate in the greatest battle of history, (so he said), and we were to do or die." Smith says dates may be confused a bit. "I'm hazy on them," he admits. They moved up in darkness, "halted and bivouacked at 3 A.M., wet as thunder Kay, and at 6 A.M. resumed the march." At dusk they arrived at the trench system and remained there overnight. Friendly troops had gone forward and "we saw batches of prisoners coming in. The ground was shell torn so as to be unrecognizable . . . I never imagined such desolation."

The 3d Division was ordered to replace the division to its front. Later Smith would learn that a new American division had advanced quite successfully, but control of the division had been lost in the advance. In his 3 November letter he says, "Circumstances required a daylight relief on ground visible to the Boche, and so it was costly."

They dug in 700 meters from the Germans, where they were shelled all day and all night, gassed at night, and lost some men. "I had my gas mask on for several hours at a time, three nights, and realized how many narrow escapes one can have without getting hurt. On the sixth [of October] we went over at 5 A.M. without artillery preparation. . . . It was very bloody. My Bn. [battalion] was an assault Bn. and before we got near the Boche, we had to pass thru their counter barrage. This was not pleasing, but necessary. D Co. lost all its officers. B Co. all but one, and C Co. several."

At one point Smith found his company well ahead of other friendlies and under fire from artillery and enemy infantry to the front. "My spirits sank. It was so dark, we were so few, and there was no one to right or left. Then out of the woods to our rear came a flock of tanks, belching fire and we hurrahed and laughed for they looked all the world like happy go lucky hippos." Advancing, he found Captain Vincent, C Company commander, "in a shell hole shot thru leg and took command of these men who were left."

Bloody assaults alternated with digging temporary defensive positions, where one was "covered every minute with M.G. [machine gunners] and snipers, so you couldn't raise your head sniped at by that artillery monstrosity, the 88 (Austrian), bombed by our own artillery, and watching my men, one by one go."

He says that on 4 October alone A Company suffered 100 casualties out of a former company strength of 250 men. Three of his five lieutenants were wounded. And there was little time to recuperate as they slogged on for three weeks, either on line or in close reserve, then called "support." But support meant one was still in artillery range. Smith's battalion commander was killed and his regimental commander wounded, indicating that American infantry commanders led from the front. The high rate of officer casualties in the companies suggests the same.

Later compilation of statistics bears out Smith's observations reported to Kay and written in his memoir. As of 30 September 1918, 4th Infantry strength was 3,662. As of 31 October it was 1,843, a difference of 1,819 men, about half of the regiment. By the end of November it was refitted and brought up to 3,515.

The other three infantry regiments of the 3d Division were also greatly reduced in strength by the intense combat of October 1918. The 38th Infantry figures were very close to those of the 4th. The 7th and 30th were only slightly less bloodied. Machine-gun battalions, while hard hit, did not suffer at the rate the infantry regiments did, and the same can be said of field artillery and engineers. The 3d Division strength as of 30 September was 27,714, and as of 31 October it was 19,908.[9] (See appendix A.)

The extremely high casualty rates, particularly among officers, meant that junior leaders, Truman Smith among them, had to accept responsibilities far beyond those for which their training and previous experience had prepared them. And they had to do that in a state of physical and mental exhaustion in almost continuous close combat with a skilled enemy. Smith passed the test with flying colors.

Casualties among key leaders made Smith commander of the 1st Battalion, 4th Infantry, to which two companies of the 7th Infantry were soon attached. His command was holding several miles of front in a fluid situation. He also had leaderless remnants of other organizations under his leadership. He was given command of one of two sectors that formed the 3d Division front.[10]

He commanded six companies of the 4th Infantry, Co. A of the 6th Engineers, four companies of the 30th Infantry, three companies of the 38th Infantry, and the 8th Machine Gun Battalion from Co. B. According to Smith, "this composite force numbered about 900 men. To command these various units there remained less than a dozen officers, so heavy had been officer casualties in the 3d Division."

His commanders retained him as provisional battalion commander even after officers senior to him became available. Lieutenant Colonel Means, a Colorado National Guard officer new to the front, supervised the logistics. Smith later wrote, "Especially gratifying to me was the fact that I knew that both my brigade and divisional commanders gave me their full trust and had refused to permit Colonel Means to take over command of my front sector."[11]

Smith's grasp of the very fluid situation, his demonstrated competence, and the success of the operation validated their decision. In his 3 November letter to Kay from the hospital, he said that Lieutenant Colonel Means "proved himself a dandy and treated me like a king."

Smith called the weather "atrocious." Constant rain and deep mud made it so. "Dysentery was rampant. Warm food never reached us. We existed on our own canned rations and captured German supplies. I suffered from hunger, cold, lice, and dysentery and lost 40 pounds during the month at the front. However, I refused to accede to the thoughtful suggestion of my brigade commander, General Fred Sladen, to turn myself into the divisional field hospital for a short period of recuperation." The tactical situation slowed a bit, allowing Smith to rest enough to continue without being pulled from his command.[12]

In a letter dated 5 November, he compared his June experience on line with October, saying that the former, characterized by "the soft fields of the Marne, the flowers, the balmy air, and the sleepy Boche wasn't really war." Of the latter experience: "It takes filth and tin cans and cesspools and corpses to make war. We got our fill in October. . . . Shaved on 2d of October and 23rd of October. Never washed my hands, whole month. Never brushed my teeth. Never took off my shoes from 4th to 28th. Never, oh never changed my socks. Kay dear—those clean, lean socks. Never had any thing hot to eat from 20th to 27th. Never had anything to eat from 4th to 7th." But he didn't lose his sense of humor. "My struggle at the front with the mud, the Boche, and the cooties (I mention them in the order of their importance) was naturally an eye opener. . . . Conducted three short hunts. In the course of said hunts, killed 400 cooties. My breed are as big as elephants and easy to catch."

Smith's outstanding performance was recognized by his superiors officially and in acts of kindness. When the 3d Division was relieved on 28 October, General Sladen sent his automobile and aide to deliver Smith to the nearest base hospital. He had stuck it out and was exhausted. On the same day, Sladen and the division commander, General Preston Brown, sent a recommendation to General John J. Pershing's headquarters that Smith be promoted to major. Smith wrote in his memoir, "Due to excessive red tape and the intervening signing of the armistice, this promotion did not become effective until April 7, 1919."[13]

The "excessive red tape" turned out to be one of those understandable—and maddening—things that happen in large organizations in periods of rapid change. When the promotion didn't happen, the commander of the 4th Infantry sent a follow-up memorandum up the chain of command. In it he outlines the case for promotion, citing, among other things, Smith's "leadership and wisdom" as battalion commander in sustained fighting while exhausted. The maddening part: "He would have been recommended for promotion to the grade of major by his Regimental Commander prior to November 11th, 1918, except for the fact that *it was impossible to accompany the recommendation with a Surgeon's Certificate of physical fitness."* Smith was being hauled about in the medical processing system as the paperwork for his promotion was adrift somewhere in the bureaucratic mill as the war stopped. The catch-22 is that Smith wasn't in good physical condition. Outstanding leadership while disregarding exhaustion had earned him the recommendation for promotion.[14]

For reasons unclear, the recommendation for Smith's Distinguished Service Cross (DSC) was downgraded to the Silver Star that he was later awarded. One suspects that with the Armistice came instructions regarding awards. It is likely that a recommendation received after the Armistice was more carefully scrutinized than one made during the shooting. In any event, Smith notes that on or about 28 October, he was recommended for the DSC by General Preston Brown, commander of the 3d Division. "However, the awards board at General Pershing's headquarters failed to approve this recommendation. Instead, on July 8th, 1919, I was cited in General Orders for bravery in action in the Bois de Foret. Later this citation was made the basis for the award of the Silver Star by the War Department."[15]

From his hospital bed, "where it is still warm and the food is good," Smith speculated on 5 November about war's end. "Certainly events are happening fast. The edifice of the German army is crumbling fast and the 'Gotterdamerning' [*sic*] approaches steadily and surely. Sometimes I wonder if another ten days might not . . . ! It would be too good to be true. I'm afraid the bad dream will last until next Spring. . . . The German army is not yet, you may be sure, beaten to her knees. Her morale is shaken, the confidence of her soldiers gone, and yet she fights on with reduced vigor but undiminished skill."

His impressions were based upon what he had just experienced, and no doubt rumors abounded as the long war largely fought from trenches in France and Belgium for more than four years became a war of movement, and Allied gains were measured in miles, not yards. In New York there was a false alarm, described by Kay, as bells of celebration rang days before 11 November 1918, possibly the consequence of "leaks" among New York elites regarding the Armistice negotiations that were taking place between Berlin and Washington. When the Armistice was at last signed, Smith was given a few days of sick leave. He was near-delirious with joy as he resurrected the possibility of Kay joining him in France (15 November letter to Kay from Nice).

In Smith's next letter to Kay (22 November), he says he is on his way to his regiment. Later, he summed up what the war meant to him personally in these words: "In this month of October 1918 I have ever since believed that I grew to full manhood and acquired a self-confidence never thereafter lost. So, despite the hunger, lice, and dysentery and especially being forced to watch the day-by-day massacre of friends and comrades, I still—in 1964—regard these terrible weeks along the Cunel road and in the Bois de Foret as the culmination of my education for life."[16]

His next assignment would take him to Germany, about which he would ultimately know more than any other American soldier.

3

Deutschland and Yearning

> Oh darling just to crush you to pieces, and love you for days on end is all I desire.
>
> —Truman Smith, letter to Kay, 29 July 1919

Smith had distinguished himself in a campaign that was brief, intense, and conclusive. As the American Army demobilized and diplomats engaged in the preliminaries to peacemaking, Truman's regiment remained in Europe to become part of the occupation force in Germany. His letters to his wife during this time reveal a new affinity to things German and his disenchantment with the French. Just as he was becoming bored with garrison routine, he was asked if he would accept a civil affairs assignment requiring close and regular contact with the German civilian authorities in and around Coblenz. He accepted the assignment and found himself in in an optimal position from which to observe Europe being reshaped in the aftermath of war. He also saw Left-Right clashes in German streets as the Weimar Republic was born. His close attention to the unfolding of these events was accompanied by his yearning for his bride and his attempts to get her to Germany.

As Smith attempted to rejoin his regiment after his hospital stay in early November 1918 and recuperation leave in Nice, he left a detailed record of his experiences in a stream of letters to Kay. Circumstances at the time permitted him to write even more frequently. His letters confirm the self-confidence he attributes to his performance in the extremely difficult close combat of October. A detached observer almost a century later is struck by his maturity and by the general clumsiness of the United States Army in France.

Educated and socialized in elite circles, Smith had limited experience with "other classes" in New York before he joined the army. That changed during his time spent on the Mexican frontier, while training later in the United States, and then in France. His soldiers earned his respect. One is reminded of the 1914 observation of

French intellectual Marc Bloch, later a distinguished historian, and still later a martyr executed by the Nazis. As a sergeant-reservist recalled to the colors at the beginning of the war, Bloch comes to respect the simple soldiers around him, remarking that in normal times his only contact with their like was when he brought his shoes to be repaired. This discovery, described in his *Memoirs of War, 1914–1915,* is shared with others who served in the trenches, among them Smith, who also learned to respect his soldiers. He was twenty-five and just three years out of Yale when he commanded 900 of them in circumstances unimaginable to his peers safe abed at home.

One commentator has noted, "The Meuse-Argonne was the greatest battle yet fought by the U.S. Army. Almost 1,250,000 American troops had participated during the course of the offensive. Casualties were high—120,000 of all types—but the results were impressive."[1] Indeed the results were impressive enough to convince German military leadership to tell civil authority that it was in the national interest to terminate the war. One can reasonably conclude that the contribution of the U.S. Army made the difference. Without it, the Allied counteroffensive in 1918 might not have succeeded. The Americans, fresh and growing in numbers and combat skills, tipped the scale in favor of the Allies on the battlefield and empowered the American president both in the Alliance and with the Germans. The Armistice, in which Woodrow Wilson took the initiative in negotiations with the Germans, was tantamount to German surrender.

But combat success and a general euphoria at the end of the war concealed serious logistical and administrative deficiencies in the U.S. Army. Poorly trained men were sent to the front, the supply system almost broke down, and the U.S. Army depended upon its allies for air, artillery, and tank support. That there would be mistakes, blunders, shortcomings under such a rapid expansion and commitment was perhaps inevitable.

Smith was not so petty as to point to the mishandling of his promotion and valor award as examples of his army's administrative ineptness, but he could have. Despite strenuous efforts to rejoin his regiment, which began on 22 November, he wrote Kay on 1 December: "The way from hospital to front is indeed devious and uncertain. Casual officers [officers not with their units because they were in transit or in hospital] all for the 3d Army are crowding every provincial city and I am lucky to get a room and some money and some blankets. France is very crowded—hotel and train accommodations since the armistice being impossible." He is eager to get to the 4th Infantry. Apparently that was the only way to get his mail! In a letter two days later (3 December) he laments that he hasn't gotten a letter from Kay in three months.[2]

At one point in his odyssey he saw King George V of England and, in a letter to Kay (1 December), expressed his increasing disdain for the French: "Finally got a glimpse of his majesty and the Princess. After these dirty-discourteous-money grubbing French race—it is a relief to meet the British." Smith's opinion of the French was widely shared with his comrades. Perhaps he believed, with Winston Churchill, that when God created the earth he wanted one perfect place, so he made France. Then, seeing what he had done, he decided that he had gone too far, so he made Frenchmen.[3]

Smith conceded, "Some few good points the French have, but as I have learned to know them, my opinion, as that of the whole AEF, has steadily sunk. Their armies nevertheless are excellent and technically the most perfect of all except perhaps the Boche army." In the coming years, he would become intimately familiar with "the Boche army" in its various guises from 1918 to 1970.

Smith's criticism of the French and his frustration at military administration and logistics were expressed during what must have been a confusing time for him and his fellow soliders of initial joy followed quickly by a return to personal concerns. Near death one day, their war was all over the next. For American citizen soldiers that meant getting home. The sudden armistice in November 1918 took almost everyone by surprise, and demobilization occurred rapidly. In the first full month of demobilization, the U.S. Army released about 650,000 men, and within nine months nearly 3,250,000 men were demobilized. But for the professional soldiers who continued to serve, it meant getting on with the new mission, getting back to one's regiment—and getting one's mail!

Before Truman and Kay Smith were reunited in August 1919 to enjoy what they later regarded as their happiest time together, Truman had to soldier on alone. It was for him a time of introspection. His letters described what he saw about him and the people he encounterd, often reverting to scenes from his October days, as though he could not get them out of his mind.

On 3 December 1918 he wrote: "Mud and filth. Night marches

. . . unreasonable orders, what a mess we went thru. One is apt to come out feeling three great thrills and a sea of dreary nothings. I blush to mention them—one changes so, up there—the attack—bayonets—blood. Your men at your elbow, and the thrill of feeling that you're where you ought to be. No flying corps S.O.S. position [a reference to a mutual acquaintance in a cushy billet]—but the glory that perhaps you'll be hand to hand with the Boche in a short moment. And then, better than the attack, the relief. Work done—head high, proud as an aviator in yellow breeches [while] muddy as a duck." And then a nip of Scotch "and we forget our troubles and criticize our generals and sit around that dear habitat of the international cootie, the German pill box, and knock all branches of the service, all conditions of life, all nations—until it comes time to take a look at F Co. or until the whiskey gives out and you roll up your coat, take a parting curse at everyone above the rank of Major and finally wander off to sleep."

Some themes from his reflections on combat would become familiar to the American general public from the Second World War, Korea, Vietnam, and the wars in the Middle East into the twenty-first century. Warrior pride, blood lust, filth, booze, various names for combat fatigue, and bonding in its several forms—horizontal, with peers; vertical, up and down an effective chain of command; and institutional, as among marines, paratroopers, fighter pilots, and veterans of good regiments and gallant ships.

Smith retained his sense of humor, though it took a turn toward the macabre at times. In the same 3 December letter he anticipates future yarn-spinning. "Now here at Toul we go over it all again until the inevitable enlargements and additions. (If it is this way now, what on earth will the stories be at Veteran's sessions in 1940?) And we linger over every gruesome detail (how Bill Jones was a damned fine soldier when alive, but he did smell his 4th day as a corpse), and how so-and-so connected with a 77 and his liver flew into Bill's lap, and he nearly died laughing. Kay, that's real wary. That's why pictures and stories don't tell the truth—that's why it's all a dim haze to you dear people at home. Society forbids all mention of dead horses and other even more disgusting sights."

Although the newly activated United States Third Army moved into Germany on 1 December 1918, to occupy the territory between Luxembourg and the Rhine River around Coblenz, on 10 December Smith still languished in France, lamenting that the last letter he

Truman wrote, "My Company A, 4th Infantry (3rd Division) taken at Plaidt, Germany, about January 1919." He was awarded the Silver Star leading that company in combat. Recruited by Colonel I. L. Hunt, he later served in the Office of Civil Affairs of the Army in Coblenz for a year and three months before reporting to Berlin. (Courtesy of Katharine Smith Coley and family.)

had received from Kay was dated 8 August. He sent her a list of the names of fourteen battalion officers killed and others known to Kay who were wounded, several more than once.

He was quite ill for a week in the middle of the month, but on 20 December he could write from Plaidt, near Andernach, "Finally in Germany and back with the 4th and one precious letter from you." From the beginning he had a favorable impression of Germans and Germany, remarking about cleanliness and the reserve but correctness of the people. Young Germans returning from the war "are all so happy it is over that they accept without question our presence." Smith was billeted in the home of a German lieutenant who had been in Serbia for three years. Although familiarity was officially discouraged, personal contacts were inevitably established between occupiers and Germans. Smith wonders to Kay what Pershing can do about that. "The French play the conquerors. Our boys can't and won't."

From the beginning of the occupation, French and American soldiers' attitudes sharply differed regarding Germans, as would the official policies of Paris and Washington regarding Weimar Germany. During the peacemaking process in 1919, and in the final draft of the Treaty of Versailles, it became clear that the Allies, particularly the French, would demand their pound of flesh, attempt to keep the Hun down, and, more specifically, to separate the Rhineland from Germany. America, the Associated Power most instrumental in getting Germany to the Armistice, was considered naive and inexperienced by its fellow Allies for apparently preferring to forgive and forget. From the American perspective, expressed by Smith, the European Allies were reverting to the bad old days of realpolitik.

Smith increasingly found the Germans more attractive than the French as people. As he became professionally engaged with German officials, he came to like, then respect and admire, Germany. In a letter of 23 December 1918 he admitted, "Germany still absorbs my interest, Sphinx-like and proud." He says that the Germans' industrious habits are showing themselves; they have little faith in their present government and are in deadly fear of "Bolshevikism"; they seem to be willing to try a republic, but they are as weak politically as they are capable commercially; financial questions, including indemnities and trade with the world, absorb them. "Germany is to me as a country more pleasant than France: more plumbing, cleaner, more industrious . . . one can feel the strength and vitality in the air. . . . Never believed such big families existed." This latter fact was not trivial. The French, Smith knew, were keenly aware of the difference in demographics. Unless France could somehow hold Germany down or break it up, time was clearly on the side of Germany.

His 25 December letter to Kay is a stream of consciousness that takes him from Christmas in Plaidt back to October days at the front, and finally to a commentary about how journalists and laymen have difficulty getting to the truth of the combat so fresh in his mind. But there is also happy surprise in his life. "God what a glorious Christmas. Woke to find the country white with snow, carols coming from a stone church echoed into my bedroom. Fir trees gleamed with candles and all seemed at peace. The old lady in my billet had fixed me up with a Christmas present of a little tree, with three candles, and I found them lighted when I arrived home. Your picture was under the Christmas tree. I was speechless." He spent that evening "before a fire in the company officers' mess with Thomas and Minnis. Both were with me in the Bois de Foret. Thomas had F—28 men. Minnis A—30 men. After I left, neither was promoted. Beastly luck to fall sick and not be able to pay the debts one owes. The fire stimulated our memories. I suppose as long as I live I shall, whenever under the influence of a wood fire, bore you with like tales. Poor Katie—the first time you won't mind it, the 250th you'll divorce me."

Thomas and Minnis had been platoon leaders in Smith's company. Due to extremely high casualties and the scarcity of officers in late October, the lieutenants took command of the remnants of A and F Companies, whose full strength had been about 250 men each. It was at this time that Smith commanded many men from many companies reduced to odds and ends. Immediately after that phase of the Meuse-Argonne campaign, when the 3d Division went into reserve, Smith would have done the paperwork required for promotions, awards, and other housekeeping chores neglected in combat. But he was in the hospital and then in transit and out of touch with the 4th Infantry for almost two months. His officers, like Smith himself, did not get the promotions and awards they otherwise would have received. That he had not been able to do right by his good lieutenants—with whom he had shared what were among the most memorable days of their lives—disturbed him very much.

Conversations among men who shared combat experiences turn to what sailors and marines call sea stories, and soldiers call war stories. Thomas resurrected Smith's "prisoners" as an amusing war story. In the midst of close fighting, Smith and his men overran German positions and a miracle of sorts occurred. Smith came upon "a Boche gift package from home." He wrote, "I halted in the mad advance, long enough to peek in—cold fried chicken, cake, honey, cheese. Remembrance of the corned willie [canned rations] eaten three days before gleamed thru me. The war was over! The grassy ravine was to be my [command post] until at least the chicken was finished off . . . I sat alone on the edge of the ravine munching the heaven-sent chicken and cake. . . . Then dimly out of the furthest corner of my left eye I became aware that all was not as it should be, and that unless I hurried I probably couldn't finish the chicken. Eight Germans fully armed were coming down the ravine. The ravine hadn't been mopped! I remember distinctly my wondering how much chicken I could eat before I surrendered. I fairly wedged it in. Not to be—they fell on their knees—threw their arms away, and I decided to postpone surrendering and begin on the honey. Shades of the five hot meals I had from September 29th to October 28th. I can still taste the chicken."

He ends this bit of self-mockery by citing exaggerated press and public relations accounts of the fighting in which he was involved as "unadulterated bunk." He adds, "this bosh is all right for propaganda, [but] there's just about the same amount of bravery and cowardice. It isn't as glorious as it sounds." Furthermore, "Truth is the rarest article in the world, and the most drab. Somewhere beneath the shroud of war, there is much heroism . . . but if you believe for a minute that our matchless army and our heroic men were the perfect celestial glory—why Katie dearest, drown it. Otherwise honey we'll fight the rest of our life."

Apparently his letters from Kay, his mother, and others were filled with tales of American heroism and glory that distorted the truth, causing Smith to write on 27 December, "I'm just moralizing and wondering if everyone back in America is as hysterical as they sound in the newspaper. The only heroes I've seen either had an unfortunate love affair, were a trifle nutty, or found some excellent Scotch." He thus confirms the old saw: the first casualty in war is truth.

But then he returns to the most pressing issue: prospects for Kay getting to Europe. He has a seven-day leave due, and wants to cut the red tape keeping Kay from Europe. "Why not try Guggenheim? She sounds like a person who could handle even a Democratic administration." As George Orwell revealed, some animals are more equal than other animals. Patricians have known that for a long time. Smith was perfectly prepared to use the political influence of a distinguished New York family to get Kay to Europe—soonest. Here we see that sense of entitlement that often accompanies noblesse oblige.

Smith's letters from mid-December 1918 to mid-March 1919 are a mix of the personal, mostly his yearning for his wife and repeated references to finding a way to get her to Europe, and regimental news about men Kay knew, gossip about friends in New York and Connecticut, and his observations about Germany, particularly the Rhineland. During this period he was back in the 4th Infantry, becoming a bit bored with the routine, but increasingly attracted to the culture, architecture, and omnipresent reminders of the past in Germany. Kay's letters, written from August to November, were still arriving in batches, and on at least one occasion, more than twenty arrived in one batch. That meant that in responding to Kay's letters Smith addressed both the issues and topics of yesterday, those rough times at the front, while registering in a more relaxed manner his impressions of life around him.

He responded to Kay's sympathetic mention of "shell shock" by saying 2.5 percent of the cases were legitimate and 97.5 percent were simple cowardice, the latter remedied by "putting a .45 [caliber pistol] to his head" (9 January 1919).

President Wilson and Germany were much on Smith's mind, and his casual observations become serious analysis, a pattern maintained throughout his life as both his prose and his analytic skills constantly improve. "Wilson is like a sheep amidst wolves at Versailles. . . . If he could dictate terms, the world would be a happier place" (26 January).

His antipathy toward France and other biases emerge: "Nothing has so impressed me with the inferiority of French Civilization as seeing Germany. The British are, in my opinion, the white people of Europe" (31 January 1919). "I am learning to speak German and forgetting my French just as rapidly" (6 February). "I'm backing Mr. Wilson and his league of nations completely and enthusiastically. Are you?" (8 February).

On 13 February, he informed Kay that higher headquarters has disapproved his Distinguished Service Cross. He is disappointed, but he says he probably shouldn't have been recommended in the first place: the real heroes are dead and maimed. In the same letter, he warned Kay again about propaganda. "My opinion of Germans is not a newspaper's opinion. It was formed on the wheat fields on the Marne and in the deep woods of the Argonne. There one got a somewhat different opinion than one sees in the *Paris Herald* or the *London Daily Mail.* This war was fought by us to accomplish the downfall of militarism. Let us not imitate other nations in having won, disgrace our knockout blow by a kick. Kay—Wilson has won me completely to his ideas—I hope France, the last stronghold of militarism will also be won to him. Strange, isn't it. Germans aren't very different from other folk."

The very next day, he is still on this topic: "I infinitely prefer an Englishman to a Frenchman. . . . Germany . . . once arrogant and overbearing, [is] now bewildered and wrestling with anarchy. We are flooded with papers evidently from French sources, urging that the Rhineland be given to France as a protection against a future powerful Germany." He goes on to say that this "would be a world disaster and directly contrary to the principles for which I fought. I'm directly behind Mr. Wilson in his great fights for ideals and a League of Nations. And the devil take Clemenceau, Orlando and that crowd of bloody Metternichs." All of Europe is rotten politically. "We may imagine ourselves as rotten, but we're not near as bad as the best of Europe." Smith excludes Lloyd George from this rogues' gallery, saying, "He too shows up splendidly."

Among the Truman-Kay collection of letters in the archives are a few written by others, one from Francis A. Markoe, a fellow officer in the 4th Infantry, to Kay on 18 February 1919. He praises Truman as one of the very best leaders. "He was just great and when the 4th was almost a thing of the past old Truman was right there to keep it going. Colonel Dorey and General Sladen both swear by him now."

Most consequential for Truman's professional development was a 12 March 1919 letter from Colonel I. L. Hunt, Office of Civil Affairs, Headquarters Third Army, American Expeditionary Forces. Hunt asked Smith if he would like to accept assignment to Coblenz for duty in the Office of Civil Affairs. Hunt said he was surprised to learn that Smith was in the Third Army and close by. He knew of Smith's "work in historical studies" and that he was "so highly thought of in your Division" that it may be difficult for Hunt "to secure the consent of your superiors for your detail." In any event, Hunt wanted "an early reply as to whether you will be interested in this kind of work, as it gives one a very excellent opportunity to study German administration at first hand. In replying will you let me know whether you took any German when in college." Smith was pleased at the prospect and accepted the job.

The timing of Colonel Hunt's letter could not have been more fortuitous. Truman had indicated to Kay that he was bored with the regimental duties he had been performing for the three years since 1916. After his high adventure and life-and-death responsibilities at the front, the mind-deadening inspections, drills, and garrison routines were a bore. Foolishness, such as that Smith reported in a letter of 18 March, caused him to question life as a professional soldier. "Pershing never did have my vote, but if he had a chance, he lost it yesterday. It was bitter cold and we stood from nine until one, without overcoats waiting for the inspection to begin." In addition, the combat veterans of the 4th Infantry were being replaced by new men. Smith's letters to Kay during this period show a marked decline in his morale. His post-combat funk may have been natural, but it was compounded by the intellectual's disease: thinking.

Smith was dubious about nonfraternization and other occupation rules in both principle and in their clumsy execution. His independence of mind was manifested in his critique of English and French newspaper reporting, which, to him, was stalled in wartime propaganda clichés that failed to capture post-Armistice realities on the Continent. Letters from home suggested that the American public, even his own circle of presumably enlightened beings, was still mired in wartime gibberish and chauvinism. His expression of support for Wilsonian idealism put him at odds with what he regarded as French revenge, Italian territorial ambitions, and Belgian desire for payback.[4]

He missed Kay terribly. That reality was exacerbated by boredom at one level, the grubbiness of realpolitik at another, and simply not knowing how long he would be a part of something that had become joyless and kept him from his wife. He was twenty-five and had been separated from his lovely bride for what seemed eons. The prospect of leaving the army is broached in several letters to Kay at about the time Hunt's letter arrived.

He was already fascinated by all things German, so the job was a good fit into his personal agenda. The icing on the cake was the paternal interest Hunt had in Smith. Nineteen years earlier, Hunt had served as a lieutenant in Truman's father's company of the 19th Infantry in the Philippines. Once again the old boys' network served him well. Smith was about to begin an enormously gratifying job that would be enhanced by Kay's arrival, making their fifteen months on the Rhine the happiest period of their lives.

4

Civil Affairs and Romance on the Rhine

> Bolshevism is the great question of the day.
>
> —Truman Smith, 1919

> The French politeness is like an overcoat that they put on for special occasions.
>
> —Kay Smith, 1920

Neither Smith nor his superiors knew how the Germans would react to occupation by foreign soldiers, nor did they know how long the occupation would last. The first question was answered early on as the Germans accepted the American presence without incident, despite the general anxiety that pervaded Germany, now defeated, hungry, and leaderless. The duration of the occupation would depend upon negotiation and acceptance of a peace treaty yet to be framed.

A more pressing personal issue to Smith was how long he would continue to be separated from his wife. His letters to Kay during this period of waiting fall into two broad categories: expressions of love and yearning, and ruminations about geopolitics and momentous events. His observations regarding how the peace process in 1919 would shape attitudes and affect the Europe of fifteen years later would prove to be prescient. And he was present at the birth and early years of the Weimar Republic. As Smith settled into his civil affairs job in Coblenz, he was sure of two things: he loved his work and he missed his wife.

The United States Third Army occupied Germany on 1 December 1918 with its headquarters in Coblenz. The American occupation zone was located between the British, with their headquarters in Cologne, and the French, with their headquarters in Wiesbaden. During the spring of 1919, nine American divisions participated in the German occupation. Since American troops had no unusual difficulties with the populace, American occupation forces were rapidly reduced soon after the peace conference ended in May 1919. At the beginning of 1920 there were about 15,000 American troops in Germany. Since the United States was not a signatory to the Treaty of Versailles, the United States was technically at war with Germany until 18 October 1921, when separate peace treaties with Germany, Austria, and Hungary were ratified. The remaining American force was gradually reduced, and the last thousand troops left for home on 24 January 1923.[1]

A general sense of disillusionment with the war and with the peacemaking process surfaced in the United States, the way a hangover follows exuberant celebration. So much was promised; so little seemed to have changed. The winners simply divided the spoils as they had from time immemorial. Americans expected more from a war that had cost so much in human lives and national treasure. Investigations were conducted in the United States to find profiteers, warmongers, and scoundrels of various stripes. And questions were raised about why American soldiers were still in Europe long after the end of the war and the signing of peace treaties in 1919. Will Rogers had a ready answer: "because two of them weren't married yet," a whimsical reference by the cowboy-philosopher to the great number of American soldiers who had married German women.

Kay Smith had a less accepting view of German-American matrimony, as noted in her diary kept for the period 19 September 1919 to 17 December 1919: "A good number of our men are marrying them. Far too many. The majority of the marriages are due to the fact that as soon as a baby is found to be on the way, the Army insists on the man marrying the girl, if she wishes. Naturally she does. The reasons for such numbers of babies arriving are due to the fact that the women are as big as horses and know nothing of taking precautions" (3). So much for Kay's initial impression of German women; so much for the nonfraternization rules of occupying armies—then and always.[2]

Truman had found a wife who pleased him very much. His problem was that she was in New York and he was in Coblenz. Separation from Kay was much on his mind as he began his work in Civil Affairs in 1919. He found it particularly maddening that he did not know how long he and American forces would remain in Germany. Therefore, he didn't know if he should send for Kay, even while half-expecting that U.S. forces would pick up and move out when the peace treaties were signed, or wait upon events. He vacillated. In his lovesick letters to Kay he often asked her to join him, and then, reacting to rumors that his army was about to return to the United States, he would change his mind. Finally, after the army sorted out personnel issues that simply overwhelmed it as it moved from frontier army to world power, Kay joined him. They set up house in Coblenz in September 1919, expecting to be in Germany for weeks or months, but they would not see the United States again until 1924.

Many of Smith's letters to Kay are eyewitness accounts and impressions of unfolding events that suggest the sophisticated political analysis and intellectual rigor that was later to characterize his professional life. He was a keen observer, and his reporting got to the essence of events. He also had the good fortune to be working in Germany, the focal point of international attention at the time, as revolution and counterrevolution erupted from Kiel to Munich and Berlin. He would live in Germany for ten of the twenty interwar years and would remain engaged in German affairs during yet another war and its aftermath. Fully half of Smith's thirty years of military service were focused on Germany and German-American relations. His personal ties to Germany and the German political-military class were the centerpiece of his professional life, ending only with his death.

Because the terms were so harsh, upon learning of the terms imposed by the victorious Allies at Versailles, Smith wondered who among responsible Germans would sign the treaty. He was not alone. American military contingency plans were made to continue the war, had that been made necessary by German rejection of the treaty and German acts of belligerence. But the treaty was signed, immediate large-scale acts of belligerence were averted, and the war was not resumed. However, early on Smith put his finger on one of the assertions that Hitler would repeat again and again: those who signed the treaty would be called traitors who stabbed the German people in the back.

The terms of the Armistice in November 1918 had put Germany in a military position so disadvantageous that only irresponsible hypernationalists would resume a war that would be fought on German soil by whatever remained of the already-demobilized German army. But anything seemed to be possible in postwar Germany. Anarchists, Bolsheviks, varieties of socialists, centrists, monarchists, and several Freikorps organizations conducted "politics" with clubs and guns in German streets. (The Freikorps were rightists whose allegiance was to a leader, usually a veteran of the trenches.) Political turmoil characterized Weimar Germany from the mutiny of sailors in Kiel in 1918 until Hitler's ascension to power in 1933, except for a period of French-German reconciliation from 1924 to 1929.

Smith had a ringside seat in Coblenz, and then in Berlin, from which he observed events as Germany went through yet another rough patch in her troubled history. His personal correspondence shows him to be a keen observer, a lucid reporter, and a responsible representative of his country, characteristics he would perfect in his professional life, soon to be unencumbered by lovesickness. Moreover, he was blessed with a wife with whom he could share the issues that mattered to him. The substance and tone of his letters to Kay indicate that she knew history and was abreast of current events.

Early in his tour in Civil Affairs there is a blending of personal concern and duty in his letters to Kay, as in this one, from 3 April 1919: "As for the Peace Conference, I am sincerely hoping the peace be of such a nature that there will be no more [American] troops in Europe. . . . I'm keen to leave the Army. I don't want to leave Kay anymore. . . . I am studying German quite hard and am getting now so I can read the newspapers. Still I am not as good at it as I am in French. . . . Col. Hunt is a very able man and an excellent one to work for. Bolshevism is the great question of the day. The government in Germany is just able to keep its head above water." He explains that the government is hard pressed by Bolsheviks who gather strength "in their fanaticism" and in the "moral and spiritual breakdown of the old order, the lack of food, and in the fact that they alone of all parties in Germany know what they want." The government must wend its way between Left and Right. "Its one source of strength is the old officer corps, and this, of course, isn't a very sure foundation for a future democratic state."

These observations in 1919 were sound. Even usually moderate political leaders in the Weimar Republic almost always came down harder on radicals of the Left than on radicals of the Right. Smith saw that, and his personal predisposition was also on the side of order and middle-class values. "Bavaria is in utter anarchy with Bolshevists [his spelling] in Munich and in the government in

Nurnberg. The Jews in Germany as well as in Russia seem to be at the head of anarchy. Heaven help and keep Bolshevism from our homes" (3 April 1919).

Smith's letters tell us how he felt about his work, what he was learning about the highly professional German civil service, and his estimate of the prospects for the peace treaty being negotiated as he wrote. "I really believe this is going to be the best job in the Army of Occupation. I am delighted, and though the work will probably be very heavy, I really feel as if I was using my mind for the first time since I came to France. . . . The Prussian officials are of all types—all extremely intelligent, of high birth, and very dignified" (4 April).

But he was pessimistic about the future of peace in Europe. "Poor peace conference. The papers are excited that it does nothing. It is a much tougher task to make peace than to beat Germany. I counsel failure" (9 April). Ten days later he expresses doubt that Germany would sign a treaty that gave the Rhineland to France. In the same letter he is surprised to find himself, quite out of the blue, promoted to major: "It was pretty tardy recognition of the Argonne, but it's something at least to have received a promotion for gallantry" (April 19).

Regular contact with French and British occupiers leads him to conclude, "I don't believe it's our genius to be able to handle a conquered people. . . . Certainly in Paris our statesmen are taking a more liberal, farsighted view than the French; to leave matters to France would be to renew this debacle in fifty years. . . . [But] the sum of matters here is that in governing a conquered people, we have much to learn from both the French and the British. A German said to me the other day, 'You should have learned how to govern us by our miserable failure in governing Belgium during the war.' That is one matter all Germans admit, the horrible botch they made of it in Belgium. We aren't as bad as that by a long shot. And America will learn. Germany wouldn't" (22 April).

In early May 1919, Smith became Colonel Hunt's chief political assistant, the person doing the actual negotiations with both the Rhineland Oberpresidium (in the American context, region or state) and the district government of Coblenz. Colonel Hunt, recognizing talent, also used Smith to draft army orders affecting the civil population.[3] All communications between the American military authorities and the government of the occupied territory, Smith told Kay on 4 May, "go through my hands. . . . My impression of the civil officials here is that they are army officers without uniforms": not a bad description of the German Beamter (civil servant). On one occasion Smith was sent to the neighboring British sector, where he had a long talk with Konrad Adenauer, who then was mayor of Cologne and, in 1949, chancellor of the Federal Republic of Germany, when American forces once again occupied Germany after a war. This was heady stuff for a man just four years out of college and with all of three years in the army. He loved it—but he missed Kay.

"Life is still as interesting as ever," he wrote to Kay on 8 May. "I have never enjoyed a position as much. If you were only here so that life wouldn't end at 5 P.M." In that letter, he was pessimistic—and sarcastic—in commenting on the treaty as the terms became public. "I've got a nice tidy little castle picked out here on the Rhine for the next fifteen years or so, and after glancing at the reparations clauses, I'm sure I can get it dirt cheap. Evidently some would-be humorist at Paris thought this war wasn't enough and decided we should enjoy another trip to Europe in fifteen years or so to help poor embattled France again. . . . France, that pure savior of civilization is certainly a sorry spectacle today. . . . Another humorist suggested Germany might sign the treaty as it is! No, I'm packing my bags tonight. We'll be on the march to Berlin in a month." He adds, "P.S. This letter is not admissible as evidence in any proceedings brought against me. I've got my fingers crossed."

Smith's pessimism continued in his next letter, on 11 May, after he had gone over the treaty terms carefully. "If the Prussian spirit conquered by the vigor of our young arms is to reappear in France, bloated, childish, self-satisfied, why these efforts and labors of ours? I feel it so deeply—it has been such a failure, all. If Wilson could have prevailed, it would have been far different. He was simply outmatched with hands tied. Let us come home! We have no place here amongst these racial hatreds. Let us get home. We came into the war so nobly and disinterestedly, and oh, it is such a mess. And the League of Nations! That too was an idle dream of mine. Certainly Germany will bide her time until the first dissension appears in the Entente, and then . . ."

He continued in this vein on 22 May. "Sooner or later, the Allies will split . . . and France will pay dearly again. France is not as industrious or as virile as Germany. . . . Her doom will come as certainly as fate, unless she sees into the future. And she has never been particularly farsighted. Let her remember 1814. [Now] is an auspicious moment to begin a period of world peace, but the whole structure has fallen to the ground. I am about prepared to see a world revolution . . . in thirty years you will see I'm right. Quite right."

Separation from Kay, personal experience with the French and Belgians, and analysis of the European situation conspired to make Smith increasingly dubious about Europeans and generally disillusioned. "But then I've learned not to expect cleanliness from a Latin. On the *moral* [emphasis in original] side I expected more, but this too disappeared" (23 May). "If Clemenceau is to have his way, we shall be in the age of Louis XIV again. Some times nowadays I wonder what on earth I was fighting for" (28 May). Smith is referring here to French use of force in the Rhineland in 1919 and the fact that after the Thirty Years War and the Treaty of Westphalia in 1648, the Germanies were small, weak states and France dominated both sides of the Rhine. He warns against a vindictive treaty, observing that in 1917 the Germans had imposed outrageous demands on the Russians, but "we are supposed to be a higher nation than Prussia. Certainly after our cries of horror at the Prussian [behavior] at Brest-Litovsk, let us be a little bit consistent" (30 May). He believed that Germany would not be able to fulfill the terms of the Treaty of Versailles and therefore would not sign it, or would renege when that was possible. Given the events of 1934–1939, Smith may be seen as prescient. He regretted that some Germans believed that the statements Wilson made to the Germans, which led to the Armistice, thanks to Clemenceau, were "tricks." He concludes, "Europe is bad business. Crush this alliance with France at all costs. I don't want a thing to do with them" (3 June).

On 22 June he informs Kay that rumors are "flying about." The big question is, will Germany sign? "All is ready to resume war, but indications point today that Germany will sign. Of course she hasn't any intentions of living up to the treaty longer than she has to, and I doubt if that will be over five years. The question now is finding someone who will sacrifice himself and sign the peace. . . . There are more future wars insured by this peace than I ever imagined. It will take Europe fifteen years to settle down, and then she won't. . . . Germany will see her old gang in power in a year." In fact, fifteen years later a new gang worse than the "old gang" was, indeed, consolidating power at home before taking aggressive actions. Smith has some kind words for England, regards France as hopelessly corrupt, and is "disgusted" by Europe. "Italy is crazy and Poland sheer mad. Topeka, Kansas for you and I Katie." (Smith is so upset that he puts a pronoun in the wrong case!)

Purely personal commentary, lovesick lamentations, and small talk about friends and family comprise a portion of Smith's letters to Kay. But the rest is about the Rhine, the Germans, the French and British, and his analysis regarding how the occupation is going and speculation about the course and outcome of the peace negotiations at Versailles. His observations regarding European affairs reflect his understanding of history, and he found it unnecessary to explain numerous historical allusions to Kay. He simply assumed she would understand. A Yale man who had done graduate work in history at Columbia, Smith had cultivated academic references and elevated prose for most of his life. What is perhaps a little surprising is that Kay, a finishing school product and debutante, now just twenty-one, seemed perfectly prepared for her husband's serious intellectual discourse and historical ruminations. Shared intellectual curiosity enhanced a relationship already solidly based on social class and physical and emotional attraction.

Kay was a clever woman. She could keep up with Truman; she was also prepared to play Boswell to his Johnson. A man who derived satisfaction in matters intellectual also derived satisfaction in his wife who, among her other charms, was as attentive as a pupil to her husband, and a protector as well as admirer of his reputation. Smith's numerous letters to Kay illustrate his evolution as a political analyst. But in the summer of 1919 he was focused on getting Kay to Europe.

The decisions made in Paris and Versailles regarding the peace terms to be offered Germany had a direct bearing on the size and location of the U.S. Army. And that, in turn, had a direct bearing on a separated young married couple. From their wedding in July 1917 until the late summer of 1919, when they were reunited in Europe after seventeen months of separation, the Smiths had been together for about eight months of their marriage. Even before Truman had deployed to France in 1917, they had made frequent moves, and his duties did not allow the couple much private time together. They were ready for a normal domestic routine.

Much red tape had to be cut to make reunion possible. Kay turned to the army for permission to get a passport. The army informed the Department of State on 5 June 1919 that the War Department had no objection. But the State Department asserted that Kay needed a written statement from the War Department saying that her husband was not scheduled to return to the United States within three months. Of course the army could make no such statement, as it, along with the rest of the world, awaited the final terms of the treaty and Germany's reaction to those terms. Then, as now and always, bureaucratic administrivia ruled.

Meanwhile Truman, whose good reputation had spread, received two job offers, one from State and one for another army assignment. At this point, looking for a way to get Kay to Europe, he may have been fishing for jobs. In any event, June to August saw a flurry of nervous letters and telegrams between Kay in New York and Truman in Coblenz, anticipating her arrival in Europe. The world kept shifting under their feet as international affairs, treaty making, the configuration of the army, and the Smiths' domestic arrangements remained entangled. The happy outcome was that Truman remained in place in Coblenz and Kay joined him there.

Among his accomplishments as a young officer, Smith could fairly take the lion's share of credit for a report written while he worked for Colonel Hunt in Civil Affairs even as he schemed for a way to get Kay to Coblenz. The report, whose official title was "Report on Civil Government of the Army" but was commonly known as the Hunt Report, would be later used during World War II by the school of military government at Charlottesville, Virginia, to train selected personnel for the occupation of Germany by the U.S. Army after that war. Colonel Hunt unselfishly gave Smith credit for the report and strongly recommended him for the job in Berlin that would later make him assistant military attaché. Smith was the author of eight of the eighteen chapters, and was also general editor of the report.[4]

Kay's first diary entry in Germany was dated 19 September 1919, as she and Truman set up house in the Coblenzerhof [her spelling], a first-class hotel built in 1914.[5] It overlooked the Rhine and faced the Ehrenbreitstein, the imposing fortress where the Rhine and Moselle rivers meet. At the first mention of Coblenz she gives the German (Koblenz), the French (Coblence), and the Latin origin (Confluentes) for the place name, further informing her diary that the city was the capital of the Prussian Rhine Province (diary 1–2).

Friends and family feared for her safety "on the Rhine surrounded by those dreadful Germans. . . . However, I was determined and felt extraordinarily brave. This added to my excitement" (136).

Her descriptions are excellent and sweeping: countryside, rivers, forests, architecture, art, table settings, seating arrangements, repartee, and social relationships. The Smiths enjoyed an active and elegant social life. They attended the theater, concerts, dinners, teas, wine tastings, and cocktail parties with interesting company: British, French, and Belgian, military and civilian. To Kay, the Rhineland was a fairy tale come to life, nature and man conspiring to give her God's raw Drachenfels, the river, hills and forests, and man's elegant twelfth-century Burg Eltz, the vineyards, castles, and natural wonders on the Rhine.

Her diary entries indicate that the social whirl in Coblenz, Cologne, and Wiesbaden was essentially like that in New York or in Greenport. She was not particularly dazzled, nor did she feel in any way inferior to the Europeans. After all, when she had seen Truman off to the Mexican border she did so in a Stutz Bearcat, an elegant automobile belonging to a friend. She called the 12th Infantry of the New York National Guard "a sort of club," with officers named Roosevelt, Auchincloss, Van Cortland, Wadsworth, Belmont, "and others of the social register." (A Belmont made an offer to present the 12th Infantry an "aeroplane." The offer was declined; 1916 military leadership saw no place for an aeroplane in an infantry regiment.)

While Truman was in Texas Kay's social life in Greenport was disrupted now and then by arguments to get in or stay out of the European war. She referred to "brave little Belgium" and corresponded with a French soldier pen pal. She made her debut in the winter of 1917, noting that "after Christmas the private parties stopped and the charity balls began."

Exotic locale and foreign languages added spice to social life in Europe, as did aristocratic titles, but the well-to-do at play on the Rhine and on the Hudson or Long Island Sound were different only in nuance. Good conversation ranked high with the Smiths. Intelligence, knowledge, charm, and wit mattered very much, but Kay also took pleasure in the material things to which she was accustomed.

An avid shopper who knew value and quality, she snapped up furniture, china, fabrics, crystal, and furs at bargain prices, some for herself and some for gifts to family members in New York and Connecticut. The dollar was strong and the Deutsche Mark was weak. Kay caught "the buying fever [that] had the whole Army of Occupation in its grip." In her diary, she noted, "The Army was paid in

German marks. As the value of the mark was steadily sinking, one had to turn one's money into real goods or lose it entirely" (173).

This was not entirely true. There was an awkward process to convert money paid in German Marks to U.S. dollars, but the fact is that Kay enjoyed visiting shops and finding bargains. She wrote proudly that she purchased "a dozen plates of Dresden china—with open-work edges" for 90 Marks, "about $2.35" (27). Not bad for two independently wealthy young people! Truman's pay as a captain in 1917 was $142.50, and the couple used that income for current expenses and pocket money. Inherited wealth was held in reserve for major expenditures and income production.

Smith was happy in his work. He liked and respected his boss, Colonel Hunt, as did Kay. One gains the impression that the Hunts treated the Smiths like their son and daughter. Truman and Kay enjoyed a second honeymoon on the romantic Rhine after a long separation. Life was good. In fact, Kay wrote, "The present was heaven" (173).

Kay's initial impressions of the German people, however, were negative. She liked the greenness of Germany and remarked on its cleanliness, but she had reservations about Germans. When a maid presumed that, because Truman spoke German he was German, she told her diary, "I was annoyed beyond description." Of German men, she wrote, "almost all without exception shave their heads till they look like escaped convicts" (diary 3).

Kay had studied German for six months at Miss Spence's School, but when the war broke out her father would not have "that damned language in his house." No doubt her views had been shaped by the drumbeat of wartime anti-German propaganda she had heard in New York. Despite Truman's numerous letters to her expressing his increasing preference for Germans and his increasing antipathy toward the French, she arrived in Germany pro-French and dubious about Germans.

In 1914 Kay, at just sixteen, was susceptible to the pro-French, pro-British predispositions of her social circle and the New York newspapers. However, after meeting polite German society she began to change her tune: "To find that they held us no animosity and were indeed ladies and gentlemen, instead of horrible cannibals was most surprising" (171). Sensitive to the bias of her parents, in her letter of 4 January 1920 she said this to them about the French: "I refrain from my opinion of the French as I realize that you are still crossing yourselves every time you mention Lafayette." A *New York Times* reporter told her that he'd lose his job if he told the truth about the French (204). But as early as September 1919, she noted, "The longer I stay here the less I think of the French. They are doing a great many dirty things to defeat the alliance" (150). The Americans in Coblenz socialized with the British in Cologne and the French in Wiesbaden, and the latter was apparently a good place to shop for furs and jewelry. Her direct contact with the French and the political climate evoked this pronouncement: "It was common knowledge that any French sentry could be bribed for a few marks" (154).

Kay's prose is as clean as the German countryside. Her powers of observation and her wit tend to prompt the reader to excuse her sometime haughtiness. In a diary entry dated 23 September she describes a woman alleged to be the daughter of Clemenceau: "I didn't know that the old 'Tiger' had a daughter. Mlle. was a sight to behold! Her dress up to her knees belied her face, which clearly was not that of a young woman. A marvelous coiffeur crowned her large head and jewels spread themselves all over her expansive bosom. Her brilliantly painted face beamed coquettishly at the tiny French officer who was nobly dancing with her. And dancing under difficulties, for that expansive bosom completely eclipsed his view of the ballroom" (diary 9).

Her criticism of the French was relentless and became increasingly harsher: "they are the most immoral and dirty-minded lot I ever saw" (214). She accuses them of behaving in the Rhine and Ruhr the way Germany had behaved in Belgium and with the same justification: "strategic reasons" that included iron, coal, and a "natural frontier" offered by the Rhine. She debunks the latter, a militarily useful defensive barrier, as "a thing of Caesar's time . . . the next war will be in the air."

The French-supported Rhineland separatist movement evoked this response from her: "The French are the most militaristic in Europe . . . a copy of Germany before this war" (222). Kay's own observations and personal experiences in 1919 and 1920 confirmed for her what Truman had been saying in his letters to her while she was still in New York. She wrote that love of the French and hate of Germans "was so carefully fostered for so many years [in the American press]," but at the end of a month spent dealing with the French, Americans can scarcely be civil to them. "French policy has been to crucify Germany," she asserted (223). But Kay was also informed by sources other than her personal feelings. In a letter to her mother dated 11 February 1920, she makes this recommendation: "Get a book called *The Economic Consequences of the Peace* by Keynes. It is absolutely the clearest statement of the case one could find. But pitiless. You can't afford to miss it. A perfect description of the situation now" (220).

That Kay, a 1917 debutante, would be reading Keynes, is indicative of her intelligence as well as her wit. She noted that very few girls of her generation went to college, and when she completed finishing school her father didn't think she should work, since by doing so she would be taking a job from someone who really needed to earn a living. She had performed monologues at school, but "no nice young women," she recalled, "would do such a thing as go on the stage." Miss Spence's School provided her with a good education: languages, writing skills, history, and perhaps most significantly, the self-confidence, poise, and intellectual curiosity that would serve her so well for her entire life. Added to those attributes was energy that ceased only at her last breath.

Her wit and sense of humor are evident even in passing observations in these diary entries. On seeing the Lorelei for the first time, as Truman pointed it out to her as they drove past it one rainy evening, Kay alluded to the myth of the Sirens: "I didn't hear them singing. Perhaps they don't like rainy nights." After meeting some French officers, she writes, "The French politeness is like an overcoat that they put on for special occasions. But the politeness of an American far less polished is innate and ever present. No one can be as rude as the 'polite Frenchman' when he hasn't got on his company manners" (diary 12). Even when being a bit prudish, her sense of humor remains evident. In a shop she observes, "Little china naked ladies on fur rugs abound, and little ladies in bathing suits and china cocks and hens doing what they shouldn't are also plentiful. This last is the final proof of the decadence of Europe" (diary 14).

Married to an infantry officer who was an intellectual, she was bitingly critical of some of her countrymen. "The general is Cavalry and most of the staff, and all they know or do is play polo. They pay no attention to or know nothing about the situation here or the work of Civil Affairs" (175).

Upon her arrival in the occupied Rhineland, as noted in her diary, Kay was often the first American lady seen there since the war ended. "Everyone everywhere stares at me terribly," she wrote.

"Coming toward them their jaws drop, their eyes nearly pop out of their heads. If I look back I see them staring after me. At first I thought it something queer the matter with me, but now I realize it is just that I am an American woman not in uniform. 'Ein [*sic*] Amerikanerin.' I am getting used to it. Now I know how royalty must feel!" (15). She was also young, pretty, and well dressed, a combination known to attract attention even outside of Germany.

Both Kay and Truman worked hard with private tutors to learn German. Truman found fluency in German to be a professional necessity, but he also seemed to enjoy the insights into all aspects of German life to which language proficiency was the key. Kay was similarly motivated, and she, like Truman, grew to like Germans very much. The joy she found in shopping was further motivation to speak the language. So was the sympathy she felt for civilian suffering.

Germany experienced serious food shortages during the war, which continued until mid-November 1919, but even later food was very expensive for urban Germans. Kay notes in her diary that when the British first occupied Cologne, "women and children were starving to death in the streets. The English General went ahead and fed the city from the soldiers' rations. He wrote a stinging letter home to the Parliament saying, 'British soldiers were not in the habit of waging war on women and children—they never had and wouldn't begin now.' Of course then the H.Q. at home made arrangements to feed the city" (diary 32).

She and Truman would become increasingly attracted to Germans and Germany in their first tour of duty in Berlin, making connections and friendships that would last a lifetime and survive yet another war with Germany.

Kay experienced two life-changing events in 1920. In February she discovered she was pregnant. She later wrote, "The thought frightened me very much, for I was sure I would be sent home" (210). But that was not to be. She would have her baby in Coblenz, but she was about to move to Berlin, another life-altering experience.

Having been asked to recommend an officer who would go to Berlin and in due course become the assistant military attaché there, Hunt recommended Smith. That assignment became the basis of Smith's major contribution to his country. After some time during which the assignment was in doubt, it was confirmed. In a letter to her mother dated 1 June 1920, Kay announced, "We are going to Berlin after all." She sums up her days on the Rhine as "the happiest, certainly the most carefree of my life" (231).

Kay's characterizing her first months in Germany as "carefree" is telling. Reunion with her husband, his satisfaction in his duties, the paternalistic concern of the Hunts, the social life, the shopping, and the beauty of the Rhineland itself made Kay a very happy young woman. She would find Berlin attractive and exciting, but she would also learn what it is to be responsible and less carefree in both her personal life and in her position as the wife of an American diplomat.

5

Berlin, Munich, and Hitler in Weimar Germany

> Germany is having a nervous breakdown.
>
> —Ben Hecht, reporting from Berlin, 1920

> It is better for America and England that the decisive struggle between our civilization [and Bolshevism] be fought on German soil.
>
> —Adolf Hitler to Truman Smith, 1922

> Germany is a sick nation, sick financially and economically, but still more sick intellectually and morally. . . . Fraught with all manner of problems for Europe and the world, the probability of a patriotic, nationalistic Germany of the future must still be faced by every thinking foreigner, European or American.
>
> —Truman Smith, June 1924

The Smiths arrived in Berlin in June 1920, when both they and the Weimar Republic were young. Everything about Berlin seemed tenuous, provisional, improvised, and ad hoc, including the American representation in the German capital. The small staff they joined had been hastily assembled under unusual circumstances. As a consequence, responsibilities normally borne by senior officials devolved on Truman and Kay. They were tested: he in observing, reporting, and representing the United States, which was still technically at war with Germany; and she in fulfilling a role usually performed by a veteran diplomat's partner. Kay was twenty-two, and Truman just four years older, when they arrived in Berlin.

Ambassador James W. Gerard had turned the safeguarding of American interests over to the Spanish Embassy when the American Embassy in Berlin was closed in February 1917 after long-simmering differences between the United States and Germany regarding German unrestricted submarine warfare. On 3 February 1917 President Woodrow Wilson announced to the U.S. Congress that he was breaking diplomatic relations with Germany. News of the president's decision arrived in Germany on 4 February and was reported to the German reading public in the *Berliner Zeitung* on 5 February. Shortly thereafter, Ambassador Gerard departed by rail to Switzerland and onward to the United States.[1]

Because a state of war existed between the United States and Germany, there was no official American representative in Berlin until a provisional arrangement was improvised after the Armistice went into effect in 1918. An astute U.S. Army colonel who was serving as a Germany-watcher in The Hague for the Military Intelligence Division (MID) of the General Staff in the War Department urged the War Department to send a major general to Berlin to look after American interests. To his surprise, MID sent that colonel instead.

Colonel Edward Davis was one of a small number of American soldier-diplomats used in successive tours as military attachés by MID. Typically, those officers had troop experience, spoke foreign languages, were good reporters, and had an independent income. Davis had all of those qualifications. He had served in combat in Cuba, in the Philippines, and on the border with Mexico. Earlier in the Great War he served in Athens. Using a great deal of initiative, he was also an observer and liaison officer with British General Edmund Allenby in Palestine. Later he would serve in Mexico City and Belgrade.

The November 1918 Armistice found Davis in The Hague, running agents in Belgium and Germany from the neutral Netherlands, which had been, as historian John Votaw put it, "the scene of a desperate battle of wits between the Allies and the Central Powers." Neither the competition in the Netherlands nor the wartime maturation of American military intelligence has gotten much attention from scholars, but Davis was conducting a professional operation that enabled him, among other successes, to predict the flight of the kaiser from Germany a full month before it occurred on 9 November 1918.[2]

Describing the evolution and development of a system for gathering intelligence and the place of military attachés in that system, Votaw concludes that by the end of 1919 "the War Department was served by a very professionally organized, staffed, and administered intelligence agency, the MID. The military attachés' role in that successful development was one of leadership and competence."[3] He might have added that the evolution in the period he describes, 1885 to 1919, paralleled the emergence of the United States as a great power.

Davis was modest about his accomplishments and witty in describing the ignorance of the U.S. Army regarding what he and his colleagues did for the army and for the United States. He said that fellow officers "did not understand what attachés did." They were seen as "nice enough fellows with more money than brains," "gentlemen-in-waiting," "absolute masters of the pink tea set." That characterization persisted among line officers then, and probably still does. Even in tactical units in the field army, intelligence (S-2 or G-2) never had the martial cachet of operations (S-3 or G-3) or command, and Military Intelligence as a branch of the U.S. Army did not exist until the 1960s.

Davis moved to Berlin under peculiar circumstances. Germany and the United States were technically still at war. Only Davis of the American group had applicable credentials; the others didn't even have passports. And Davis, in accordance with usual diplomatic practice, was accredited to The Hague, not Berlin. Nevertheless, if the Germans in Berlin were to deal with an official of the American military, Davis would be that official. Moreover, the Americans were Germany's best bet for a friend in court. He reports that the Germans treated his group with courtesy. As the senior American quasi-diplomat of rank, he opened the old Embassy for the first time since it was closed, "somewhat indignantly, by Ambassador Gerard in 1917."[4]

Under Armistice terms the Allies established the Inter-Allied Control Commission, consisting of American, French, British, Italian, and Belgian officers, but, Davis reports, the Americans never filled the slot assigned to them. This enabled him to maintain freedom of action from the Commission in a tumultuous period characterized by a new and questionable form of government in Germany saddled with poor economic conditions, threatened by both armed remnants of the German military and a communist movement intent on revolution. The unique position of the United States, an "Associated" rather than "Allied" power, is underlined in Davis's account of a meeting with War Minister Gustav Noske, who suppressed bloody disorders in the early days of the Weimar Republic. He regarded Davis "curiously as the first American government representative he had received." Davis says that one of Noske's first remarks was, "You Americans got us into this hole, and I think you ought to get us out." That was the prevailing opinion of thinking Germans. They believed that the Americans had turned military stalemate into German defeat. However, they also realized that the Americans would be far less vindictive than the French and Belgians in dealing with them. The British took a middle position: more forgiving than the French, less so than the Americans.

Initially, the American postwar representation in Berlin was the "American Commission," a body of "Observers" that would become the American Embassy once a treaty was signed ending the war between Germany and the United States. Because of their social position and Truman's assignments, the Smiths came into contact with a great number of people who were well known at the time of their meeting and later. Several of the Americans who served in the Commission later became quite famous, as did some of the Europeans.

Hugh Wilson was counselor of embassy when normal relations resumed. He had served in Berlin before the war. The Wilsons and the Smiths established a friendship in the early 1920s that was continued when Wilson became ambassador and Smith was military attaché in Berlin in the late 1930s. Allen W. Dulles, a junior Foreign Service officer later prominent in the Office of Strategic Services (OSS), as director of the Central Intelligence Agency (CIA), and as the brother of John Foster Dulles, Secretary of State, assisted Wilson in Berlin.

Another luminary was William F. Halsey, Admiral "Bull" Halsey, later famous in World War II for leadership in the Pacific. He was briefly Naval Attaché but had to leave his station because his wife had tuberculosis. Kay writes, "Bill tended her with great care. How ironic this strong determined man should have so frail a wife."[5]

Aviation pioneer Benjamin Foulois, the corporal in the company of Smith's father when Captain Edmund D. Smith was killed in action in 1900, was Chief of Air Service and a major general in the Great War. It was a great coincidence that he was Attaché for Air in Berlin when Truman and Kay arrived there. Kay writes that he was the son of an employee of Truman's Aunt Jenny Platt and was coached by Truman's father to become an officer. Foulois almost certainly felt a sense of debt to the Smiths.[6]

Davis had direct contact with German leaders, some already famous, some whose fame would come later. He was an eyewitness to the 1920 Kapp Putsch two months before the Smiths arrived on station, remarking that Captain Hermann Ehrhart's Marine Brigade—a free corps that refused disbandment—was decisive, well disciplined, and intelligent. The German Army's unwillingness to suppress revolution from the Right as vigorously as it suppressed revolution from the Left was an early indication of the tilt to the Right that ultimately would be the death knell of the Weimar Republic.

Major Friedrich von Boetticher was Davis's point of contact in the German War Office.[7] Boetticher, later a lieutenant general and longtime German military attaché in Washington, became a friend of both Davis and Smith. Boetticher and Smith maintained their friendship between the wars and into the post–World War II period.

Davis met Field Marshal Paul von Hindenburg several times, once bringing Army Chief of Staff General Peyton C. March to Hindenburg's house for a private meeting. Davis includes in his papers a collegial note from Hindenburg to the American as Davis ended his tour in Germany. He also met General Erich Ludendorff, who used almost the same words as Hindenburg to describe the American soldier as a man of reckless bravery, dismayed by few obstacles, only partially trained, and awkwardly handled. Ludendorff added that the United States saved France twice, once when Pershing arrived on French soil in 1917 to revive the hopes of the French people, and once again when huge numbers of fresh American troops in 1918 shaped the fortunes of war.

Colonel Davis was a skilled and experienced soldier-diplomat. He was also a compassionate man, the kind of officer known in the army as "old shoe," the opposite of a martinet. As Kay Smith prepared for the move from Coblenz to Berlin, she informed her mother that she and Truman would be staying with Colonel and Mrs. Davis until the Smiths found suitable housing. She noted that Mrs. Davis was the only "official" American woman in the delegation at that time. The Davises demonstrated a parental interest in and affection for the Smiths that was reciprocated with respect and fondness by the young couple. The Smiths were fortunate in having, in the Hunts in Coblenz and the Davises in Berlin, chiefs—and their wives—who were also mentors. The elders seem to have recognized the potential

Smith in Berlin in 1920, looking every inch Yale 1915. His duties in Coblenz from 1918 to 1920 included liaison with German officials and editing and writing the "Hunt Report" on civil-military operations during the occupation. He would interview Hitler in Munich in 1922. (Courtesy of Katharine Smith Coley and family.)

they saw in Truman and Kay. In any event, the Smiths had optimal role models in leadership during their assignments in Germany. The willingness of the chiefs' wives to assist the young couple was appreciated, and the skill of the old soldiers in cultivating Truman by giving him responsibility is noteworthy.

Kay was pleased to report that the men in the Embassy are "all

Yale or Harvard." She notes in a letter sent from the British Officers Club Resthouse in Cologne dated 20 June 1920, "we are ordered to Berlin as 'Official Military Observer,' and attached as assistant military attaché to the Netherlands. This last is an excuse to draw attaché extra entertaining pay as there is no embassy at Berlin. Supposedly it is a mission."[8] She was right about the observer status, but the accreditation to the Netherlands was done to provide official status and a diplomatic passport, not to legitimize funds for entertaining. However, the American government was notoriously frugal with funding. That is why those of independent means were selected for attaché duty.

Truman Smith's memoir account of his June 1920–April 1924 assignment in Berlin is succinct: only four double-spaced pages—including just a single page on his 1922 interview with Adolf Hitler in Munich. Fortunately, as we shall see, he was more expansive elsewhere.[9]

From 1920 to 1922, the military observer office was part of the diplomatic mission headed by Ellis Dresel. Smith's title was Assistant Military Observer until mid-1922 when, with peace having been restored between Germany and the United States, the diplomatic mission became an embassy with Alanson B. Houghton of the Corning Glass family as first postwar ambassador. Smith's title became Assistant Military Attaché. In his memoir, Smith recalls his activities during this period:

> My reports on these developments [revolution, siege, and fighting all over Germany] brought me to the attention of the Military Intelligence Division of the War Department in Washington. I also became a sort of authority on the postwar German army. I not only studied all sorts of German military manuals but read widely on their operations in the World War just concluded. During these years I became acquainted with a considerable number of German officers, some of whom were to continue as friends until 1964. I also traveled widely in Germany and saw a good deal of the transformation of the Kaiser's army into the small but highly effective Reichswehr under General von Seekt's direction.[10]

During this first tour in Berlin, he came into contact with several notable figures. In 1921, Smith twice came into contact with

Monsignor Achille Ratti, "who only a year later became Pope Pius XI (1922–1939)." Benjamin Foulois, Smith believed, was "the most outstanding officer" in the Observer/Attaché office, "far abler and more experienced than any other army officer in Berlin."

As for William F. Halsey, Smith found him "genial, hearty, and impetuous. Both Kay and I liked him immensely. However, I must confess that I did not foresee his later fame. Nor did Kay."[11]

In November 1922, Ambassador Houghton sent Smith to look into "a new German political group in Munich which called itself the National Socialist Party" and to "interview the party's leader, Adolf Hitler, and evaluate the present and future importance of National Socialism and its leader."[12] According to Smith, "Mr. Houghton seems to have had, even at this early date, a premonition that the [National Socialist] movement and its leader might play an important role in the disturbed Germany of the early twenties," despite the prevailing view that Hitler was "an uneducated madman" who would fade into oblivion as Germany settled down after the transition from monarchy to republic.[13]

Upon Smith's arrival in Munich, he called on the acting consul, Robert Murphy, for orientation on the local political scene.[14] Smith interviewed several editors and key political figures, such as Crown Prince Ruprecht of Bavaria, General Erich Ludendorff, Alfred Rosenberg (later Nazi political philosopher), and gadabout Ernst F. S. (Putzi) Hanfstaengl. The highlight of the trip was Smith's meeting and subsequent interview with Hitler on Monday, November 20, 1922, at 4:00 P.M. in a house and room at Georgen Strasse 42, "drab and dreary beyond belief, akin to a back bedroom in a decaying New York tenement."[15]

Smith found Hitler to be "a marvelous demagogue." He added, "I have rarely listened to such a logical and fanatical man. His powers over the mob must be immense." Smith wished "with all his heart" that he could have foreseen the course of history, but of course he didn't.[16]

One wonders how it could have mattered. Smith and Hitler were rather minor figures in the great scheme of things in 1922. Had either of them foreseen and publicly announced what was to happen in Germany over the next two decades, they would have been rightly consigned to a madhouse.

Two of the ten points Smith put into his notebook from the Hitler interview leap out: Hitler believed that "Parliament and parliamentarianism must go. No one can govern with it in Germany today. Only a dictatorship can bring Germany to its feet." Accordingly, immediately after assuming power in January 1933, Hitler began to destroy all opposition and to make the Reichstag a Nazi rubber stamp as he established his dictatorship. He also told Smith, "It is better for America and England that the decisive struggle between our civilization [and Bolshevism] be fought out on German soil."[17]

The next time Smith saw Hitler was on a September day in 1935, when Hitler addressed 70,000 "fanatic followers" in the Nuremberg Stadium at the annual Parteitag. Then, on 3 March 1937, he accompanied old friend and newly appointed American ambassador Hugh Wilson to the chancellor's palace as Wilson presented his credentials to Hitler, after which there was a reception. As Smith passed down the reception line, he shook hands with Hitler and was about to pass on, when he felt a hand grasp his sleeve. "Have I not seen you before?" Hitler asked. "Yes, Mr. Chancellor, in Munich in 1922," Smith replied. "Oh, yes," replied Hitler. "You introduced me to Hanfstaengl." Then, Smith recalled, "another member of the embassy staff stepped up to shake hands with the chancellor. I never spoke to Hitler again."[18]

A more expansive account of Smith's 1922 interview and analysis is found in the formal report Smith wrote and sent to MID five days after his interview. (Its full title is "Conditions in Bavaria: The National Socialist Labor Party Service Report, 1922.") Each evening in his hotel room Smith organized the notes he had taken of his observations, conversations, and impressions from that day. His report was roughed out in Munich. When he returned to Berlin, he took three days to write the report, which he submitted to his boss for approval and forwarding to MID in Washington. This was Smith's working method for his entire life. He was scrupulous in editing and rewriting until his product was as close to perfect as he could make it.

His analysis is sophisticated and nuanced. He identifies Hitler's aim: to establish a nationalistic dictatorship. To achieve that, it would be necessary to win the workers from the parties of the Left to the National Socialists (NS). He described the growing importance of the *Stosstruppen* (storm troops), saying that the *Stosstruppen* was created to secure NS meetings from attacks by Leftists, but soon thereafter they were used to break up meetings of the National Socialists' enemies, particularly socialists and communists.

Smith notes that the National Socialists were very strong south of the Danube, and Munich was their center. The Bavarian government was sympathetic to NS philosophy and activities. Moving north in Bavaria to the industrial cities of Regensburg, Nuremberg, Wuerzburg, and Hof, the SPD (German Social Democratic Party) was well embedded. As one moved further north, however, the NS movement had not yet taken root. Northerners were described as "interested but waiting." Smith asks himself if Hitler's National Socialists can play a role in Germany equivalent to the Fascisti in Italy, concluding that it was not possible to answer the question in 1922.

Smith wondered about Hitler's ability to maintain control of his movement. "It seems certain that with the great influx of party members now going on, the task of maintaining the purity of the party's national aims will require not only a great orator, such as Hitler is, but a political genius, with a deep knowledge of human nature. One can not say as yet that Hitler's possession of this quality is proven."[19]

Smith posed the right questions. With the hindsight of today's observer, one can say that Smith's reporting is thorough. His analysis is rigorous, insightful, and prescient. For example, some competitors for power in Hitler's party would emphasize the "socialist" of the National Socialist, and others the "nationalist." Hitler maintained control by crushing all such competitors.

Later, in June 1924, Smith drafted a magazine article, "The German Fascisti," that was unpublished until 1984. He does not say why he wrote it, or why he did not have it published, but we may find answers to both questions in the text and in Smith's nature.

It was perfectly natural that after almost six years in Germany, a man intellectually curious, well positioned, and skilled as a writer would attempt to comprehend the ebb and flow of the chaos he had witnessed in a country that he had come to know and care about. To assess what he had seen, to describe the current state of affairs, and to speculate about the future were probably irresistible impulses in a man who throughout his life ordered his thoughts by writing.

Furthermore, Smith drafted his article while he was alone in Berlin. Kay, pregnant for a second time, had returned to the United States in December 1923 to avoid travel in advanced pregnancy and in order to give birth in a hospital in New York. Her sister had had two miscarriages, and Kay and Truman had lost their first child, a daughter named Alling, at the age of two, in Berlin in April 1923. Kay was understandably careful with this second pregnancy.[20] Truman remained in Germany until April 1924. It is reasonable to surmise that during this period he had the time and inclination to put his thoughts about Germany on paper, beginning in Berlin while separated from Kay, and continuing while in the unchallenging job to which he was assigned later that year at Fort Hamilton, New York. The article was a summing up of his observations, a net assessment of what he had witnessed.

Those familiar with the course of German history in the decades after 1924 will appreciate the insights found in Smith's official reporting and the lucidity of his presentation. But there is a bonus in the draft article. He is analytical, as usual, but he is noticeably less constrained than in his official reporting; he feels freer to offer opinions and speculation about the future. He gets Hitler, the National Socialists, and Germany of the 1930s right—in 1924.

Smith begins his article with the initial meeting of the second Reichstag of the German republic on 27 May 1924, an event that, in his words, "opened a new era in the history of the German republic," as the extreme Right of the house sat in a compact mass of thirty-five deputies "whose lung power in no way gave precedence to that of their communist opponents. . . . For this time the communists had met their master in the game of parliamentary rowdy tactics."[21]

Ludendorff was at their head, "for their true leader, Hitler, still languished behind Bavarian fortress walls" (that is, in confinement). Hitler and his Fascisti, as Smith refers to the National Socialists, had nearly 2.5 million voters in the Reichstag election of 1924. "The handful of followers in Munich in 1921 had become a formidable array." They symbolized defiance to any attempt by the German government to bow to the will of the Allies and were the beginning of a change of fortune for the German state.[22]

Smith warned that those who considered the German extremists on the Right as a force that "will disappear with the returning financial and political stability" were wrong. "Desperate economic conditions such as have prevailed in Germany since the autumn of 1918 always tend to fertilize the ground for extreme political doctrines," he wrote. "The foreigner in Germany could readily sense the yearning of the masses to escape at all costs from the abyss of political and economic collapse and could understand, though decry, their readiness to give ear to any agitator who could promise relief from their misery, a living, and the possibility of saving a due portion of their earnings." He goes on to note that "a still more important cause for the party's astonishing growth is its pandering to a dawning German patriotism . . . pride in race and state is dawning today, a patriotism far different from that slavish discipline with which peasant and *Burger* followed the beck of the warlord to their place in the sun in 1914."[23] Smith anticipates here the frightening hypernationalism that swept Germany a decade later, stunning friends of German culture.

And, about the party: "Determination, relentlessness, not seldom the most intemperate radicalism, have carried the day against moderation and wisdom. . . . It would be a daring observer who today would state that the revolution had yet spent its course and the German ship of state come to anchor in the calm waters of a final constitutionalism." But were the "Hitler of beer garden fame" and his friends more akin to "the black-shirted followers of Mussolini south of the Alps" or a "Germanic Ku Klux Klan, striving to purify their race by bringing about a new exodus of their Jewish fellow citizens? Or perhaps even a recrudescence of the Wilhelm-Ludendorff conception of a world Germanic empire coupled with a ruthless overriding of the rights of others?" Smith is not sure. But, he suspects, in private conversations "they would probably even claim themselves to be a part of the new world movement, seeking eternal peace through the collaboration and mutual respect of super nationalistic states (purged of Jews)."[24]

Reference to a "world movement" in connection with Jews may have been an exaggeration, but Mussolini and Hitler certainly would have European imitators: the Iron Guard in Romania, various Fascist groups in Hungary, Franco and the Falange in Spain, and Action Française in France. Even Britain had Sir Oswald Ernald Moseley and his British Union of Fascists. These reactionary movements in Europe shared a superheated nationalism, and contempt, or worse, for Jews.

Smith allows himself some amusement in noting the superficial similarities with the Italian movement, and a difference not at all amusing. The Germans' uniforms, military formations, Roman greetings, and the "never-ending demonstrations aiming to influence the masses" have been taken en bloc from the Fascisti. But Mussolini's "theatricalism so correctly pitched to the Italian temperament [eludes] crude Teutonic imitation, much like those Swabian copies of Swiss watches which flooded world markets before the war." To fill the gap, "a militant, relentless anti-Semitism" is found in National Socialism and "has struck a resonant chord somewhere in the German people." Smith believes that "Unless a moderate degree of economic prosperity soon returns . . . it is entirely possible that the fanaticism and strength of the Racialism will gain intensity and volume."[25]

Economic prosperity did not return; racialism did gain in intensity.

Smith outlines the program of "this new German messiah, Hitler": defy the Allies by rejecting the Treaty of Versailles; achieve economic independence; damn the international and German bankers and brokers; fight socialism; spread extreme German nationalism; achieve dictatorship; continue anti-Semitism. Smith notes that "intelligent America" may smile at the serious promotion of such "absurdities," but Hitler's converts numbered only few among the German intelligentsia. It must be understood "that Germany is a sick nation, sick financially and economically, but still more sick intellectually and morally."[26]

One can speculate about the possibility of German recovery had there been no Great Depression, but there was a Great Depression and Germany remained "a sick nation."

Smith then goes on to explain the growth of Hitler's party, which he has been calling "the Racialist movement." For the first eighteen months after the November 1918 revolution, he notes, "every energy of [the] bourgeois parties was required to repel communist attacks. No countermovement gained an appreciable following." Beginning in 1920 several parties of the Right were active in Germany. The National Socialist Party in Munich "had already become a breeding ground for reactionary experiments. The communist wave had spent itself, and [Rightists, including Ludendorff] had begun to unveil war monuments and review parades of steel-helmeted veterans. The National Socialists were at first regarded in Berlin as another beer fantasy, and perhaps they would still be inconsequential had it not been for the curious, demagogic personality of their leader, Adolf Hitler."[27]

Smith describes Hitler's appearance as that of a "German middle-class shopkeeper. The appearance is saved from mediocrity by dark eyes, gleaming with fanaticism, intense and unceasing. The eyes, coupled with the voice, for it is as a speaker and agitator before hostile audiences that Hitler is in his element, have brought him to the forefront. His derisive, rasping, often angry voice, his feeling for the dramatic, and a veritable genius in sensing the temper of his audience carried Munich by storm during 1920 and 1921. . . . Hitler's personality and his National Socialism soon were a force to be reckoned with in Bavarian politics, to the surprise of the government, which had at first tolerated the movement as a possible antidote for the socialism of the workers."[28]

In the summer of 1923, Smith wrote, "the North German Racialists and the Munich National Socialists joined forces, Hitler being unanimously accepted as leader. Ludendorff's adherence to the new party soon followed, and while his reputation for political wisdom has long been under a cloud, there is no gainsaying even today the influence of his name in officer circles, a class always to be reckoned with in Germany."

Smith calls Hitler's "Beer Hall Putsch" of 8 November 1923—part of a nationalistic response to the French and Belgian occupation of the Ruhr in January 1923—"the most ludicrous of all revolts." But, he says, "The policy of the Bavarian government at the trial of the ringleaders was doubly farcical." Hitler was permitted to use his propaganda skills during the trial to the advantage of his movement. "Respectfully Ludendorff was acquitted amidst scenes of rejoicing, and Hitler was given a minimum confinement in a Bavarian fortress." The tide turned. From low ebb weeks earlier, the trial resulted in "astounding success in the [April 1924] Bavarian state elections" that put Hitler, Ludendorff, and the party in "the new Diet second in strength only to the long dominant Catholic group." Then, as a result of the 4 May 1924 Reichstag national election, thirty-five of Hitler's party were seated as deputies on 27 May. From then onward, the National Socialists counted for something at the national level in Germany.[29]

Concluding the article, Smith emphasizes the reawakening of the patriotism of the German people. "Fraught with all manner of problems for Europe and the world, the probability of a patriotic, nationalistic Germany of the future must still be faced by every thinking foreigner, European or American. In the days when a beaten, despairing army recrossed the Rhine and communist bands plundered and ruled, a new Germany was born. Its growth gathered untold impetus on the day General Degoutte marched the hosts of

France into the Ruhr. Its future lies still unrevealed somewhere in the distant years."[30]

This is impressive political analysis, identifying Hitler's themes and National Socialist characteristics in 1924.

Why didn't Smith publish the article then?

Army officers of the 1920s and 1930s were famously apolitical, at least publicly. Smith was a serving officer. His article dealt with sensitive issues regarding a foreign state. Such a report by a political officer in an American embassy would not be made public, nor would Smith have published it while in Germany. Lacking direct evidence, Smith probably considered it too politically charged for publication under the byline of a serving U.S. military officer.

During his visit to Munich in 1922, Smith spent time with Ernst F. S. (Putzi) Hanfstaengl, a curious figure who was a Harvard graduate and later Hitler's foreign press chief. Years later, Smith wrote, "Hanfstaengl states in his 1957 memoirs, *Unheard Witness,* that 'it was I who brought [Smith] into contact with Hitler.' This may well be so, but the actual facts of this introduction are not firmly fixed in my memory."[31] Truman and Putzi would meet again in Germany in 1935.

Smith liked to stick to the facts. While in Berlin and throughout his military service, his writing and analysis were used primarily to produce official reports for MID in Washington, and later to produce intelligence and briefings as a part of MID during World War II. We shall see that even while writing professionally under his own byline for a brief period in 1941, he continued to be a very disciplined writer.

Kay, by contrast, often blended objective fact with her observations and impressions. Sometimes she just was having girlish fun in her letters or diary entries. For example, she described Mrs. Beehler, the wife of a naval attaché, as "a great success with the diplomatic corps. She fulfilled all their previous ideas of an American, since she said so many frank, often crude things."[32] Used in tandem with Truman's writings, Kay's recollections add rich background and color to his scrupulously tight writing, just as anchovies bring zest to Caesar salad.

But Kay did her homework. There is an unexplained reference to an article she wrote while in Berlin that she sent to her mother, apparently to have published in New York. But, cautioned Kay, "You can't tell my name or my connection here."[33] Nothing came of it, but there is no doubt that she was attentive to serious matters. (After all, it was on this tour that she learned how to make and drink martinis.)

She was honest, even self-deprecating, about her naiveté in matters small and large. Told that a woman across the room was the widow of Karl Marx, Kay admits, "I never heard of him." But she adds that she later became more familiar with his work and influence. Marx simply was not part of the curriculum at Kay's finishing school, where French subjunctive conjugations presumably took precedence over learning about a German malcontent in the British Museum scribbling the obituary of her social class.

Kay sketches recent political events in Germany for her correspondents like a schoolgirl boning up for final exams or dishing gossip with friends: Philip Scheidemann declaring the German Republic; General Wilhelm Groener promising support of the army; Friedrich Ebert as president; Gustav Noske as minister of war; the Wolfgang Kapp Putsch.

Her correspondents were justifiably concerned for her physical security in the midst of street fighting around Germany—including in Berlin—which they were reading about in the American press. She describes staff members, the rooms and decor of her apartment, domestic help, and prices, how food from the commissary in Coblenz was sent to Berlin by train each month. And she records less mundane events: her meeting the Papal Nuncio in Berlin, Eugenio Pacelli, later Pope Pius XII (1939–1958); Truman's playing bridge with another future pope (Monsignor Ratti, later Pius XI). Diplomats and their wives and lovers are described, as are meals, furnishings, dress, and jewelry. She even describes the way she dealt with a middle-aged Lothario whose hand found its way to her thigh under the table at a formal diplomatic dinner. (He was French.)

Memories of the recent war were fresh and painful. It didn't take much provocation to bring them to the surface. On Bastille Day 1920 the French hoist the Tricolor; an indignant German crowd pulls it down. The French ambassador protests. The German government responds by sending an honor company to march by the embassy and salute the French flag. Amends made—but then the German troops sing "Deutschland über alles" as they march away. The French protest.

Kate Wilson, Mrs. Davis, and Kay were for some time the only women at the American mission. At the age of twenty-two, pregnant for some of the time and then caring for a very ill child, Kay carried out social, quasi-official, and official tasks usually performed by the wives of senior officials of middle age. Her education and socialization in the upper strata of society had prepared her well for the life she experienced, and her poise was enhanced by her honestly inquiring mind. It is always flattering to respond to a person who really cares about one's special knowledge—particularly if the earnest listener is a young and attractive woman. The Smiths' two memoirs provide abundant evidence that Kay and Truman regularly discussed serious political issues with each other. Truman's observations were refined in conversations with his intellectually curious wife. He took the intellectual and analytical lead, but theirs was a marriage of peers.

In her memoir, Kay relates a story intended to explain one of the reasons why Truman was so warmly received by German officials, particularly by German officers, early in his first Berlin tour of duty. Rochus Freiherr von Rheinbaben and Edgar Graf von Matuschka were directly involved in the 15 January 1919 murders of Karl Liebknecht and Rosa Luxemburg, leaders of the Spartacus Union, which became the Communist Party of Germany (KPD). Liebknecht and Luxemburg were murdered in Berlin while in the hands of the army, one shot in the back "while trying to escape," the other clubbed with a rifle butt and thrown into the Landwehr Canal. According to Kay, Rheinbaben and Matuschka fled to Coblenz and surrendered to the Americans there. Truman, learning of their precarious situation, had them transported to an American prisoner of war camp for their protection. Rheinbaben and Matuschka were treated well there and were grateful; in fact, Smith may have saved their lives. It is unclear precisely how much Smith knew about events in Berlin at that time, but after the two fugitives returned to Berlin, they spread the word of Smith's actions and friendly behavior toward German officials, who were already predisposed to think kindly of the Americans. Kay says of herself, Truman, Rheinbaben, and Matuschka, "We became close friends."[34]

Major General Henry T. Allen, Commander of the American Forces in Germany and the American Representative on the Rhineland High Commission, in his book *The Rhineland Occupation* noted the provisions of the Armistice regarding the relationship of German and occupation authorities. The occupied areas of the Left Bank of the Rhine were "to be administered by the local authorities under the control of the troops of occupation." The Americans enjoyed a reputation for scrupulously avoiding interference with purely internal German politics. But in the immediate aftermath of the war it wasn't always easy to know who the "local authorities" were. In some places, pre-Armistice conditions applied; in other places Soldiers' and Workers' Councils were the de facto "local authorities." The situation was further complicated by the French encouragement of the Rhenish separatist movement.[35]

American evenhandedness made the American area of occupation in Germany a safe haven for political activists of all stripes. The two officials involved in the murders in Berlin probably realized that, until things cooled off in Berlin, the American-occupied area near Coblenz was the safest place for them in revolutionary Germany.

The need for security and stability in the chaos of Weimar Germany had much broader implications for the future course of German history. As historian Gordon A. Craig has noted, General von Seekt, "while carefully refraining from putsches, made the army an autonomous body within the state, with policies that did not always accord with those of the state." In the general turmoil in the early days of the Weimar Republic, President Ebert and War Minister Noske depended upon support from the Army Supreme Command and Free Corps volunteers to maintain order. Threats from Russian Bolsheviks and Poles on Germany's frontiers, and revolutions in almost every part of Germany, made political authority unhealthily dependent upon military force. The tilt to the Right existed from the very founding of the Republic, even by longtime socialists who were part of the government. Craig calls the elections of June 1920 "a catastrophe for the Weimar Republic" because of the country's turn to the Right.[36]

The essence of thinking on the Right in 1920 Germany is captured in this pronouncement by General Walther Freiherr von Luettwitz: "[The government] is acting irresponsibly in permitting the last pillars of the state to be undermined. If the Free Corps are dissolved and, in addition, half of the regular army is disbanded, the country will be left defenseless vis-à-vis the threat of Bolshevism."[37]

Kay and Truman were unquestionably conservative by upbringing. They felt a kinship with European elites steeped in a shared Western culture and, for the most part, conditioned to similar social conduct. They established personal and official relationships with German officers, both those who would not fit well in the coming social order of the Nazis and those who would. But the Nazi social order came later. Given the chaotic conditions they witnessed in the immediate postwar period, it is not surprising that they would tilt in the direction of order and good manners, preferring gentility to the bombast, riot, and revolution associated with the Left. But although they were naturally conservative, they were also broadminded as a result of their formal education, close observation of the world around them, serious reflection, and a refusal to accept clichés as a substitute for rigorous analysis. A sin of elites is condescension and a sense of entitlement; a virtue is noblesse oblige. Evidence suggests that the Smiths had generous dollops of each.

Pregnancy returned Kay to the United States at the end of December 1923; Truman's orders relieving him from duty in the embassy arrived a month later. He was to report for duty at Fort Hamilton, New York, in April 1924. Alling, their first child, born in the Coblenz army hospital in November 1920, had died in April 1923 in Berlin of an undiagnosed mouth infection, and her ashes were returned to Connecticut for burial. (See appendix B.)

After the death of Alling, Kay was determined to have another child. On 15 May 1924 Katharine Truman Smith was born at the Sloan maternity hospital on West 59th Street in New York City, close to Kay's parents' residence on 58th Street. "Ever afterward," wrote Truman, "she was to be called by the nickname we gave her at birth, Kaetchen," the German diminutive for Kay.[38] (She used the spelling *Kätchen*.)

6

Years of Preparation

> Truman loathed this duty. He knew nothing of animals and cared less.
>
> —Kay Smith, on Truman at Fort Hamilton

> [Fort] Benning became one of the greatest experiences of our lives.
>
> —Kay Smith

> Personally I found the [Leavenworth] course to be far less interesting than the one I had completed the year before at Fort Benning.
>
> —Truman Smith

The Smiths' European adventure of the early 1920s was a rich personal and professional experience; the same cannot be said of their next assignment. Truman later wrote, "The ensuing year and a half spent at Fort Hamilton was altogether the dullest and least professionally rewarding of my whole army career. The only relief from garrison boredom was the summer training periods at Fort Dix, New Jersey."[1]

Smith's later assignments, to Fort Benning and then Fort Leavenworth, were far more gratifying than the dull routine at Hamilton. He, along with some military contemporaries who shared his intellectual curiosity, were able to escape tedium by attending a succession of professional schools. The army education system was, and is, designed to train and educate officers for successively greater responsibilities as commanders and staff officers. As an infantry officer, Smith attended the advanced course at the Infantry School at Fort Benning, Georgia (1926–1927), to learn how to lead a company or battalion in combat, with emphasis on tactical effectiveness.

At Leavenworth (1927–1928) he would attend the Command and General Staff College (C&GSC) to learn how to employ brigades and divisions and to understand how a corps functions, with emphasis on how to coordinate the efforts of the various arms and specialties in a division to accomplish the mission assigned. Upon completion of C&GSC, Smith was pleased to return to Benning to serve on the faculty of the Infantry School (1928–1932) under the leadership of George C. Marshall, along with many officers who would become senior commanders in World War II, among them Omar Bradley, Courtney Hodges, "Vinegar Joe" Stilwell, Matt Ridgway, Joe Collins, James Van Fleet, and Walter Bedell Smith.

At the Army War College (AWC) (1932–1933) in Washington, D.C.—which, along with the Naval War College in Newport, Rhode Island, were the two "senior service schools" in the period between the world wars—Smith took his place among carefully selected officers who were educated to think in terms of national and theater strategy and to write war plans. Throughout this phase of his professional life, Smith did very well both as a student and as a teacher. Peers and faculties respected him for his mature good judgment, his communications skills, and his knowledge of Germany.

This "schools period" was followed by command of a battalion of the 27th Infantry (Wolfhound) Regiment in Hawaii (1933–1935) before his assignment to Berlin as the military attaché (MA) (1935–1939). In her memoir, Kay called this 1924–1935 period of their lives "Years of Preparation" that positioned Truman well for the future. But before good things happened, they had to get through the 1924–1926 tour of duty at Fort Hamilton.

The contrast between the life they had known in Europe and what they found in Brooklyn was pronounced. Truman had lived life on the edge in combat in France in the Great War. Then his performance in Coblenz and Berlin in demanding jobs had revealed his talents as a perceptive observer and accurate reporter. Those assignments had also revealed that his background, education, and personality made him particularly well suited to yet another role: representation. Eleven years after his return to the United States in 1924, he would return to Berlin to observe and report on Hitler's Germany and to represent his country there.

As dull as Truman found Fort Hamilton, Kay found it unspeakably duller and a shameful waste of what she correctly recognized as her husband's considerable talents. She observed, "The Army shrank once more to a small guard. Officers were reduced in rank [Truman from major to captain]. I was furious. It seemed such a mean petty thing to do, but Truman took it as a matter of course. . . . Hamilton was an anachronism. I seemed to have moved back a century. I felt displaced in time. It was my first experience of life on an Army post."[2]

Her recorded reaction to the mundane and uninspiring tour at Fort Hamilton is honest and personal, as usual. And it is understandable. Coblenz was romantic; Berlin was exciting; Hamilton was Brooklyn—and mules! At the same time, however, one can say that Kay's gradual integration into the army subculture, including her discovery of the concept of "for the good of the Service," begins during her stay at Fort Hamilton. Her journey from purely personal gratification to the loftier aspiration of Service to something beyond oneself reminds the reader of her diaries and memoir that she was a very young woman when she went to Europe and just twenty-five when she returned and wrote so scathingly of Truman's stateside assignment. But she maintained her sense of humor and confessed her vanity.

Kätchen's birth had gone very well, but Kay responded to her mother's jibe about her shape in pregnancy with these words: "I hated that part of it, the grotesque change in my body."[3] Presumably storks would have been the preferred mode of delivery.

There was a related problem with the housemaid the Smiths had brought with them from Germany. Ella had earlier had an abortion, and became pregnant again, causing Kay to remark that "she was incurably susceptible to the male sex." Ella's employment in the Smith household was terminated, and she returned to Germany.[4]

Living in New York was convenient for Truman and Kay, for the birth of their baby and for reunion with friends and family, but Truman's duties were a far cry from the great events the young couple had witnessed in Germany, with the Weimar Republic in its infancy amidst revolutions from the Left and the Right. Kay was bored, observing, "Little time was spent on troop training, and certainly the Service Company was involved in maintenance."[5]

Truman's narrative of his Fort Hamilton days gets all of a page and a half of typescript in his memoir, and half of that is spent on his application and acceptance to the advanced infantry course at Fort Benning, Georgia. He reports glumly that at Hamilton he was placed in command of Service Company, 18th Infantry, with sixty horses and mules, a motor transport platoon, and regimental supply maintenance personnel. After commanding a large body of American soldiers in desperate fighting in the greatest American battle on foreign soil to that date, his puny command in a backwater was a tremendous letdown. He describes Hamilton as "an antiquated stone New York harbor defense fort of 1830" located on the Long Island side of the Narrows, across from Staten Island, and then adds, "Our old fashioned, roomy quarters has [*sic*] since been torn down to make room for the eastern pier of the Verrazano Bridge."[6]

Kay found it difficult to accept, almost insulting, that her gifted Truman was forced to command a herd of horses and mules, and in Brooklyn, no less. The horses were probably acceptable; it was the mules that got to her. Fortunately, Kay had a baby to care for and her old New York social circle to which she could retreat in escape from the ignominious mules and Truman's mundane housekeeping duties. His duties and responsibilities in Europe had been out of all proportion to his age, rank, and experience. But the army has a way of teaching humility, even to its high-fliers; and although Kay clearly did not like the Hamilton assignment, she showed signs of adapting to army ways. As she later wrote, "I learned that those in the Army truly lived 'for the good of the Service' and concern for the newcomer was part of that good of the Service."[7]

One of the highlights of the Hamilton assignment suggests that Truman remained both an unreconstructed historian and a romantic. At a review at Fort Dix, Smith was pleased to meet and talk with General E. S. Godfrey. Smith describes Godfrey as "a very ancient retired officer" who was a survivor of Custer's defeat at the Little Bighorn, an action for which he had been awarded the Medal of Honor. "Godfrey seemed to me when I met him a heroic figure out of that distant past when our army was battling against the formidable Sioux nation, the finest light cavalry of all history."[8] His meeting with Godfrey may have reminded him that his father was also among the last of the Indian fighters.

Truman, typically, presents us with a fact of life, the inspection visit of the division commander. Kay, describing the same event, shows directness and her ambition for Truman in turning it to her husband's advantage via the old boys' network. Truman mentions that his 1st Division Commander, Major General Preston Brown, had commanded the 3d Division in the latter part of the Meuse-Argonne offensive. Brown, a Yale man, was "regarded as one of the most brilliant officers of the army, but also an unreasonable martinet." However, Truman says that Brown was "most friendly" and recommended Smith for the advanced course at Fort Benning.[9]

Truman probably did not know at the time what Kay describes in her memoir regarding Brown's visit to Fort Hamilton. She was keenly aware of her husband's discontent with his routine tasks and the damned mules: "Truman loathed this duty. He knew nothing of animals and cared less." When Brown attended a reception during his inspection visit to Hamilton, Kay writes, "I dressed myself in my best evening gown. I was determined 'P' Brown should know Truman was an old Eli." She informed the general of that fact and believed that brandishing the old school tie made a difference and led to her husband's assignment to Fort Benning.

It is more likely that Brown was fully aware of Truman's outstanding war record and background, including his education at Yale and Columbia. In any event, Brown and Colonel Edwin Croft, Truman's regimental commander and later chief of infantry, strongly supported Truman's application to attend the Infantry School. Kay said, "We were eternally grateful to Colonel Croft for his insistence. Benning became one of the greatest experiences in our lives."

It began with a memorable trip to terra incognita. The Smiths bought a Dodge automobile and accompanied it on a ship that took the family from New York to Savannah, Georgia. Her description of the drive on the unlighted, unmarked, improved dirt road from Savannah to Columbus, Georgia, located on the Chattahoochee River, is memorable for its local color. A novelist might capture this portion of Kay's memoir with a chapter entitled "Benning: Blacks, Booze, Broken Body, and Brother Officers." Life in Germany was more familiar to both Smiths than life in Georgia. Now these two Yankees who found themselves in the Deep South for the first time would add a bit of Americana to their repertoire.[10]

Truman reported for duty at the Infantry School in September 1926. He is characteristically concise in describing his student year at Benning in a few paragraphs. He studied hard and was one of the top students of about ninety officers, doing particularly well in military history and tactics. He was sent the following year "to the army's most sought-after educational institution, the Command and General Staff School at Fort Leavenworth, Kansas. What I did not know at this time was that I had also been placed on a special list of officers from which future Benning instructors were to be chosen."[11]

Kay's account of life at Benning and her impressions of the

The staff of the Infantry School, Fort Benning, Georgia. Front row center, Colonel George C. Marshall; third from right, Major Forrest Harding, chief of Smith's section; second from left, Major Paul E. Peabody; third row, fifth from right, Smith. This was one contingent of "Marshall's men." (Courtesy of Katharine Smith Coley and family.)

American South are far more expansive and colorful than Truman's. Her stark pronouncements on race are simplistic, unencumbered by research, and probably representative of the views of her social peers in New York and New England. "Negroes have green thumbs. They can grow anything. . . . The proportion of Negro to White [in the area around Columbus] was nine to one . . . all polite to one another . . . when drunk, a Negro is apt to go berserk." Her "Colored maid, Maud," was "inefficient but pleasant and very faithful." Of the two regiments at Fort Benning, the 29th Infantry supported the training conducted by the Infantry School. The 24th Infantry, officially designated a "Colored" service regiment, took care of stables and post chores. So much for race relations in the army and in the Deep South in the 1920s.[12]

She is amusing on the subject of alcoholic beverages. In Coblenz she discovered the martini to be a powerful and interesting alternative to the fruit of the grape. In Georgia she discovered an alternative to both in a southern version of the nectar of the gods. She says

Georgia was a "dry" state even before Prohibition, but "to obtain a gallon of corn whiskey, one had only to put a quarter on a stump in a pine 'clearin,' go away, return in ten minutes and there was your whiskey." That important discovery led to another in a form of chemistry. "Georgia corn liquor, when first from the still, is raw-burning, horrible-tasting with a most unpleasant odor, but aged six months in a charred oak keg, into which has been added a can of drained charred apricots, it becomes a pleasant drink. The older, the smoother, the pleasanter the flavor and aroma."[13]

This dissertation on the (illegal) stimulation of the local economy exists alongside much more serious passages in Kay's memoir, one dealing with her recovery from serious injuries she sustained in an automobile accident in mid-March 1927. The accident left Kay with multiple fractures: pelvis, left leg, ribs, collarbone, wings on vertebrae, plus a dent in her forehead. She was in traction for two months. Her mother stayed in Columbus for a couple of months to be near her, and Truman's mother took care of Kätchen in Stamford until the following September. It was feared that Kay would never walk again and might be condemned to life in a wheelchair. But her

Kay was seriously injured in an auto accident while at Fort Benning and hospitalized for months there and in Walter Reed Army Hospital in Washington, D.C. However, Truman and Kay enjoyed the Benning assignment very much. Marshall and Smith maintained contact over the years. (Courtesy of Katharine Smith Coley and family.)

toughness and determination, plus the extraordinary care she received at Walter Reed Hospital in Washington, resulted in her total recovery, making "Booze and a Broken Body" humorous relief from a very serious situation.

While Kay was in the hospital in Columbus, Truman's old comrade, Joe Patch—whom Truman had killed off and resurrected in letters to Kay during the fighting in France—commiserated during one of his many visits, in the course of which he referred to his experience of being badly wounded and left alone for many hours in no-man's-land in the Great War. He concluded by regretting that there was nothing he could do for Kay. Kay corrected him. In fact, there was something he could do: put a keg of whiskey under her hospital bed. Then visitors would remain longer and be more relaxed.

This was done.

As a result, visitors did indeed remain longer. And they were relaxed. Kay recalled that Truman charmed a martinet nurse to turn a blind eye on the rather unusual activities in Kay's hospital room.

One night Kay's doctor, extremely fatigued, came to her room for a drink. He asked Kay how to get the whiskey from the keg under the bed. Kay told him that the enema tube was used for that purpose, among others. Grateful, the doctor had a nip and went about his errands of mercy somewhat refreshed. "Grace under pressure" is the way John F. Kennedy defined courage—a fitting description for the belle of Greenport and Manhattan.[14]

Kay relates another humorous booze tale from the Smith odyssey. When they reported to Benning to join the Infantry School faculty in 1929, Kay was aware that the new school assistant commandant, George C. Marshall, had made it known that he expected the Infantry School to be "dry." Kay said Marshall's reputation was that he was able, ambitious, and demanding. She decreed there would be no alcohol in the Smith quarters. Truman objected. He felt obligated to have liquor for their guests, to reciprocate for the alcoholic beverages they surely would be offered in the quarters of their friends and colleagues. Kay put her foot down: no booze. Apparently she was far more concerned with Marshall's dictate than with the fact that prohibition was the law of the land from 1919 to 1933.

They had been exploring their assigned, but not yet completely furnished, quarters for about an hour when there was a knock on the door. A captain from the Fourth Section of the Infantry School, Truman's section, informed the newly arrived couple that they would be the guests of the officers and wives of the section at dinner that night. The next day they would be guests for all their meals. After that, it was expected that their furniture would be in place, and they would be on their own.

As the captain departed he said, "Look in your cellar. The Fourth Section takes care of its own." Kay wondered what that meant, so she went to the cellar. "There before my horrified eyes lay a five-gallon keg of Georgia corn. I was already defeated. Not five minutes in the house we had whiskey in it! How hard it is to go 'straight.'"[15]

Kay writes of the Fort Leavenworth assignment, "At Benning everyone in the class had put on his preference list for next assignment, Fort Leavenworth, the Command and Staff College. Truman received this longed-for assignment."[16]

Truman's remarks about his Leavenworth experience confirm that success in the course was, indeed, career enhancing. He called it "a plum." The upper half of the approximately 150 officers in the course would be placed on "the General Staff eligible list," meaning that they were eligible to serve on the War Department General Staff in Washington. Competition was intense. Smith says, "Up to the year 1926, when the publication of marks achieved was ended, successive classes had averaged about one suicide a year. But even in my class, in which no officer was supposed to know where he stood, the mood of fierce competition continued."[17] Kay also alludes to suicides, "but not this year." Suicides at Leavenworth, due to the pressure of competition and demanding work, were and continue to be a part of army folklore, perpetuated despite lack of evidence. Why spoil perfectly good mythology with facts?

Truman, as usual, worked hard. "Written problems were given almost daily," he notes. But he believed that at Leavenworth intensity was confused with quality. "Personally I found the course to be far less interesting than the one I had completed the year before at Fort Benning. I also regarded Leavenworth educational methods as archaic. In particular they seemed to me to present war as a chess game which was to be solved by mathematical formulas." This latter point and his criticism of the methods used would cause him soon to embrace George Marshall's methods at the Infantry School. And Marshall valued Smith's approach to using history and what we would now call case studies to teach tactics.

Smith, German exchange student Adolf von Schell, and Marshall would arrive at similar methods, emphasizing flexibility and the need for troop leaders to react to the constantly changing situations that characterize actual combat. Lengthy written orders and formulas were the very antithesis of the Marshall years at Benning. That was also Smith's conviction. "The written problems [at Leavenworth] I thought were stereotyped and artificial. Nevertheless, I studied hard each night from eight to midnight. I and three close friends formed a study group in which we quizzed each other every evening with merciless severity." The other members of this group were Paul Peabody, Richard Tindall, and Ralph Smith, "all later destined to be general officers in the Second World War."[18]

The Command and General Staff Course year was not a joy for the Smiths. The quarters were uncomfortable, the weather atrocious, the recreation limited; and the many prisons in the neighborhood made the place gloomy. "My wife regards this year at Leavenworth as one of the most uncomfortable of her thirty army years," Smith wrote. But his talents and self-discipline ranked him fourth in his class. He was very pleased to get War Department orders in the spring of 1928 to the Infantry School for duty as an instructor in the Military History Department of the fourth section of the school. "The ensuing four-year tour of duty was about the most pleasant of my entire army life," he recalled. "My wife shares this view. It also influenced markedly, I think, my subsequent army career."[19]

7

Marshall's Men

> I will give you pastors according to mine heart, which shall feed you with knowledge and understanding.
>
> —Jeremiah 3:15, King James Version

The people and the work made Smith's Benning assignment "most pleasant." Kay was relaxed, and Truman thoroughly enjoyed his job. Many of their friends, colleagues, and students became the top army leaders during and after World War II, and there was an unexpected bonus. Truman's already close connection to the German Army was strengthened by an official visit to Prussia and by meeting Captain Adolf von Schell, who was the first German exchange officer assigned to Fort Benning after the Great War. Schell became a lifelong friend of the Smiths. But the most important aspect of the Benning assignment for Smith was his introduction to George C. Marshall. Smith admired Marshall at Benning, and that admiration increased over time. Marshall reciprocated, discovering in Smith personal and professional qualities that made him one of a group called "Marshall's men," soldiers who would exercise power and bear great responsibilities in the Second World War.

Marshall never published a memoir. He didn't want to repeat the race to glory and the finger pointing that followed the Great War in a battle of memoirs, which, as a close associate of General of the Armies John J. Pershing, Marshall was in a good position to observe. Fortunately, Forrest C. Pogue has given us a biography of Marshall in four volumes that provides great insight into the man.[1]

Generals in times of war make decisions of consequence, creating clusters of friends and enemies, cheerleaders and snipers. However, in the century and more that have passed since his commissioning in January 1902, and the sixty years plus since he left public service in September 1951, Marshall's copybook is strikingly free of blots. Considering the scrutiny of his decisions, the events in which he participated, and his high posts in momentous times, including army chief of staff, secretary of state, and secretary of defense, the absence of ad hominem criticism is remarkable. Professionalism and rectitude defined his career from beginning to end. He personified the Prussian motto "Sein Statt Schein" ("Be, rather than appear to be").

In 1901 Marshall was first captain at the Virginia Military Institute (VMI), served with distinction in the Philippines at the beginning of his career, and was first in his 1907 class at Fort Leavenworth, remaining to serve on the faculty there until 1910. Despite the fact that his work brought him to the attention of luminaries before the Great War—Hunter Liggett, who would distinguish himself as first army commander in the Great War in 1918; J. Franklin Bell, commandant, General Service and Staff College (1903–1906); Tasker H. Bliss, chief of staff and later American military representative in the Supreme War Council; Leonard Wood, Medal of Honor recipient, Harvard Medical School graduate, friend of Theodore Roosevelt, and army chief of staff; Henry L. Stimson, secretary of war under Presidents Taft, F. D. Roosevelt, and Truman among them—at thirty-five Marshall was still a lieutenant and would remain one until his promotion to captain on 14 August 1916 after fourteen years as an officer, nine as a first lieutenant. Then-Lieutenant Henry H. (Hap) Arnold, later chief of army air forces in World War II, said of Marshall in a letter to his wife in 1913 that he had just seen a future chief of staff in action.[2] Another peer called him "one of the finest tacticians and strategists in the Army . . . with the quickest and best answers to tactical problems of any officer I ever met."[3] These accolades did not prevent him from considering leaving the army. Discouraged by slow promotions and the prospect of a mediocre career, he considered resignation from the army in a 22 November 1915 letter to VMI superintendent and mentor General E. W. Nichols, who replied, "I would advise you to stick to it. If you do, I am sure in time you will be among the high ranking officers in the service."[4]

Though his requests for command in the Great War were denied, Marshall distinguished himself as an organizer and staff officer as a colonel. After the war, he reverted to major as the army was severely reduced. Pershing selected him to serve as a kind of personal chief of staff in 1919, a job he did for the next five years, one of the longest tours of his military career. He was promoted to lieutenant colonel, again, in August 1922. In 1924 Marshall asked for and got an assignment he long desired, duty with the 15th Infantry in China. The trip to China from New York was long, but it was punctuated by a visit to Panama, where General Fox Conner, often credited with being the mentor of Dwight Eisenhower, entertained with lots of champagne. In San Francisco General Hunter Liggett, who successfully commanded a corps and an army in France, hosted the Marshalls. In Honolulu they visited General and Mrs. Charles P. Summerall, an artillery innovator of the Great War. While at sea Marshall received a message sent from Paris, which read: "Au revoir, Affectionately, Pershing." Clearly, change of station was effected at a leisurely pace in those days, and networking was as important then as now, perhaps more so then. Later, centralization of selection for schools and command slots reduced the clout of the old boys' network considerably.

Marshall was assigned as executive officer of the 15th Infantry, but immediately upon his arrival he acted as interim commander for two and a half months until the new commanding officer arrived. There would be a similar period of command when his colonel was later relieved of his duties. During what was essentially a happy tour with troops (1924–1927) and a three-year shopping expedition for Mrs. Lily Marshall, momentous events were unfolding in China, to which Marshall would return during and after the Second World War. In 1927, the Kuomintang-Communist split took place, effectively beginning a civil war in China that would end with Communist victory in 1949. Meanwhile, foreign garrisons and regional warlords compounded the complexity of events during Marshall's tour, as would Japanese interventions just a few years later.

Lily Marshall saw more of her husband in China than she had since before the Great War. Despite the "convulsions shaking China," life in the American compound was generally relaxed and pleasant. But Lily's health, never robust, took a turn for the worse. In the early summer of 1927, the Marshalls returned to Washington, where he was to lecture at the Army War College. In August, following what had been expected to be a minor operation, Lily Marshall died. The couple had been married for twenty-six years. Marshall was shocked by Lily's unexpected death. He felt an emptiness in his life that caused him to say later, "At a War College desk I thought I would explode." He knew that he needed intense physical and mental activity that would totally absorb him. He was offered several options—remain at the War College, become corps chief of staff in New York, or take a post at Fort Benning. "I thought it best professionally and in my present frame of mind to go to Benning," he noted. So he went, and threw himself into the Infantry School with great energy and a clear sense of purpose. It was at Benning that Smith was able to take the full measure of Marshall, even while Marshall was noting and remembering the strengths and weaknesses of his faculty and students.

Smith observed in his memoir that although Marshall was assigned as the assistant commandant at the Infantry School, under the two generals who commanded while he was there, "Marshall had almost a free hand to mold the course and direct methods of teaching as he wished." Marshall took full advantage of the opportunity and in four years revolutionized educational and training methods "backed by as able a group of officer-instructors as our army ever gathered together at one time." Smith considered it "an honor and a privilege to have been a member of the faculty and also to have contributed my bit to the Benning 'revolution' which was inspired and directed by George Marshall."

The entire faculty was loyal and devoted to their chief, "with the possible exception of Joe Stilwell," whom Smith describes as "an odd man . . . loyal to no one but himself . . . a thorn in Marshall's side." This insight, gratuitously provided by Smith, who did not engage in petty gossip, is all the more interesting since it had been Marshall who brought Stilwell from the 15th Infantry to Fort Benning. Stilwell, always difficult and ever the antithesis of a diplomat, later famously referred to Chiang Kai-shek as "Peanut Head." Less well known is the fact that Stilwell had spent ten years in China before World War II, spoke and wrote Chinese, and was a skilled and hard-driving infantryman. Marshall could have had a more congenial man assigned, but he chose "Vinegar Joe" for his tactical skills. It is said that Stilwell was the only general who called Marshall "George."[5]

It has become a mantra of American military historians to say that an extraordinary number of Marshall's men became famous American commanders in World War II, many of them household names. From the 1927–1932 period, some 150 of his students and 50 of his instructors became general officers. And there was a multiplier effect, as Marshall's teachings were carried to the army in the field by those men and anonymous others who did not get to the top of the military hierarchy.

While Marshall unquestionably deserves top marks for his teaching and influence, it must be noted that that the trained officers of the interwar period were perfectly positioned to become the flag officers of World War II. Who else would lead a vastly expanded citizen army—and navy—composed of millions of amateurs? Marshall later, as chief of staff, did not tolerate senior Regular Army, Reserve, or National Guard officers who were unable to adapt to the speed of modern war. The ordinary types who couldn't keep up were shunted aside to perform necessary but routine tasks, or they were retired. They are, for the most part, forgotten. Moreover, some famous leaders of World War II, but for timing, would have joined the ranks of retired lieutenant colonels and colonels.

Marshall was as pleased with his assignment as Smith was with his. Soon after arriving at Benning, Marshall had two interesting job offers. Governor General Dwight F. Davis asked him to go to the Philippines as chief of constabulary, a prestige job that paid well. Secretary of State Stimson had proposed him for that post. In addition, Virginia friends asked that Marshall "allow his name to be presented for the superintendency of VMI." He declined both offers. He wanted the Infantry School at Benning.[6]

Marshall agreed with Smith regarding the quality of his faculty. The Infantry School "was composed of the most brilliant, interesting and thoroughly competent collection of men I have ever been associated with."[7] Marshall also reveled in having "an unlimited field of activity, delightful associates, and all outdoors to play in."[8]

Kay Smith, in her memoir, adds this cogent insight: "One of the great blessings of Benning was the opportunity for so many young officers of the same age and rank to learn to know each other thoroughly. When World War II came these men knew on whom to rely, knew their capabilities of command and their ability in leadership, planning, and decision making. The life-long attachments formed and assessments of each other were nearly as important as the school training."[9]

Marshall was a teacher who made a difference by opening minds. He was also modest about his accomplishments, finding himself "in the embarrassing position of seeming to be the one who knew." He did not feel that he was the originator of much that happened on his watch, saying, "I furnished the directive and drive and the arbitrary orders it must be done."[10] It is true that his men got it done, but Truman Smith saw it otherwise. He said that Marshall used his instructors to carry out his ideas. He would tell them what he wanted and then they would do it. Smith said there was something about Marshall that made one *want* to do what he wanted done.

Pogue notes that Marshall's three decades of professional experience in a variety of assignments informed him that it would be best to proceed "quietly and gradually." There was opposition to overcome. Some officers preferred "the even tenor of their theoretical ways. . . . To issue an edict or regulation would probably do more harm than good. The job must be a personal one, to be affected slowly as faculty minds, physical means, and other tangible factors are gradually rounded into shape for each step. Sudden changes in an educational plant are bound to be destructive, and any material changes must be timed by the men on the ground."[11]

Those intimately familiar with the army schools system will note wryly that more recently and more typically army "educators" are inclined to pull a plant up often—preferably annually—to inspect its roots. Last year's curriculum or syllabus is presumed to be outdated, so last year! Moreover, highly centralized command, enabled by an ever-increasing technical ability to reach from top to bottom, threatens to kill initiative in the chain of command and create fear of failure. That is precisely what Marshall did not permit. Typically, if an instructor asked how he could do what was wanted, Marshall's response was, that's your problem. He told his instructors *what* he wanted and trusted them to figure out *how* to get it done, a point amusingly made by Smith, who, in addition to being one of his instructors at Benning, was also Marshall's tennis partner. In "The Facts of Life" Smith reports that one day Marshall said, "Smith, it would be nice if we could hold a big tournament at Benning and procure 'Big Bill' Tilden and 'Little Bill' Johnston as participants." Without much thought, Smith replied, "How on earth could we obtain such famous players way down here in the South?" Quick as a wink Marshall shot back, "Smith, that's your business." Smith made it happen.

The essence of Marshall's influence on tactical training is found in two words: simplicity and flexibility. As long as the nation's defense relied upon an expandable army, in time of mobilization that army would consist of a small professional core augmented by a mass of citizen soldiers: National Guard, reservists, volunteers, ROTC-commissioned officers, and conscripts. Marshall's experience convinced him that a citizen army must concentrate on learning the essentials of tactics. Its leaders had to know how to think clearly about problems on the battlefield without being entangled in elaborate techniques, long planning, and the distribution of elegant, printed orders. It was Marshall's opinion that the American Army in France became wrapped up in form because it was anxious to *appear* professional to its allies. As Pershing's aide, he reviewed the army's needs and concluded that equipment, administration, and training were all too complicated for anything but a purely professional army. Similarly, after five months with the 15th Infantry in China, he wrote to Pershing, "I find that the officers are highly developed in the tactical handling or functioning of weapons, in target practice, in bayonet combat, and in the special and intricate details of paperwork or administration generally, *but that when it comes to simple tactical problems, the actual duties of troop leading, they all fall far below the standards they set in other matters.*"[12]

In 1933, after his Benning tenure, Marshall continued to express his concern for embedded institutional focus on the petty and merely formal. He wanted to "get down to the essentials, make clear the real difficulties, and expunge the bunk, complications, and ponderosities [*sic*]; we must concentrate on registering in men's minds certain vital considerations instead of a mass of less important details. *We must develop a technique and methods so simple and so brief that the citizen officer of good common sense can readily grasp the idea.*"[13]

He refused to present battle to junior leaders as an organized and predictable affair, identifying two deadly sins. First: too much information about the enemy was provided in classroom situations, when in fact combat leaders typically operate with incomplete intelligence, inadequate maps, and other important unknowns. Second: officers must not leave the Infantry School believing they have canned school solutions for all tactical situations in their backpacks; the real problem, Marshall held, "is usually *when* to make a decision not *what* the decision should be." The leader's estimate of the situation is just that: an estimate. Based on that estimate he acts expeditiously by deciding and issuing his order. Waiting for complete information allows the moment to pass and the situation to change.[14] Smith called Marshall "a foe of the military 'scholasticism' which had dominated Leavenworth."[15]

Setting aside for the moment the differences between preparing company-grade officers for combat at the platoon to battalion levels, and the preparation of field-grade staff officers at division level and above, Marshall emphasized tactical decision making in constantly changing battlefield conditions. And, whatever the circumstances, officers were to accept responsibility. (As army chief of staff as of 1 September 1939, Marshall streamlined his staff and simplified decision making at the very top of the army as well. The army staff learned that clear presentation of an issue brought to Marshall was necessary but not sufficient. The chief wanted the staff officer to tell him what he should do about it. Dumping the problem on Marshall's desk was unacceptable. The staffer needed the guts to take responsibility for a decision.)[16]

Even now, in the twenty-first century, one continues to hear the essence of Marshall's legacy in references to the Fort Benning KISS formula: Keep It Simple, Stupid. The dirty, unclear, and dangerous world of the infantryman is generally not an environment that can tolerate leisurely production of long or complex orders. The leader enters the fight with a plan, but timely, fragmentary orders are constantly issued in reaction to an appreciation of constantly changing circumstances. Orders can't be complicated and often are simply, "Go there. Do that." A second best plan, a well-executed simple one, is generally preferable to an optimal scheme requiring coordination almost certain to break down in a setting that makes even the simplest of tasks difficult.

Marshall also emphasized flexibility. On the face of it, there seems to be a contradiction in teaching simplicity and flexibility. The former assumes that the leader knows and communicates what is to be done. Flexibility assumes that the leader will almost certainly encounter something unexpected that affects his plan or course of action. This indeterminacy is what Clausewitz called fog. Smith made a major contribution in teaching the means by which Marshall's desired flexibility in junior troop leaders could be achieved while maintaining simplicity. Smith's training in history and his infantry experience were an optimal combination that provided Marshall with a specific means to accomplish ends simple to express but difficult to realize. Today we would call what Smith did the case study method of teaching: presenting a case from the past that is rather like a situation addressed in the present. The "rather like" is important. The past case was not a blueprint; it was only similar.

At Benning, Smith joined the Fourth Section of the Infantry School, History and Publications. For his first two years he was an assistant in the Military History Section; in the final two years of his assignment he was its chief and, he later wrote, "succeeded in obtaining as my assistant the gifted Richard Tindall, who had been a member of our Leavenworth study group."[17]

In the small Regular Army of the interwar period, an officer could be familiar with most officers of his branch and most of his grade in the entire army.[18] Moreover, the rather small group of front-runners attending branch schools, staff colleges, and the War Colleges knew one another or knew of one another. Alternating school and field assignments, living together "close to the flagpole," made the social life of this group somewhat inbred. They were constantly meeting friends of friends, assisting one another in personal crises, celebrating promotions, and experiencing the ubiquitous hail-and-farewell of the nomadic professional soldier. This intimate subculture, as Kay noted in her memoir, meant that one's personality, style, strengths and weaknesses, and character were all revealed to others.

That old boys' network can be, and has been, abused by those who allow friendship to blind them to mediocrity or incompetence, or enmity to blur judgment in other ways. Marshall's men were selected on the basis of their being the best qualified for the tasks he had in mind, then and later, when he led the entire U.S. Army. Despite being a burr under the saddle, Lieutenant Colonel Stilwell led First Section, Tactics.[19] Second Section, Logistics and Communication, was led by Lieutenant Colonel M. C. Stayer, a medical doctor. Third Section, Weapons and Weapons Doctrine, was led by Lieutenant Colonel Omar N. Bradley, a quiet-spoken man, as different in temperament from Stilwell as it is possible to imagine. The Bradleys and the Smiths were next-door neighbors, but not intimates.

Lieutenant Colonel Edwin Forrest Harding, "another China friend of Marshall's," wrote Smith, "a charming and scholarly officer, to whom during the ensuing four years I became deeply devoted," led Fourth Section.[20] A very literate man, Harding amused friends around the world with his humorous poetry and activity in theatricals. He edited the *Infantry Journal* from 1934 to 1938; and planned, supervised, and edited the 1934 book *Infantry in Battle* and was consulted for the extensive revisions of the version published in 1938. A man of many parts, Harding commanded the 27th Infantry (Wolfhounds) Regiment before World War II and the 32d Division in that war. He was the first chief of military history, U.S. Army, and retired a major general, as did so many of Marshall's men.[21]

In a rare instance of Smith's permitting himself to take a bow, in his memoir he cited Pogue's description of what was happening at Fort Benning in the Marshall years:

> History properly presented could also underline for students the real problem of decision amid the confusion of battle. Marshall was delighted when one of his staff, Major Truman Smith (later distinguished as the United States military attaché who watched and perceptively reported the rearming of the Third Reich), worked out several lectures in which a historical battle was described and the part played by a small unit outlined. On the basis of the actual fragmentary information the students were required to explain what they would have done had they been in command. Major Harding's section later carried on the idea and compiled a book of examples from history (published as *Infantry in Battle*).[22]

In his instruction, Smith used some of the opening battles of movement of the Great War involving small units of German and French infantry regiments, before the war of movement gave way to trench warfare, believing that few students would have knowledge of the course of the battles or their outcomes. Confusion and uncertainty in battle were stressed, just as Marshall wished. Smith reports that Marshall was almost always present and usually rose during the class to emphasize his own ideas. Smith gave credit to his colleagues Tindall and Major Gilbert Cook, but it was he who was singled out for the good work, and it was he who was sent out to share the teaching technique in lectures he gave to National Guard and Reserve officers at Jackson, Mississippi; Birmingham, Alabama; Macon, Albany, and Atlanta, Georgia; and Tampa and Jacksonville, Florida. Marshall was ever conscious of the need to teach and train the citizen officers who would vastly outnumber the Regulars after mobilization. Smith also delivered one or two lectures at the Air Corps Tactical School at Maxwell Field near Montgomery, Alabama.

In his memoirs, Smith mentioned that he had two "subsidiary duties." He taught public speaking, saying that in so doing he taught himself how to handle both friendly and hostile audiences, a great help in every stage of his later career as an officer and still later as a candidate for public office. He was also school librarian, a job he enjoyed. Marshall wanted a great military library; Smith recalled that Marshall "turned over to me each year very considerable sums for the purchase of books . . . between twenty and thirty thousand dollars on books in three years, if my memory does not fail me."[23]

It isn't clear if modesty or a failing memory explains why Smith failed to mention in his memoirs that he also collaborated with Leroy W. Yarborough during this period to write a history of the Infantry School from 1776.[24]

More interesting regarding training, however, are Smith's German connections. They placed him in the center of Marshall's quest

Marshall sent Smith to observe the Reichswehr. From right: Smith, General Werner von Blomberg, and Colonel Schaumburg, commander of the 1st Prussian Infantry Regiment at Arys, East Prussia, 10–13 July 1931. Contacts made on this trip were extremely helpful to Smith's access to key officers in Berlin, 1935–1939. (Courtesy of Katharine Smith Coley and family.)

for methods to teach tactics and made both Smith and Marshall aware of General Hans von Seekt's similar efforts to teach tactics. The story of the professional and personal relationship of Marshall, Smith, and German captain Adolf von Schell, a 1931 Advanced Course graduate, begins with Marshall's appointing Smith as aide to visiting German general Werner von Blomberg during Blomberg's visit to Benning in 1930. Blomberg (later Hitler's war minister, deliberately disgraced and relieved of his duties by the Nazis) invited an American officer to visit Germany for the 1931 First German Division maneuvers at Arys in East Prussia.[25]

Marshall sent Smith, both because Smith could afford to pay for the trip that Marshall could not fund and because of Smith's apparent rapport with the Germans. While in Germany Smith was invited to the Field Artillery School by General Friedrich von Boetticher, whom Smith had known since 1920. Boetticher was later a longtime military attaché in Washington. He had great affection for the United States and was Smith's close friend. Smith recalled, "I profited greatly from the two weeks spent in these military visits, renewed my acquaintance with many German officers, made several new friends later destined to prove useful, and brought myself generally up to date on German military thinking. The following winter Colonel Marshall directed that I deliver at Benning several lectures on German military developments. This I did."[26]

Marshall reciprocated by inviting a German officer to attend the Advanced Course at the Infantry School. Captain Adolf von Schell was that officer. He had fought in Belgium and France as a platoon leader until he was wounded in October 1914. As of February 1915, he was a company commander in the winter battles of the Mazurian Lakes, in the assault that climaxed with the fall of Warsaw, and in the drive east that took him to the Beresina River. In 1916 he operated with Austrians in the effort to stop the Brussilov offensive in Galicia. In 1917 he was in the Carpathians, and in 1918 in the Ukraine, the Crimea, and the Caucasus. The Armistice found him fighting the Bolsheviks. As Major General Campbell King put it, "There is probably no officer in our army who has participated in so many widely varying types of military operations as Captain von Schell."[27]

Kay Smith provides insight to Schell's nature and his relationship to Truman, to her, and to Marshall that began in Schell's year at Benning. That year was followed by his study of the production methods at General Motors, followed by his rapid advancement to positions of great authority and responsibility in the motorization and mechanization of the Reichswehr and the Wehrmacht.

She recalled that Schell barely spoke English upon his arrival at Benning and so gravitated to the German-speaking Smiths. He was grateful for their hospitality and valued their friendship. That friendship later gave Truman a key source of intelligence when the Smiths returned to Berlin in 1935. The relationship also saved Schell's life in the immediate post–World War II period, when Smith and Marshall personally intervened to prevent the British Army from turning Schell over to the Russians as a POW. A photograph of Marshall inscribed "To my friend Adolf von Schell" and signed by Marshall upon Schell's departure from Fort Benning figures prominently in the story. The British confiscated the photo before Smith-to-Marshall-to-Churchill communications intervened and kept Schell in the British-occupied area of Germany. Marshall then sent a replacement inscribed photo to Schell, which Schell treasured, not least because Marshall called him "friend."

Kay said that Schell admired Marshall almost immediately. That observation came from the poised and confident lady who confessed, "Colonel Marshall rather intimidated me. He is one of the few men with whom I have been uneasy, yet he was always friendly. . . . Friendly as he might be, there was always a reserve. Those who understood him gave him life long loyalty."

Smith and Schell understood him. Marshall reciprocated with loyalty to them. In contemporary jargon, these quintessential professionals "bonded." Marshall's use of the word "friend" in his inscription to Schell will strike those who know something about him as unusual: Marshall was a distant man, always formally addressed by title and always calling subordinates by their family names. Smith, as close as he was to Marshall, was always "Smith" in direct address, never Truman, and "Dear Smith" in letters.

Kay departs from strict chronology in her memoir, skipping from 1931 to the mid-1950s, as though she could not wait to tell this follow-up story: "When Truman was sent by General Trudeau to Germany in 1955 on a special mission [Smith was vetting German officers for key posts in the rearming of the Federal Republic of Germany's new army, the Bundeswehr] we saw Adolf again. As each [of his children] was introduced, each sank to a knee, kissed our hands, saying, 'We thank you for our father's life.' Tears clouded my eyes as I raised the young women to their feet, quite overwhelmed."[28]

Returning to the Benning years and Schell's arrival there, she writes that Schell reveled in the great adventure. "He had never seen a Negro 'til he reached Georgia, and his eyes never left a maid of color who was serving at dinner. . . . When we took [him] to see [a fourteen-foot-long alligator in the wild], his eyes popped."[29]

Schell enjoyed driving on post and in the countryside, and appreciated being regularly rescued by classmates and faculty as his car, apparently frequently, broke down. Kay reports an observation Schell made that occurs to many Europeans who don't quite know what to make of Americans. "He thought Americans the most friendly and helpful people he had ever met. . . . But by the end of the year Adolf decided the Americans were the most difficult of all people to really know. They are most friendly, call one by one's first name on meeting, go out of the way to be helpful, but no one gets any closer than at the first meeting."[30] Perhaps, but the Smith-Schell-Marshall relationship belies the generalization. Their link was the lasting soul-to-soul connection captured in the best of Russian literature. (See appendixes G and I.)

Kay wrote that in six months Schell was lecturing to standing-room-only classes at the Infantry School. Of course as the first postwar German doing a course at Benning, he was something of a novelty. But she reports that people were seen standing on boxes outside of lecture halls while looking through windows to see and hear him for what he had to say about decision making in close combat. His audience of American Regulars recognized that this German professional soldier had fought a long war in its many forms, including movement to contact and dynamic battles of movement on the Eastern Front.

Schell's lectures were presented precisely in the manner Marshall sought, Smith evolved, and Erwin Rommel later popularized. A unit combat action within a battle actually fought was the scenario. Schell would state his teaching point, for example: "In war, obscurity and confusion are normal. Late, exaggerated, or misleading information, surprise situations, and counter-orders are to be expected." He would then describe an action, calling it an "example," and provide the source: who fought the battle, where, and when. Then, in a short "discussion," he would draw out what was learned in the action. In a later, printed version this is accomplished in about three pages, one of which is a hand-drawn sketch clearly matched to the example.[31]

Smith, in his own classes, added a twist. At a decisive moment in the narrative, he would stop, choose a student, and ask, "Captain, what are your orders at this time?" The student had the information available to the leader at the time of the action, no more. The student would respond. Others were then drawn into thinking through the problem, with Marshall himself routinely in attendance and participating. The point was clearly made: combat leaders had to be flexible. Rommel's technique, similar to that just described, is perhaps more widely known than that outlined in the Fort Benning–produced text *Infantry in Battle.* Rommel's *Attacks* was first published in Germany in 1937 as *Infanterie Greift An.* It went through eighteen printings by 1944 and was translated and published by the U.S. Army in 1943 under the title *Infantry Attacks* and again in 1979 as *Attacks.* Rommel briskly narrates a combat action, including sketches and hand-drawn maps. Then, in italics, he follows with "*Observations,*" drawing teaching points from the action just described. The same technique was applied in the field. After a training exercise a critique followed in which the instructor highlighted good points and bad, inviting further discussion by students. There did not need to be agreement. The point was for participants to engage the situation, to think it through. It is no wonder that the work of Schell and Smith pleased Marshall. They gave him means and method to produce a simplicity in orders for small units to overcome the friction of their immediate environment while simultaneously appreciating the infinite variety of battle. Most important, Regulars were being prepared to train citizen-soldiers in leadership.

There was a good reason why the Germans had a leg up on the Americans regarding tactical training. General Seekt, father of the Reichswehr (1920–1926), the German Army, which was limited to 100,000 men and 4,000 officers by the Treaty of Versailles, in 1921 directed study, analysis, and the publication of a series of army field and training manuals known as *Heeresdienstvorschriften,* abbreviated HDV. Their purpose was to incorporate into German training what had been learned in the recent war. HDV 487, also called *Feuhrerschaft in Gefecht,* abbreviated FG, was translated as *Leadership in Battle* (though *Gefecht* actually suggests more a fight, an engagement, an encounter, what is sometimes called "minor tactics," rather than a Jena or Waterloo level of battle). Schell was the link between what Marshall wanted to accomplish in the late 1920s and early 1930s and what Seekt had directed be done in Germany in the early 1920s. Smith was familiar with the armies of both countries, and would watch both as they would later mobilize and expand.

Defeat, like the prospect of hanging, tends to focus one's attention. So did Germany need to organize, on a completely new basis, a small, all-volunteer, long-service army without the conscript-centered and highly organized reserve system that characterized the armies of the major European Powers before the Great War. The German Army early on in the midst of political chaos conducted scrupulous study, with a focus on tactics.

The American Army experience of 1917–1918 was an introduction to trench warfare followed by the final counteroffensive on the Western Front that ended the war. In sharp contrast, then-junior German officers, such as Rommel, Albrecht Kesselring, Ewald von Kleist, Erich von Manstein, and Karl von Rundstedt, had extensive experience on the Eastern Front in battles of movement involving cavalry and infantry. Future British and French leaders were almost entirely conditioned to static war by their long fight in the trenches of the Western Front. Those differences shaped training in the various armies between 1919 and 1939 and the conduct of operations in the next European war.

Reichswehr officers, forbidden to participate in policy formulation, turned their energy to the operational side of war. Practically every issue of *Militaer Wochenblatt* in the 1920s included articles on tactics and weapons. Small-unit tactics of all sorts were emphasized. Rommel, for example, never served on the General Staff. He was an instructor at the Infantry School in Dresden from 1929 to 1932—interestingly, while Marshall was at Benning's Infantry School—and wrote several pamphlets based on his combat experiences on three fronts that were assembled in book form as *Infanterie Greift An.* All of these factors turned the attention of German officers, Schell included, to tactics. (One could argue that emphasis on tactics and operations enabled the Germans to fight very well in ill-conceived strategies, a topic for another day.)[32]

Tactical expertise and ability to teach made Schell a perfect fit in Marshall's Infantry School. Smith's academic, cultural, and combat background meshed nicely with Schell's temperament and experience to realize Marshall's concept: teach Regulars a simple method of decision making in combat so that it could be passed on to the citizen-soldiers who would be the junior leadership in a mobilized mass army. Trust, respect, and essential compatibility among the German and the two Americans, Marshall and Smith, survived tension and war. All three left Fort Benning with satisfaction in a job well done.

8

Army War College and Command

> General McNair used to call those guys, the ones that had gone through the War College, the Ph.D.s of the Army. Anything that came up, there was some guy who just knew a hell of a lot about it. It was the one place where you could sit down and think.
>
> —General Thomas T. Handy, 1974

Smith's gratifying years at Fort Benning with Marshall, Schell, and other first-rate professionals were focused on training and tactics. That assignment was followed by a year at the Army War College, where his focus was on national strategy, military strategy, and an expansion of his already considerable expertise regarding Germany, just as Hitler was coming to power and consolidating his grip on all aspects of life in Germany. Upon completion of the academic year in Washington, Smith returned to troop duty as a battalion commander in Hawaii, a place he had earlier visited and remembered fondly. The pattern of his assignments was consistent with the army's practice of providing Regular Army officers a range of experiences from a "place where you could sit down and think" to a place where one's boots got muddy in the field in the company of soldiers.

Smith was pleased to be selected for the Army War College (AWC). He described the college as being the peak of the pyramid of army schools. It was a place where even casual social interaction was professional development, because one interacted with men who were still in the race to the top of the profession. Among military professionals there is a seamless segueing from professional to social to personal and back without differentiation. Kay and Truman saw life as an integrated whole, the center of which was unreserved faithfulness to duty. His classmates knew of his German expertise, that he was a decorated infantryman, that he was one of Marshall's men, and that he was on the fast track.

Successful completion of the Leavenworth course, indeed high standing in one's class there, and an impressive record of performance over almost twenty years of service was necessary to qualify for General Staff duty and for appointment to the AWC. The officers selected to attend were regarded as prospective generals and key General Staff officers. That's the way it was from the beginning, when John J. Pershing graduated with the first class in 1905, and that's the way it continues to be into the twenty-first century.

In the period between the world wars, class size at the AWC was generally eighty-five officers: seventy-nine army and six navy and marine corps. Reciprocally, usually six army officers attended the Naval War College in Newport, Rhode Island. The army school was in Washington Barracks, later renamed Fort McNair, and a short trolley ride to War Department headquarters near the White House. The thinking and writing Truman Smith did there in his academic year solidified his already established reputation as the most knowledgeable officer in the U.S. Army regarding Germany.

Smith later recalled that in sharp contrast to the Leavenworth Command and General Staff College Course, "there was no competition among the students at the [Army War] College."[1] Class work was performed in committees and subcommittees consisting of several students each, who would work together for several weeks on some aspect of a prospective war, such as, for example, manpower and industrialization, estimates and surveys of a potential enemy's war capabilities and limitations, or American war plans. When the assigned task was completed after analysis and the preparation of a paper, findings and conclusions were presented orally to the class in a plenary session and subjected to criticism and discussion by students and faculty. Then, student committees were reconfigured to work a new problem with different classmates. In the course of the year, one worked closely with nearly all of the other students. During Smith's time at the War College, this resulted in familiarity with just about all of those who would lead in World War II. About 75 percent of the War College graduates from 1933 to 1940 attained flag rank.[2]

Study, analysis, production of papers, and presentations by the student committees alternated with presentations by academics, diplomats, journalists, educators, elected officials, industrialists, and senior leaders of the uniformed services. For example, one of the guest speakers in Smith's academic year (1932–1933) was Colonel Hunt, Smith's former boss in Coblenz, who spoke on civil affairs in an occupied country. Probably the greatest challenge to most Army War College (AWC) students, then and now, was the requirement to write a paper roughly comparable to a master's thesis. In Smith's time at AWC, it was called the Individual Staff Memorandum, or ISM.

Upon reflection years later, Smith indicated that every effort had been made by the college to expand the intellectual horizon of those chosen to be the future leaders of the army. He was certain that he personally benefited greatly from the experience. For reasons he did not explain, he was particularly drawn to lectures on industrial mobilization, about which he had previously been only dimly aware. Witnessing the German experience in the transition from mass army to a smaller force of 100,000 stimulated his interest in transforming an army, but he was also filling what he saw as a gap in his professional knowledge base. In any event, the knowledge of both manpower and industrial mobilization he acquired at the college was particularly useful to him in his position as military attaché in Berlin (1935–1939) as he observed, analyzed, and reported on Hitler's rearmament of Germany. That rapid rearmament strengthened Hitler's confidence and accelerated his estimates of German readiness for war, which in turn accounted for aggressive German diplomacy during Smith's second tour in the American Embassy in Berlin.

The course of study at the Army War College was not designed specifically to prepare Smith to be military attaché in Germany, but in retrospect it appears to have been almost perfect preparation for that assignment. Some of what he studied there was right on target, that is, focused on Germany and in which Smith played a leading role. But the studies not specifically addressing German issues in which Smith was engaged illustrate the breadth and substance of the course. Among them, for example, were such topics as a strategic survey of the Soviet Union, a comprehensive examination reported to the rest of the class on 20 December 1932;[3] War Plan Red Coalition (Britain plus allies), reported on 14 April 1933;[4] concentration of enemy manpower on the North American continent (with special focus on ports, rail, transportation, and shipping nodes), reported on 22 November 1932;[5] joint and army strategic war plans (German, French, and British pre-World War I planning and the United States' present planning and plans), reported to the class on 23 September 1932;[6] and manpower, U.S. employment of women, and use of Negro manpower in military service.[7]

Students tackled problems in all General Staff areas: G-1 (personnel); G-2 (intelligence); G-3 (operations and training); G-4 (logistics); and War Plans. Some effort was made to focus on areas of a student's special competence, such as Smith's taking the lead in a Strategic Survey of Germany topic; and some where a student was relatively ignorant, such as Smith's introduction to industrial mobilization.

Conceptually, the course was divided into two broad areas: preparation for war, and conduct of war (the classic distinction in the spheres of military activity first identified by Clausewitz). Smith worked on several specifically German problems. One, "Joint German Operations, Oesel Island, 10–24 October 1917," was an analysis of a German amphibious operation in the Baltic Sea and Gulf of Finland that could have served as a template for German, Russian, and Finnish planners of operations in that part of the world in the Continuation War.[8] Another was "Counter-Offensive Vistula-San Operations, 28 September–27 October 1914,"[9] reported to the class on 17 February 1933, an analysis uncannily similar to German operations in the same area in September 1939 and described in the November 1939 issue of the *Cavalry Journal.*

Two major efforts of Smith's during his academic year highlight both his knowledge of Germany and his remarkable prescience. One was a committee he chaired that produced a paper called "A Strategic Survey of Germany," which was reported to students and faculty on 20 December 1932.[10] The second was his major individual paper, the ISM he wrote entitled "Germany and Hitler."[11]

The stated purpose of "Strategic Survey of Germany" was to arrive at "conclusions as to the maximum military effort that country could initiate and maintain; where its most vital interests lie, and how they coincide or conflict with those of Blue [the United States], and what would be its probable action in wars in which Blue might be involved."[12] Smith's report was impressively thorough. It began with an analysis of political geography: a survey of German territorial losses in Europe and its loss of colonies; the fact that Germany bordered on ten countries; an explanation of its existing political boundaries and subdivisions (*Läende,* or states within the Weimar Republic); and the fact that the Treaty of Versailles reduced Germany's population by 10 percent and its territory in Europe by 12 percent. It surveyed Germany's birth rate, climate, minerals, manufacturing, trade, transportation, communications, finance, banking, debt, financial stability, foreign relations, and system of government.

Smith's six-man committee, like all students at AWC, had ready access to almost unlimited sources of information due to the proximity of the college to civilian and military government agencies in Washington.

His committee, in its consideration of the current internal political situation in Germany, recognized that the Weimar Republic was in conflict with a potential Fascist dictatorship and reported that most recently rule in the country had been by decree. A parade of chancellors ensued. President Hindenburg had named Heinrich Bruening and then General Kurt von Schleicher as Reich Chancellor during a period of increasing instability, frequent elections, and the shuffling of cabinets. To fully appreciate Smith's insights it is important to note the date of his committee's report, 20 December 1932. Hitler came to power in January 1933.

In the committee's analysis of the German Army, we hear Smith's voice. The year before arriving at the AWC, Smith had spent the summer of 1931 in Germany focused on training, particularly on German methods used to teach tactics. There he found an emphasis on leadership, intelligence, flexibility, and initiative. "They escape the teaching of generalities by a rigid adherence to the case method," the committee report stated. "The German aim is always the same, 'to teach how, not what to think' . . . small reliance is placed on the rifle and bayonet and comparatively great reliance placed on supporting weapons."[13] These methods of suppression would be encountered by American infantry troops a dozen years later.[14]

The committee report also noted that the Germans favored small units with a high ratio of leaders to led. "Swift decisions, quick issuance of orders, and prompt execution" characterized German infantry tactics. "Small organizations, small staffs, and a marked absence of stereotyped form . . . surprise and mobility are their two tactical keystones." That, too, would impress chroniclers of German tactical performance in combat in World War II.[15]

At a time when the legal limit of Germany's army was 100,000 men, the survey concluded that on mobilization (M-Day) the Germans would field 210,000 men; at six weeks, 350,000; and in twelve months, 2,312,000. The source of men beyond the 100,000 limit imposed on the Reichswehr would be storm troops, police at various levels, Einwohnereinheiten, and Einwohnerwehr, the last two armed resident self-defense organizations. In Germany's Weimar Republic period from 1918 to 1933, legal police and military forces competed with ad hoc veterans groups and armed bands of political parties, mostly from the extreme Right and the extreme Left. Politics included activity at polls and in elections, but also thugs of various stripes who engaged in "politics" with clubs and rifles in the streets and beer halls.

In the question-and-answer session following presentation of Smith's committee survey, questions were posed regarding Austria, the Saarland, and German-French cooperation. The authors of the survey answered each in turn. The Austrians, they stated, reprint German training regulations as soon as they are published. "It is generally believed that about 90% of the people in Austria favor union as soon as possible. As soon as a favorable moment arrives, I am sure the movement will come to the fore in Austria for union with Germany."[16]

Regarding the Saar plebiscite planned for 1935: "there isn't much doubt about the results, that it will go overwhelmingly for Germany."[17] That was an accurate forecast. The French would try again after World War II, in 1955, with the same result. The French-German people of that area preferred to remain a part of Germany.

A question about German-French relations elicited a response from Smith's team that is both a look at the past and a hint at the future. "Ever since 1921," they noted, "there have been groups of German industrialists and bankers who have built visions of a Franco-German alliance upon Ruhr coal and Lorraine iron and have foreseen a close economic entente between Germany and France."[18] That shared aspiration anticipated the Schuman Plan and the German-French Iron-Coal Community established in the years following World War II, which were among the first steps in the direction of European cooperation and, ultimately (it was hoped by many) union.

This bravura performance of Smith's team, impressive at the time, was even more impressive as it was proved right in the coming years regarding all the issues that were discussed in the Q&A session with peers and faculty: the struggle between republic and dictatorship, Germany's rapid mass mobilization, the Austrian-German Anschluss, the Saarland plebiscite, and the German tactics that many in the class would personally experience in combat within a decade.

Smith was also chairman of one of four subcommittees that examined the joint plans and army strategic plans of major belligerents before World War I.[19] The object of the exercise was to examine the degree to which those belligerents demonstrated joint planning, "joint" meaning the army plus other departments of government. Smith chaired the subcommittee that addressed the joint plans and army strategic plans of Germany just prior to the Great War. Two other subcommittees did the same for France and Britain. A fourth subcommittee examined American joint army and navy strategic plans. One obvious difference was that the United States, unlike the Europeans, had no plans on the shelf prior to the war for involvement in a great continental war in Europe. Therefore, the fourth subcommittee used contemporary thinking about joint planning as of 1932.

Smith's team cited Grand Admiral Alfred von Tirpitz, who said of pre–World War I German military planning, "The government left every department to itself, and quite in the dark as to the views or intentions of the others." He added, "I was not even informed of the invasion of Belgium." The report, signed by Truman Smith, concludes, "No agency . . . had the direct function of preparing joint war plans, and none were prepared." The point is that the German Army and Navy did not cooperate. There was little to no coordination in the *planning* of political, economic, and social instruments. The report strongly suggests that casual talk, even serious discussion, is not planning. Smith used an excellent schematic to highlight the lack of "jointness." It shows a number of separate lines from the kaiser to his Naval Cabinet; the secretary of state; the navy; the Admiral Staff; the General Staff; the war minister; and the Military Cabinet. On the chart is an empty box in red with the caption "Joint War Planning Agency—NONE."

The group reporting on French joint planning just prior to the war concludes that the French planning was good, but things went wrong due to "lack of flexibility in the Army Strategic Plan to meet the blow."

The group reporting on the British concludes that "agencies established for war planning were excellent instruments . . . war plans were adequate and complete . . . [but] all planning agencies had failed to envisage the magnitude of the impending war. . . . Faulty estimate as to the force and direction of the initial blow and the rapid advance of the German Army." British peacetime planning was good, but the AWC student group opines that the senior officers in the Expeditionary Force "were not familiar with the details of the army plans." Joint French-British planning "was particularly effective." (Later in the twentieth century, in the American military lexicon "joint" came to mean the several services of a nation, such as army-navy planning; "combined" came to mean bi- or multinational, such as the French-British planning described here.)

The fourth subcommittee, the one that examined real-world American 1932 joint and strategic army plans, consisted of three members: a soldier, a sailor, and a marine. It concluded that war planning must take "four forces" into account: armed, economic, political, and social. In fact, and unfortunately, they concluded that only the army and navy take any such war planning seriously. Creation of the Office of the Assistant Secretary of War for Industrial Mobilization by the National Defense Act of 1920, said the committee, is a step in the right direction, but "the State Department has failed to cooperate in war planning." However, "the G-2 Division, WDGS [also called MID for Military Intelligence Division, War Department General Staff], and ONI [Office of Naval Intelligence] maintain close liaison with it [the State Department] and, through attaches, keep in touch with the world political situation." As for "social forces," the committee was referring to the importance of influencing popular opinion and using propaganda. Measuring public opinion was new, and not only to military planners. George H. Gallup in 1935 began reporting the polling of public opinion, and others soon followed. Polling as a method to measure public opinion was promptly "discovered" and later used by students at AWC in strategic planning after 1935. Radio was used to great effect by Hitler and Roosevelt, among others, to influence public opinion.

The committee focusing on U.S. joint planning went on to say, "Germany, France, and Britain had only one plan to consider seriously. Our situation, on the other hand, is such that a number of plans must be so considered." Of course, that statement is not entirely true. Germany had to plan for war on two fronts. France planned for war on the European continent and to protect its colonies overseas. Britain likewise had continental and colonial interests and, as an entrepôt nation, had to maintain a sea lifeline. The observation does, however, show an awareness of American worldwide interests, without reference to specific enemies. And there was a hint of what would come much later, the unified commands and theater commanders, in the assertion that "the designation by name in time of peace of theater operations commanders is worthy of serious consideration." This subcommittee also noted—with envy—that the British and French senior military reported plans to the heads of the respective governments to ensure material, political, and, via elected governments, popular support. The American planning process represented only the thinking of the army and navy and stopped at a uniformed dead end, the Joint Board, which did not have access to the head of government. The subcommittee believed that fear of militarization of the government explained this state of affairs in the American system.

In his oral presentation, the committee chairman presented a synopsis of what had been gleaned from the four subcommittees regarding joint and strategic planning, and concluded the following: Economic, political, and social forces are "not treated to their full value" in the formulation of joint plans. Present joint plans are inadequate. Current Joint Planning Committee (JPC) membership is unlikely to take cognizance of economic, political, and social forces.

The recommendation that follows anticipated the national security apparatus that would be established in 1947 and 1949: "That an agency directly advisory to the President in war planning and charged with the coordination of the four forces [armed, economic, political, and social] and all government instrumentalities concerned is highly desirable but is considered impracticable of present realization." One sees a nascent national security council in this recommendation, but, accepting a response that it is "impracticable of present realization," the subcommittee settles for half a loaf: the JPC could be expanded to include four forces "as coordinate entities," and this "should furnish the first step in the evolution towards the agency mentioned above."

Commandant Major General George S. Simonds attended the presentation and participated in the Q&A session that followed. He was an experienced professional, a soldier-diplomat-intellectual. He had been assistant commandant of the AWC in 1922–1924; chief of the War Plans Division, War Department, General Staff (WDGS), 1927–1931; Army Chief of Staff Douglas MacArthur's deputy for a year; and he was serving as military advisor to the American delegation at the arms limitation conference in Geneva in 1932 when he was appointed commandant of the AWC. (To illustrate the importance of this position, on 2 October 1935 Malin Craig went directly from being AWC commandant to MacArthur's successor as army chief of staff.)

Simonds agreed with the committee's recommendation that civilian officials had to integrate the political, economic, and social instruments into military planning, if planning were to be truly joint. But, he warned, the JPC could get too big, too cumbersome, and too bureaucratic, which would get in the way when agility and quick response were required. He also made the point that political, economic, and social instruments, seemingly "impracticable" for use in the calm of peace, "could be brought forward if the Army and Navy made the case for an emergency emerging or present."

He provided an example of getting the full attention of a civilian leader. The JPC briefed an ambassador designee, Simonds, recalled, and gave him "detail as to the political, economic, and social conditions of the United States and Japan." Simonds said, "He told me afterward, 'You have it summed up there in the best form I have ever seen.'" Based upon his extensive experience at that place where military judgment meets civilian authority, Simonds was advising his younger comrades at AWC to keep their powder dry. In an "emergency emerging or present," our civilian friends will learn that we have thought things through and they "could be brought forward." That's not a bad summary of just what happened on the eve of war and in the early days of World War II.

Smith attended and participated in all of the class plenary session presentations and discussions of war planning before World War I. From 1939 to 1941 he would serve on the General Staff as the United States once again considered its options as events in Europe and Asia posed the possibility of American involvement in yet another war.

Smith's major individual writing effort, his Individual Staff Memorandum (ISM), was entitled "Germany and Hitler," which he submitted on 29 April 1933.[20] It is organized in staff study format:

1. Purpose.
2. Facts bearing on the study.
3. Conclusions.
4. Action recommended.

These are presented in five pages. Supporting evidence appears in nine appendices in which Smith addresses nine issues in seven pages to flesh out some of the stark assertions made in the body of the paper. The staff study format forces a logical process and very tight writing. Smith's insights are, again, prescient. One cannot know all of Smith's sources, but we do know that Friedrich von Boetticher, his old friend from 1920 whom he visited in Germany in 1931 and who was now sitting in the German Embassy in Washington as Military Attaché, was useful in informing Smith's paper and in making it current. Boetticher had been appointed by the previous German government at the end of 1932 and arrived in Washington as 1933 began. He would serve on station until December 1941, when Germany declared war on the United States and he returned to Germany. Smith's friendship with Boetticher was renewed after World War II and lasted until Smith's death.

Smith's purpose in his ISM was to say what conditions brought the Nazi Party into being and to estimate what effect the Party might have on Germany's internal affairs and external relations. The rise of the Party was mainly a consequence of the lost war; but, writes Smith, the "Hitlerite revolution" was more in keeping with the German tradition of authoritative government than was the "unaccustomed Democracy" of the Weimar Republic. In Germany, says Smith, the purpose of government is more about social peace and order than individual freedom. "The Republic was weak from the start in that it did not suit the temper of the German people."

Economic chaos in Germany—first reparations and indemnities, then the Great Depression—resulted in massive unemployment, created a new sort of proletariat of the educated poor, and provided fertile ground for recruitment by communists and Nazis, both revolutionary parties. Moderate parties complained about, but complied with, the Treaty of Versailles. Hitler, by contrast, demanded abrogation of the Treaty. According to Smith, "Hitler's call has been to youth, the patriotic, and the dispossessed." A "new Teutonic golden age" would come from a "skillful combination of planks" in Hitler's platform: abrogation of the Treaty; purging the country of Jews; "authoritative dictatorial government"; "a vaguely outlined regime of Social Justice"; and a "vague promise of the socialization of unproductive capital."

Regarding prospects for Germany in the future, Smith writes that Hitler will make immense internal changes; "for the time being" it is improbable there will be radical change in foreign policy. Hitler will establish a personal dictatorship and "diminish materially the importance of legislative organs of government." He will, asserts Smith, make the State supreme in all fields; annihilate Socialist, Communist, and Republican parties; "abolish every vestige of Internationalism within Germany" of the Moscow or Capitalistic variety; "compel all Germans to worship at the shrine of a beneficent all powerful state"; leave untouched for the present the issue of monarch or republic; reduce Jewish influence in all phases of German life; and complete the centralization of the German state begun by Bismarck. (Smith notes that Bavaria, the best example of regionalism in Germany, then and now, "has already been captured by the Nazis.") Smith believes that "hostile elements of the population will be reduced to impotence" by political bribery, propaganda, and, where necessary, force.

In an appendix headed "The possibility of dissensions in the Hitler party," Smith dismisses the idea of an impending breakup of Hitler's party, which had been reported in the press. "A revolt of less important Nazi elements would be crushed by Hitler in a single blow, provided past occurrences are any precedent for the future."

Indeed they were crushed. Historian Gordon Craig provides one example of Nazi ruthlessness: when SA commander and tough soldier of fortune Ernst Roehm challenged Hitler, Hitler tried to bring him around by appointing him minister without portfolio in the Reich Government in December 1933. When that failed, "in the Night of the Long Knives (30 June 1934) Roehm and dozens of other SA leaders were snatched from their beds and shot by SS troopers."[21]

In the body of his paper and in another of his appendices, Smith says Hitler will intensify the already existing friendly understanding with Italy. The Anschluss question (that is, Germany's absorbing Austria, an action prohibited by the Treaty) will remain dormant temporarily, but Smith foresees the growing strength of the Nazis in Austria and a change in Italian policy. "Hitler has paid for Mussolini support by surrendering Teutonic claims for the return of South Tyrol, in which there is a strong German minority. . . . Up to now Italy has opposed the Anschluss, but some observers profess to believe that Mussolini will shortly change his policy, inasmuch as now a sister Fascist movement rules Germany."

About Czechoslovakia, he had this to say: "As the German speaking population of the country exceeds three millions, the possibility of a strong Hitler movement is not to be neglected."

Before presenting his five conclusions, Smith makes two final points in the section "Facts bearing on this study." First, Hitler's immediate objective is to secure equality of armaments, that is, abrogation of the military clauses of the Treaty. He says that Hitler will press "aggressively though warily." Hitler will get support from Italy, will try to gain British support, and "would appear to believe that *France will not resort to war . . . unless she is actually assaulted by Germany*" (italics added). These assertions of Smith's, made in early 1933, would hold true later in the decade. Smith would be in Berlin in March 1936 when Hitler acted on his gut feeling and sent German troops to remilitarize the Rhineland, a place the Smiths knew well from their happy Coblenz days of 1919–1920. As Smith foresaw, the French failed to take decisive action at this clear, if not quite last, chance to slow or stop Hitler. Hitler tested the water and found it to his liking.

Finally, notes Smith, "Germany is liable to do all in her power to conciliate America, *short of changing her Jewish domestic policy*" (italics added). He concludes his appendix on "the anti-semitic question" with this statement: "It is not believed probable that the power of International Jewry will prove strong enough to alter materially the Hitler anti-semitic measures. These will probably cause a marked decline in the power and prosperity of the German Jews."

His conclusions are as follows:

> I. The Nazis will continue to solidify their internal position in Germany and regiment German public opinion behind their foreign and domestic policies, to an extent no German government since the war has succeeded in accomplishing.
> II. Germany's economic situation will continue to depend upon the world situation.
> III. Neither political nor economic domestic issues are likely to unseat Hitler.
> IV. Germany's immediate foreign policy will be directed to secure equality of armaments.
> V. The possibility of a European war in the near future does not revolve around territorial settlement, but on the question whether France and her Allies by force will seek to prevent German rearmament.

Clearly, Smith had a remarkable understanding of Germany's domestic and foreign policies. He had it right in his unpublished article in 1924, and he had it right in this paper submitted in April 1933, which he prepared as Hitler and the Nazis consolidated power after January 1933. In no small part, Smith's feel for the situation in Germany can be attributed to the excellent German sources that he nurtured throughout his time on active duty and beyond.

In his memoir, "Facts of Life," Truman dedicates less than a page to his year at AWC. He takes no bows for his documented appreciation of political conditions in Germany in 1933, which was accurate and available to policy makers then and to scholars now.

Kay is more expansive in her own memoir, "My Life." Most of her recollections have to do with family and friends, but her personal political outlook emerges in bits and pieces from her prose. During Truman's time at AWC, the Smiths were living at 3318 N Street NW, a block west of Wisconsin Avenue, in Washington, D.C. At one point a group of veterans known as the Bonus Marchers assembled in the city to demonstrate. Kay wrote, "While sympathizing with their need, we felt no group should be allowed to disrupt the city and menace the Capital. We felt even more sympathy with the Army obliged to enforce the disagreeable duty of marching against veterans." Of course, the situation was mainly disagreeable for the veterans, but it appears that, for Kay at least, order trumps the needs of the ragged at the bottom of the human pecking order. *Ordnung muss sein* (There must be order).

Kay's mother, who lived with the Smiths for the year in Washington, attended the inauguration of Franklin D. Roosevelt on 4 March 1933. Kay recalled her mother exclaiming, "He was wonderful!" and "holding up her hands in joy." But, Kay quickly added, "Her faith in him did not have long to last. For two years he blundered about with his 'New Deal' left-leaning policies . . . he copied Hitler's plan of Arbeitskorps in founding CCC [Civilian Conservation Corps] Camps . . . WPA [Work Projects Administration] 'the shovel leaners' were everywhere visible . . . FDR never solved the economic problem. Hitler rescued him through war."

Kay was more lighthearted on the subject of liquor in those Prohibition years when alcoholic beverages were illegal. "I never went to those places [speakeasies]," she wrote. "We drank our Martinis, doing our bit for individual freedom, quietly at home . . . my friends gave my name to a 'reliable' bootlegger from Baltimore. . . . I did not tell Truman the name of the bootlegger, nor would I let him go

Assignment to Hawaii (1933–1935) followed graduation from the Army War College. Smith's caption: "The 2nd Battalion, 27th Infantry (The Wolfhounds) pass in review at Schofield Barracks, Oahu with the Waianai Mountains in background." He was a succesful commander, and Kay loved Hawaii. (Courtesy of Katharine Smith Coley and family.)

downstairs to my little meetings in the reception room. I did not want him involved in the remotest way in my shady doings."[22]

Like much of the rest of the country, the Smiths didn't take the Volstead Act (1919, later repealed in 1933), very seriously. She conducted her "shady doings," keeping her husband out of the booze-related transactions, protecting her officer and gentleman in this small matter as she would protect his reputation in all other ways, then and always.

From the time Smith left Benning, he knew that after graduation from the War College he would be due for foreign service and duty with troops. "I had set my heart on returning to Hawaii," he wrote later, "which I remembered happily from my summer visit while at Yale to my friends, the von Holts. Honolulu was not an especially popular army garrison, and my request was granted readily by the War Department."[23] Considering his satisfaction with the tour, his pride in the regiment, and Kay's unreserved joy while there, his comment about Honolulu's not being a popular garrison is puzzling.

In his typical style, Smith describes his two years as battalion commander in the 27th Infantry (Wolfhound) Regiment in three succinctly written pages. Also typical is Kay's more leisurely recollection of a very happy time; her descriptions of the colorful place and the warm friendships made in Hawaii take up forty-one pages of "My Life."[24]

Truman credits the "semipermanent corps of non-commissioned officers, many of whom had served continuously in the regiment for decades," with the outstanding "morale, discipline, and unusual esprit de corps." (James Jones, in his novel *From Here to Eternity,* saw morale and esprit in Honolulu otherwise from the ranks just a few years later, but he would agree that the NCOs ran the companies.) "It was pure delight for me to command the 2nd Battalion," continued Smith, "which accomplished every task I set for it."

A personal highlight of his command was a successful tactical feat by his battalion that was recognized by his superiors. It played the part of aggressor in a force-on-force field exercise in which Smith demonstrated the validity of his division commander's conviction (always a splendid idea) that good infantry could, in fact, penetrate terrain generally regarded as impassable. Kay took girlish delight in Truman's success. "The 27th had covered itself with glory. The men had climbed holding a rope to keep them together. The battalion was proud of itself. . . . They had lived up to the Wolfhound's reputation for daring and vigor. Truman was pleased."[25]

Not all of Smith's experiences were as positive. While Hugh Drum commanded the Hawaiian department, Smith's regimental commander from the Meuse-Argonne offensive of 1918, now Major General Halstead Dorey, assumed command of Smith's division. Reunion was fine for old times' sake, but Dorey seemed to Smith to be past his prime, to put it politely. That made Truman uncomfortable.

He was tasked with organizing and directing the umpiring of a major field exercise. The experience reminded him of his army's deficiencies. "To my astonishment, I discovered immediately upon taking up this new duty that the American army possessed no regulations or pamphlets telling how an umpiring service should function. I had to improvise an organization and then write a directive covering the duties of the umpires. . . . later on in Germany, I witnessed an umpiring service function in a maneuver involving four times as many soldiers as in Hawaii. . . . At its [the American exercise] close I felt dissatisfied with the performance of my umpiring service, though my superiors seemed to be pleased enough with my work."[26]

One notes in passing some differences in American soldiering before World War II and in the second half of the twentieth century. Two leap out to those intimately familiar with military service. Command, since at least the 1960s and increasingly so with passing decades, is extremely stressful. For commanders at all levels, it is career make-or-break time. Centralized selection for schools and command—a system in effect since the early 1970s—is an impersonal process, with advantages and disadvantages. The advantage is fairness: the old boys' network cannot so easily protect incompetent friends. The disadvantage is that central selection depends upon paper files, meaning that it is a bloodless affair highly dependent upon the writing skills of the seniors who compose the report cards of the rated officers. Both Smiths report a thoroughly relaxed mood for Truman's entire time in command. That would be unusual in more recent times.

Another striking difference is pace. The Smiths spent twenty-eight days in travel by sea from New York to Honolulu, which allowed time for socializing with old friends in Panama and San Francisco. When it was time to leave Hawaii, another month was spent aboard ship, with the same ports of call and socializing. The old way was inefficient; but it also was genteel, and allowed one to decompress and shake off the dust of the old before confronting the new. The new way begins and ends with shock.

Kay's ruminations once again provide a colorful backdrop to Truman's more objective reporting. "Truman had been a member of the water polo team at Yale," writes Kay, "with Herman von Holt, Carter Galt and Archie MacLeish. After graduation [from Yale] Truman and Brad Coley [a lifelong Yale friend who would become the father-in-law to Truman's daughter, Kätchen] visited Herman and Carter [who would later provide the Smiths entree to bankers, Dole pineapple executives, and planters in Hawaii]. This memory of magic days and events never left him. Now he was to return."[27]

Passing through the Panama Canal "should make any American's heart beat fast with pride . . . a tremendous demonstration of our capability and the power it brings us. . . . The Zone is beatific, but beyond the fence, what a contrast. Trash, rotting food thrown about, monkeys running over food stands. Nobody seemed to mind." San Francisco revealed the "Golden Gate all shrouded in fog," friends, rest, elegant dining, views, entertainment. Aboard ship Kay was entertained by "troops singing, boxing."[28]

Upon their arrival in Hawaii, the Smiths were introduced to their Japanese cook named Sugita, who found a maid and trained her. Kay wrote, "Do you suppose the Japanese have less sensitivity to pain than we?" (For the record: the Japanese did not seem to enjoy internment just a few years later, or the effects of flamethrowers.) Kay got horses and taught Kätchen to ride, saw sharks, watched Japanese spear fishermen, and enjoyed the military band and the daily retreat ceremony. She became a veritable cheerleader for the regiment. "Officers wives appeared at sports events in the Battalion Quadrangle every night, usually boxing. I became quite knowledgeable and thoroughly enjoyed it. Supporting regimental morale was everyone's job. The 27th was a happy regiment, proud of its past martial record. Perfect day succeeded perfect day."

After a few months, recalled Kay, "we made a number of congenial friends. BG and Marian Greeley, Colonel and Mrs. Virgil Peterson, Percy and Laura Black [the Blacks would rejoin the Smiths in Berlin and later in Washington] and ourselves formed the habit of meeting at one another's house for cocktails before dinner. 'The Brain Trust,' we were called." Of a rented beach house she said, "Oh! The beachcomber's paradise. One lived in bathing suits."

The Smiths also made navy friends. "From our height above we looked down on the entire fleet anchored in Pearl Harbor, with the exception of the Midway [*sic*], too wide to come through the narrow channel, anchored close to the shore. The ships lay at anchor as closely packed as furniture in a room. It was a sight I shall never forget." At a dinner one evening, Kay found herself sitting near the navy chief of staff at Pearl Harbor. Kay recalls that she said to him, "It gives me cold shivers to see all our fleet tucked up in Pearl Harbor. One single Japanese freighter loaded with scrap could scuttle herself and bottle you all up. (There were always several Jap tramp steamers loading our waste scrap.) Quite angrily he replied. 'You are a very silly woman. We wouldn't be in Pearl Harbor if there were any thought of war. Ticklish talks would be going on between us. We would keep the fleet at sea.'"[29]

Soon enough, recalled Kay, "In the midst of this happy life a sudden bombshell exploded. Truman came home with a letter he had received from Colonel Barnett, in command of G-2 in Washington, asking Truman to consider going to Berlin as military attaché.

'Of course you won't do that' was my immediate reaction, remembering the years of discomfort of 1920 to 1924. 'Well, I am thinking about it.' He went on to say that there were important things going on in Germany, very grave things. 'Colonel Barnett thinks I am the man he needs there now.' I don't care for interfering wives. But I secretly hoped we would not go. I believed it would not prove financially possible. A second letter shattered this hope. It was feasible and Truman accepted. He was ordered to Washington. We were to leave in June."[30]

Truman's recollection is about the same as Kay's, but he adds that it was not entirely a surprise to him. Friends in the War Department had told Smith that he was being considered for assignment as the military attaché in Vienna. He had decided he would refuse if offered that job, but the Berlin assignment was "a different matter." Hitler was secretly expanding the Reichswehr. Smith knew that Berlin would become a post of military importance.[31]

Smith did not report this in his "Facts of Life," but Kay describes Truman's interview with Chief of Staff Douglas MacArthur as he departed Washington for Berlin, saying it was what Truman had told her. "I was shown to General MacArthur," Kay quotes Truman as saying. "He was seated at his desk, his jacket of loud tweed, smoking a cigarette. He looked at me considering, waved me to a chair, and began pacing the room back and forth, as was his custom when considering a problem, smoking furiously. He stopped in front of me. I rose. 'You are very young to be going to Berlin.' 'Yes, sir.' Pacing again. I sat down. 'You have no rank.' 'Yes, sir.' 'Well Smith, I have only this to say to you. I have long noted when young officers go abroad they very soon end up in the British pocket. Now Smith, my advice to you is never to go to bed with a corpse.' He waved me away."[32]

9

Hitler Takes Power

> I knew quite well that there were rugged and trying years ahead for me in Germany.
>
> —Truman Smith, on events in 1935

The chief of staff's enigmatic pronouncements must have puzzled Smith as he prepared to take up his post as military attaché. After all, MacArthur had been a brigadier general when just thirty-eight and superintendent at the United States Military Academy a year later. Smith was about to turn forty-two in 1935 when he had his audience with the great man. Others had noted that as early as 1911, MacArthur was inclined to "strike attitudes to impress the spectators."[1]

In letters to his wife from the Pacific in World War II, General Robert L. Eichelberger, who referred to MacArthur as the "Big Chief" or "Sarah" (for Sarah Bernhardt, the histrionic actress), wrote, "Shortly after I arrived in Australia, General MacArthur ordered me to pay my respects to the Australians and then have nothing further to do with them," a xenophobic or anti-British order akin to his warning that Smith not "end up in the British pocket." MacArthur famously ordered Eichelberger to combat command with these words: "Bob, I'm putting you in command at Buna. Relieve Harding [Major General Edwin F. Harding, one of Marshall's men, then commanding the 32nd Division]. . . . I want you to take Buna, or not come back alive."[2]

One is inclined to recall admonitions about not sleeping with corpses and not coming back alive, particularly if conveyed melodramatically and directly by one's Big Chief.

Smith was disappointed by the two weeks of preparation spent in Washington in the Military Intelligence Division—after another monthlong voyage from Honolulu "on the aged army transport *Republic,* whose utmost speed was 12 knots." That trip began in May and included social calls in San Francisco and Panama before ending in New York. He described his course of instruction on the duties ahead as "cursory and quite inadequate." He learned something about codes and office administration, "but naught else." He did, however, find his two weeks in Washington useful, in that he "saw at first hand how inadequately organized, staffed, and financed the Military Intelligence Division was." The MID was, in his words, "the orphan branch of the General Staff and [of] the army as a whole and military attachés lacked prestige and were little regarded or listened to."

Colonel Barnett, chief of the attaché section of MID, had handpicked Smith because of his qualifications for the job, and he had figuratively twisted his arm by sending a second letter to encourage him to take the Berlin assignment. Kay, as noted earlier, had reservations, but that did not deter Truman. He knew the job was important, however inadequate the immediate preparation for it. Even as he was preparing for the posting, the press was reporting that a vast rearmament was under way in Germany. Smith declared, "I decided that come what might, I would make my voice heard in the War Department even from faraway Berlin." Through his research and writing about Germany and Hitler at the Army War College and scanning current reports from the Berlin attaché's office, Smith could tell that "the Hitler rearmament was not only large, but that a revolution was proceeding in matters of organization, weapons, techniques, and tactics. This realization spurred me on."[3]

His appreciation of the hard work that lay ahead—to observe and report German rearmament and the military revolution that would strengthen Germany's political position and possibly lead to war—contrasted sharply with the commonly held notion that attachés were engaged in a Noël Coward scene of cocktail parties, clever repartee, and elegant uniforms. Furthermore, Smith unfortunately arrived in Berlin after his predecessor, Colonel Jacob W. S. Wuest, had departed. That meant that Smith was denied the direct hand-over, debriefing, and useful insights he could have had from a man who had personally observed Hitler and the Nazis from 1929 to 1935, during which period they took and consolidated power.

Further evidence that in MID one hand did not know what the other was doing was the fact that the Smiths were aboard a slow boat from Hawaii to New York just as Colonel Wuest was addressing officers of the War Department on 10 May 1935 regarding conditions in Germany. He reported that the German people strongly supported Hitler, that German despair had become hope, and that no European nation was willing to antagonize Hitler. He further opined that the French were disorganized and politically divided, that the Czechs were afraid, and that Germany and Japan were exploring the possibility of an alliance.[4]

There were additional indications that Hitler's Germany had a favoring wind at its back—and that Hitler sensed it. The Germans and Poles had signed a nonaggression treaty in January 1934, a breach in the French alliance system in eastern Europe; Hitler had met with Mussolini in Venice in June 1934, with no short-term pay-off but with ominous implications for the future alliance of the Fascist states; and in June 1935 the Anglo-German naval agreement was signed, indicating a British acceptance of German renunciation of Versailles, which drove a wedge between Britain and France.

The January 1935 plebiscite in the Saarland found 90 percent of the voters choosing reunion with Germany, not France. The return of the Saarland to the Reich, with which the other Powers did not interfere, marked a new and bolder phase in Hitler's policy. Historian Gordon Craig describes Hitler's readiness to test the waters after the plebiscite at the very time that Smith had considered, accepted, and was preparing himself for the Berlin job. Hitler, writes Craig, "had survived his period of extreme vulnerability unscathed, and, thanks to the distractions and differences of the other Powers, his own tactical skill, and a good deal of luck, had been able in the course of two years to free himself from the restraints of the European security system, while at the same time proceeding with the policy of *Gleichschaltung* and the arms build-up that were the necessary prerequisites for his future plans. Now he was ready to test the resistance of the Western Powers to those extensive designs."[5]

Wuest estimated that it would take several years for the German army to organize, train, and equip as it grew from the Treaty-imposed army of 100,000 men to become the preeminent army in Europe. Smith, once on the ground in Berlin, shared Wuest's opinion regarding the pace of German rearmament, saying that the constantly growing and improving army needed time to be combat ready. The American attachés arrived at that conclusion for the best of reasons: that was the view of senior German officers, the source of both Wuest's and Smith's insights and estimates. In fact, the

Americans were wrong because their German sources were wrong. Although German military leadership was cautioning Hitler about the readiness of his army for general war, he was prepared to disregard professional military estimates and to bank on the lack of resolve among his neighbors.

Hitler, trusting his intuition, was impatient with any experts who would slow him down, including his generals. From the time he came to power in 1933, and during Smith's tenure as Military Attaché, Hitler routinely acted boldly as German senior military leadership advised caution. That was true of estimates of army readiness for combat, diplomatic initiatives, and, finally, his use of the military. Until his decision to invade the Soviet Union, Hitler's boldness intimidated Germany's neighbors and produced an uninterrupted series of successes.

Well before Smith prepared to assume his duties in Berlin, Germany was already a recognizable hot spot of interest to the United States. Given that fact, failure to ensure a direct exchange of views between Wuest and Smith was particularly unenlightened and validated Smith's low regard for MID's competence.

As Smith later ruminated about his Berlin assignment, he cast a rare backward glance at what might have been had he not accepted that job. He did not know in 1935 that he would be diagnosed with diabetes in 1939, nor could he have known the degree to which the lifestyle of the diplomatic corps in Berlin contributed to his illness. The diplomatic cocktail circuit is not the prescription a doctor would have written for him.

Nor did he know that army regulations pertaining to physical condition would effectively block an opportunity for him to command troops and thus keep him from a potentially great wartime career, once his diabetes was diagnosed. In fact, by regulation he should have been medically retired in the summer of 1939. Only personal intervention by Chief of Staff George Marshall permitted Smith to be retained on active duty and his subsequent assignment to intelligence duties in Washington during World War II.[6]

Smith's return to Washington, Marshall's intervention, and Smith's assignment to MID will be taken up in greater detail later, but it is worth noting—as Smith surely did—that most of his contemporary front-runners went on to become stars, several elevated to the top positions in what became the defense establishment. Fort Benning colleague and AWC classmate Omar N. Bradley got five stars. Another 1933 AWC classmate, Jacob L. Devers, got four stars, as did twenty-one others from the AWC classes 1934 to 1940. Of the 657 graduates from 1934 to 1940, 436 became generals.[7]

Smith's talents were widely recognized among his peers and superiors; MID was not the only General Staff agency that wanted him. At Christmastime 1934, Chief of Infantry general Edwin Croft, who had been Smith's commander at Fort Hamilton between 1924 and 1926, wrote: "I had hopes of bringing you here to my office for duty during the next year, but the Intelligence Section made such strong demands for you to go to Germany and as they assured me that this was in accordance with personal desires, I gave in and let them have you. I know of no man better qualified for the job and I hope you enjoy it."[8]

Had Smith joined the Chief of Infantry's office in the position Croft had in mind for him, writing infantry training regulations and manuals, he would have been well positioned for almost certain regimental command and possible division and higher command early in the war. On the infantry command track, the sky was the limit. In Berlin he was, in later bureaucratic jargon, out of the loop. It is also likely that infantry assignments in the field might have been healthier than the cocktail and canapé circuit in Berlin. One cannot know how circumstances might have shaped his career otherwise, but the door to troop command and martial fame enjoyed by many of his contemporaries effectively slammed shut upon Smith's arrival in Berlin with Kay and Kätchen in mid-August 1935.

Smith later called his three and a half years in Berlin "the most nerve-racking and tumultuous years of my life." He also believed that he "succeeded in influencing (beyond my fondest original hopes) the military policies of my country." The patrician and professional soldier must have taken enormous gratification in being able to make that statement. It comes close to the Prussian military ideal modestly expressed as: *Ich diene* (I serve).

He had a ringside seat in those tumultuous years as he observed and reported the military revolution taking place in Hitler's army, the transformation of German society, and the shifting relations among nations. His tour was filled with many surprises, requiring mental agility and thorough understanding of Germany in order to comprehend the significance of events and pronouncements. Earlier, while at the War College, Smith had written that Hitler would first focus on internal actions to solidify his base and purge his enemies. Then he would remove the impediments to German rearmament with increasing confidence and indulge his characteristic inclination to bold strokes. Smith's assessment was correct. A general outline of some major events and trends in the interwar period that paralleled Smith's career provides a useful backdrop for what Smith would observe and report from 1935 to 1939.

Smith was in Coblenz and Berlin during what historian William L. Langer later called "The Period of Settlement" (1919–1924). Smith was dubious at the time about French efforts to keep the Hun down, predicting in one letter to Kay that the United States would be asked to again rescue France from another European fire in about fifteen years. He believed that rubbing salt in German wounds was a very bad course of action for France and for Europe, since that would be followed by eventual German recovery and predictable renewed German military ascendancy.[9]

Langer called 1924 to 1930 "The Period of Fulfillment." Gustav Stresemann, who served in every German cabinet from 1923 until his death in 1929, was identified with this period of relatively good Franco-German relations, as was his French counterpart, Aristide Briand. Germany was admitted to the League of Nations in 1926 and in 1929 accepted the terms of the Kellogg-Briand pact, renouncing aggressive war. In this period, Smith was attending army schools and teaching tactics at Fort Benning, sharpening skills useful in command that would prove invaluable to an observer-reporter of a foreign army.

Continued German yearning for authority, paternalistic government, and "the good old days" of Empire was manifest in the election of Field Marshal Paul von Hindenburg as president in 1925 and in his reelection in 1932, when he was eighty-five years old. Hindenburg, born in 1847, was a veteran of Germany's 1866 war with Austria and the 1870–1871 war with France. He had retired from the army in 1911, before being reactivated for command in the Great War, and had retired once more from public life in 1919. He died in office as president on 2 August 1934 at the age of eighty-seven. That was just one month after Hitler had purged his ranks in the Night of the Long Knives, a purgation met with approval by Germany's military leadership because a rival quasi-army—the SA—

was reduced, if not eliminated. On 19 August a plebiscite approved Hitler's assumption of sole executive power and his preferred title, *Führer* (Leader). He then required every soldier to swear a personal oath of allegiance to him.

Attendance at the War College and battalion command demanded Smith's full attention in the first half of what Langer called "The Period of Repudiation and Revision" (1930–1939). But Smith kept current in German affairs through personal contacts, including the America-friendly German military attaché in Washington, and by almost constant research and study. Germany had become a habit, a hobby, and an almost constant part of his personal and professional life. The "repudiation" aspect of Langer's taxonomy was a consequence of the worldwide economic depression, the connection between inter-Allied debts and reparations, and the fact that European governments saw Herbert Hoover's moratorium "as acknowledgement that inter-Allied debts and reparations would stand or fall together." Simply expressed, there was a tacit recognition in the early 1930s that inter-Allied debts would not be paid and that Germany simply could not pay reparations. "Revision" of the Treaty of Versailles would take place by degrees, at first by evasion and deception by the Weimar Republic, then successively by rhetorical defiance, threats, and troop deployments as Hitler sensed weaknesses and boldly exploited them.

The Reichstag elections of 14 September 1930 marked the emergence of Hitler's National Socialists as a major party. Moderate parties in Germany lost heavily, reflecting the polarization of German politics and society. National Socialist and Communist bands clashed in the streets; disorder reigned; and a succession of cabinets failed in a parade of chancellors and new elections.

On 30 January 1933, Hitler became chancellor in a coalition cabinet that was widely expected to fail as earlier coalitions had failed. Hitler's assumption of power, writes historian Gordon Craig, "caused no great sensation in the international press, which was less interested in what was happening in Berlin than it was in Franklin D. Roosevelt's arrival in Washington and in the preparations for the World Economic Conference in London."[10]

The Nazis had only three seats in the coalition cabinet, "an insecure power basis to ensure long tenure in office." Moreover, it was assumed that responsibility would tame Hitler, and his revolutionary posturing would be set aside. In any event, it was thought that conservatives and the army would position themselves to capture the Nazi movement and control its leader. A political enemy, Franz von Papen, who was chancellor in 1932, remarked, "We have framed him in." Historian Gordon Craig opines, "The remark should be included in any anthology of famous last words."[11]

10

Hitler's Germany

> The "small town" Hitler, whom I had talked with in Munich in 1922, was now absolute ruler of sixty million Germans, a people as gifted scientifically, industrially, and militarily as any on the globe.
>
> —Truman Smith, on the Hitler of 1935

Smith had thought through Hitler's influence and Germany's future in his 1924 article, "The German Fascisti," which remained unpublished until 1984. In it he warned that "critics and scoffers" who proclaimed Hitler's doctrines as artificial "bunkum" "may well be too optimistic." He concluded, "The probability of a patriotic, nationalistic Germany of the future must still be faced by every thinking foreigner, European or American."[1] Later, as a student at the Army War College, Smith's 1933 paper "Hitler and Germany" was again right on the mark regarding key issues: the dictator's consolidation of power at home before undertaking military action; Hitler's irrevocable decision to deny Jews property and status as Germans; and the Nazi movement's being a grab bag of inconsistencies designed to appeal to all components of German society. While in Hawaii from 1933 to 1935, Truman's attention was dedicated to his soldiers and to enjoying two bucolic years in paradise with Kay. But neither the world outside nor Germany held still.

Franz von Papen was neither the first nor the last to underestimate Hitler. The speed with which Hitler consolidated power, as well as his sheer audacity, stunned his enemies and energized his supporters. He also won over many who, even if generally indifferent to politics, were tired of the years of defeat and drift and were ready to take a chance on a leader who exuded a sense of purpose and appealed to pride in being German. He was unscrupulous in his readiness to seize every opportunity to enhance his position and to *destroy*—not defeat—his *enemies*—not opponents. He moved swiftly, making assurances of noninterference to the Reichswehr while installing Hermann Goering as Prussian Minister of the Interior, giving Goering control of the police, who were directed to cooperate with the SA, the SS, and Stahlhelm (a veterans' organization) to combat the Left. He was not subtle. Hitler's order to the police was to shoot first and ask questions later: "Every official must bear in mind that failure to act will be regarded more seriously than an error due to taking action."[2] If that was not clear enough, this was: "I am not concerned with both sides. I see only those who are for National Socialism and those who are against it, and I know how to deal with the latter."[3]

The fox was guarding the henhouse. The men with the guns were with Hitler. He exploited the 1933 Reichstag fire—the cause of which is still debated, though it is likely that an SA/SS *Sondergruppe* did the deed—by blaming the communists, arresting 4,000 Communist officials, and getting President Hindenburg to sign an emergency decree passed by the Reichstag, the Enabling Act, on 23 March 1933, that effectively suspended the basic rights of citizens for the duration of the emergency. The temporary measure became a permanent part of Nazi rule. The SPD, casting the only nay votes against the Enabling Act, might as well have posted a sign saying, "Out of Business until 1949." The National Socialist Party was declared Germany's only political party on 14 July 1933. Hitler's dictatorship was established in less than six months.

Hitler touched all bases—courting labor, agriculture, industry, women, youth, veterans, the military—and made brilliant use of radio and film to win mass support by underlining his very real accomplishments. Strikes were prohibited, for example; but so were lockouts. More significantly, the new regime eliminated unemployment, chiefly by opening labor camps and performing visible public works. The *Kraft durch Freude* (Strength through Joy) social program provided worker vacations and entertainment. Germany withdrew from the League of Nations on 14 October 1933, an action validated by the German people in the (unopposed) Reichstag election of 12 November 1933, as 92 percent voted for the Nazi list of candidates and 93 percent approved of the government's decision to leave the League. On 7 April 1933, Hitler promulgated a "Law for the Restoration of the Professional Civil Service," which effectively purged Jews, SPD members, and enemies of the Nazis from the civil service. The Reichstag, singing the Nazi tune, became, as Gordon Craig put it, "the most expensive glee club in the country."[4]

The passion of German electoral politics in the early 1930s, in too-frequent elections, is depicted here. The lower left poster says, "Vote the National Socialist List." The two men in uniform struggle for the New Germany. (Press and Information Office of the FRG, 1980.)

"Do not buy from Jews!" (Press and Information Office of the FRG, 1980.)

Gleichschaltung, getting everyone "coordinated" in the same gear (or "with the program" in today's vernacular), was the objective, another way of saying that no opposition would be tolerated in the new order of things. There was no room for a loyal opposition; opposition was disloyalty.

Moreover, the federal system, which had been in place since the unification of Germany under Bismarck (when several of the states, or *Laende,* were kingdoms), gave way to the establishment of centralized authority. Hitler stated his position unequivocally: "National Socialism has as its historic task to create the new Reich and not to preserve the German States."[5]

Support of the army was essential to Hitler. And, to its regret and Germany's, the army made a deal with the devil. Despite Hitler's assurances in February 1933, the army remained concerned about the SA as a competing armed force. On 30 June 1934, Hitler addressed the army's concerns and at the same time purged radical dissidents and tightened his personal control of the party. Variously called the Great Blood Purge and the Night of the Long Knives, a number of Hitler's potential rivals around Germany, most of them roused from their beds in the middle of the night, were summarily executed by the SS. Among them was the SA's leader, Ernst Roehm, who, on 6 August 1933, before a parade of eighty thousand SA men on the Tempelhof Field outside of Berlin, responded to Hitler's pronouncement that "revolution is not a permanent state of affairs" with this defiant answer: "Anyone who thinks that the tasks of the SA have been accomplished will have to get used to the idea that we are here and intend to stay here, come what may."[6]

Hitler had made his choice between loyalty to an old fighter and total control of the party and Germany. Roehm had to go. So did Gregor Strasser, and other enemies, such as army General Kurt von Schleicher. Reliable SS men did the Nazis' dirty work, but the army was complicit. On 1 July 1934 the defense minister, General von Blomberg, praised the führer's "soldierly decision and exemplary courage" in destroying "mutineers and traitors." A month later Hindenburg died, and Hitler amalgamated the offices of chancellor and president under his preferred title, führer. Then, every officer and man in the armed forces bound himself to Hitler with this oath: "I swear by God this sacred oath, that I will yield unconditional obedience to the Führer of the German Reich and Volk, Adolf Hitler, the Supreme Commander of the Wehrmacht, and, as a brave soldier, will be ready at any time to lay down my life for this oath."[7]

One wonders how often in the following decade German soldiers reflected on the oath or connected the words to the deeds expected of them. The language is certainly unambiguous. On 20 August 1934, the army got a formal promise from Hitler "to fix the army as the sole bearer of arms in the nation." He may have meant it, but the SS would become a more formidable competitor for the army than the SA ever had been.[8]

Josef Goebbels, Reich Minister of Propaganda, touted Hitler's accomplishments through many means, but he exploited radio for propaganda purposes with special success. Hitler's rhetoric and voice seemed made for that medium. (The same can be said of Franklin D. Roosevelt, who also effectively presented his Fireside Chats on the radio at about the same time.) Film director Leni Riefenstahl captured the sense of Germany's being on the march again under the leadership of Hitler in her classic film of the 1934 Party Convention in Nuremberg, *Triumph des Willens* (Triumph of the Will). Hitler's considerable personal magnetism and mesmerizing oratory are amplified by her lighting and staging of the ceremony, pageantry, flags, and music at the rally. Anyone who has seen the film will understand how a down-and-out human being might find hope, unity, and pride in viewing it. She directed that film and another, covering the 1936 Olympics held in Berlin, at Hitler's request. The latter, a tribute to youth, fitness, and competition, also served to document the restoration of Germany's position in the world under Adolf Hitler's leadership.

Radio and film were still-emerging methods of projecting a message, but Hitler, in his book *Mein Kampf,* had already expressed his views about the message itself: "Effective propaganda must be limited to a very few points and must harp on slogans until the last member of the public understands what you want him to understand. . . . [If you] try to be many-sided, the effect will piddle away."[9] Accordingly, Hitler made no qualifications to his argument, no concessions to the other side, and he focused on a few targets in direct language: the Versailles Treaty, the League of Nations, parliamentary democracy, communists, and Jews.

Even the briefest description of conditions in Germany after 1933 must emphasize Hitler's unique personality. What mattered most was not his appeal to reason but his intuition and supreme self-confidence. One of Hitler's true believers said what affected him. "He who once looked into Hitler's eyes, he who once heard him, will never get away from him again."[10]

Many others spoke of Hitler's mesmerizing, hypnotizing gift. The dispassionate Smith said of his 1922 interview with Hitler that he was "deeply impressed by his personality and thought it likely that he would play an important part in German politics." His timing, disregard of risks, and skill in enlisting the masses were at the heart of his successes at home and abroad. (One wonders where his gifts came from; one hesitates to call them god-given.) Yet reliance upon those characteristics that brought him to absolute power also produced the hubris that later doomed him—and Germany.

A famous man of the Right foresaw that, like the Pied Piper leading rats to their death, Hitler would lead the German people to misery. Two days after Hindenburg's appointment of Hitler as chancellor, Erich Ludendorff, who had marched with Hitler in 1924, wrote this to Hindenburg: "I solemnly prophesy to you that this damnable man will plunge our Reich into the abyss and bring inconceivable misery down upon our nation. Coming generations will curse you into your grave because of this action."

But historian Joachim Fest describes Hindenburg as a "doddering old man" and calls him "cold, self-centered." He adds that Hindenburg was satisfied that Hitler was doing away with "wretched undisciplined party nonsense." Hindenburg, the president of the Republic, obviously held republics, parliaments, and political parties in contempt.[11]

Émigrés left; second-raters succeeded them; the masses were barely distinguishable from sheep. What about the decent Germans who remained and were ashamed, alarmed, or both? It is difficult to contemplate, and near impossible to plan, active resistance to a government having a monopoly of power, a government that demonstrated repeatedly a readiness to use that power ruthlessly against real and imagined enemies, a government that despite its excesses enjoyed the support of large segments of the German public and scant opposition from neighboring nations as the years after 1933 moved on to 1939.

It is cheap talk for outsiders to speak of resistance. Most people are not martyrs. Consider the father of a family, a man lucky enough to have a job or career in bad times, who deliberately risks his job, status, family, and life itself in resistance as neighbors cheer the Pied Piper and other governments treat the dictator of his country with more deference than had been shown the Weimar Republic. That is a rare human being, one to be revered. It is not most of us, who do what human beings do most of the time: go along to get along.

Christopher Isherwood captures in simple prose the ordinary person bending with the wind in this description of his landlady as he leaves Berlin in 1933, after spending several years there.

> It's no use trying to explain to her, or talking politics. Already she is adapting herself, as she will adapt herself to every new regime. This morning I even heard her talking reverently about Der Fuehrer to the porter's wife. If anybody were to remind her that, at the elections last November, she voted communist, she would probably deny it hotly, and in perfect good faith. She is merely acclimatizing herself, in accordance with a natural law, like an animal which changes its coat for the winter. Thousands of people like Frl. Schroeder are acclimatizing themselves. After all, whatever government is in power, they are doomed to live in this town.[12]

There were those opposed to Hitler in their hearts who found expression of their feelings by means of mental reservations rather than direct action, an attitude later called "inner migration." Others served without reflection in response to undeniably bad times, called to the colors to "defend" the homeland, and only later brought mature critical judgment to what they had experienced. The creative ones became eyewitnesses who would later give literary testimony. That was not as heroic as storming the barricades, but the writings of such authors as Guenther Grass, Heinrich Boell, and Siegfried Lenz, from 1948 onward, forced post–Third Reich introspection among Germans, when forgetting—or at least keeping quiet about the Nazi time in the immediate postwar period—was the preferred way to escape responsibility. War-weary German survivors wanted to put Hitler and the war behind them and proceed with what became the *Wirtschaftswunder,* the economic miracle of the mid-1950s; they wished to earn the respect of the international community by *not* talking about the bad old days. They would warn that Germans should not foul their own nest. Those who brought up the dirty linen were considered soft-headed or were dismissed as agents of the enemy camp to the east. Novels such as, for example, Grass's *Local Anaesthetic,* Boell's *The Clown,* and Lenz's *The German Lesson*, forced newly prosperous Germans to think and talk about the then of the Hitler time and the now of the self-satisfied citizen, and perhaps to reflect upon the shallowness of what is called civilization. There are a number of variables to explain why the Bonn Republic would succeed where the Weimar Republic had failed. One is the work of artists who refused to allow Germans to forget. But that all came later.

Hitler had told the world in innumerable speeches—and in his book—that he would revise the Treaty of Versailles, and his career showed that he meant exactly what he said. His actions would match his words. The Western Powers, in the period of Smith's second Berlin tour, would consistently undercut potential German domestic resistance by capitulating to Hitler's demands. As early as 1931 a Berlin report from French ambassador Andre François-Poncet warned his government that "the eternal agitator will not escape the necessity of acting." The essence of Hitler was the necessity of acting. British ambassador Sir Horace Rumbold on 26 April 1939 said that Hitler "would probably be glad to suppress every copy [of *Mein Kampf*] today," since that book explained what would soon start happening in the foreign sphere "sooner than contemplated."[13]

Hitler's blueprint was available in a book published and sold in the millions, but it was dismissed. Hitler was masterful in allaying the suspicions of his neighbors in order to buy time for *Gleichschaltung* and to make the first preparations for the all-out rearmament that would come later. Other governments thought that if they treated Hitler adroitly, they could tame him. They were as wrong as his domestic foes about who would tame whom.

Historian Alan Bullock called the period 1933–1937 "the Counterfeit Peace" in Europe, adding that although 1938–1939 was the period in which Hitler more aggressively addressed *Lebensraum* (living space) for the German people, "Hitler was ready to risk war and started preparing for it from the day he came to power."[14] That is true, but his timing was exquisite in its blend of menace and conciliation, which kept foreign governments constantly off balance. His confidence, never in short supply, grew with each success. On 30 January 1937, after four years in power, he could present an "impressive balance sheet of achievements" before the Reichstag and boast, "Our language is being understood again only since we have a large army. . . . We move through the world as a peace-loving angel, but one armed in iron and steel."[15]

The intellectual and cultural cost for Hitler's absolute rule was enormous. Writers Thomas and Heinrich Mann, and Arnold and Stefan Zweig; painters; architects; musicians, such as Kurt Weil; pioneers in film, including Josef von Sternberg and Fritz Lang; historians Hajo Holborn, Theodor Ernst Mommsen, Felix Gilbert, and Hans Kohn; film stars Marlene Dietrich and Peter Lorre, among many others from the Weimar film industry, which compared favorably to Hollywood—all left Germany, bestowing on American students and patrons of the arts the benefit of their intellectual energy and imagination. (Your current writer is a grateful student of expatriates Sigmund Neumann, Karl W. Deutsch, Georg Halm, and Ernst L. Presseisen, the latter a Dutch victim of the Nazis.)

The German press, through laws and intimidation, fell victim to *Gleichschaltung.* Hitler's contempt and distrust for intellectuals resulted in demoralized universities, and admissions to the university and gymnasium were increasingly determined more by party fealty and membership in the *Hitlerjugend* (Hitler Youth) than intellectual capacity or talent. Second-raters took the place of the first-rate in Germany. The works of Marx, Heine, Freud, Remarque, Kaestner, and Tuckolsky were burned in front of the Kaiser Wilhelm University in Berlin.[16]

The *Manchester Guardian* on 19 May 1933 devoted a whole page to list the names of 196 professors and academics who had been dismissed from their university posts in Germany within a period of three weeks. (Gordon Craig writes that 45 percent of the established positions in German universities changed hands from 1933 to 1938.) For many scholars and intellectuals—not to mention artists, Jews, communists, and socialists—Britain was merely a staging post on the route to America. Other staging posts (or, in some cases, permanent residences) were Switzerland, Sweden, France, and elsewhere in Europe and the Western Hemisphere. Willi Brandt went to Norway. Novelist Erich Maria Remarque fled to Switzerland, then to the United States.

Many kept a step ahead of the Germans by going, for example, first to Paris, then to London, and then to New York, Los Angeles, or some bucolic college campus in the United States. Far more Jews of distinction settled in America than in any other country. Five scientists who had already won the Nobel Prize and six who would subsequently do so went to the United States.[17]

By the time Smith arrived in Germany in 1935 for his second assignment to that country, Hitler was firmly in the saddle. As Smith put it, "When I reached Berlin, I found myself catapulted into the very center of one of the most dramatic and world-shaking periods of modern political and military history. The 'small town' Hitler, whom I had talked with in Munich in 1922, was now absolute ruler of sixty million Germans, a people as gifted scientifically, industrially, and militarily as any on the globe."[18]

The Smiths were still settling into an apartment and Truman's new job when the Nuremberg Laws (15 September 1935) were passed, depriving Jews (including those of one-quarter Jewish extraction) the right of citizenship. All intermarriage with Jews was forbidden. Many Jews left the country and their property. These draconian laws were no surprise to Smith, who had written in his War College "Germany and Hitler" paper (29 April 1933) that a desire to conciliate America would not change Hitler's "anti-Semitic measures. These will probably cause a marked decline in the power and prosperity of the German Jews." And conditions got worse.

The 1972 film *Cabaret* shows a scene of two Jews, one of whom is about to open a door to his house, discussing what the Nazis, who are on the brink of coming to power, will do about German Jews. As he passes through the door he looks back to his friend, shrugs, smiles, and asks, "What will they do, kill all of us?" The screen goes black.

Smith was right in 1933 about the Nazis consolidating their internal position, regimenting the German people, and getting public opinion behind their foreign and domestic policies; right in saying that Hitler would not be "unseated," when many expected him to fail and depart quickly, as his predecessors in the office of chancellor had done; right in identifying equality of armaments as Germany's immediate foreign policy objective. Finally, he was right in putting his finger on "the question whether France and her Allies by force will seek to prevent German rearmament." By the time Smith returned to Germany, consolidation of power and Hitler's survival were accomplished facts. The answer to the question regarding whether the French would be willing to use force would come with Hitler's remilitarization of the Rhineland seven months after Smith's return to Germany. The answer was "No."

Milestones on Hitler's road from consolidation of power to his remilitarization of the Rhineland include the plebiscite in the Saarland that emboldened him, the testing of the will of the Western Powers that further encouraged him, and the challenge in his remilitarization of the Rhineland in March 1936, when he was convinced that France was unlikely to fight unless actually attacked.

The Saarland plebiscite, which set Hitler on a more aggressive foreign policy course, had taken place in January 1935. Shortly thereafter, on 8 March 1935, Hitler, in the first of what became known as "the Saturday Surprises," announced that he had a new military air force. A week later he announced that he no longer intended to abide by the military clauses of the Versailles Treaty regarding Germany and was expanding from the Treaty-mandated strength of 100,000 to a force of thirty-six divisions and about 550,000 men. Despite the French call for talks, Britain, France, and Italy failed to speak with one voice to reject this unilateral abrogation of the Treaty and to restrain Hitler. Relations between Britain and France were strained because of the recently signed Anglo-

German naval treaty. And when the League of Nations condemned German policy, Hitler ordered the doubling of his air force, showing his contempt for that organization and its member states. He blended bold actions with conciliatory words. Some simply feared him. Some showed "an almost pathetic readiness" to believe his conciliatory words.[19]

In England there was an attitude—going back to 1919 and the early 1920s regarding the Treaty and France's behavior in the Rhineland and Ruhr—that perhaps the Germans had been rather badly treated. Moreover, the British had an Empire to worry about. One can speculate about what closer French and British cooperation from 1919 to 1939 might have meant, but from the beginning there were differences in their German policies.

Italy became engaged in armed involvement in Abyssinia in December 1934 and later invaded that country. Mussolini was persuaded that the Italian heirs to Rome had a right to regard the Mediterranean as "our sea." A French general later wrote that, when he first joined the General Staff, his immediate superior took him aside and said, "By the way, the general [Maurice Gustave Gamelin, French general and chief of the General Staff] has no guts."[20]

Hitler was aware that his army was not quite ready, but his intuition told him that the psychological conditions were propitious. France would not fight unless invaded. Britain would not intervene if France did not fight. Mussolini was busy in Abyssinia, and his objectives, in any event, were in the Mediterranean littoral.

So, as Gordon Craig wrote, with "a total strength of 22,000 men plus 14,000 local police (a far cry from the 265,000 troops that Gamelin maintained were under German command in the Rhineland), Hitler had effectively destroyed the post–First World War security system." The psychological effect was immense. German prestige was enhanced. French defensive strategy was revealed, causing Belgium to seek relief from treaty obligations and to abandon plans to extend the Maginot Line into Belgium as Belgium set a course to return to neutrality. France's friends in Middle Europe "began to weigh the advantages of getting on to Hitler's bandwagon."[21]

Hitler later confessed, "If the French had marched into the Rhineland, we would have had to withdraw with our tails between our legs, for the military resources at our disposal would have been wholly inadequate for even a moderate resistance."[22]

The French did not march. The Germans did.

Historian Gerhard L. Weinberg has called the period from 1933 to 1936 "a diplomatic revolution." In 1933 Germany was "a barely accepted equal on the European stage."[23] By 1936 Hitler's Germany was the dominant power on the Continent, and "Germany's determination for war had become the central theme of world diplomacy."[24] Hitler's purpose: to acquire land for agricultural settlement by Germans. His method: to win a series of wars against isolated enemies, to increase resources, and to terrify others.

As Truman and Kay took up residence in Berlin in 1935, each noted the great changes in Germany since 1924 and others that were under way. Kay's account of the Smiths' first year back in Germany adds a human dimension to what we know of the place and period from professional diplomats and historians. She was perfectly suited by nature and experience to be a full partner to Truman, whose work was both demanding and important to his country.

11

Kay, Germany, and Ambassador Dodd

> One felt a hurry in the air and a certain tenseness.
>
> —Kay Smith, on her first impressions of Berlin in 1935

> I have seldom met a man for whom I developed so much contempt. . . . He was small with wrinkled, dried up colorless skin and hair. (His soul was the same.)
>
> —Kay's description of Ambassador William E. Dodd

Katharine Alling Hollister Smith used Alling, her mother's maiden name, and Hollister, her own maiden name, on the title page of her memoir, "My Life," presumably to make it clear that she was not just another Smith. She describes her and her husband's second tour of duty in Berlin in a single-spaced document of 286 pages.[1]

Kay's unpublished memoir is analytical, with generous helpings of gossip, but always evocative of the drama of Hitler's Germany from 1935 onward. She is an observant, engaged, intelligent, and informed recorder of matters large and small. The biographer welcomes her fondness for name-dropping and character assessment (and sometime character assassination), but she often omits the precise dates of events the historian craves, requiring some detective work to get them right. But that is quibbling. "My Life" is a unique document that provides contemporaneous human responses to Hitler's bold strokes and international reaction to them or, more accurately, the international failure to react.

The Smiths' earlier service in Berlin, as the Weimar Republic was being born, at a time when anything seemed possible, gave Kay a sense of ownership. So did the fact that the Smiths in 1935 were widely known among Germans in high places, with some of these individuals soon to be famous—or infamous. She is proud, even vain, projecting a sense that she deserved easy entree into elite circles. She is often critical, but she is generally not mean-spirited. (She makes an exception for Franklin D. Roosevelt. She hated him and held Ambassador William E. Dodd, a Roosevelt appointee, in contempt.) Her usual attitude is analogous to the finishing school senior appraising the new freshman girls.

Kay's constant and unqualified loyalty to her husband and to his legacy, and her high opinion of his skills and integrity, seem justified. She also had blind spots. For example, although she had Jewish friends, she did not mention the Nuremberg Laws, which deprived Jews of citizenship, laws promulgated just weeks after the Smiths returned to Germany. Because she had a strong sense of responsibility and was well aware of her high visibility in her representational role in the diplomatic community, she was critical of official Americans who made little effort to learn German and those who failed to represent the United States well, including Ambassador Dodd and his entire family.

She was also quite capable of doing well while doing good. In both tours in Germany she was a vigilant bargain-hunter, monitoring currency exchange rates as she found the best deals in luxury items such as furs, clothing, jewelry, crystal, house furnishings, and tableware—at someone's expense. What wasn't available in Berlin could be (and was) ordered from New York City: books from Brentano and clothing from Best & Company. But most significantly, Kay was her husband's confidant and later his Boswell. Truman shared his views with his wife, often trying his ideas out on her. She listened as attentively as Boswell had, and reported, if not as famously.

Kay's estimate of the situation upon returning to Berlin after a twelve-year absence began with the Esplanade, "the best and nicest hotel in Berlin." The Smiths always went first-class. She notes that Berlin "was all the same yet not the same. The streets, the buildings were all as I had known them. But now no more shabby fronts and broken fences. All was clean, freshly painted and in August blooming with leafy trees and window boxes full of flowers." In addition, she noted "the streets jammed with cars where before there had been nothing but broken down cabs. The crowds well dressed, the people looking well nourished, energetic. One felt a hurry in the air and a certain tenseness. This I became aware of more and more as the days passed, and I myself was caught up in it. The tempo grew faster and faster, until in 1938 and 1939 events rushed on with the tempestuous force of a river nearing a great Falls. One was swept along with the river well knowing of the Falls whose thundering already pounded in our ears, battling with all one's power to keep one's little craft from being swept over with the stream onto the rocks below. But at first it was not like that at all."[2]

Those impressions are consistent with what historians record. In Hitler's first two years he focused on consolidation of his power and reducing unemployment by putting people to work on public projects that were visible both in the doing and in the result. Kay's initial description captures the energy and high morale that later became tenseness. Her impressions in 1935 contrasted sharply with the chaos she had witnessed in the early 1920s: "Berlin was a very safe city at this time, as all the drunks, bums, and homosexuals, etc. had been put in concentration camps. This was the original purpose of the concentration camp, to house *arbeits scheu* (work-shy people, those who didn't want to work)."[3] These are the same people that Kay's friends in New York would accuse of being "the shovel-leaners" of the New Deal's WPA or CCC, content to be living on the dole while faking honest work. She's a bit disingenuous here, perhaps not yet fully aware of what was happening. Socialists, communists, Jews, and anyone else who resisted *Gleichschaltung* in word or deed joined the "work shy" in German concentration camps.

At first, Kay relied more upon hearsay than evidence, and reflected the views of her sources. The trains ran on time. Things were looking better. Unemployment in Germany fell from 6 million in 1932 to 1.5 million in 1936. Industrial production doubled in the same period under Hjalmar Schacht, president of the Reichsbank and, as of August 1934, Minister of the Economy. Hitler had improved the lot of most Germans. Most significantly, he had restored their pride and made hope possible. The importance of Hitler's restoration of hope and pride cannot be exaggerated. Kay saw that improvement.

But, writes a scholar with the advantage of hindsight in 2009, "Behind the gleaming achievements . . . the autobahns, the Volkswagen, the Junker bombers, and the Messerschmidt fighter planes . . . the Nazi economy was a rickety machine plagued by shortages and relying on rationing to allocate scarce consumer goods."[4] When Schacht tried to slow Hitler's arms buildup, he was fired in November 1937.

As noted earlier, an American military attaché assigned to a European capital in those days needed deep pockets. The Smiths' household staff, the required entertaining, the elegant apartment in Berlin, and private schooling for Katchen—at first in Germany and then in Switzerland—clearly required an income far greater than the pay of an army major (or a general, for that matter). His government gave Smith's office a total of $250 per annum for entertainment for five officers, working out to a princely $50 per attaché per year (later doubled). And there were further personal expenses for memberships in tennis and riding clubs for Truman and Kay and riding, piano, and language lessons for their daughter.

The household had a live-in staff: Jenny, the cook, described by Kay as a monarchist, and Robert, the driver, "stolid, stout, a communist." Emma, a waitress to whom Kay assigned no political affiliation, engaged in nonpolitical extracurricular activities. There was a butler, "but he and Emma carried on so that Jenny complained she could not sleep. Besides, he stole whiskey and cigarettes. So I got rid of him and made do with a cleaning woman and an extra butler for dinners."[5]

Kay settled into a routine of entertaining that included dinners for ten to twelve on Fridays each week, recording and monitoring the menu so that her guests would not be subjected to a repeat meal. The Smiths also hosted receptions in their apartment for as many as two hundred people. For one of these receptions Truman personally mixed five hundred martinis to be sure they were done right. If Kay's recollection is correct, assuming not all of the guests shared in the Smith martinis, and further assuming the drinks were consumed, that reception was a missed opportunity for world disarmament declared by the mellow international guests in the Smith apartment.[6]

At first the Smiths accepted almost all the invitations they received to dinners, teas, and receptions, so that the diplomatic corps would come to recognize the tall officer and his attractive wife, the new Americans in town. Even later, when they were more selective about accepting invitations, the pace of their lives was hectic. Kay writes, "Events were happening so fast, dinner after dinner, reception after reception, crisis after crisis; ever more and more people; more and more demands on one. . . . Our minds were fixed on the necessity to enlarge one's circle, to get more and more news to send home." She might also have mentioned the daytime activities that took up her time and on which she spent energy, such as afternoon teas, receptions, ladies' social activities, and escorting official or quasi-official American visitors around town or to places of interest in Germany. One may question how the social activities were connected to official duties. Kay offers an illustration to help explain that connection.

One evening Kay was attending a dinner in a large hall, seated next to an officer she did not know and never saw again. "During the course of conversation," she wrote, "it developed that he was under a great pressure as he was involved in building the Siegfried Line. He said his superiors were not satisfied with the pace of construction. *'Ach, noch nicht fertig. Das ist interessant'* (Oh, not yet complete. That is interesting.) There was that in my tone and voice which made him jump. *'Wer sind Sie?'* (Who are you?) he demanded bruskly. I handed him my place card saying, *'Die Frau der Amerikanische Militaer Attache.'* I thought he would choke. He looked scared to death. I went on to assure him. 'You needn't worry. I am not going to repeat this to any of the other attaches.' His dinner was ruined. Evidently he had come up from Baden for the occasion and did not know his way around Berlin." Truman must have gotten an earful when they went home that night.[7]

If the key to real estate is location, location, location, the key to the military attaché game is access, access, access—to contacts, particularly, but not exclusively, with host nation officials. Attachés exchange information, but with Smith that would be, for the most part, a one-way street. He had more useful contacts and better access to the German Army upon his arrival than most attachés would have at the end of their tours. This was particularly important because, as Kay noted, "in order to prevent the pumping of officers by foreign attachés, etc., the German Army and Navy had passed a rule forbidding an officer to frequent the home of a foreigner unless he had known the foreigner previously or been entertained by the foreigner in that person's home while the German was in that country." This effectively made knowledgeable official German sources unavailable to attachés in a congenial social setting. Kay continues, "Our own Naval Attaché, Captain Dutton, had none. [He] had to content himself with the official contacts [trips, visits, receptions arranged by the War Ministry, and handouts they provided] and cutting items from newspapers or what he could glean from the press. . . . Later more leeway was allowed the Italian and Japanese Attachés. Both the British and French were remarkably bare of contacts. They relied more on paid spies."[8]

Smith benefited from knowing many German officers from his days in Coblenz and his first tour in Berlin, and Schell from his Benning days. Particularly useful was knowing Chief of Staff General von Blomberg, who in 1931 had invited him to Germany for maneuvers. Smith spent two weeks in 1932, Kay recalled, "with nearly all the upper echelon of the [German] Army." Therefore, said Kay, "this rule [regarding German officers' social contact with foreign officials] was useless as far as Truman was concerned. . . . his house was thrown open to the Army without hindrance." And his excellent old contacts passed him on to new contacts. Truman was discreet in handling his privileged access and scrupulous in avoiding any semblance of being a spy.[9]

Aside from Smith's personal relationships, Germans were generally kindly disposed to Americans. They were grateful to the Americans for their occupation after the Great War, which was gentler and more sympathetic than the French, the Belgian, and even the British occupations. Germans of rank both high and low recognized America's great wealth and military potential, which they felt might be useful in an unknowable future in which one fact was certain: Germany would remain a country in the midst of many squabbling neighbors. There was no point in alienating America. And of course many Germans had a relative in New York or Milwaukee wh'o had made good and was *der reiche Onkel in Amerika.*

Among Smith's contacts were interesting (and some odd) Germans and Americans, including Nazis, who were essential to his mission: understanding what was happening in Germany and reporting it. But, as we shall see, when Smith returned to the United States in 1939, he would be accused of being pro-Nazi.

"After we were settled in our apartment," Kay wrote, "the first German who came to call was Rochus von Rheinbaben. (His story is found in our Coblenz-Berlin period of 1919–1924.) He was older but as amusing and lively as ever. I noticed he wore in his lapel the *'Blut Orden,'* a round insignia, a red band on the outer edge, a white center with a black *'Hackenkreuz'* [swastika] in the middle. 'Yes,' he said, 'and very proud to wear it. There are not many here in Berlin who joined the Party so early and fought for it when it was unpopular to do so and dangerous. There are many more in Bavaria than here. Those of us who wear it are favored as the advanced guard.'" Kay rather blithely adds, "Rochus had had a bitter time with the communists in Berlin in 1918, and so it was natural for him to become a member of the anti-communist party."[10]

She asked Rheinbaben to explain to her the theory of National Socialism. (Her friend Bobbi Buggenhagen had earlier told Kay that "Hitler had taken the Red Flag and put the Hakenkreutz on it.") "I listened carefully," recalled Kay, "for I wished to understand this movement, to me still completely unknown. After he finished I said, 'But Rochus, what is then the difference between National-Socialism and Communism?' He threw up his hands. *'Hush, Katie. Das darf man nicht sagen.'* (One may not say that.) He had some job with the party, I forget what, not important."[11]

Kay was not alone in her failure to comprehend the theory of National Socialism. Much ink has been spilled to explain the components and contradictions of the Nazi Party. Perhaps it is best understood as superheated nationalism born of resentment, political drift, and economic deprivation causing otherwise rational Germans to follow the Pied Piper.

She called on Rheinbaben's wife, an old friend, and found her "very disturbed." Her son had been put in the Hitler Youth. "A staunch Catholic," Kay's friend objected, not least for reasons of religion. "At that time," Kay explained, "the Party was trying to substitute the old Germanic religion in place of Christianity. This effort sponsored by Rosenberg was a real mistake. . . . Germany is really a religious country and these actions against the church aroused strong feelings against the Party." The mother learned that instead of saying grace at meals, a Nazi youth leader had the children say, *"Lieber Jesu, bleib uns fern, wir essen ohne dich ganz gern."* Kay translates: Dear Jesus, stay away from us. We eat quite gladly without thee. "She was outraged," Kay continues, "but caught in the State trap she could only instruct them differently at home."[12] "Caught in the State trap" is a fine formulation, suggesting the plight of those seemingly without recourse. The thugs were in control.

Rheinbaben's reference to the strength of the Nazis in Bavaria and the favored positions enjoyed by the Old Fighters is another useful insight. Germans south of the Main River, as well as the Austrians, the Roman Catholic parts of German-speaking Europe, were the incubator of the Party in the early days when the choice seemed to be between the communists and the parties of the right. Even now, in the twenty-first century, Bavaria takes pride in being unique, conservative, and Catholic. In the period between the world wars, there were probably more monarchists in Bavaria than in any other land (state).

Kay writes, "the churches were filled on Sundays as they had not been for some time. Dr. Jakoby preached in the Gedaechtnis church near us. I went to hear him in the early days. The church was packed with a most serious congregation. He preached a sermon for freedom and the duty of the individual Christian to stand against paganism and state control." She wondered why the Party tolerated that, and her friends told her "they did not dare to arrest him."[13]

Kay's excursions into regionalism, religion, and education in conversations with German friends were interesting as an intellectual exercise that provided further insight into German society. But having a school-age child made the selection of the right school a very important practical matter.

Katchen at first attended a private school in Berlin, and her mother described the arrival of an official who went to the school specifically to teach the children the Party salute. The Party closed that school at the end of the academic year. The Smiths then sent Katchen to a school in Switzerland.

One of the first people the Smiths arranged to see upon their return to Berlin was Putzi Hanfstaengl, a Harvard-educated, musically talented, enigmatic character. For a while he was close to Hitler, and he knew Hitler in Munich in 1922. Martha Dodd, the ambassador's daughter, called Putzi "the personal clown and musician to Hitler himself." She also wrote that he arranged for her to meet Hitler in a social setting, before Hanfstaengl's fall from grace.[14]

Kay wrote that Hanfstaengl was head of the Press Department in charge of foreign correspondents, "or some thing like that." When the Smiths visited his "very nice small apartment" that backed up to the place where Hitler had his office and apartment, Truman hung his hat on a large bust of Hitler. "Putz hastily snatched it off," recalled Kay. "This was lese majeste!" They had coffee, cakes, and a good chat to catch up on things. "It was plain that all was not rosy between Putz and Goebbels. Putz intimated that Goebbels was jealous of his, Putz's influence over Hitler and was keeping him away from Hitler." The Smiths didn't see much of Hanfstaengl in the ensuing years. "We were frightfully pressed for time and he did not seem anxious to take up our erstwhile fairly close though spasmodic connection. He felt he was skating on thin

From left: Smith, Ernst "Putzi" Hanfstaengl, and Carl von Wiegand. Putzi was Harvard's gift to Hitler for public relations. He would return to North America claiming that he had attempted to civilize the Nazis. Wiegand was born in Germany, was raised in Iowa, and covered Weimar Germany for Hearst. All three knew Germany well. (Courtesy of Katharine Smith Coley and family.)

ice. Truman did see him off and on. One time Putz asked him to coffee with Carl von Weigand, respected dean of the United States Newspaper Correspondents."[15]

The fact that Hitler was firmly established when the Smiths arrived in 1935 did not mean the end of *Gleichschaltung*. Ever-increasing regime control of the population was palpable. Kay recalled, "At first when we came, people did not hesitate to criticize the regime. After two years they thought it wiser to hold their peace. . . . [Then] it was no longer safe to remain silent when criticisms were made by someone else. One had to deny the remarks loudly and clearly or be reported as condoning anti-government sentiments." Even conversation with close friends required discretion and prompted behavior later associated with life behind the Iron Curtain, when the world had become more familiar with life under totalitarian regimes. "Frequently I would call for [her old friend Baroness Bobbi von Buggenhagen] in my car and we would be driven to the Gruenewald where we would walk for an hour . . . one was sure not to be overheard [and] one can see from afar anyone approaching. This made it a safe place to talk of dangerous matters."[16]

One of these dangerous matters was a "dreadful aftermath" of a dinner party at the Smiths' apartment. One of the guests, air force officer Walther von Etzdorf, who was assigned to the German Attaché section of the staff, in after-dinner conversation "extolled Hitler's internal reforms but condemned his foreign policy as likely to lead to war." He also said that he was a member of the *Deutsche Glaubungs Bewegung* (German Faith Movement), Rosenberg's revival of the old German paganism. Weeks after the event, in a telephone conversation Bobbi told Kay that "something terrible had happened to her but would not talk [about it] over the telephone. Would I take her for a walk in the Gruenewald?" Kay assented. Once together in the car, Kay asked what was wrong. Bobbi responded, "I have had trouble with my stomach," putting her finger to her lips and pointing to the driver. They made small talk until they walked in the forest, where Bobbi told this story.

She had been called by the Gestapo and was required to report to a prison the following morning to make a statement about Etzdorf's remarks at the Smith dinner party, and sign it. Then Etzdorf was brought in to read the statement. Bobbi had called him a patriotic German and made reference to his membership in the *Glaubungs Bewegung,* so, after reading the statement he "drew his heels together, bowed over my hand, and said, *'Ich danke Ihnen als eine treue Deutsche Frau'* (I thank you as a loyal German woman) and gripped my hand in a firm handshake. I bowed to him and was ushered out. Oh Katie! It was all so *echt Deutsch,* so stiff, so formal. I could have laughed had it not been so frightening. I was so thankful to get out of the prison! My knees shook all the way home." Etzdorf was let out "a day or so later." The two ladies went over the guest list together and concluded that one of the women guests, "a determined Nazi," was the culprit who reported Etzdorf's remarks made at the Smith dinner party.[17]

To Kay's dismay, the word got out. Some weeks later, an American woman whose husband was in Berlin for an American bank said to Kay, "I hear that one of your guests was reported on. Have you a spy in your house?" Kay was thunderstruck: "I was paralyzed." She abruptly told the woman that that was a very dangerous thing to say and advised her not to repeat it. Apparently the woman forgave Kay's abruptness. Years later, Kay wrote, "when we met in

New York she asked me to join the Colonial Dames." Kay's concern in Berlin was that if the story spread, Truman's contacts would dry up. Fortunately, they did not.[18]

Kay's remarks about Jews reflect personal connections, impressions rather than profound and abstract ruminations about justice and morality. A case in point, with an odd ending, concerns Gladys Baker of Rhode Island, whose father had been governor and whose sister was a friend from Fort Benning days. "Gladys had married a cultured wealthy Jew, Felix Friedheim," wrote Kay. They were neighbors in Berlin. Kay asked Gladys if they had any trouble with the Party. "She was quite airy about it. Said they had come to arrest Felix to take him to a concentration camp but that she persuaded them to take the 'young one' instead. She had gone out to the camp every week taking cigarettes and chocolates. According to her it was quite informal, rather like a cantonment for soldiers during World War I. They had movies. After a while they let her son out. (This turned out to be a cock and bull story. I found out later that . . . when they emigrated to the United States he was arrested in Washington for indecent exposure!)"

The Friedheims returned to the United States in 1938. They said they were returning to attend a wedding, but Kay presumed that was an excuse to get out of a Germany increasingly hostile to Jews. To Kay's surprise, they returned to Berlin. When Kay told Gladys she was surprised that they did not remain in America, Gladys said, "Felix wouldn't. He likes the trees in Berlin." The story gets even more bizarre. Eventually they did get out. "They could not take any capital with them, but they did take all their silver and other things. But the most amazing thing of all, Gladys came back alone! She stayed in her apartment all through the war! Felix had put everything in her name and she stayed to hold on to it. And she succeeded." According to Kay, Gladys's friendship with a high official's wife made that possible.[19]

Among Kay's contacts in Berlin were several seemingly directionless and inbred Americans of independent means who were at least as "Lost Generation" as Ernest Hemingway's characters in *The Sun Also Rises* or F. Scott Fitzgerald's in *Tender Is the Night*. They all seemed to know one another, either from schools—usually Ivy or finishing—or through classmates, friends of friends, spouses, or former spouses. They personify the old-name, moneyed constellation comprising the northeastern establishment.

One such rudderless naïf, who would become totally estranged from his country, was Douglas Chandler. He was the second husband of Laura Wurtz of Pittsburgh, whose father had been ambassador to Japan. Laura had gone to school with Kay's sister Dorothy. Her first marriage was to Bradley Coley, Truman's Yale classmate, lifelong friend, and later father-in-law to the Smiths' daughter. While stationed at Fort Hamilton in 1926, the Smiths attended a cocktail party at the Chandlers' on 58th Street, across from Kay's mother's residence. "Of all the guests at the party," wrote Kay, "I only remember Sinclair Lewis and then only because he was so homely with tobacco stained teeth and pocked or acne-marked skin."[20]

Another future celebrity the Smiths met through the Chandlers, this one in Berlin, was Philip Johnson, who was studying in the Bauhaus School of Architecture in Berlin. "He was the most nervous individual I have ever seen," Kay recalled. "He sat silent most of the time listening intently to the conversation, biting his fingernails and cracking his joints. . . . He has since become a great success . . . his anti-Semitism has never been noised about."[21]

Chandler lost his Wall Street job in the 1929 crash "and took to his bed with a nervous breakdown." The Chandlers lived on the Riviera, in Greece, and in the Black Forest, where Chandler took up photography. He became good enough to go on several assignments for *National Geographic*. "He was extremely anti-Semitic and made several lecture trips for the Nazi Party on a voluntary basis to Scotland, where he was well received." Word of this got back to *National Geographic*, "which cancelled his assignment. Of course this made him more rabid than ever."[22]

One day Chandler asked Kay how she liked Katchen's school in Switzerland. He was considering where to send his girls, who had finished their German schools. Kay recalled, "I said he should send them home to be Americanized and to make friends. He said he did not want them to be Americans; he was thinking of taking German citizenship. I told him he was a great fool. The Germans treated him well now, because he was doing propaganda for them on a volunteer basis, but that once he was a German citizen they would take away all the privileges now accorded him, that he would find it most uncomfortable." He said he didn't like the way the United States was developing. "I said that he had better think again, that war was coming."[23]

Kay, "to finish the subject of Douglas Chandler," picked up her story in Washington in the summer of 1939. Truman had a good radio while working in G-2 in the Pentagon so that he could listen to broadcasts from Germany. "One night," wrote Kay, "I heard a program announced from Germany as Paul Revere. A horse neighed, a man's voice announced himself as Paul Revere." He then warned that the Jews were taking over America and concluded his talk with a poem. "I listened spellbound. . . . The horse neighed again and the program ended."

"Truman, that was Douglas Chandler," said Kay.

"You must be mistaken. He couldn't do such a thing."

"I am certain," she insisted.

"What makes you so sure?"

"The poem," she replied. "Don't you remember when Eddie abdicated the British throne and married Wally, Douglas recited a poem he had written, beginning:

An American whore
from Baltimore
led Edward
bedward.

"This poem tonight is in the same meter. The voice I know was his, the anti-Semitic feelings . . . "

Kay was right. After the war Chandler was arrested, tried, convicted, and confined in Danbury prison. Chandler's daughter asked Truman to testify for her father. Truman refused. He could not testify on behalf of anyone who had betrayed his country. Kay reported that Chandler spent "many long years in jail and was the last person released who had been an agent of a foreign government." He was in prison even longer than Tokyo Rose. He was freed when Bobby Kennedy was attorney general. Kay intimates that it could have gone worse for Chandler: "Lord Haw-Haw, the British counterpart of Chandler was executed by the British."[24]

Kay found the members of the Military Attaché Office, particularly Captain James Crockett and Major Koenig, "most attractive, helpful and kind," but she had not one good word for Ambassador William E. Dodd, nor for his family. Since Dodd served in Berlin for four and one-half years, two and one-half of them while the Smiths were there, a brief evaluation of his service is useful in understanding him and Kay's assessment of the man.

Crystal Crockett, the wife of one of Truman's assistant military attachés, who gets high marks from Kay for representing the United States well, told her to "look out for Mr. Dodd, our Ambassador." He had asked Colonel Wuest (Truman's predecessor) constantly to the Embassy to entertain for him, which Wuest had done to the tune of $10,000 out of his own pocket. When Wuest left, Dodd sent "a miserable efficiency report on Wuest to the State Department, and that after making Colonel Wuest think he liked him very much." Mrs. Crockett also said that Dodd had the house he was living in from a Jew, ostensibly to safeguard the property, but that he paid the poor man no rent.

Kay's assessment of Dodd is unambiguous: "I have seldom met a man for whom I developed so much contempt. . . . He was small with wrinkled, dried up colorless skin and hair. (His soul was the same.)" In addition to these imperfections, he was a pacifist; he did not permit his military and naval attachés to appear in uniform when attending official ceremonies with him; "his cronies were the professors." Kay adds that "most of his time was spent writing the Life of George Washington (at taxpayers' expense)." Upon meeting the ambassador and his family for the first time, Kay reports that Dodd said:

"Mrs. Smith, you have come just in time."

"In time for what, Mr. Ambassador?"

"In three weeks Hitler is going to be thrown out."

"Oh, how interesting. I thought he was quite popular. I did not know anything of this."

"Yes, in three weeks this regime will be thrown out and it will all be ended."

"Well, I am glad I shall be here to see this."

She concludes by saying, "This was the first of many things he told me that were the exact opposite of what happened."[25]

Kay was less cruel in her description of Mrs. Dodd, calling her "the poor lady" who was out of her depth. Kay made herself useful by translating French and German for her and otherwise supporting the ambassador's wife. Kate later wrote, "When the Ambassador and Mrs. Dodd finally ended their tour of duty and we went to say goodbye to them, Mrs. Dodd threw her arms around my neck and kissed me, saying, 'You are the only one who ever helped me.' She had tears in her eyes. I felt sorry for her." Kay adds: "Mrs. Dodd died insane which did not surprise me."[26] No one else mentions that

Dodd's wife suffered from insanity. She died of a heart attack in her home in Round Hill, Virginia, on 28 May 1938.[27]

The Dodds had two grown children, William and Martha. Kay reports that William had returned to the United States at the request of the German government. "It was said the government had reason to believe he had carried papers back and forth to Russia for the Communists under his diplomatic immunity." Of his sister, Kay writes, "Martha had a way with the gentlemen and, it was said, no scruples. As time went on I heard rumors that she entertained men at all hours in her apartment. . . . She had tried to have affairs with young men in the German Foreign Office, but they had been warned that if they were known to have been seen with her, they would be dropped from the Service. . . . It was believed she did some service for the Russians."[28]

Journalist William L. Shirer writes that Dodd "could not stomach the Nazis. He was frank and blunt about it, which did not endear him to Hitler or his henchmen or, he told me, to the striped-pants bureaucrats in the State Department in Washington, who thought he ought to be more diplomatic." Shirer liked the frankness and bluntness, as any journalist would. "We soon became good friends and he an important source for me."[29]

Scholar Oliver Lubrich corroborates Kay's comments about Martha Dodd: "In Berlin the diplomat's daughter seemed to have affairs not only with various Nazis, but also with a Russian diplomat who was apparently assigned to her." He adds that Martha continued her espionage activities, was "watched by the FBI," and moved to Mexico in 1953, to Prague in 1957, to Cuba in 1962, and back to Prague, where she died in 1990.[30]

Historian Franklin L. Ford provides a nuanced description and assessment of Dodd as the American ambassador in Berlin. To round out an evaluation of Dodd in Berlin, Martha Dodd's book and Ambassador Dodd's diary are useful first-person sources for the period from a year before the Smith's arrival in Berlin and the 1935–1937 period described by Kay Smith.[31]

Ford sheds light on the reasons for Dodd's behavior and also provides comparisons to his French and British peers. Dodd was a history professor at the University of Chicago when he was selected by the recently elected President Franklin Roosevelt in 1933 to be ambassador. Dodd had earned his PhD at the University of Leipzig in 1900 after three years of hard work, crowned by a dissertation on Thomas Jefferson's return to politics in 1796 (*Jefferson's Rueckkehr zur Politik*). Historian Charles A. Beard hits the nail right on the head: "Mr. Dodd's function was to strengthen and rally the moderate elements in German society then bewildered, no doubt, but not yet solidified and *gleichgeschaltet* under the iron regime of Chancellor Hitler and his party. The task may have been hopeless from the beginning." Roosevelt, fully aware of Dodd's background, chose not to appoint a businessman, a party contributor, or a career Foreign Service officer to be his man in Berlin. He knew just what he was getting: an academic kindly disposed to Germany and well connected there. Interestingly, Dodd had already been designated to serve as president of the American Historical Association. He was at the top of his academic game.[32]

Dodd insisted that his family should live in Berlin on his salary of $17,500. Moreover, according to Ford, "A combination of nervous indigestion and boredom at formal affairs led the ambassador to keep his personal routine as simple as possible, given his position." After two interviews with Hitler (one on 17 October 1933 and a second in March 1934), Dodd "still believed in a wide range of future possibilities" and "maintained normal social contacts with leading Nazis."[33]

But the Blood Purge of 30 June–1 July, when Hitler solved the problem of resistance in the Party by killing his former comrades, changed all that. In an 8 July 1934 diary entry Dodd questions how he could work for peace and better relations "so long as Hitler, Goering and Goebbels are the directing heads of the country. Never have I heard or read of three more unfit men in high place. Ought I to resign?" Of Hitler, he wrote on 13 July 1934, "I have a sense of horror when I look at the man. . . . He is such a horror to me, I cannot endure his presence."[34] He never again had a private interview with the führer, though they met at large receptions for the entire diplomatic corps. That was the Dodd Kay Smith saw when the Smiths arrived in 1935.

Dodd refused to attend the Nazi Party Congresses in Nuremberg. The State Department overruled him while he was in the United States on leave in 1937, directing that an American official from the embassy attend that Party Congress. Understandably, the State Department did not appreciate the direct correspondence between President Roosevelt and his man in Berlin, the lunches they shared when Dodd was in Washington, and the personal relationship with the president that allowed Dodd to make end-runs and to assert himself in dealing with the Department. Moreover, for his last two and one-half years in Berlin, Dodd, wrote Ford, "remained hostile and despondent." He never concealed "the hostility he felt toward most career diplomats and businessmen in the Foreign Service. His diary bristles with remarks about 'rich men,' not only those in the Department or other missions, but certain of his principal aides as well." The Smiths, not mentioned by Ford in this connection, fell neatly into that category.[35]

The Smiths were aware of the sense of Dodd's opinion confided to his diary on 18 August 1934, one year before the Smiths arrived. After attending "a nice little party" hosted by Captain Crockett, Dodd wrote: "Army and Navy Attaches here, and I think all over Europe, are utterly unequal to their supposed functions. They simply have never received good training except in drill and tactics. They may know a little formal history, but they really do not grasp the social and economic problems in countries to which they are accredited. Nor are they clever enough to spy on German military performances. Spying is what governments expect in such fields."[36] He was wrong about Smith's grasp of all aspects of Germany and wrong about spying.

Smith's extensive reporting, private correspondence, and published and unpublished articles provide ample and unambiguous evidence of his understanding of all aspects of the country to which he was accredited. As to spying, everything he did was visible to his German hosts. He could play the game according to the rules because he held an excellent hand: extraordinary contact to German sources. His observing was open; his reporting was confidential.

Kay perceived Dodd's attitude and resented it, confiding to her diary (that became the basis for her memoir) contempt for Dodd and hate for Roosevelt. She was engaged in a kind of quiet class war with Dodd and resented FDR. Add to that her experience in Berlin fifteen years earlier, when she was a very young woman simultaneously playing the roles of belle of the ball and grand lady. In 1935, her official position was more subordinate in a bigger embassy in which neither her husband nor his office was close to the ambassador and key staff officers. This was in sharp contrast to relationships in 1922, when Truman was sent to Munich to interview Hitler. Dodd's frugality, low regard of the military, and unwillingness to engage the Nazis offended her. She considered Dodd an ineffectual academic unsuited for the high position he occupied. And she relegated him to the inner circle of evil occupied by the New Dealers and that traitor to his patrician class, Franklin Roosevelt.

Both Dodd and Roosevelt overestimated the capacity of Dodd—or any American—to influence German policy. As Smith wrote in his 1933 Army War College paper, Hitler was set on a course of consolidation of power at home that would be followed by testing the will of his European adversaries. Consolidation of power and *Gleichschaltung* were accomplished quickly. The United States was peripheral in Hitler's thinking. Dodd nevertheless believed that he had failed in his efforts to moderate German political behavior, to somehow return to 1900, to realize the Germany of *The Student Prince.* After the Blood Purge, Dodd brooded in the realization that some aspects of the Germany he loved from his student days had become personally odious to him.

A diplomat's tasks are more modest than those Dodd set for himself. A diplomat represents, reports, and negotiates. During the period that the Dodd and Smith tours of duty overlapped, the ambassador did none of those tasks well. He was not the contemptible bumpkin Kay describes; he was a broken man. Dodd left Berlin on 28 December 1937, quietly, without notice in the German press, and missed by no one. He had been in Berlin to do America's business with Germany, not to restore the land of thinkers and poets. He was successful in neither task.

Smith knew his ambassador's views. He instructed his subordinates "that he himself would handle all matters which arose between his office and Dr. Dodd." Smith says, "not once in the two ensuing years of Dr. Dodd's service in Berlin did the ambassador make any request of the military attaché to furnish him data on either the German army or air expansion." But, Smith adds, "Dr. Dodd never interfered in any way with the activities of the military attaché or his air assistant." The relationship was always formal, distant, and courteous.[37]

Truman's clear prose and detached professionalism taken with Kay's personalized commentary gives us a sense of the time and place. They shared an unfavorable impression of the ambassador, but Truman separated his personal feelings from an official and necessary relationship as, at least in this instance, Kay could not. As a soldier, Smith could work with and for someone not quite his cup of tea. Liking the boss was a bonus, not a requirement. Kay, conditioned to privilege as a normal condition of life, could become quite waspish when displeased with others or when she felt she was denied her due. There was a bit of the willful young girl in her. He was analytical; she was descriptive. His sure touch in getting at the essence of things informs his reader. Her descriptions of the unfolding drama enhance the reader's feel for time and place, and frequently add a generous dollop of charm and wit.

A social event in the Smith Berlin apartment was one of many such receptions and dinners there, but Kay's first reception was an insight into how the diplomatic game was played in Berlin in a totalitarian system. Kay told the story this way in 1992.

Major Rabe von Pappenheim, in Kay's words, "was the officer in charge of the Military Attaché Corps . . . keeping tabs on what everybody was doing, I suppose." That is one way to put it. In fact, it was Pappenheim's duty to be polite and helpful to foreign officers whose job it was to know more about the German military than the German military wanted them to know. To further confound matters, Pappenheim and his wife Hildegard became "great friends, the four of us."

Early in 1936, Pappenheim informed Truman that, in accordance with Berlin diplomatic practice, it was about time for Smith to give a reception for the other attachés. Smith agreed and drew up a list of guests. Would Pappenheim be so kind as to have his secretary look over the list to be sure titles and addresses were correct? Of the 190 guests, about 100 were German officers. The real unspoken question Smith was putting to his friend was, "Are you going to give these Germans permission to come?" The blanket rule at the time was just what Kay earlier described. German officials could accept invitations to the home of a foreign official if the foreigner had been a guest of the German at some earlier time. Smith had enjoyed social relations with many Germans from 1919 onward, so Pappenheim approved the list.

According to Kay, "When the other attachés came and saw the amount of German officers that were there, they started turning green." Among the guests were Chief of Staff Werner von Blomberg "and his second in command," Field-Marshal Wilhelm Keitel. This was clearly a coup for the American major Smith. But there is more to it than this.

The Smith reception took place just before German troops

marched into the Rhineland, in clear violation of the Treaty of Versailles. Kay believed that the Germans, particularly those at the very top, "wanted to show that their minds were carefree." What she described as Smith's coup was part of a German deception plan. It contributed to the surprise of the *Einmarsch*.[38] This reminds one of an unofficial definition of a diplomat: a gentleman sent abroad to lie for his country.

Twenty years before her interview, Kay had told the same story in her memoir, and there she was more expansive. She writes that at the reception she heard General Renondeau, the French attaché, ask Pappenheim point blank, "Are you going to reoccupy the Rhineland?" Pappenheim replied, "No. Surely not, *mon General*." "Do you swear on your honor?" "*Ich schwere*" (*sic*). Later Pappenheim told her that "he hated to swear, but how could he betray the plan known but to a few." Kay went on, "I could scarcely wait to tell Truman that the reoccupation was certain."

Smith had earlier made his suspicions regarding the reoccupation of the Rhineland known to MID. According to Kay's memoir, "After the event [the reoccupation], Ted Barnes of the *New York Times* came to the apartment to talk to Truman about it. 'I scooped you, Ted,' Truman laughed. 'I sent my cable four days before.'" Kay says that there were only five copies of the plan to reoccupy and that the chief of staff had handwritten the plan himself, but she provides no source for that information.

She also reports that the day after the reception, Hitler made a long speech to the Reichstag, rehearsing the history since World War I, "his customary practice." At the close of his speech, according to Kay, he dropped his voice and announced the entry of German troops, "now crossing the Rhine bridge. And then we heard the bells of Cologne cathedral ring out. It was a dramatic close to a dramatic speech."

Truman rushed to the Embassy.

Ambassador Dodd, wrote Kay, "shut himself up in his library."

When Truman returned to the apartment, he asked Kay how fast she and Katchen could "get away from here." Estimating how long it would take to pack furnishings, Kay said three days. Truman said she would have thirty minutes, if the French react with force. "The bombers will be here in half an hour. Pack two suitcases. Tell Robert to put enough cans of gas in the car to take you to France." Truman would stay with the Embassy. "I was numbed at the sudden possibility of immediate war," recalled Kay. "I said no word more but carried out my orders."

Truman concluded at the time that if the French did not come at once, they would not come at all. Kay noted, "Hitler was right. He had sensed [the French] weakness. The Army had been wrong. Hitler's stock soared with the German people and rose considerably all over the continent." Not knowing for sure what the French might do, Kay's suitcases remained packed and the gasoline cans were kept at hand. Kay accused the French of being all talk, and she holds them—and the British to a lesser extent—responsible for not challenging Hitler at this time, the last clear chance, in her view, to stop him.

She was pleased to note the discomfort of Ambassador Dodd, whose professor friends showed satisfaction in the restoration of German pride rather than wringing their hands at the unilateral military action. According to Kay, Dodd retreated to privacy, "leaving matters to others."[39]

Kay, an opera lover who had fond memories of the rich cultural life in Berlin she had enjoyed in the early days of the Weimar Republic, regretted that her demanding social life as the wife of the military attaché allowed little time to indulge her appetite for music and theater. However, right after the entry of German troops into the Rhineland, Kay attended a performance of Richard Wagner's *Der Meistersinger von Nuernberg,* an opera with arias telling ordinary Germans to "wake up, the day is coming," and the day will "dawn alight with Rose colors." She reports that in the last act, as Hans Sachs finished his impassioned praise of German art, "The audience went mad. Interrupting the performance . . . they rose to their feet spontaneously as one person, cheering themselves hoarse, waving handkerchiefs, in an outburst of national enthusiasm. After years of humiliation, awakened national pride poured itself out in this tremendous demonstration lasting fully five minutes, renewed once more when Sachs made his curtain bow at the end when the curtain had fallen. It was amazing to witness and showed plainly the feelings of people concerning the reoccupation of the Rhineland. Hitler, by this action, had stirred hidden depths as he was to do over and over again in the years to come."[40]

Kay's real-life experience reminds one of the musical *Cabaret*. In one scene, an idealized German youth—complete with *Urdeutsch* trappings: Aryan (actually Nordic) good looks; wearing *Lederhosen;* prepared to *wander;* standing *unter den Linden*—begins to sing a ballad. Solo. Softly. Sweetly. The tempo picks up. Other voices join in. The sweet ballad becomes a march. All join in, lustily singing "Tomorrow Belongs to Me" and marching with their countrymen to a better future.

Kay almost certainly conflates what she observed and reported in Berlin, from her arrival in the summer of 1935 to the reoccupation of the Rhineland in March 1936, with her memories and impressions of conversations over the years on the same subjects. Moreover, it is literally impossible for even the most objective reporter to be unaffected by the events of the 1940s, 1950s, and 1960s in looking back and attempting to reconstruct the Berlin of 1936. Nevertheless, Kay's memoir puts flesh and blood on the skeleton provided by historians and analysts of the Hitler time. Her description of the audience's reaction to *Der Meistersinger* is particularly powerful. To one aware of Truman's 1924 article, "The German Fascisti," it calls to mind his prediction of "the probability of a patriotic, nationalistic Germany of the future."

12

Hitler Arms, Smith Reports

> The most complete account of the official phase of my life in Berlin is to be found in a sworn statement I prepared in 1945 in Fairfield for the use of the War Crimes Commission.
>
> —Truman Smith, 1964

In 1935, Smith knew with absolute clarity that he was in Berlin in Hitler's time to observe and report on German rearmament. In retrospect, he realized that he had been close to the center of world-altering events in the decade after 1935, a period covering his assignments in Berlin and in Washington from 1939 to 1945. Nevertheless, he donated his papers to the Yale University Library in 1957 and 1961, believing them to be no more than the next chapter of the Smith family chronicle, of interest primarily to family members. But in 1964, at the age of seventy-one, he changed his mind. He added selected unpublished documents to an existing typescript of his memoir, noting, "My files still contain in 1964 a considerable number of reports and letters dating from the period 1935–1939. Most of these are of interest solely to historical students of this period. Others are of a technical nature and scarcely likely to interest my family. Yet, in some form or another, a record ought to be left of this important chapter of my life."[1]

He continues: "The most complete account of the official phase of my life in Berlin is to be found in a sworn statement I prepared in 1945 in Fairfield for the use of the War Crimes Commission. . . . This sworn statement was written six to ten years after the events described. It made use however of a large number of contemporary documents still in my Fairfield files. My memory of these events was far fresher in 1945 than it is in 1964" (77).

Once Smith reached his seventies, mortality was on his mind. So was posterity. His account provided the War Crimes Commission with a clear sense of the bee-like activity that was Hitler's Germany on the march in the late 1930s. It lays out the history-shaping events of the period. But between the lines, Smith seemed to be asking: Why were Hitler's actions a surprise? Hitler had stated clearly in his book, *Mein Kampf,* what he intended to do, and then he did it. He repeated what he planned to do in countless speeches before and after he came to power. Then he did it as the world watched. Smith could have congratulated himself for the insights and predictions in his 1924 unpublished article and in his 1933 Army War College paper on Hitler and Germany, but he didn't even refer to them in his 1945 statement. That sworn statement suggests, but does not ask: Who, reading my reports, could not see that Hitler's words of 1935 became his aggressive actions from 1936 onward? The time to stop Hitler was not after the invasion of Poland or the fall of France, or during the Battle of Britain. The train had left the station with Germany's unopposed remilitarization of the Rhineland in 1936.

Smith's "function" in Berlin, in his own words, was to "keep abreast of the strength, organization and training standards of the German armed forces, and to keep myself advised of all economic, political, and military activities and trends that might have a bearing upon German capabilities and intentions of waging war" (80). His inclusion of economic and political activities and trends in Germany makes his mission statement much broader than Kay's characterization of it in her memoir. She sought to distance her husband from any connection with the Nazis or politics in Germany in the 1930s, describing his job as being purely military. There was good reason in the period 1939–1941 for Kay to depoliticize Truman's Berlin duties. However, to do his job there he necessarily had to have contact with all knowledgeable sources, including Nazis.

Kay's efforts to protect Truman's reputation are understandable, considering the tumultuous period when Truman's association with Charles A. Lindbergh caught him up in American partisan politics, as the proper role of the United States in the war in Europe was debated with passion from about 1 September 1939 to 7 December 1941. This is a tangled story, connecting Smith's service in Berlin, accusations of his being pro-Nazi, larger-than-life foreign and American personalities, sensationalist media commentary, and a tense period when Americans were watching dramatic events in Europe and Asia, wondering how events in faraway places might affect them. From the invasion of Poland to the Japanese attack on Pearl Harbor, most particularly after the fall of France and during the battle in the air over Britain, U.S. policy toward belligerents was hotly debated as "interventionists" and "isolationists" clashed. This phase of Smith's life will be taken up in detail when we return the Smiths to the United States from Berlin in 1939.

Smith said of his Berlin reporting that for the most part his findings were based upon personal observations, augmented by conversations with important German military and political persons, reports prepared by the State Department representatives throughout Germany (consulates), German manuals and publications, and, to a lesser extent, newspaper and magazine articles. American journalists, travelers, and businessmen were further sources of information that rounded out his appreciation of what was happening in Germany. His reports were sent to the War Department's Military Intelligence Division (MID, later called G-2.) MID collated and analyzed the reports and tasked collectors to fill intelligence gaps.

Copies or extracts of reports of particular interest to an official or staff section were passed on to those interested, sometimes at their request, sometimes at the initiative of MID. For example, reports on German Army motorization were of interest to the War Department G-3, the War Plans Division, the Chief of Cavalry, and the Chief of Infantry. Personal letters between Smith and General George C. Marshall contain "off-line" information Smith passed directly to Marshall and comments by Marshall telling Smith that some of Smith's collection tasks were due to specific questions Marshall had posed to MID. During the time Smith was in Germany, Marshall was chief of the War Plans Division for three months, then deputy chief of staff as of 15 October 1938. On 1 September 1939 Germany invaded Poland; that very day Marshall became chief of staff, was promoted to permanent major general with two stars, pinned on four stars, and met with President Roosevelt. When Smith returned to the United States some months before, in April 1939, Marshall was about to reorganize the War Department General Staff and lead the army in World War II.[2]

Smith wrote in his memoir that upon his arrival in Berlin in July 1935, he saw "unmistakable and compelling evidence that the German program of building up its army, air force, and war industries had been going full blast long before 1935." In March 1935 Hitler had announced in two "Saturday Surprises" that Germany no longer considered itself bound by the provisions of the Versailles Treaty, which limited the size of its military establishment and the extent of its war industry. Smith believed that the German rearmament program "had been going on since at least 1933 with an intensity of purpose and concentration of effort unparalleled up to that time in modern history." He is explicit in interpreting what was intended when Hitler took off the mask of secrecy in 1935. He planned to use the modernizing and expanding German military to impose his will on Europe by blackmail or by the direct use of force: an "overwhelming military position was a prerequisite to a successful and aggressive diplomacy" (80). Secrecy was for the earlier period, a time of German weakness. Advertising German military power and stating a willingness to use it was deliberate policy, not bluster.

Each year the Nazis held a Party Congress in Nuremberg at which was staged an imposing military pageant called *Tag der Wehrmacht* (Armed Forces Day). Smith attended in 1935, 1936, 1937, and 1938. He found it interesting that at the 1935 display "the secrecy as to tanks, armored cars, and modern heavy artillery was lifted" (82). In 1936 the air force was featured, with flyovers and antiaircraft units marching and showing their weapons. He concluded that the purpose of these pageants was to reveal to the world the deliberate policy of the German government: that Germany was rejecting the Treaty and that German armed forces were large and ever increasing. Smith wrote, "I considered it *my most important function* as Military Attaché to keep abreast of the status of the German rearmament program in all of its details: strength, order of battle and rate of expansion of the German army and the German Air Force, status and rate of increase of German war industries, and development of the German war economy" (82; italics added).

Early on, he was struck by the "urgent sense of immediacy which was everywhere apparent." He concluded that, while arming for the future "with almost feverish haste," Hitler wanted at all times to be ready for any emergency that might arise from his aggressive foreign policy. This need for constant readiness to back words with actions explained to Smith why Germany continued to field outmoded aircraft even while designing and producing the most advanced models. In fact, the sense of urgency that pervaded the entire rearmament program was exemplified by the German air force and the air industry (82).

In July 1936 Smith estimated that the German aircraft industry had a productive capacity two and one half times of that of either Great Britain or the United States, the result of the policy adopted

Smith with Marshal von Blomberg at the Nuremberg Party Day, 1935. "Behind us a mass of 20,000 German soldiers," wrote Smith. Leni Riefenstahl's 1934 classic propaganda film, *Triumph of the Will,* captures the passion and the power of Hitler's speeches and the mass surrender to him. She also directed *Olympia,* the film of the 1936 Berlin Summer Olympics. (Courtesy of Katharine Smith Coley and family.)

by the German government in 1933. That is remarkable. Germany had practically no air force and a very small air industry in 1933, since armaments clauses of the Treaty of Versailles had specifically denied Germany an air force. Germany had devoted 90 percent of its air industry to commercial aviation, while doing some work on military aviation in secret laboratories or abroad in disguised German factories (83). Glider clubs trained pilots; German and Soviet outcasts secretly cooperated. Smith says that the Germans believed the basis of air superiority in any future war would depend not primarily upon the aircraft that began the war, but upon the ability of the nation's aviation industry to produce quality aircraft during the war. Therefore, the Germans decided that the foundation of its air arm must be an "overwhelmingly large and efficient air industry." Germany, Smith determined, had these alternatives: "she could try to catch up on foreign design in designing room and laboratory, waiting for mass production until her designs were equal in quality to those of France, Great Britain and the United States; or, sacrificing quality, she could immediately go into mass production" (83). Germany chose the latter course of action, because from 1933 on,

Smith (3) at the Taunus Maneuvers, October 1936, introducing U.S. Colonel Paul Peabody (4) to Colonel General Beck (2). Beck had recently been appointed chief of the German General Staff. Rabe von Pappenheim (1), the top of his head cropped in this photo, was the staff officer who dealt with military attachés. He was a lifelong friend of Smith. Jim Crockett, also shown here (7), was Smith's assistant. (Courtesy of Katharine Smith Coley and family.)

she wanted to be in a position to fight at any time. That explained why the Germans continued to produce obsolete aircraft even as the latest in technology and performance already existed in prototypes.

Another clue to the catch-up striving that characterized German rearmament was the great effort made in 1936 and 1937 by the German arms industries, backed by the government, to regain a leading position in world markets. Germany's domestic market was too small to support the immense production that was the national objective. New weapons systems are usually treated as highly classified military secrets and are not exported. That was the way France and Britain treated their latest systems. But the Germans, said Smith, chose to develop a large and thriving arms industry at all costs, including the shipment and sale of "first class weapons, even if by so doing certain German military secrets were necessarily sacrificed" (83).

Centralization of Germany's economy went much further than

the modernization of the Luftwaffe and aircraft industry. Smith noted in September 1936 "that German finance, commerce, and industry were being conducted entirely in accord with the needs of building up the German war machine" and that this could not be measured "by usual commercial yardsticks." In January 1938 he observed the influence of the German War Ministry in every phase of commercial and industrial activity. "The Army, Navy and Air Force," he wrote, "claimed their share of raw material imports for conversion into cannon and airplanes; their share of labor for the construction of fortifications, machine guns and bombs; and their share of the government budget to make these programs possible." Developing this war economy "was unequivocal proof that Germany intended to be the strongest military state in Europe." He added that the German effort was "without precedent in history." The country's singleness of purpose in forging its war machine "had much to do with the amazing speed of the German rearmament program" (84).

Smith gives the Four Year Plan decree of 18 October 1936 much of the credit for the speed and thoroughness of the German preparation for war. Reich Marshal Hermann Goering was given extraordinary powers, "similar to those previously exercised by Schacht in controlling the German economy and directing it toward war" (84).[3] Germany's internal supply of raw materials was limited in both kind and quantity, as had been revealed by the British maritime blockade in the Great War. The main goal of the Four Year Plan was to broaden the country's domestic raw material base and to make Germany self-sufficient.

Smith saw an economic transformation in little over a year (by November 1937) and the prospect of continued success regarding specific commodities (gasoline, rubber, copper, the substitution of porcelain and glass for iron and steel). Where natural materials were unavailable, synthetic substitutes would be found. Smith wrote it was evident to him that "under no circumstances would the government abandon the Plan or stir one inch from its resolve to make Germany as self-sustaining as possible" (85).

In a speech delivered in the Reichstag on 20 February 1938, Hitler reported the economic progress in Germany in the first five years of the National Socialist regime. He provided statistics indicating specific gains in areas such as iron, gasoline, and oil. Smith was particularly impressed by the production of synthetic gasoline and noted, "While Hitler was not the most truthful of speakers and often dealt in half-truths, I found that in the case of economic statistics he could be relied upon" (85).

Hitler again addressed self-sufficiency in a speech in Nuremburg on 5 September 1938 in which he claimed that "the German economy has been so organized that as a whole it can at any time exist wholly independent of other nations and stand on its own feet . . . we will cling to the principle that it is better to skimp a little here and there, if necessary, rather than to become wholly dependent upon foreign powers." Smith's observations confirmed Hitler's claims, as his travels revealed new autobahns under construction; old roads being repaired; new factories, barracks, and workers' settlements rising; and old factories being enlarged. "This visual picture of increased industrial activity," he contended, "was fully borne out by official statistics" (86).

Smith was pleased to report that in the fall of 1938 his old Fort Benning friend, Adolf von Schell, "was appointed as dictator of the German automobile industry." Schell told Smith that in a presentation to Hitler on or about 15 October 1938, Schell convinced Hitler that there were too many small firms and too many types of motor vehicles being produced in Germany. According to Smith, "Col. von Schell stated to me that in April 1939, he intended to select from all existing German types, the best trucks in the one ton, three ton and five ton classes. . . . From then on, these three would be the only permitted truck classes which would be allowed to be built in Germany" (86–87). Licensing arrangements would allow the losers in the competition to share in the building of the winning models. The advantage of such a system in the transition from peace to war was obvious. "It was axiomatic to Col. von Schell that private truck factories must produce in peace the same vehicles they would be called upon to produce in war and that the war production program of a factory must merely foresee the enlargement of its peace time production." Schell reckoned that six months in the industrial mobilization process could be saved by this scheme. And, Smith added, "This is the very system then employed in the German aircraft industry [that] had produced such favorable results" (87).

The *Reichsautobahnnen* (Federal Motorways) were another intelligence target of strategic significance to Smith. In 1936 he made a study of that system, concluding that it was superior to the network of roads in "the eastern states of the United States in 1936, and infinitely better than anything built or planned in Europe" (87). The layout of the roads and their engineering features were strongly influenced by the General Staff. The network as a whole provided alternate north-south and east-west routes to provide redundancy in the event that hostile air strikes took out bridges and viaducts. Smith was struck by the absence of autobahns in the border areas, especially roads paralleling frontiers, and their absence on the west bank of the Rhine between Cologne and Mainz, where they could be as useful to the French as to the Germans. Also, he noted, throughout the system, the routes selected were kept out of artillery range. In addition, the "Berlin Ring," the circle of autobahns surrounding Berlin, represented the outer arc of antiaircraft defense of the city and also made it possible to route military traffic around the city (87).

By the end of 1938, 3,062 kilometers of autobahn were open. The obvious military utility of the system was demonstrated in the rapid German concentration against Czechoslovakia in September 1938. On 25 September the 29th Division (motorized) from Thuringia was routed south over the Leipzig-Munich autobahn and onward over Salzburg to Linz. Traffic was closed to other traffic as the division moved in four columns, using all lanes. Five antiaircraft batteries were observed in fields near the Berlin Ring on 27 September, further indicating to Smith that the ring was the outer line of defense of the capital. He noted in December 1938 that the originally planned network of 10,000 kilometers had been increased to 14,000 kilometers, due in part to the extension of the road system into Austria and the Sudetenland and then from Breslau to Vienna across the narrow neck of Czechoslovakia in the vicinity of Bruenn. The point is that the roadways served a distinctly military purpose (88).

German industry was relocated in accordance with national defense needs. In fact, all features of German life were being subordinated to the military program.

In September 1936, Smith made an assessment of what he had personally witnessed in the preceding twelve months he had spent in Germany. He noted a steady consolidation of the position of the Nazi Party within Germany and an increase of German prestige throughout Europe. There was little doubt in his mind that "the growing might of the German armed forces" contributed to both Germany's internal consolidation of power and to its status abroad. Smith concluded his 1945 sworn statement by explaining how economic, psychological, and political elements of national power were transformed to measurable military clout.

It was also in September 1936 that Smith received official information that on 10 October 1936 the German Army would expand from 24 to 36 divisions. Significantly, on that day the conscripts of the class, or *Jahrgang*, of 1915—that is, those born in 1915—reported to the colors along with a large group of volunteers from other classes. "The class of 1914 was not released on that date," noted Smith, "as would have been the case if the one year's term of service had remained in force, but remained with the colors." By this action, the army was roughly doubled. He estimated that at the beginning of 1937 the active army would be at least 600,000 men strong (89).

Smith and his assistants constantly studied and estimated the military strength of Germany. Since no official or unofficial statements of exact strength were available, he relied upon his personal sources, his knowledge of the tables of organization for the various types of German units, and a "Station List," which his office kept as up to date as possible. He arrived at these manpower strengths:

Active Army:	541,700
Reserve:	1,330,000
Air Force:	110,500

In February 1937 he made these estimates of how the German Army would take to the field in the event of a major war:

36 active divisions	620,000 men
12 reserve divisions (within 10 days)	205,000
12 Landwehr divisions (within 10 days)	145,000
Line of Communication troops	200,000
Frontier formations, Landsturm, etc.	150,000
Total, Army	1,320,000
Air Force	110,000
Total, Air Force and Army	1,430,000

He estimated that the Field Army could be reinforced within 60 days by the following units:

24 Reserve divisions	410,000
24 Landwehr divisions	335,000
Air Force Reserve units	30,000

Thus, Smith estimated that a total of 2,205,000 men would be available at M+60. He further estimated that about 500,000 men of the SA and SS should be added to this figure at M+10, "since they could be used for frontier protection in quiet sectors" (89–90).

In November 1938 he estimated the strength of the army at 850,000; the air force, including antiaircraft artillery (AAA), at 280,000; and the navy at 55,000. (In the Wehrmacht, and later in the Bundeswehr, antiaircraft artillery is in the air force.)

Noting, again in November 1938, "The German Air Force was also growing by leaps and bounds," Smith updated his estimates as follows:

Combat planes	as of date
1,212	May 1936
1,400	November 1936
1,956 to 2,198	June 1937
2,400	15 July 1937

The personnel strength of the German Air Force was also increasing. In January 1937 he estimated the strength to be 100,600 men, broken down as follows:

Air Force	45,600
AAA	40,000
Air Signal Corps	15,000

By March 1937 he increased this estimate to 110,000 men, and later to 280,000. The AAA strength of 55,000 men, which Smith estimated in January 1938, particularly impressed him. So did the fact that the material had not been introduced earlier than 1933, meaning that it was state-of-the-art. He noted, "It was believed in Berlin that the strength of the German AAA as of 1 January 1938 was already in excess of that of any other two European powers taken together" (90–91).

From left: Smith, his assistants Paul Peabody and Jim Crockett, and two German soldiers in the field in 1936. Confident in his knowledge of the German Army, Smith's office lacked the technical skills required to assess aviation and the burgeoning Luftwaffe. Charles Lindbergh accepted Smith's invitation to observe all aspects of German aviation. (Courtesy of Katharine Smith Coley and family.)

That was the way Smith concluded his 1945 sworn statement, which he regarded as the most complete account of his service as military attaché in Berlin in 1935–1939. In brief, he knew the German Army very well and had excellent sources among German officers, several of whom were lifelong friends. His interest in economics and industrial mobilization, awakened during his student year at the Army War College (1932–1933), was just what was needed in his job as he observed, interpreted, and reported the motorization and mechanization of the German army that was taking place before his eyes under the leadership of his old friend Adolf von Schell, the fellow who tinkered with autos while at Fort Benning just a few years earlier. The paper Smith wrote on Hitler and Germany while at the Army War College, an assessment that benefited from the advice of another old friend, Friedrich von Boetticher, then the German military attaché in Washington, confirms Smith's currency in German politics between his tours in Berlin. Some of us are blessed in finding professional tasks congruent with personal passions. Truman Smith was such a person.

In addition to the pages Smith devoted to his record "of this important chapter of my life," he devoted the last six of the twenty-eight pages he added in 1964 to the human dimension of life in Hitler's Germany.

His and Kay's penthouse apartment at 4A Cornelius Ufer in the Tiergarten section of Berlin was elegant. It had belonged to a pair of famous German actors, Max Pallenberg and Fritzi Massary, both Jewish. The couple had emigrated from Germany before the Smiths arrived in Berlin. (The apartment was destroyed by bombs in 1944.) While in Berlin, the Smiths were kept under constant German surveillance, and Smith thought his phone was tapped. But, he writes, "I never let the surveillance interfere with my work or social life; particularly as there was no way to avoid it" (99).

Their daughter Katchen's education in a dictatorship presented problems. She first attended a private school that was soon closed, then was instructed by a tutor in Berlin, and finally was sent to the excellent Grand Verger School in Lausanne, Switzerland.

In his writings Smith described some of the people who were important to him, reminding us that individual personalities matter. "Documents," he asserted, "however important, do not of course tell the whole story of Kay's and my life in Berlin between August 1935 and April 1939. Seldom do the personalities with whom one associates, day in and day out, emerge clearly in official reports and communications" (99).

Major Albert Vanaman, his air attaché, got high marks from Smith and became an air force major general. Major Herman Kramer, an American student at the Kriegsakademie, was later a division commander. Major John Ratay, in Berlin doing research in the German war archives, also became a general. In his memoirs Smith wrote, "Captain Albert C. Wedemeyer, who was a student at the German Kriegsakademie, became Theater Commander in China. He and his wife Dade ever since those Berlin years have held a firm place in our circle of friends" (102).

Official relations with Ambassador Dodd, Smith admitted, "were at times strained, but my personal relations with him were pleasant enough" (102). Dodd's successor, Hugh Wilson, was an old friend from Smith's first tour in Berlin, and they remained friends

Ambassador Hugh Wilson, front and center, with his staff in 1936–1937. Smith is third from left in the back row, the tall man. The next man to the right is Major Arthur Vanaman, Smith's assistant for air. Kay was pleased to be rid of the Dodds and delighted to be reunited with the Wilsons, who were friends from Smith's first Berlin assignment. (Courtesy of Katharine Smith Coley and family.)

until Wilson died in 1949.[4] Commander Paul Pihl and his wife, Charlotte, the sister of 1940 presidential candidate Wendell Willkie, became friends of the Smiths for life. Smith also had kind words for others, less well known, in his "official family."

He recognized several fellow military attachés as men of "exceptional ability." Five of them, he noted, became their country's ambassadors or ministers in Berlin between 1935 and 1939. "The most famous of them was Oshima, the Japanese military attaché who became Ambassador to Germany. It was he who effected the Japanese-German alliance. In 1946 he was executed as a war criminal" (103).[5]

Smith adds that "my closest friends in the attaché corps were General Renondeau, the French military attaché; the Swede, Colonel Juhlin-Danfeldt; the Pole, Lt. Col. Anton Szymanski; and Colonel Hotblack, the first of several British attachés. One of the British assistant attachés, Major Kenneth Strong, became the G-2 in General Eisenhower's headquarters" (103).

The short man in the center looking at the folder held by the German officer is the Japanese military attaché, General Hiroshi Oshima. He was later Japanese ambassador in Berlin and had direct access to Hitler. In 1946 he was tried, convicted, and sentenced to life imprisonment for war crimes. He was paroled in 1955 and died in 1975. (Courtesy of Katharine Smith Coley and family.)

He considered two successive Italian attachés, Colonel Mancinelli and General Efisio Marras, to be able officers. Both became chiefs of staff of the Italian army after the Second World War.

Smith's remarks about one man are rather poignant. "The assistant Russian military attaché Colonel Gerassimoff," he writes "was a pleasant man though obviously born a peasant. He sought me out at all diplomatic parties. [He] seemed lonely and craved friendship. I hope with all my heart that his liking for me and certain other attachés was not the cause for his being recalled to Moscow in 1939 and his subsequent execution" (104).

His observation of another famous and controversial figure is worth quoting in full.

> In any gathering of the diplomatic corps, its doyen, the Papal Legate, Cardinal Pacelli, with his aristocratic mien, his ascetic face and his brilliant crimson robes was the center of all eyes. On one occasion at a reception in the British embassy in 1938, he sent a Monsignor aide to ask me to come to talk with him. I was astonished when, upon joining Cardinal Pacelli, he quizzed me in perfect English as to the state of readiness of the Luftwaffe. One of his questions I remember distinctly was, what did we Americans think of Germany's new two motor fighter: the Messerschmidt 110? Just a year after this conversation, Cardinal Pacelli was elected Pope and became Pius XII. (104)

Germany's future war leaders were often guests at Kay's Friday dinners for ten or twelve, or receptions—for 200 in their penthouse apartment! Of these, according to Smith, "only Field Marshall Walter von Reichenau and General Colonel Walter Warlimont [among the very top men] were close personal friends. I had often played tennis with the former in the years 1923–1924 . . . and I had known Warlimont when he had visited Fort Benning in 1928" (105).

Smith also knew Colonel Hans Speidel, who later became Rommel's chief of staff. After the war, Smith would vet Speidel and other German officers when Germany was rearmed and the Bundeswehr came into being in the mid-1950s. Speidel became the commander of the ground forces of NATO in Europe. "Colonels Rabe von Pappenheim and Horst von Mellenthin showed me repeated favors," wrote Smith. "They and their wives are still close and loyal friends in 1964" (105). (Horst, later general, was the older brother of Major General Friedrich-Wilhelm von Mellenthin, author of *Panzer Battles*.) Smith recalled, "Another German friend, Col. Kurt Hesse was a gifted military writer who had published several books on the psychology of soldiers at the front. I had seen much of him in Berlin in 1922. Four years before that, in June 1918 Hesse and I had faced each other in battle in the dense wood on Hill 204 northwest of Chateau Thierry" (105).

But it was an American, more famous than any of the Europeans Smith knew in Germany, who figures prominently in the story of how Smith penetrated the Luftwaffe and the German aviation industry. Smith called the story of his aviation intelligence coup the most important one of his Berlin years. He would pay a high personal price for his intelligence prize shortly after his return to the United States in April 1939. So would his source and accomplice.

13

Smith's Trojan Horse

> [The annual aviation report] took no account of the extremely rapid development of the Luftwaffe, in which expansion could be noted almost every week.
>
> —Truman Smith, on reporting from Berlin, 1935

In the summer of 1953, seven years after his retirement from active military duty, Smith was approached by the Intelligence Division of the General Staff with the request that he furnish them all pertinent facts regarding the connection of then-Colonel Charles A. Lindbergh, Army Reserve, with Smith's office in Berlin between 1935 and 1939. The Intelligence Division was particularly interested in what Smith called "a half-mythical document which our press in the years 1939, 1940, and 1941 often referred to in their columns but never quoted from directly." Smith was skeptical that such a Lindbergh report existed, "as were both the Army Intelligence and Historical divisions."

Smith's initial reaction to the request lands somewhere between petulance and recalcitrance. The official effort to get to the truth regarding Lindbergh is commendable. The record could and should have been captured in print. But by 1953 it was much too late to prevent the damage done to Lindbergh's reputation and to Smith's integrity a dozen years earlier.

"After much hesitation," Smith continued, "I decided to meet the wishes of the army, but in my own time and way. I decided to prepare at my leisure a record of the air intelligence activities of my Berlin office and, in the course of the research necessary for this project, ascertain the true facts concerning the so-called Lindbergh Report."[1]

One can visualize the clenched jaw and the steam coming from Smith's ears as he seized the opportunity to right what he regarded as a grievous wrong. He worked deliberately, taking from September 1954 to September 1956 to research and write a report with a very carefully worded title—"Air Intelligence Activities, Office of the Military Attaché, American Embassy, Berlin, Germany, August 1935–April 1939"—and an equally carefully worded subtitle: "With Special Reference to the Services of Colonel Charles A. Lindbergh, Air Corps (Res.)." The order of mention—"Intelligence Activities" before "Lindbergh"— is deliberate and noteworthy. Smith put Lindbergh's service in the context of the military attaché's intelligence collection efforts regarding the German Air Force and the German aviation industry. He intended to clear Lindbergh of charges that he was pro-German, if not pro-Nazi, in the years between the German invasion of Poland and the Japanese attack on Pearl Harbor.

Smith's intent is emphasized at the very end of his foreword to the long report: "I wish to leave an accurate account for history of the services of Colonel Lindbergh to American intelligence in connection with the birth and development of the Luftwaffe. It is my sincere hope that Lindbergh's future biographers will read this record and evaluate its facts before they attempt to describe or comment on his activities in Germany and America between 1936 and 1941."[2]

The full implication of these words emerges from the details of Smith's intelligence methods described in this chapter. Smith's use of Lindbergh to observe, analyze, and report the war potential of German aviation had unexpected personal and professional consequences for Smith, who found himself a target in the heated debate between isolationists and interventionists in the United States from 1939 to 1941. The national issue at that time was war or peace; the personal issue was, and continued to be, integrity. Subsequent chapters examine the political role played by Lindbergh when he returned to the United States in April 1939.

As Smith warmed to his description of air intelligence activities, he began with his assessment of the strengths and weaknesses of his office after one year as military attaché in the American Embassy in Berlin. In a nutshell, he was confident in the accuracy and comprehensiveness of his reporting on German army expansion. He had been observing the army for eighteen years with an intensity that varied only in degree. He had excellent, well-placed sources and assistants, both full-time assistants and the American army officers, like Albert Wedemeyer and others, who attended a two-year course as exchange students at the Kriegsakademie and were available to him during academic breaks. They were quality officers who knew

Germany and spoke the language, and Smith knew their worth, writing, "I had more than my share of top-notch ground force assistants in the Berlin office from 1935 to 1939 to help me cover the German army expansion." However, while he usually had three or four assistants covering the army, he never had more than one aviation officer. The "gathering of air intelligence concerning the very rapid expansion of Goering's Luftwaffe" was a tantalizing prospect.[3]

Smith had visual evidence that something very important was going on right under his nose. He saw the new blue-gray air force uniforms in Berlin and as he traveled elsewhere in Germany. Barracks were springing up near airfields. Factories were being modernized or built near those airfields, presumably to construct aircraft. But he lacked the means to observe and report about the air force the kinds of things he knew about the army: order of battle, organization, training, and logistics; and, perhaps most important, he lacked the expertise to analyze the technical characteristics of aircraft, both current and those in development. Smith noted that in an open society it is possible to get much useful information from newspapers and appropriation bills passed by a legislature, but in Hitler's dictatorship such open-source information was simply not available. Smith and his assistants agreed that both the German army and the Luftwaffe construction programs were gigantic. They had chapter and verse on the army, but they had only general impressions and rough approximations regarding the air force. His assistant for air intelligence, Captain Theodore Koenig, got high marks from Smith as a military officer and as a man, but he lacked intelligence experience, reporting skills, and "knowledge of aeronautical science and engineering."[4]

In Washington, Smith noted, "G-2 treated [air intelligence] as a foster child, and the special intelligence group in the office of the chief of Air Corps was small, poorly organized, and given little or no recognition for its work." Unsurprisingly, given this situation, "most of the officers of the [air] corps suitable for this type of service preferred to serve in almost any other position."[5]

Scholars and soldiers will agree with a rueful smile that it is more fun to do loops and spins, punching holes in the sky, than it is to shuffle papers at a desk of the General Staff. Military intelligence specialists routinely lament that they are ignored in peace and castigated in war by those who had ignored them in peace. Invariably, in an action-oriented organization, operations are more fun and more professionally rewarding than intelligence. The institutional attitude of a flying organization can be summed up easily: there are pilots, and there are passengers.

General Henry H. (Hap) Arnold's belated appreciation of the Luftwaffe illustrates the point. In his memoir he complained of the inadequacy of prewar intelligence; but there is no indication that he, either as assistant chief of the Air Corps (January 1936) or as chief (September 1938), made any effort to send his best officers to intelligence jobs. In fact, he wrote that a conversation with Lindbergh in May 1939 was a revelation to him. He called Lindbergh's remarks "the most accurate picture of the Luftwaffe . . . that I had so far received," thus revealing that he was ignorant of Smith's reporting on German aviation, which was largely based on Lindbergh's observations and analysis, and was in the hands of G-2, the War Department General Staff, and available for the asking.[6]

Smith saw two deficiencies that could be fixed. One, in his own office, was simply a matter of organizing the products of the collection effort. He had his assistant for aviation establish a systematic approach that included a card index file of factories, airfields, units, and technical data for each type of aircraft.

Another deficiency was externally imposed by what he regarded as a faulty air intelligence reporting system. A surprisingly small number of air reports, far fewer than reports on the German army, were being sent to Washington. His assistant for air was directed by Washington to produce a voluminous annual report that took up most of his time and energy. It was prepared on a form provided by the Air Corps and, wrote Smith, called for "a mass of statistical data on every conceivable aviation matter. It was unintelligible to anyone who had not received technical aviation education." Smith believed that this annual report was imposed because of the lack of trained analysts in Washington to consolidate and analyze numerous individual reports. He concluded that the annual report "took no account of the extremely rapid development of the Luftwaffe, in which expansion could be noted almost every week." The very fact that this core report was delivered just once a year indicated to him the inadequacy of the system.

Compounding this bit of bureaucratic bumbling, personal letters that the assistant attaché for air received from his friends in the office of the chief of Air Corps made light of Goering's new Luftwaffe and German technical aviation developments. This information, passed on to Smith, suggested to him that his office was failing in its efforts to convince Washington that German air expansion was formidable and "likely to change the balance of European power."[7]

Smith's education and experience enabled him to fully appreciate that a large and modern air force was becoming a powerful diplomatic weapon, which the opportunistic Hitler was prepared to use. Truman's energy and sense of purpose drove him to do something about it.

In the winter of 1935–1936, Smith raised with Colonel Charles Burnett, the chief of the Attaché Section of G-2, the question of obtaining a replacement for the assistant for air. It pained him to do so, but the situation in Germany required it. The new man, he told Burnett, had to have knowledge of both aircraft and engines. Such a qualified person was not immediately available, but Burnett told Smith he'd have someone by early 1937. Major Albert Vanaman was that man.

The generally friendly attitude of the Luftwaffe, Goering included, regarding America and Americans could be exploited. Smith identified this friendliness as "the one strong card in his hand." It also helped that the only air force officer Smith knew very well from previous association was Colonel Friedrich Karl Hanesse, who, in 1935 was chief of the Attaché Section of the German Air Ministry, the very section with which Smith had to deal on a routine basis. Smith would play that card deftly.

In April 1936 Berlin was abuzz with preparations for the summer Olympic games to be held there. It was obvious to Smith that the games would be a propaganda opportunity for the Nazis, who were eager to show the world the revitalization of Germany under Hitler's leadership.

As Smith recalled, about the middle of May 1936, while he and Kay were at breakfast in their Berlin apartment, Kay called Truman's attention to an item on the front page of the *Paris Herald,* which reported that Colonel Charles Lindbergh had visited French aircraft factories. Although that news produced no immediate action on Smith's part, it must have stuck in his mind, because he found himself a few days later wondering if he might somehow get Lindbergh to Germany to visit aircraft factories there.[8]

Kay's recollection of the Lindbergh connection is consistent with Truman's, though she adds some relevant personal considerations that he omits. She wrote, "By now Truman felt that he was on top of the expansion of the army. He had a large order of battle chart, units identified, weapons, training methods, lists of officers, their characters showing what types of decisions they were apt to make, etc. The work was well organized and well under control. Therefore he now turned his attention to air developments and was appalled to find his air assistant had done nothing of this kind."[9]

She, too, praised Koenig's personal attributes, describing him as "the nicest man possible, an excellent flier, and [someone] who spoke good German." But, she added, "he could not identify engine types nor could he pump his [German] friends to find out things he should. He felt 'this was not a very nice thing to do.' Surely not. But essential to his job at this time."

Smith made some estimates of German aviation to which Colonel E. R. Warner McCabe, assistant chief of staff, G-2, responded by saying that the Germans were pulling the wool over his eyes. "They could not have such a production as he had estimated," Kay recalled. She added that her husband "felt this was a reprimand. This was depressing. He felt that no matter what he said Washington would not believe him for they knew he was not an Air Corps man."

Kay attempted to console Smith, but he insisted that this was far more than a personal matter. The United States was vastly underestimating German aviation expansion. "So much distressed was he to feel that Washington was not giving weight to his reports," wrote Kay, "that in November [1935] Truman got leave to return home, paying his own way."

Paying his own way was less indicative of the seriousness he attached to the issue than the fact that Smith had been on station less than four months when he insisted on a face-to-face meeting with his boss in Washington. Upon his return to Berlin, he told Kay that the trip had been worthwhile. "From that time forward Colonel McCabe, and after him General [Sherman] Miles trusted him completely. They were alerted to the situation in Germany."[10]

Charles Lindbergh's was just a celebrity name to Smith, though he knew that Lindbergh was much more than a daring young man in a flying machine. He was qualified in the technical aspects of aviation and current in aviation developments around the world, including the selection of routes for the young commercial aviation industry. Lindbergh was also an army reserve officer, and Smith suspected he would therefore probably be willing to assist the American military attaché in Germany if invited to do so. It was Smith's impression that the German Air Ministry would be happy to score points with Hitler by presenting the world-famous aviator as the special guest of the Luftwaffe at the Olympic games. Smith was acting on a hunch, and it paid off.

On his next routine visit to Colonel Hanesse, chief of the Attaché Section, Smith broached the subject of a Lindbergh visit to the German Air Ministry in a casual and informal manner. Hanesse liked the idea very much and said he would run it by Minister Goering and Goering's principal air assistant, State Secretary Erhard Milch. Later the same day, Hanesse called Smith to say that the Germans were delighted at the prospect of the visit and were prepared to show combat units and factories to Lindbergh. Smith had hooked his fish!

The swift response indicated the Germans' eagerness at the prospect of a propaganda coup, so Smith arranged for another meeting with Hanesse on the following day. He wanted to be sure that Lindbergh would be shown "air establishments beyond those which were displayed customarily to foreigners." In a discussion that lasted over an hour, Smith got an agreement with Hanesse as to exactly the combat units, factories, and research installations the Air Ministry would show Lindbergh. The agreement was written down in an informal note, and Smith emphasized that the promise "was kept religiously when the visit occurred three months later." Colonel Hanesse also agreed to Smith's request that "either he or Captain Koenig be permitted to accompany Lindbergh wherever the latter was taken." Tentative dates for the visit were set, although at the time Smith did not know Lindbergh's personal plans or even if the famous man would accept the invitation.[11]

Smith next sought the approval of the embassy. Fortunately, Ambassador Dodd, who might have been a stumbling block to the proposed visit, was on leave in the United States. Mr. Ferdinand Mayer, an experienced diplomat who understood precisely what Smith was up to and the difficulties in getting current information on the Luftwaffe, was acting as chargé d'affaires and approved the scheme. (Mayer and Smith, who remained close friends and frequent correspondents until Smith died in 1970, would later recall fondly the dramatic years they spent together in Berlin.)

Smith decided to write directly to Lindbergh and invite him

to Germany. Only after getting Lindbergh to agree to come would Smith inform Washington of his plans. He was confident that his recent trip to Washington had cleared the air and that McCabe would appreciate the utility of Smith's plan to get information and access.

Smith knew only that the Lindberghs had rented a country residence somewhere in England; he did not know just where. But this did not deter him from preparing a letter to Lindbergh on 25 May 1936, conveying Goering's oral invitation to Germany. He sent the letter to the assistant air attaché in London, with a personal note asking him to get the letter to Lindbergh.

Kay called the letter "masterful," and it was.[12] It was masterful in being honest even while shading facts, giving Lindbergh every reason to accept. Smith made it appear that the initiative was from the Germans and left the impression that Goering had dealt directly with Smith in extending the invitation. It appealed to Lindbergh's known interests in research laboratories, test stations, civil and military air schools, factories—and to his patriotism.

The letter was also sensitive to Lindbergh's great aversion to publicity, dating from the time of the kidnapping and murder of his toddler son in New Jersey and the sensationalist and relentless press coverage he so deeply resented. Escaping the American press was what had motivated the Lindbergh family's move to a quiet corner of England. Smith wrote that Germany could provide "more privacy to your person than can a visit anywhere else in the world," thus making a virtue of totalitarian information control.

Smith offered his own house or that of Mayer to Lindbergh and his wife, Anne, or a bachelor apartment in the German aviation club should he prefer to visit without Mrs. Lindbergh. He suggested that the aviator could fly his own plane to a military airfield in Berlin, "where you can preserve your incognito better than on civil airfields. During your stay in Berlin your plane will be kept at the Staaken airdrome of the army in a western suburb of Berlin." Smith also put Captain Koenig "entirely at your disposal during your visit, meeting you at the frontier and assisting you during your stay in every way possible."

He baited the hook with this pronouncement: "It is my distinct impression that the present air program here is by far the biggest the world has ever seen." Dates in late June were proposed for Lindbergh's visit.

Lindbergh had an offer he could not refuse. He accepted gracefully, proposing a change in dates to after 21 July, when a plane he was building in England would be completed. "A rented plane," he remarked, "is never very satisfactory." He expressed his gratitude to Goering for recognizing his wish to avoid "the sensational and stupid publicity" he had so often encountered in the past, and, he added, "I hope that General Goering does not feel it is necessary to provide any special entertainment as far as I am concerned. . . . As a matter of fact, I thoroughly dislike formal functions and have not attended one for several years."

The details of the visit were sorted out to the satisfaction of all concerned. Smith had no difficulty in getting Colonel Hanesse to accept the change in dates to 22 July through 1 August, the opening day of the Olympic games. Smith wrote that he was "dismayed" at Hanesse's insistence that Lindbergh would be expected to attend the opening ceremony as Goering's guest, an event that would be attended by 100,000 people.

So much for privacy!

Smith was concerned that the publicity-averse Lindbergh would bolt, but an exchange of letters between Lindbergh in England and Smith in Berlin resulted in Lindbergh's approval of the dates and events, as well as in the housing arrangements. The famous visitors—prolific and popular writer Anne Morrow Lindbergh was becoming increasingly well known in her own right—would be houseguests of Major and Mrs. Smith. Lindbergh was thus assured privacy, and Smith had control of his prize.

Only after all the details of Lindbergh's visit had been arranged did Smith seek the approval of Colonel Burnett in Washington, to which Burnett replied "without delay" with the hope that air intelligence from Germany would improve. Smith was very pleased that Mayer, the highest-ranking American diplomat in Berlin, was entirely supportive and corresponded with Lindbergh to offer all courtesies.

Smith wrote, "It was in no case to be a social visit." He summarized what he hoped to get out of the famous flier's visit (which eventually became several visits between 1935 and 1938):

—prestige with and access to the Luftwaffe and the German aeronautical world for himself and Captain Koenig;
—for Lindbergh and Koenig to see as many factories and other air establishments as possible;

—for Koenig to be at Lindbergh's elbow as the latter met the elite of Germany's aeronautical scientists, designers, engineers, and air officers;
—Lindbergh's "considered opinion as to the quality of the German air rearmament."[13]

Crudely expressed, the Nazis would get the propaganda they valued; Smith would get aviation intelligence and access to the German key players in aviation. Smith's account shows that he and the United States got everything he wanted during Lindbergh's visit. In addition, the halo effect gave him and Koenig ready access to the top men of German aviation after the visit. There was also the mixed blessing of the professional relationship that blossomed into close friendship among the Smiths and the Lindberghs.

Lindbergh got the royal treatment, literally and figuratively. He met members of the old aristocracy, the Hohenzollerns, as well as the new Nazi aristocracy of Goering, State Secretary of the Air Ministry Erhard Milch, and Chief of the Technical Office of the Air Ministry Ernst Udet. On the first full day of his visit (23 July 1936) he was honored by a luncheon attended by high-ranking American and German dignitaries, including Germany's ambassador in Washington, Hans Bieckdorf, who happened to be in Berlin. Lindbergh was called upon to make a speech (which he had carefully prepared and cleared with Truman Smith, a fact that nourished their budding friendship). His theme was the responsibility of all who were engaged in aviation. He said, "Our libraries, our museums, every institution we value most, are laid bare to bombardment" and cautioned, "We do not destroy the very things which we wish to protect."[14]

Smith noted that the speech was printed in many European and American newspapers, adding, however, that no German paper commented on it editorially, "possibly because it ran counter to Hitler's expansionist and bellicose policies." Similar remarks by Lindbergh would make enemies of those Americans favoring intervention, or at least material support of Britain and France in the European war, particularly in the period 1940–1941.

In the days that followed, the Germans honored their word as Lindbergh, always accompanied by Smith and often by Koenig, saw fighter squadrons soon to receive the new ME 109, whose charac-

Charles Lindbergh and Kay Smith, flanked by German officers, inspecting the Olympic Village outside Berlin in July 1936. (Courtesy of Katharine Smith Coley and family.)

Lindbergh in the cockpit. Hitler and Goering rolled out the red carpet and gave the American celebrity access to research, production, and the latest Luftwaffe aircraft. Lindbergh, while in Germany, flew many of the planes with which Germany fought World War II. (Courtesy of Katharine Smith Coley and family.)

teristics (later confirmed) were briefed to the visitor (to the delight of Koenig, who immediately reported them, among other things, to Washington).[15] That aircraft would become the German fighter workhorse of World War II. Both Koenig and Lindbergh were particularly impressed and surprised by the German progress in aircraft engine design.

Smith would later regret that the significance of Lindbergh's queries about rocket development at a research institute eluded Smith and Koenig. Lindbergh had worked for some years with Professor R. H. Goddard, a pioneer in the field. Rockets, to Smith and Koenig, were probably the stuff of Buck Rogers comic strips. Their focus at the time was on manned military aircraft.

The American group saw and was briefed on all types of aircraft, including the JU 87, the later-famous STUKA (a German acronym for assault support combat aircraft) dive-bomber that provided close air support to German ground forces in Poland in 1939 and in France in 1940. (Smith later noted that the American emphasis on strategic bombers made for a blind spot in his country's appre-

Smith escorts Lindbergh. Smith made a deal with his German hosts: Lindbergh would appear at the Olympics; Lindbergh and Smith's office would get access to German aviation. Done! Smith reported German aviation information to Washington, and the Lindberghs returned to Germany several times before the war. As a bonus, the Lindberghs and the Smiths enjoyed a lifelong friendship. (Courtesy of Katharine Smith Coley and family.)

Lindbergh in Berlin, 23 July 1936. The Lone Eagle always drew a crowd. His penetration of German civil and military aviation exceeded Smith's expectations and resulted in detailed and accurate reporting to Washington on the aircraft with which the Luftwaffe entered World War II. (Courtesy of Katharine Smith Coley and family.)

ciation of the dive-bomber potential for ground combat in Europe. However, building an air force primarily to achieve air superiority on the Continent and to support combat ground forces would work to the Germans' disadvantage in the Battle of Britain, when strategic bombers were required.)

Smith was prepared to admit that he had failed to assess correctly some of the practices and products he saw. For example, none of the Americans could figure out why the Germans manufactured an excessive number of "the quite obsolete JU 52 bomber." They observed that Lufthansa used it extensively for European commercial traffic. The answer came later, when the Germans used a huge military transport fleet as an integral part of the Luftwaffe. The JU 52 was intended to carry parachute battalions and airborne divisions. Smith later wrote that the JU 52 bombers he and the other Americans had observed under construction at Dessau in 1936 "were constructed so as to be readily convertible to military transports. Throughout the whole course of World War II, these JU 52s did excellent work."[16]

This German postcard shows Hitler at Hermann Goering's wedding. Goering once took Smith aside, Smith wrote, and "with moist eyes and a voice tinged with emotion, he turned to [me] and said, 'Smith, there are only three truly great characters in all of history: Buddha, Jesus Christ, and Adolf Hitler.' This remark reduced [me] to speechlessness." (Courtesy of Katharine Smith Coley and family.)

Smith recalled that despite his efforts to restrict Lindbergh's social obligations to an absolute minimum, "the strictly intelligence visits and inspections consumed less time than the purely social activities." But there was an intelligence payoff to Smith for Lindbergh's discomfort at such events, as Smith was able to deepen his relationships and understanding of some of the key players in German aviation. The personalities of leaders are of interest to intelligence analysts because they are useful to political leaders, who want to know as much as possible about what makes their opposite numbers tick. Smith's thumbnail sketches capture many of the personality traits of those men.

Goering was the second figure in the Third Reich hierarchy. Hitler called him "my Paladin." That is more than a reference to a brave knight. To educated Germans it is a link to Charlemagne, a revered figure. Goering was air minister, minister-president of Prussia, presiding officer of the Reichstag, commissioner of the four-year plan, minister of forests, director of the state theaters of Prussia, and, most important, heir apparent. Smith, who recalled that he had "only four opportunities to talk at length with Goering," called him "formidable . . . dangerous and a killer." But "he made a definite effort to behave like a gentleman" and, in Smith's opinion, "frequently was successful in his aim."

On one occasion in 1937, Smith was summoned to Goering's coffee table after a large formal dinner. Goering was in a talkative mood and wished to discuss Hitler. "With moist eyes and a voice tinged with emotion," Smith wrote, "he turned to [me] and said, 'Smith, there are only three truly great characters in all history: Buddha, Jesus Christ, and Adolf Hitler.' This remark reduced [me] to speechlessness."

Smith had the impression that Goering "would have been in his element as a sixteenth-century renaissance prince . . . every aspect of his character and personality would have seemed quite normal if Goering had been the despot of an Italian city-state in that age—his will to power, his love of luxury, his desire to be a patron of the arts, his geniality, his readiness to kill anyone who crossed his path." The world "would do well not to write him down as a clown, a boaster, or adventurer."[17]

In sharp contrast to Goering, Erhard Milch, State Secretary of the Air Ministry, general of the Luftwaffe, and Goering's right-hand assistant, was staid and dependable in the tradition of the German civil servant whose allegiance was to the state. Smith found him intelligent, penetrating, firm, and affable. Before Hitler came to power in 1933, Milch had managed Lufthansa. He knew America well, admired its aviation achievements, liked Americans, and was quite open with them.

The third important leader of the Luftwaffe was Ernst Udet, one of the foremost German fighter pilots of World War I, along with Baron Richthofen.[18] Udet came out of a background of motorcycle racing before the war and "barnstorming" after the war, when he appeared as a stunt flier in America. He was also a good cartoonist, who enjoyed drawing sketches of fellow guests at dinner parties. Smith called him a "good mixer" and a great flier, but he had reservations regarding Udet's qualifications as chief of the Technical Office for the Air Ministry, a position that gave him considerable power to decide the types of aircraft Germany would produce. Smith says that he and other attachés believed that Udet had been elevated to a position beyond his abilities, probably due to his close relationship with Goering. His personal charm and naturalness struck foreigners as being unmilitary and un-Prussian.

On his first full day in Germany in 1936, Lindbergh was guest of honor at what Smith characterized as a "state" luncheon attended by Hermann Goering, Erhard Milch, and Ernst Udet, among others. Smith said that the luncheon "was an important milestone in the air intelligence progress of [his] office. From this day on, an even closer liaison developed between the American officers and the Air Ministry. The credit for bringing it about was Lindbergh's." It was he who gave the Americans the privileged position they enjoyed in the Berlin attaché corps.

It was good to have easy access; it was vital to get the facts right and report them. Lindbergh and Smith would rehash the day's activities over a drink in Smith's spacious apartment, often with their two wives chiming in with questions and observations. Lindbergh and Smith also met with Captain Koenig in Smith's office "almost every morning." The air intelligence gained the day before was reviewed during these sessions, with a shorthand stenographer taking notes. Doubtful or contradictory observations were discussed, thus providing Koenig with Lindbergh's observations as well as his own. Smith recalled that the most interesting features of these morning meetings were the comparisons Lindbergh frequently drew between his personal knowledge of British, French, and American planes and what he had seen the previous day in Germany. Smith tellingly points out that usually "an attaché is in a position to see only what transpires in the country to which he is accredited, while that which is happening elsewhere remains obscure." Lindbergh showed extraordinary patience in explaining the significance of technical details to Smith with great clarity so that a layman could understand, "no matter how much ignorance the military attaché displayed," Smith said of himself, thus giving him "a panorama of German, British, American, and other European aviation developments."[19]

Koenig's reports to Washington "became more colorful and convincing" due to the confidence he had in their correctness. It became apparent to Smith in the fall of 1936 that Air Corps headquarters in Washington was attentive to the reports and "at least aware of the imposing rearmament program. The skepticism previously shown in letters received by Captain Koenig from friends in the Air Corps suddenly vanished." The new receptiveness to Koenig's reporting from 1936 makes Arnold's seeming surprise at Lindbergh's personal report to him in 1939 as he returned from Europe something of a mystery.

An avalanche of questions from Washington followed Lindbergh's first visit to Germany, Smith wrote, and "a veritable pilgrimage to Germany of prominent personalities of the American aviation world" followed in the spring of 1937. A partial list includes aviation pioneers Glenn Martin, Laurence Bell, Igor Sikorsky, as well as several academics, G-2 officers, army and navy aviation test pilots, and assorted experts.

Smith was very satisfied with the dramatic improvement in air intelligence. On 1 August 1936, just before Lindbergh departed Germany, Smith asked him to return in about a year. In September 1937, Colonel Hanesse told Smith that Goering "would be most gratified" if Smith could induce Lindbergh to be present as a guest of the German government for the Lilienthal aeronautical society congress to be held in Munich 12–16 October 1937. In due course, Lindbergh accepted and attended.

The German invitation played nicely into Smith's hands. On 25 August 1937, Major Albert Vanaman of the Air Corps replaced Koenig as Smith's assistant for air. That meant that early in Vanaman's Berlin assignment he would accompany Lindbergh on an extended tour of factories and air establishments planned to take place after the Munich conference.

While in Berlin, the Lindberghs were guests once again in the Smiths' apartment, but the first five days of their second visit to Germany, from 11 to 25 October 1937, were spent in and around Munich. For the remainder of his visit Lindbergh continued to have almost unlimited access to civil and military aviation activities, usually with Major Vanaman in tow. Udet seemed pleased to show Lindbergh around personally. In addition to a test station and other facilities, Lindbergh visited the Foche-Wulf factory in Bremen (where he saw a helicopter), the Henschel factory, and the Daimler-Benz and BMW engine factories. He was shown seven different types of aircraft and was permitted to examine the cockpits. Smith highlighted Lindbergh's inspection of the DO 17, the ME 109, and the JU 87 and the fact that Lindbergh flew a short takeoff-and-landing aircraft. "Udet was apparently anxious to obtain Lindbergh's estimate of the new artillery-infantry liaison and observation plane known as the 'Storch,'" Smith wrote.[20] The ME 109 made a deep impression on Lindbergh. He estimated that the next forward step in the Luftwaffe program would be the appearance of twin-engine fighters. He was right. The twin-engine ME 110 existed in prototype, but he did not see it in 1937.

Before Lindbergh left Berlin in late October 1937, Smith—for the first and only time—had Lindbergh participate in the preparation of a formal intelligence report for MID, a general estimate of the progress of German aviation. With Lindbergh's cooperation, the four-page report was prepared in three days and was known as the General Air Estimate of 1 November 1937.[21] Smith signed and sent the report, which was deliberately "couched in dramatic rather than technical terms." It was his intention to get the attention of "the chief of staff of the army, the secretaries of war and state, and perhaps even of the president himself." With Lindbergh at his side, he said he felt confident to "assay the task."

He succeeded in getting the attention of army chief of staff General Malin Craig, who questioned him at length in Washington during Smith's visit while on leave late in 1937. Smith later wrote that the bulk of the thoughts expressed in the report were merely the attaché's interpretation of Lindbergh's views. The whole panorama of German air development was covered in the document, which addressed aeronautical science, the capacity of industry to produce aircraft and aircraft engines, the performance of combat aircraft, and the training level of personnel. It also compared the combat value of the Luftwaffe to the RAF and the French air arm. Tables and statistics were provided to support the analysis.

Smith got what he wanted from Lindbergh's visits to Germany: detailed information on the Luftwaffe and German aviation in general. In brief, his report said: Germany is now a power in the air; that country has outdistanced France in almost all fields; it will soon surpass Britain; and it will catch up to the United States in 1941 or 1942.

The Germans also got what they wanted: respect for—even fear of—German military capabilities. Hitler's renunciation of the Treaty of Versailles in the "Saturday Surprises" of March 1935, in which he announced expansion of the German army and creation of an air force was coupled with dramatic expansion of the military and increasingly aggressive words and deeds. Hitler was deliberate in letting the world know that Germany once again had a strong military, which he was prepared to use. And Smith's report did not end on a technical or military note. It concluded that the development of German air power is "of the first diplomatic importance."[22]

Smith's political antenna had been fine-tuned over the years, most recently by Hitler's unilateral militarization of the Rhineland by decisive action and French dithering. Hitler saw the utility of air power as leverage in the diplomatic jousting that would be conducted in the next two years. Britain and France would blink; Hitler would not. He would use military power first as a diplomatic tool and later to make war.

14

The Lindbergh-Smith Friendship

> Among the most interesting of the American friends we made in these Berlin years were Charles and Anne Lindbergh.
> —Truman Smith

Truman Smith was enormously grateful to Charles Lindbergh for the air intelligence gained by the aviator's visits to Germany in 1936 and 1937. Later Lindbergh visits in 1938 and 1939 were icing on the cake, but Smith singled out his 1 November 1937 report on Nazi air power as his crowning achievement. Lindbergh's visit had validated and fleshed out what were Smith's unsubstantiated 1935–1936 impressions of German aviation development. It opened the door to Luftwaffe leadership for Major Albert Vanaman's further reporting and gave Smith and his Berlin office credibility in Washington with the G-2 and with his own army's air corps. Smith believed that his report on German aviation was right on the mark. He further believed that Lindbergh never got the credit he deserved for the intelligence coup and was, in fact, very badly treated by FDR and the American interventionists in the early stages of World War II.

Smith was too self-critical after the war in noting his personal failure to highlight an important fact: that the German prewar Luftwaffe was not a long-range air force built around heavy bombers, that it was designed primarily as a supporting arm for ground warfare in Europe. Intelligence specialists, however, would almost certainly credit Smith with a masterful job of information gathering. It was the analysts in MID and in the Army Air Corps who should have been more thorough in evaluating the strategic implications of the capabilities and limitations of the air force the Germans designed. Smith's job was to collect intelligence, which he did magnificently.

The professional relationship of Smith and Lindbergh blossomed into a close and lasting friendship that included their wives, Katharine Smith and Anne Morrow Lindbergh. The details of the relationship provide insight into what life was like for American officials in Hitler's Germany, an oblique look at German leadership, and some human dimensions of the individuals, all from eyewitnesses.

That friendship was deepened in Lindbergh's visits to Germany in 1938 and 1939 as the Germans continued to give the famous American flier the royal treatment and a wealth of aviation information that was passed on to Washington via the office of the military attaché. Lindbergh flew his personal aircraft from Berlin to Paris on 18 January 1939, ending a two and one-half year connection to Smith's office in Berlin. He would not return to Germany until the very end of World War II, and from late 1938 onward Lindbergh's once-glowing reputation became tarnished. Smith's close association with him would later cause Smith to suffer extensive and unfair criticism as he was drawn unwillingly into the public battle between interventionists and isolationists that dominated American politics.

While sharing many of Lindbergh's geopolitical views, Smith would have preferred to remain both invisible and mute regarding politics, as was expected of an American military officer. The problem that later arose was that the personal connection between Smith and Lindbergh was made public, while Lindbergh's major contribution to American intelligence was not public knowledge at the time. Smith's friendship with Lindbergh, his general agreement with him, and Smith's sense of honor made it impossible for him to denounce Lindbergh. At the same time, his officers' code of discretion would not allow him to speak out in defense of Lindbergh and against his commander in chief. As a consequence, some of the slings and arrows meant for Lindbergh hit Smith.

The patter of Noël Coward, the songs of Cole Porter, and the acting of Cary Grant and Katharine Hepburn suggest the tone of the meetings and commentary of Truman, Kay, Charles, and Anne. True to character, the players describe the relationship in their idiosyncratic voices; but mutual respect, affection, and trust are at the root of the friendship. Truman is objective, analytical, and professional. Kay is colorful, feeling, witty. Anne is the professional writer putting scenes into the larger context of the play. Charles is brief, direct, pragmatic—and dogmatic.

Truman pointed out that his and Lindbergh's professional relationship is detailed in the "Air Intelligence" report, but his feelings toward Lindbergh were not. "These should properly be mentioned in this memoir," he wrote. "I saw Lindbergh on seven occasions between 1935 and 1939, each time for several days or, on a few occasions for a week or so. The Lindberghs stayed in our apartment during four of their five visits to Berlin. We also visited them in 1937 at their rented English home, Long Barn, near Knole in Kent and in 1939 in their Paris apartment." He called Lindbergh "a genius, an explorer and adventurer worthy to stand along side Columbus." The precision of his thinking and wealth of knowledge "constantly astounded" Smith. Lindbergh believed that America ought to build up its military power, especially air power. "I came to share these views of Lindbergh," wrote Smith.[1]

But, said Smith, the aviator was "a lone wolf." One had to allow him to go his own way. "He was in no sense a team man." Smith doubts Lindbergh's suitability to be an effective secretary of air or a satisfactory president of an airline. "Yet, he seemed to me to be capable of seeing further and truer into the future than any man I had ever known." Lindbergh repeatedly told Smith that if in the war, which he felt was "certain to come," Germany were destroyed as a military power, the Soviet Union, which he feared even more than Nazi Germany, would fill the vacuum created by Germany's destruction and become the dominating power in Europe and indeed in the whole Eastern Hemisphere.[2]

Superpower confrontation for the half-century following the beginning of the shooting war in 1939 make Lindbergh's views prophetic and Smith's concurrence understandable. Ten years after defeat and disarmament, the Federal Republic of Germany would rearm and become a member of the North Atlantic Treaty Organization (NATO), whose purpose it was to be precisely the bulwark between the Soviet Union and Western Europe envisioned for Germany by Lindbergh in the 1930s. The division of Germany and membership of the German Democratic Republic in the Warsaw Pact underlined the centrality of Germany in Europe. But in the shorter term, Lindbergh's and Smith's views regarding European security would diminish the aviator's popularity and harm the soldier's reputation.

Lindbergh's geopolitical views, his frequent visits to Germany, and his familiarity with the Luftwaffe and its leaders would result in charges that he was far too cozy with the Nazis. In fact, he would be called a Nazi in the press and in the letters by irate citizens sent to the president of the United States in the months before the United States entered the war. But that was later, after the friendship of the Smiths and the Lindberghs was firmly established. The beginning of the turn in public opinion against Lindbergh can be measured from two events in late 1938, which will be discussed in detail in the next chapter.

"Both Kay and I liked Anne immensely," Smith wrote in his memoirs. The Smith's Cornelius Ufer apartment was large enough to allow the Lindberghs a separate suite of rooms "at the far end of the apartment" where they each recorded their day-to-day experiences in detail, much of which was later published. Anne's book *North to the Orient* had just been published, and this was to be the first of thirteen books she published in her lifetime, five of them her published diaries and letters. Her books *The Flower and the Nettle*, covering 1936–1939, and *War Within and Without*, covering 1939–1944, are the two works of hers most relevant to our story.

When not engaged in official business, the foursome toured Berlin museums, "which fascinated both of them," Smith recalled, and took brisk walks along the canal that ran in front of the apartment and in the nearby Tiergarten. The Lindberghs were civilized and sensitive, Smith says. He and Kay "loved to be in their company, but we recognized also that the Lindberghs needed much privacy and that one must never seek their company but rather let them always take the social initiative."[3]

Kay's recollections of the events leading to Lindbergh's first visit to Germany are recorded in her unpublished memoir, "My Life." They are consistent with Truman's observations but more detailed, often adding a personal dimension and some embellishment to her husband's concise and precise reporting of facts.

Shortly after Truman's return from his late 1935 trip to Washington, Kay saw in the *Paris Herald* that the Lindberghs had left their home in England for a visit to France. She mentioned that to Truman, and he responded quite spontaneously, "There's the man who could help me if he would!"[4]

Smith sent a letter of invitation to Lindbergh via Colonel Raymond E. Lee, the military attaché in the American Embassy in London (who would later be G-2 and Smith's boss in Washington.) Lee wrote back that he had forwarded it, but he doubted Lindbergh would come, as he was living very much in seclusion. The Smiths were in Sweden (he was accredited to Sweden, the Netherlands, Belgium, Denmark, as well as to Germany) when, to Truman's great satisfaction, Lindbergh accepted.

Kay was a keen observer, but now and again she declaims on issues without evidence. For example, her thoughts on Sweden may have been prompted by her views of socialism: "Perhaps what ails Sweden is that so much of her good blood emigrated to the United States. There are more Swedes in America than in Sweden. During World War II Sweden owed her immunity from Germany to the fact that Goering's first wife, Karen whom he adored, was Swedish." As much as the folks of the upper Midwest might approve, Swedes might object to the first part of her pronouncement regarding "good blood." And German policy may have been determined by issues aside from Goering's admiration for his first wife.[5]

Knowing that Lindbergh "was afraid of newspaper publicity and being bothered by reporters," Kay and Truman were pleased that the Lindberghs chose to stay with them during their first visit to Germany. Daughter Katchen stayed with friends to provide space and privacy for the guests. "Jennie, Emma and Robert [the household staff] were terribly excited that the Lindberghs were to stay with us. It was a great feather in their caps."[6]

Kay recalled "feeling a little apprehensive as Lindbergh was reputed to be so difficult." However, "after the first hour we found we could get on very well together. He was interested in everything and so was she. As we sat there in the warm evening light we found we would have no difficulties with each other and my apprehension vanished." After the official activities, there was time for sightseeing. Kay was pleased to see Charles's interest in art. "This was the man whom I had been led to believe was interested only in nuts and bolts!" Truman was charmed by Anne, "as everyone is."[7]

The first reviews of Anne's book *North to the Orient* were forwarded from England while the Lindberghs were in Berlin. One day Truman, Kay, and Anne returned from a walk to find Charles with reviews spread all over a bed. "He looked up his face shining. 'They are fine. Splendid.' He was as happy as if it had been his own book," Kay recalled.[8]

Because Truman had agreed that American reporters would come to his office every day at a specified time to get the plan for the day's activities, everyone was satisfied with the amicable arrangements. Lindbergh even asked to meet the American reporters one evening. There was no problem with the German press. They tried to follow Lindbergh one day, but Truman called Hanesse and it never happened again.

Goering hosted a formal lunch. "A large black open Mercedes car came to take us to the Air Marshall's residence," Kay wrote—"motorcycle outriders and all." The air heroes of Germany were there, the meal was sumptuous, Kay and Anne flanked Goering at the table. Goering tried to speak Swedish to Lindbergh, who said, "I am an American." Goering asked who was his copilot and navigator on the trip described in *North to the Orient*. He was much surprised when Kay told him that Anne was. Kay translates his response: "I find that [causes me] to laugh to death."[9]

When Kay complimented Goering for the new Air Club at which she had recently been a guest, Goering was delighted. He explained that when his officers had requested 80,000 marks to furnish a villa they had selected, he told them to leave it all to him. Among his positions was president of the Prussian State Parliament. He said, "It occurred to me there are two places in the world where the most nonsense is talked, in parliament and in clubs. So I turned the [Parliament] building into the Air Club. I despise from the bottom of my heart the parliamentary system. As for [the price of] decorations, I simply added a zero on the end." Kay adds, "He smiled with satisfaction. He knew it made a good story."[10]

Either Lindbergh had asked to see the Goerings' pet lion, which lived in the house with them, or Goering wished to show it to him. Accordingly, Kay wrote, a young lion "about three feet high, his body about four feet long without counting the tail" bounded in. Kay reports that Goering called, "Come here, Augie." The lion sprang onto his lap, put his paws on his shoulders, and licked his face. "Suddenly an aide laughed. The startled lion let loose a flood of yellow urine all over the snow white uniform! A wave of red flowed up Goering's neck. He tossed the lion from him with a wave of his arm and sprang to his feet. The lion bounced off the opposite wall." Frau Goering had to calm him down by saying the lion was like a little baby and there were too many people. This mollified Goering. "Yes, it is like a little baby," he said. "Then," recalled Kay, "we all laughed pleasantly."[11]

Kay added that during this incident, Lindbergh turned to a far corner of the room and proceeded to ask an aide about a picture on the wall. "Very adroit," she said, realizing that Lindbergh was attempting to spare Goering any embarrassment. She notes that Frau Goering "was most pleasant and natural with considerable charm. He was a formidable personality but with a likeable quality in spite of his obesity, temper and domineering nature. I could see he had leadership, that intangible quality so necessary and so infrequent."[12]

On a visit to a school for glider pilots, the ladies were included. Kay noticed that the young officer who was delegated to take Anne and Kay about was straining to hear what Charles, walking in another group consisting of men, was saying rather than being attentive to the ladies. Kay, knowing that Anne had a glider pilot's license (as well as being a fully qualified aircraft pilot), asked Anne if she had a glider license. That seemed improbable to the young man, but the ladies then held his attention for the rest of the tour. Kay was aware that Anne, who made no fuss about it, was sensitive to the German inclination to (politely) shunt the ladies aside from their man's world.

During his first visit to Germany Kay said that Lindbergh made only "one error, and it was a stupid one." The crown prince at Potsdam invited him to tea. Truman tried to dissuade Lindbergh from going, pointing out that the prince still had hopes of some form of restoration and that he was persona non grata with the present government, which was, after all, Lindbergh's host. Smith further said, "The Prince had no great reputation for brains." Charles insisted, however, so they went. Also in attendance, recalled Kay, was Louis Lochner of the Associated Press, "a great pal of the Prince."[13]

Lochner reported from Berlin from 1921 to 1941. Well connected, with a German wife, Lochner was bilingual, and later was editor and translator of *The Goebbels Diaries,* among other accomplishments. He may have been the best-informed American in Germany, and his book *What about Germany?* is a source of many fascinating yarns and penetrating insights. For example, he noted that Hitler's creation of the German autobahns not only provided employment for Germany but also "were designed from a military-strategic point of view, to make possible the blitz offensives" of 1939, 1940, and 1941.

His remarks about Hitler, whom he interviewed several times over the years, are similarly incisive. "The fact is," wrote Lochner, "that Hitler needs the adulation of the masses as a fish needs water. He grows stale unless he hears the cheering crowds, unless he can harangue them, unless he can take their frenzied salute." He noticed that when one interviews Hitler "he looks up at the ceiling. He has a vision of the masses. He is no longer speaking to an interviewer, he is addressing multitudes." Lochner, who also covered Mussolini, noticed a difference between the two dictators in their relation to the press: "Genius at propaganda and publicity as he is, Hitler seems to dislike the press as much as Mussolini likes it."[14]

Lochner was a friend of Hjalmar Schacht, president of the Reichsbank, and once remarked about the new face in the president's outer office. "Oh, don't you know him?" Schacht said nonchalantly. "That's a Gestapo officer who must watch me." That a sophisticated man such as Schacht would accept a spy in his front office defines the totalitarian state.

Lochner followed German forces into Poland, Denmark, Holland, Belgium, France, Yugoslavia, Greece, and Russia—missing only Norway (which was covered by an AP colleague). After the German declaration of war on the United States in December 1941, he was interned along with other Americans in Bad Nauheim for five months. They were repatriated in exchange for Germans in June 1942. Smith and Lochner knew one another; they both shared and competed for information.

Kay warned Charles that he was "in for it" when she spotted Lochner at the lunch with the crown prince and distracted Lochner by talking "right into his ear both loudly and constantly so that in spite of his straining every nerve to listen to Charles he couldn't hear very much." However, at the end of the tea the prince asked Charles if he would mind having a snapshot taken for the prince's memory book. Charles assented. But instead of an informal snapshot, Kay wrote, "a man with a camera on a tripod, a professional type of camera, popped out of the bushes, put a black cloth over his head and focused on the Prince and Charles as they stood together."

Smith called Lochner as soon as they got home, attempting to prevent publication of the picture, but Lochner expressed regrets that it was already on the way to London and he could do nothing about it. The picture was immediately published in London and in the United States. "It had all been a put up job in an effort to make the Prince popular with the people who thought him more or less as an ass," Kay asserted. Lindbergh was embarrassed by his own foolishness. Fortunately, when he explained to the Air Attaché Of-

From left: Anne Morrow Lindbergh, the Hohenzollern crown prince, and Charles A. Lindbergh in Potsdam in 1936. Smith warned that the crown prince was persona non grata with the government and "had no great reputation for brains." Photos of the "casual" meeting were taken and published in the United States, but the Lone Eagle's reputation was not damaged—at that time. He was later called a Nazi. (Courtesy of Katharine Smith Coley and family.)

fice what had happened, they just laughed, saying that the prince had always been a fool and dishonest.

Kay said that Lindbergh was so pleased with what he had learned in Germany about aviation and how the visit was handled that "he came back to visit us again a number of times in the next two years." He urged the War Department and aircraft manufacturers to go to Germany to see for themselves the quantity and quality of aircraft production. As a consequence, according to Kay, "the following year one after another they all came to Berlin [Bell, Martin, Sikorsky, etc.]. We had our hands full taking each one around, but Truman was happy to do this. General Arnold of the Air Corps was awake to the danger."[15]

Not quite. More accurately, General Arnold *should have been* awake to the danger. In his book, *Global Mission,* Arnold wrote, "I never did see Lindbergh's memorandum myself, though I believe the State Department sent it to G-2 of the General Staff." He refers here to a "carefully written report" Lindbergh prepared regarding German aviation, which he gave to Colonel Martin Scanlon, Air Attaché, and Colonel Raymond Lee, Military Attaché, in London. "Ambassador Kennedy was so impressed by its wealth of detailed information and its general critique that he forwarded it to the State Department," Arnold wrote. But Arnold himself never saw the report! Arnold contends that "one day in May, 1939," he met with Lindbergh and got the most accurate picture of the Luftwaffe he had so far received.[16]

That "accurate picture" was available for the asking years earlier in G-2, War Department General Staff, the location of the many reports from Smith that had been vetted—indeed dictated—by Lindbergh, including the very thorough and comprehensive Air Estimate of 1 November 1937. Smith's low opinion of MID might be more broadly applied to other General Staff sections.

Kay, writing years later, confesses, "My first impressions of Charles and Anne are now a little blurred. It is difficult to separate the first from later knowledge, since for so many years we became intimately associated in a close friendship." That admission is important. The storyteller, whether historian, biographer, or memoirist, is routinely confronted by the need to deviate from chronology to address important themes that have a past and a future, and loose ends that defy strict adherence to chronology. Impressions cascade almost simultaneously, but sentences are written one at a time in sequence. Kay is taking us with her as she attempts to sort out initial impressions from later knowledge of the Lindberghs.

"I do remember that I found out very quickly Charles was not a person with whom one made light conversation, remarks simply to fill silences as one does in society," she writes. When asked a question he would think it over carefully before responding, and when he asked a question he was direct in trying to obtain information. For all his disdain of social conventions, however, "he was very aware that blue, blue grey, suited him best." His clothes fitted him well. He kept a comb in his upper breast pocket and combed his hair before entering a house to call. His black shoes were suitable for long walks. He took no coffee, tea, or liquor because they were habit forming. He kept himself in shape to be able to walk out of any place in case of a plane crash. He carried a filled rubber water bottle and a few chocolate bars for the same reason. He was, according to Kay, fond of cheese and sweets, but otherwise indifferent to food. He had excellent manners and a firm handshake, but "he did not like close bodily contact."[17] All of this adds up to a rather unusual personality, which Kay generously ascribes to fame.

Somehow the public learned that Lindbergh could be sent mail at Smith's address. Charles asked Kay to translate the letters to him that were written in German and French. She was amazed that many asked for money, and "one was so scurrilous my color changed as I read it." He insisted upon hearing all of them. When she asked him why, he told her, "In case we should have any trouble in the future I keep these in sacks and send them to St. Louis. I get them all the time." She writes that it gave her "a sudden pang to realize that he and Anne had to live all the time with this horrible experience and had to be prepared for a repetition. It was not until several years later that the kidnapping was mentioned between us."[18]

Charles and Anne's first child, a son, had been kidnapped and murdered several years before they met the Smiths. It was to escape the constant press coverage in America that the Lindberghs eventually took up residence in England and France and would seriously (though briefly) consider living in Germany. Even while living abroad they made frequent long flights, just the two of them, in aircraft he owned.

Lindbergh's fame—for his solo transatlantic flight, for the kidnap and murder of his and Anne's child, and for the flights he and Anne made to determine routes for the nascent passenger-airline industry—is certainly a partial explanation of his personality. But some of his quirky behavior is just plain odd. During a car trip in England, with Charles driving and the Smiths in the back, Truman opened a newspaper. Charles reached over and put a cigarette lighter to the paper, causing it to erupt in flame. As Truman put out the fire, Charles laughed. Anne later told Kay that Charles had done that before.

Another time, sightseeing in Paris, while descending the Eiffel Tower Truman noticed that a small son of the Lindberghs was fatigued, so he picked up the little boy. Charles abruptly told Truman to put the boy down, saying he had to learn to be tough and walk down on his own. Kay noted on another occasion at a meal that the boy was expected to cut his meat at an age when little boys should not use a sharp knife. Kay noted similar incidents in passing. For all of his merits, there was something of the geek about Charles Lindbergh, but she accepted him as he was, warts and all.

Idiosyncratic attitudes and conduct, to which Lindbergh may have been entitled in his private life, sometimes spilled over to national policy without his recognition of the difference between public and private expression.

After a visit to Russia, having been shown his usual first-class treatment, Lindbergh was accused of making indiscreet remarks about the quality of Russian aviation at a social event upon his return to Britain. The alleged remarks were reported in the press. The U.S. military attaché in Moscow, who had arranged the Lindbergh visit as a way to get information about Russian aviation, got wind of the remarks and cabled Raymond E. Lee, the U.S. military attaché in London, Lee later wrote, "begging me to have Lindbergh retract this statement." The Moscow attaché believed that as a result of Lindbergh's indiscretion, his "sources are likely to be shot." Lee told his counterpart in Moscow that Lindbergh had already left for Berlin. The Russian attaché then asked Smith to get Lindbergh to modify his statement "in such a way that the [Russian] officers who had been his sponsors would not lose their lives." But Lindbergh "never did say anything to modify his criticism."[19] He was ever suspicious and contemptuous of journalists, and so failed to make a distinction between his personal antipathy and the dangers to his Russian hosts in the midst of Stalin's purges of civil and military leadership at the time in Moscow.

Kay gives us a word picture of Anne Morrow Lindbergh, who made an unambiguously positive impression. "Lovely brown eyes, dark brown slightly wavy hair, pointed chin, retroussé nose . . . small and slight she was actually sturdy and strong though giving the impression of one rather fragile. She was shy or gave that impression but as tough-minded as she was sturdy of frame. She was retiring, very silent, especially when he [Lindbergh] was present." She was also a good listener. Kay remarks, "This art of listening is one few cultivate. The charm of the attentive, interested listener surpasses the charm of beauty or wit." And when Anne spoke she "put her finger on the significant point, bringing it forward to more significance."

Kay recalls once inadvertently hearing parts of a discussion in which the Lindberghs were engaged behind closed doors. Charles seemed to be trying to persuade Anne to do something. Her voice rose loudly above his: "No, I won't promise anything. No." Kay says she "scurried silently away not wishing them to think anyone could have overheard them. But she was holding her own."[20]

Kay's point is that Anne and Charles, like the Smiths, were in a marriage of equals. The husbands were the headliners, but neither Kay nor Anne was the submissive little woman. Anne Morrow came from a prominent family. Her father was a partner at J. P. Morgan, maintained residences in Englewood, New Jersey, and New York City, and was appointed ambassador to Mexico during Anne's last year at Smith College (1927–1928). Her mother would later serve as acting president of a college. After Anne's 27 May 1929 marriage to Charles she mastered the skills required to act as copilot and navigator as just the two of them made many flights to almost every part of the world. Both she and Charles were shy people, and in public she deferred to the air hero. But Kay makes it clear that Anne was self-reliant and tough, and could hold her own with Charles.

In Anne's book *The Flower and the Nettle,* we learn that that respect was reciprocal. During the Lindberghs' second trip to Germany in the fall of 1937, while driving on a day trip to Berchtesgaden, Kay and Charles were discussing courage, how much is physical and how much mental, how much inherited and how much trained. Of Kay Anne commented, "I feel in her tremendous courage, beyond her strength. It is the strongest thing I feel and what I admire the most in her."

The next day, said Anne of the Smiths in her diary, "They are both remarkable with people, observant, sympathetic, able to make people at ease. She more unconsciously, spontaneously; he more consciously. I feel too that he is not so much interested in people's conversation as he is in people themselves, skipping the steps of conversation and jumping ahead with sheer perception. She follows the paths of observation and conversation, but both come to the same end."[21]

Later, in a 29 October 1938 entry in her diary, Anne wrote, "I feel really fond of Kay. She has been such a brick on this trip [to Germany]. She manages her life with great courage and sense and real devotion and selflessness in regard to her husband."[22]

The professional relationship that became close friendship would have unanticipated consequences when the Lindberghs and the Smiths returned to the United States. But 1938 and 1939 found both couples still in the midst of dramatic events in Europe.

15

Hitler Is Ready

> Anne gave it but a fleeting glance and then—without the slightest trace of emotion—remarked, "the Albatross."
>
> —Kay Smith, on Anne Lindbergh's reaction to her husband's receiving the Service Cross of the German Eagle, 1938

Truman Smith's promotion to lieutenant colonel in 1938 was good news, as were two more visits to Berlin by Charles and Anne Lindbergh, during which they were once more guests of the Smiths. The visits were a source of personal pleasure for both couples. Anne wrote on 1 April 1938 that living in England for two and a half years had given the Lindberghs the peace and quiet they wanted, but she added with obvious regret, "I had not made a single friend." She had found a friend in Kay Smith in Berlin.[1]

The purpose of the Lindberghs' visits to Berlin was to gain even more access to German leadership and more information about the Luftwaffe. Hitler's never-ceasing expansion of his control of all instruments of power in Germany and his bold initiatives in Austria and Czechoslovakia were important events that demanded Truman's constant, careful attention and drained his energy. Nothing held still, as a torrent of dramatic events in Middle Europe shared headlines with Italian neocolonialism in Africa, Japanese aggression in China, civil war in Spain, and Stalin's show trials in Moscow, all during the worldwide economic depression that persisted through the 1930s.

The timing and publicity of an otherwise minor matter, Goering's handing Lindbergh a German medal, became bad news with damaging consequences for both Lindbergh and Smith. The results of Smith's physical examination, required for his promotion in December 1938, brought more bad news. It revealed diabetes, a revelation with decidedly unhappy consequences.

Truman didn't know much about the disease when he was diagnosed with it, but he did know about half a dozen high-ranking

German generals who were diabetic but were still holding important positions in the German army and air force. He presumed that he would simply be treated and allowed to continue on active duty. But Kay, in retrospect, called the diagnosis "a stunning blow . . . a crushing blow" that made her ill with anxiety.[2]

Smith, who hadn't been feeling well for some months, observed, "I doubt whether I had ever worked so hard in my life as I did in 1938."[3] The cocktail circuit and his smoking habit no doubt aggravated his poor physical condition.

Anticipating his scheduled relief from Berlin in the summer of 1939, he wrote to General George C. Marshall for help in getting an assignment to troop duty at a western post where he could have more physical exercise and outdoor activity. Smith did not know at the time that by army regulations, diabetes required medical retirement from the army.[4]

Of course the reason for his strenuous exertions in Berlin was the near-impossible task of keeping up with Hitler, who was all about action and movement. He was unrelenting in consolidating power at home and in taking bold measures in Middle Europe, measures that repeatedly took Europe to the brink of war.

To ensure his control of the army, Hitler removed War Minister Werner von Blomberg and commander of the army Werner von Fritsch and replaced them with more pliable men. There is an interesting sidebar to Hitler's changes at the top of the German military hierarchy at the beginning of 1938, told by Kay in her memoir. She and her husband, who was on an official visit to The Hague in 1938, took the opportunity to meet with Rabe and Hildegard von Pappenheim in Brussels. (Rabe had been assigned from the attaché office in Berlin to be military attaché in Brussels.) The couples spent a pleasant evening together.

When the Smiths came down for breakfast the next morning, Kay wrote, "Hildegard, at the head of the table, had red eyes and tears were on her cheeks. Rabe was very agitated." Asked what had happened, Hildegard said, "General Blomberg was recently married and now the Party charges him with marrying a whore! A licensed whore! What makes it worse, Hitler was his best man and now feels he has been insulted. Blomberg is to be dismissed. The entire Army is disgraced through this." Kay added, "It turned out there had been those who did not like Blomberg who was a fine man and a gentleman."

Blomberg, Truman's sponsor and host in Germany in 1931 and later a guest in the Smiths' apartment in Berlin, had been set up. Kay remarks that the army "remained Christian, had reinstated obligatory church service attendance by the regiment as a whole. The Party hoped through this disgrace of the Chief of Defense [*sic*; Kay means Minister of War] to break the spirit of independence in the Army. And it succeeded. Their pride was humbled." Hildegard's advice, as she wiped away her tears, was: "In my opinion he must commit suicide. There is no other honorable way for him."

Kay, not as shocked as later generations of Americans might be by this "honorable way," simply remarked that Blomberg did not take that advice and was "shunned by everyone." She adds, gratuitously, "His son, a flyer and a fine young man was killed in World War II."[5]

She had this to say about the relief of Fritsch: "It was now that the Party ganged up on General von Fritsch, accusing him of homosexuality. Although he was acquitted completely, nevertheless his usefulness was at an end and he retired. Hitler took over the post of Supreme Commander himself and also head of Defense, appointing General Keitel to carry out his orders. The Army's spirit had been broken, its independence and opposition to his plans a thing of the past. To act against the Supreme Commander and Commanding General of the Army was treason."[6]

At the foreign office, Joachim von Ribbentrop replaced Constantin von Neurath. The army and foreign office were even more subordinated to the Nazi Party, and the new men favored the bold policies that resulted in the invasion and annexation of Austria in March 1938. Historian Gordon Craig wrote of the Foreign Office, "its prestige and influence sank to their nadir" in the period from mid-1936 to 1938.[7]

Kay confided a personal note to her memoir, another comment that humanizes great events. She said that since the dismemberment of empire things had gone so badly that "had I been Austrian I would have been sympathetic to the idea of the Anschluss."[8] Her remark captures the feelings of others about truncated Austria.

The Nazis, with increasing intensity, had choreographed internal and external agitation regarding the German minority in Czechoslovakia. Then the Czech security situation was completely changed by the German annexation of Austria: Czechoslovakia was flanked on three sides by the new German Reich.

The shorthand for what followed is "Munich" or "appeasement," words used and abused since 1938, indicating a proclivity to use buzz words and sound bites that save thinking through complicated issues. The last phase of the dismal story began with a 12 September speech by Hitler in which he laid claim to the Sudetenland and its German population in accordance with the right of self-determination, a guiding principle in the redrawing of borders after the Great War. That territory was fortified, and it was the most favorable defensive terrain the Czechs owned that faced west, that is, toward Germany. Hitler, however, described it as a dagger pointed at the heart of the Reich.

Munich was actually the last of three conferences dealing with the German minority in Czechoslovakia. Adolf Hitler, Benito Mussolini, Neville Chamberlain, and Edouard Daladier attended the 29 September Munich conferences; Czechoslovakia was not represented. The result was concession by the French and British to the Germans at the expense of Czechoslovakia, a result that was warmly received when the Western diplomats returned home to cheering crowds that chose to believe that Hitler had gotten what he wanted, would be satisfied, and would therefore adopt a less bellicose posture. That perception caused Chamberlain to famously announce that "Munich" meant "peace in our time."

Winston Churchill saw it otherwise. He addressed Chamberlain with this pithy declaration: "You were given the choice between war and dishonour. You chose dishonour and you will have war." However, British service chiefs probably would have noted at that time that "Munich" was necessary to give Britain eleven months in which to prepare for the coming war with Germany.[9]

Hitler certainly gave every indication that Germany was prepared and willing to fight. The French and British were neither prepared nor willing—and their governments knew it. The details of what followed in Middle Europe are as fascinating and complex as they are important, but they are beyond the scope of our story. Suffice it to say that the net outcome of Hitler's use of diplomacy and force in Austria and Czechoslovakia was that Germany emerged as the strongest power on the Continent.

Lindbergh's third visit to Berlin, from 11 to 29 October 1938, followed closely on the heels of the German diplomatic victory in Munich. Like his first two visits, it was a triumphant tour during which the Nazis treated him with great deference. Smith writes that from an intelligence standpoint, the timing could not have been more propitious. "After their diplomatic victory at Munich, the Germans were more anxious than ever to display their new air might to the American aviator."[10]

Smith's need for Lindbergh's help in 1938 was not as pressing as it had been in 1936 and 1937. As noted, the earlier visits provided the Military Attaché Office with the first accurate appreciation of the progress being made by the Luftwaffe, gave Major Albert Vanaman access to sources that continued after the famous aviator's visits, and won the confidence of the people in G-2 who were reading the Berlin reports. Nevertheless, the new round of inspections of air factories, research establishments, and Luftwaffe experimental and operational aircraft made Vanaman's reporting of current developments very useful as well, since intelligence requires continual updating. Accompanying Lindbergh also enabled Smith and Vanaman to refresh their own contacts with the top men in the German aviation industry and in government.[11]

Lindbergh climbed into the cockpits of the latest German civil and military aircraft, took notes, and debriefed Smith, who wrote that Udet and Goering gave Lindbergh permission "to pilot Germany's premier fighter, the ME 109. This must be termed a unique coup in American military intelligence." (Smith consistently calls the Bf-109 the ME 109.) He puts the value of this visit in perspective: "These seven airplanes inspected or observed during October 1938 represented the complete first-line equipment of the Luftwaffe, which in 1939 and 1940 destroyed Poland, occupied Norway, Denmark, Holland, and Belgium, drove the British expeditionary force from the continent, and annihilated the French army and air force. Not until the autumn of 1941 did airplanes not observed by Lindbergh and Vanaman during this 1938 series of inspections take their place in the combat units of the Luftwaffe. Indeed many of 1938 vintage continued in front-line service until the spring of 1945."[12]

However, an unexpected pro forma award of a medal would take on vastly disproportionate importance, affecting both the Lindberghs and the Smiths, and serves as a reminder that acts need to be understood in context. We are also reminded that the road to hell is paved with good intentions.

Kay was delighted when Hugh Wilson replaced William Dodd as the American ambassador in Berlin in January 1938. According to her, the Dodds departed "to the joy of everyone on the Embassy

Staff." She liked the sophisticated Wilson and his wife, Kate, even more than she disliked the Dodds, whom she had written off as hopeless provincials. "Kate [Wilson], thin, red haired, vivacious, tense and witty was universally popular. What a relief to have them here! How fortunate to have Hugh as the new Chief!" The Wilsons and Smiths were friends in Berlin "way back in 1920" and "became quite close" when Wilson was counselor to Ellis Dresel, who headed the American mission in Berlin before the official end of the war and the designation of the American representative as ambassador. Wilson was a skilled and experienced diplomat whose professional expertise was crowned with personal charm.

Kay writes that at Truman's suggestion, "Hugh called regular meetings of all heads of departments so that knowledge could be pooled and everyone obtain valuable assistance in this manner." In addition to establishing what would later be called "the country team," Wilson, unlike Dodd, showed real interest in military developments in Germany. He accompanied Smith on some trips and demonstrated trust and confidence in his military attaché, unlike Dodd, who was inclined to see soldiers as mindless furniture cluttering up the embassy. A personal relationship between the Wilsons and the Smiths obviously made Truman comfortable with the ambassador, who knew German history and current affairs very well. Wilson's experience in the early days of the Weimar Republic, when the government was under assault from Left and Right and barely hanging on by its fingernails, contrasted sharply with the centrally controlled German government and the very visible Nazi uniforms and symbols of 1938 he now witnessed. It should be emphasized that he was a professional diplomat.[13]

The German Air Ministry invited Lindbergh to attend a session of the Lilienthal Society, to be held in Potsdam and Berlin between 11 and 14 October 1938. By happy coincidence Ambassador Wilson had earlier expressed to Smith the desirability of a Lindbergh visit to Germany. Wilson was anxious to establish a personal relationship with Goering, something he had been unable to do, Smith recalled, "because of Foreign Minister Ribbentrop's jealousy of his own prerogatives, especially that of himself handling all diplomatic matters with foreign embassies."[14]

Wilson's stated purpose was to get Goering's support for measures desired by the U.S. State Department to ease the financial plight of many Jews being forced to leave Germany "in a penniless condition." Wilson, for reasons unclear, believed that Goering was the only leader in the Nazi government who might be won over to such a humanitarian gesture. With Goering's support, Wilson felt that Hitler might be convinced. Smith was pleased to be a party to the humanitarian effort and at the prospect of increased access to Luftwaffe and aviation leadership by nourishing the personal relationships among Goering, Lindbergh, and Wilson.[15]

Accordingly, a dinner given by Ambassador Wilson for Minister General Goering took place in the American Embassy. In attendance were the Italian and Belgian ambassadors; Prof. Dr. Paul Heinkel, Erhard Milch, and Ernst Udet from the Air Ministry, as well as several other German officers; Igor Sikorsky, American aircraft designer and manufacturer; a sprinkling of American diplomats; and the naval and military attachés.

Goering and his adjutants arrived late. After exchanging greetings with his host and shaking hands with the other guests, Goering, accompanied by the ambassador, made a beeline to Lindbergh and at once began a speech in German. He took a red box from an aide-de-camp and handed it to Lindbergh, who, not understanding German, "appeared nonplussed," recalled Smith. Some American German-speakers stepped forward to interpret. To the surprise of all, Goering had presented the Verdienstkreuz Deutscher Adler (Service Cross of the German Eagle), a high decoration for civilians, to Lindbergh for his services to aviation and particularly for his historic solo flight across the Atlantic.[16]

The presentation of the award was unremarkable considering that Lindbergh had received many awards, honors, and medals from kings, princes, and officials of foreign governments. Moreover, both Smith and Wilson, the latter in a 4 August 1941 letter to Lindbergh, said that no American present "had any previous hint that the presentation would be made." There was no graceful way for Lindbergh to reject the decoration without personally affronting Wilson, his host for the evening, and Goering, his host in Germany.

Smith adds, "At the moment, the award of the medal seemed quite natural. It should be remembered that October 1938 was a month of much diminished international tension. Europe, after the Munich accord, was relaxing. The prospect of war had receded into the background. The notorious anti-Semitic riots of 9 November 1938, which were to shock the world, lay still some weeks away."[17]

Smith says that the award was more or less taken in stride as a pro forma event by the men at the dinner. Not so the Lindbergh and Smith wives! When Truman and Charles went home that night to the Smith apartment, Charles, without comment, drew the medal box from his pocket and handed it to his wife. Anne, Kay recalled, "gave it but a fleeting glance and then—without the slightest trace of emotion—remarked, 'the Albatross.'" Kay shared that view and later that evening pronounced to Truman, "This medal will surely do Lindbergh harm."[18]

The Nazi persecution of the Jews came to a head on a night just weeks after the dinner at which Lindbergh was awarded the German medal. It is ironic that Lindbergh, unknowingly a party to an attempt by the American ambassador to benefit German Jews, would have his public image severely damaged by the conflation of press accounts of what occurred at the dinner and what happened to Jews on what became known as *Kristallnacht,* the Night of Broken Glass.

On the night of 9–10 November 1938 the Berlin synagogue was reduced to a burned-out shell, and synagogues all around Germany were damaged or destroyed. Over 7,000 Jewish businesses were destroyed. Jews were killed, beaten, and intimidated. Goebbels called it a "spontaneous" response to the killing of a German diplomat in Paris by a seventeen-year-old Jew (who ostensibly was avenging the deportation of his father from Germany to Poland in a boxcar). The pogrom was in fact directed and coordinated from Berlin. Hitler's architect, Albert Speer, said, "Something was beginning that would end with the annihilation of one whole group of our nation."[19]

Smith says the award to Lindbergh was covered by the press in October, days after the event, as a routine matter, with little criticism of Lindbergh. But after the events of 9 November, described by Smith as a "far-flung government-organized series of anti-Semitic riots and fierce Nazi repressive measures," there was a strong anti-Nazi reaction around the world, "perhaps most intense in the United States. A number of American newspapers at once launched simultaneous violent attacks on Colonel Lindbergh for having accepted a medal from Goering." Both Smith and Ambassador Wilson were disturbed, feeling that they had inadvertently set Lindbergh up by using him as bait to bring Goering to Ambassador Wilson to ease the plight of the Jews. But they agreed that no explanation of the circumstances surrounding the decoration should be made. As Smith put it, "The ambassador and the military attaché had had ulterior purposes of their own in bringing Lindbergh to Germany, motives which could not be aired in the press under any circumstances."[20]

Lindbergh had returned to Paris from Berlin on 29 October. Learning of the pogrom in early November, when he was seriously considering living in Germany, he telephoned the Smiths to say that he would not take a house in Berlin. Kay recalled that he was "vehement." She added that the Germans had earlier promised that Speer would build him a house if he couldn't find one that pleased him.[21]

Typically, Lindbergh made no public response to the press uproar. He later said that if it weren't the award, his enemies "would have found something else. I always regarded the fuss about it as a sort of teapot tempest. If my memory is correct, both the French ambassador and Henry Ford got one at about the same time."[22]

Smith disagreed; it was not a tempest in a teapot. Lindbergh was obtuse in not connecting the timing of the award and the reaction to the pogrom. On 14 November 1938, Ambassador Wilson was recalled to Washington "for consultation" and never returned to his post. On 18 November, the German ambassador in Washington, Hans Dieckhoff, who reported "a hurricane is raging here" in reaction to the pogrom, was recalled to Berlin and likewise never returned to his post.[23] Kay says that Kate Wilson, the ambassador's wife, was asked to stay on in Berlin—and did—to avoid the appearance of a complete break.[24] But it was obvious that the United States took the pogrom very seriously.

Smith believed that by not speaking out, Lindbergh afforded his enemies "a most convenient tool with which to attack him" between November 1938 and December 1941 "in scores of articles. Most of these were of an untruthful and scurrilous nature, quite misrepresenting the situation at Ambassador Wilson's dinner."[25]

Before and after this incident, Lindbergh reacted to press attacks with indifference stemming from a conviction that he was right, saying that rebuttal would merely fuel the fire. For example, not long before his third visit to Berlin, the brouhaha described earlier arose regarding remarks Lindbergh allegedly had made in England upon his return from a visit to Russia denigrating Russian aircraft and air capability. The wires burned with traffic between the American attachés in Moscow, London, and Smith while Lindbergh was in Berlin, but Lindbergh chose not to make a public statement. Anne Lindbergh "did mind Charles being misquoted . . . and I worry about

[Philip] Faymonville [the American Military Attaché in Moscow]. It will kill him and his work up there."[26] But Anne knew that when her husband dug in his heels, it was futile to argue with him. In private Lindbergh told Smith and intimates that the charges were muddled and false, about what he expected from the press. His attitude regarding the press would hurt him again when he became actively engaged in the debate about American intervention in the war in Europe. And it got still worse for him after the shooting war in Europe began on 1 September 1939.

The Smiths had promised their daughter, Kätchen, a trip to Paris before they returned to the United States. From 29 December 1938 to 4 January 1939, the Smiths were the guests of the Lindberghs. They toured Paris and vicinity with them and had a fine time, even while noting Lindbergh's quirkiness in private. Kay remarked to Charles that it struck her as amusingly incongruous that Charles, "the rugged one," slept in a charming but quite feminine bed. Lindbergh was not amused by this remark. She also was surprised to see that Charles insisted that his son Jon manage all sorts of things without adult assistance. Nevertheless, Kay admired Charles for his grand visions despite his views regarding child rearing.

During this visit to the Lindberghs, Truman and Kay found time to lunch with some French members of the diplomatic corps assigned in Paris. Kay was "sick at the ignorance of these people who after all were in a position to know more of the facts than the man in the street." The conversation was about how Hitler's "bluff" should be called. Kay was aware of Germany's formidable forces, Hitler's readiness to use them, and the unpreparedness of Britain and France for war. It was precisely this kind of willful ignorance about Germany that accounted for Smith's great efforts to get the facts right and report them, even at the cost of his health.[27]

Shortly after the visit to Paris, Lindbergh was again in Berlin, this time on a mission from the French government to make a deal with the Germans to buy engines for French planes. Charles did not want to involve Truman in this scheme (which did not pan out), so he stayed at the Esplanade Hotel—not with the Smiths—while representing the French position to the Germans.[28] Kay's memoir entries in January 1939 describe this improbable plan, which is confirmed in Lindbergh's journals. The seemingly naive notion—it was little more than that, but it had the blessing of senior officials in both countries—was that trade would somehow decrease the likelihood of war between Germany and France, even so late in the game.[29]

It is noteworthy that Lindbergh, a private citizen, was asked to carry out this task, underscoring the fact that he had contacts with an impressive list of powerful people around the world, including the inner circles and ruling classes in Britain, France, and Germany. He also had the ears of the American ambassadors accredited to the countries named, as well as military aviators, scientists, aircraft manufacturers, and leaders in all aspects of civil and military aviation.

In the vernacular of more recent times, the Smiths were also well-wired insiders. Kay's vanity about her linguistic skills and sophistication often surfaces in her writings, even if she sometimes confuses Slovaks and Slovenes and is not alone in her bafflement in declining German nouns, articles, and pronouns. And she is something of a name-dropper. Nevertheless, the Smiths knew many famous and powerful people and were close to the center of important events unfolding in London, Paris, Berlin, and Washington in the late 1930s. Reference to just a few of these individuals is striking, even without counting the many German and American officers, diplomats, and journalists Smith knew so well for so long.

Kay says that while in Berlin, she heard her husband and Albert Wedemeyer discussing how the United States would attack Germany in the coming war. "Straight across the Channel at its narrowest point," said Wedemeyer. They analyzed problems, estimated casualties, and debated solutions. She says it was the first she heard of Roundup or Overlord, "but [I] did not breathe a word to a soul."[30] She writes as if the operational plan were signed, sealed, named, and delivered in her Berlin living room instead of what it was: two professional soldiers engaged in some what-if speculation. It may be an example of Kay's readiness to enhance her husband's reputation, a gilding of the lily well after the fact.

The Smiths met Herbert Hoover in Germany, and they became friends, often dining with him later at the Waldorf Astoria when the Smiths resided in Connecticut after the war. Smith served on the post–World War II Hoover Commission, whose purpose was to reorganize government. The Sikorskys, too, were counted as good friends from Berlin days and into Smith's retirement. Bernard Baruch wrote glowingly of Truman's reporting when he learned of it during the war. Clare Boothe Luce was a close friend; she held the congressional seat that made the Smiths her constituents. (Smith would run for that seat in 1946.) Anne Lindbergh was becoming increasingly well known as her books were published, and her friendship with the Smiths deepened. Truman's Yale classmates, Dean Acheson and Archibald MacLeish, were heard of later. The Smiths personified the WASP/Wall Street/Ivy/northeastern establishment.

Kay reveled in wit, repartee, human folly, and pure gossip. A little levity was needed to maintain balance. She spun yarns that are fun to read and are probably more or less true. She enjoyed retelling some stories, like the one about the dinner at which she was seated next to a short, chubby, rosy-cheeked French consul general. "During the meal I felt an exploring hand on my thigh. Turning to him I said blandly in French, 'I am an American. . . . Try your neighbor on the other side. Perhaps you will have more luck.' He turned quite red. I went on calmly eating my dinner."[31]

Nor did she spare her Nazi hosts. On 2 June 1938, Frau Goering gave birth to a girl. The baby was named Edda, after Mussolini's daughter. It was alleged that Goering was impotent due to a war wound. Jokers said his daughter's name, EDDA, was an acronym for *Ewige Dank dem Adjutant* (Eternal thanks to [Goering's] adjutant).

Kay reports that after Germany's annexation of Austria without war, fantastic legends about Hitler made the rounds: Did you know that out of the graves of the führer's parents a giant tree sprang up overnight? Once in a hundred years such a man as Hitler is born. And a clear day was called "Hitler weather."[32]

The personal asides of serious and sensitive Anne Morrow Lindbergh about Germany in her book *The Flower and the Nettle* also provide a humanizing view of the time and place. In her introduction she says, "Eric Maria Remarque's *All Quiet on the Western Front* made an indelible impression on me and convinced me that war was the ultimate evil." Her initial impressions of Germany on 22 July 1936 were of newness, neatness, order, trimness, cleanliness, very different from France. "The Hitler Youth were tanned and strong-looking," she wrote. She is surprised that "there are lovely-looking German women" and equally surprised by their wit, humor, and charm. (That remark echoes a similar comment by Kay in her first exposure to Germany in 1919.) "I keep forgetting about the humor of the Germans. It comes as a surprise every time, next to their earnestness, and thoroughness and seriousness and sentimentality; and yet there it is—a sharp quick sense of the ridiculous." She finds Mrs. Dodd, the ambassador's wife, all suffering, weary, as though it were just a little bit too much for her.

Her 1936 observations and comments about German officers reveal the insight of an artist. "I begin to realize the difference between the old Army and the new—the sharp line between them: on the one side, aristocracy, manners, tradition, sophistication, weariness. On the other, strength, energy, crudeness (sometimes), natural insight, ability—youth." She engages in extended conversations with German General von Falkenhayn, whom she finds to be quick, observant, and intelligent, "with a nice gaiety and lightness of touch that seems quite un-German to me." And Erhard Milch she finds "quick as the crack of a whip; but he has a kind of pure knifelike directness that knocks the wind out of you. Like the first breath of air walking out of doors on a cold bright winter morning. Pure, clean, bright—and freezing."

Constantly attentive and observing, she notes of one of her German dinner companions in October 1938, Otto Merkel of Lufthansa, that he trusts two things to keep us out of war: aviation (fear of it) and radio (hearing the other person's point of view.) The irony is chilling. War was a year away. Aviation would give us Pearl Harbor, Coventry, the Blitz, Dresden, and Hiroshima. Radio was most useful to Hitler and to Roosevelt to communicate the leader's point of view and to mobilize all of a nation's resources for total war.[33]

Without prior consultation, the Smiths departed Germany and the Lindberghs left Paris to return to the United States at the same time, April 1939. Even a cursory assessment of the individual views of Kay, Anne, Charles, and Truman regarding the proper policy position of their country concerning Europe shows commonality on major points, though they came to their conclusions via different routes and use of evidence. A general sense of their political convictions and national security predispositions is useful in understanding what happened to Truman Smith between April 1939 and December 1941.

Kay was convinced that after the failure of the French to prevent the German remilitarization of the Rhineland in 1936, Britain and France had effectively given Hitler a free hand in Middle Europe. If the Western Powers would not assert themselves on contiguous western real estate, how and why would they become more assertive in places far away and harder to get at? She liked the British and regretted what she saw as the frittering away of their former great power and influence. She had friends from several nations, including many Germans. In many ways she was an anachronism, valuing social class, sophistication, manners, and good conversation above all, but also loyalty to family and country. She was highly critical of command economies, though recognizing that the Nazis had accomplished much in a very short time while the United States was still in deep depression. Visible and well-publicized material accomplishments had taken Germany from despair and chaos to hope and a sense of purpose. She predicted—and regretted—that the centralized economies of Bolshevism and Fascism were the wave of the future. She damned President Roosevelt, seeing the New Deal measures to combat the Great Depression as steps toward socialism. The world was changing in ways that would reduce the power and influence of her class. She knew that and didn't like it.

Anne Lindbergh, in her own words, saw war as the ultimate evil. Her flights with Charles to many corners of the world and her interaction with foreign elites in many capitals, where Charles was given red-carpet treatment, inclined her to internationalism. Living in England and France in a kind of exile, essentially hiding from publicity after the kidnap and murder of her son, reinforced her citizen of the world attitude. Had the overt persecution of Jews in November 1938 not occurred, the Lindberghs probably would have moved to Berlin. Had the bombs not fallen on Pearl Harbor in 1941, she probably would have been a declared pacifist.

Charles applied mathematics and logic to all aspects of the human condition. His technical knowledge of aviation, and the access to the Luftwaffe plotted by Smith and permitted by Goering, informed him that Germany had the best air force in Europe and would likely catch up to the United States to have the best military aviation in the world. He told that to the British, the French, and anyone who would listen. He said, "Germany now [1938] has the means of destroying London, Paris, and Prague if she wishes to do so. England and France together have not enough modern warplanes for effective defense or counter-attack. . . . I am convinced that it is wiser to permit Germany's eastward expansion than to throw England and France, unprepared, into a war at this time."[34]

Upon his return home Lindbergh met immediately with Hap Arnold to give the chief of American military aviation an update on the Luftwaffe. A few months later, the Germans invaded Poland. Lindbergh thought that the French and British declarations of war on Germany bordered on madness. He believed they should have stopped Hitler on the Rhine when they could have. Instead they simply watched Hitler's military buildup, particularly the creation of the best air force in Europe. Then they decided to intervene where they could not. The acrimonious debate between interventionists and isolationists was joined by Lindbergh, who advised that the United States stay out of the war in Europe and worry about "America First."

Truman Smith was the quintessential military professional. He found no conflict between true and lifelong friendships with Germans and doing the job he was sent to Berlin to do: to gain access to reliable sources in order to observe and report on the German Army and Luftwaffe. He did that job about as well as it could be done. He was conservative and would run for Congress in Connecticut as a Taft Republican after the war and after he retired from the army. But his party-political views were kept in a private compartment, as was generally the case with serving American officers in the interwar period.

The details and soundness of Smith's geopolitical analyses will be discussed in a later chapter. Future events were obviously unknown—that is, Hitler's choices regarding whom, when, and where he would attack, as well as in what sequence, were yet to be determined. In advance of that knowledge, Smith believed that the German Army and Air Force were the best on the Continent. And if forced to choose between the two obvious dominant powers—Germany and the Soviet Union—he would choose Germany. These views, like his party political preferences, were not advertised, but they roughly coincided with Lindbergh's.

When Lindbergh went public with his views on the proper American course of action regarding the war in Europe, Smith was sucked into the fray. His life would be complicated by charges of being a Nazi sympathizer at the very time that his health affected his future in uniform, and at the very time he was playing an important part as one of Marshall's men organizing the defeat of Germany. His life and career were played out in World War II in two phases separated by the attack on Pearl Harbor.

16

Welcome Home

> Had [diabetes] not intervened, I have little doubt that Smith would have risen to high rank and might have played a role equal in influence to Eisenhower's during World War II.
>
> —General Albert C. Wedemeyer

> My mother was his number-one drill sergeant. He [Smith] loved steak and Old Fashioneds—both no-no's for diabetics.
>
> —Daughter Kätchen Coley

> The collapse of France on 22 June 1940 was the prelude to the most unhappy period of my life. Almost at once, one columnist after another, among them Drew Pearson and Walter Winchell, launched personal attacks on me for being pro-German and anti-American. . . . I was also told at this time that [Justice Felix Frankfurter and Secretary of the Interior Harold Ickes] had suggested to the president that I be court-martialed.
>
> —Truman Smith

Despite the discovery of diabetes in the course of his physical examination, Smith was promoted to lieutenant colonel with a backdated effective date of rank of 1 July 1938. Date of rank in the interwar U.S. Army of slow promotions was important to Regulars. Retention on active duty was one administrative matter of concern to Smith; his place in the hierarchical pecking order was another.

In February 1939, he received orders to return to the United States and to report to the Walter Reed Hospital in Washington in April. Exhausted by his efforts over the previous three and a half years, he decided to take a three-week cruise in the Mediterranean on the Italian steamship *Saturnia.* Smith later wrote that at the time of the cruise he was unaware of "the inflexible rule of the army doctors that officers suffering from diabetes were to be retired." But he did know that he needed a rest.

At the conclusion of the cruise, he and Kay returned to Berlin, paid their official departure calls, and departed from Germany on a United States line steamship. He reported to Walter Reed Hospital on 24 April 1939. After a thorough physical examination found him suffering from "a moderately severe case of diabetes," he was placed on a strict diet and given injections of insulin. It was apparently only then that he realized how life-altering his illness would be. "Now I learned for the first time that my retirement from the army was inevitable."

However, after a fortnight in the hospital Smith was in for another surprise. He was ordered back to duty in G-2. In his words, "This was an astonishing development." Each morning a car took him away at eight and returned him to the hospital in time for supper, a routine ordered by General George C. Marshall. Smith's job title was "Special Consultant on Germany."

By mid-November 1938, Smith believed that the situation in Europe was becoming progressively more serious and that war would come in 1939. It did. On 1 September 1939, Germany invaded Poland, and French and British declarations of war on Germany followed. The United States was not to be a formal belligerent, however, for another two years, during which debate raged in the United States regarding American policy. Simply expressed, the choice seemed to be between intervention in the European war or neutrality.

Meanwhile, a medical board had met at Walter Reed on 29 August and recommended that Smith be ordered to present himself to an army retiring board. That was a formal administrative step leading to separation from the army, now fully expected by the doctors and Smith. Those were the rules of the game. But Marshall again intervened. According to Smith, "[Marshall] called for all the medical papers and having read them, placed them in his personal file, neither approving or disapproving the recommendations. Simultaneously he ordered me to resume full duty in G-2 and told me to hunt for quarters in Washington."[1]

Marshall was not about to send away the American soldier most knowledgable about Hitler's Germany just as the shooting war in Europe was about to begin. "Marshall," wrote Smith, "doubtless felt that no matter whether the doctors approved or disapproved this action, my service at this particular moment of history could not be spared." Smith knew Germany; Marshall knew Smith; it was not a hard decision to make. But it violated policy.

Smith enjoyed special status as a consultant on Germany ever since he had resumed work in G-2 in May, even as Marshall and the doctors considered his possible medical retirement. He was, as he put it, "part of G-2, but yet not of it." This suited him perfectly. He and the chief of the German section of G-2, Colonel Hamilton Maguire, got along splendidly. Maguire managed the normal business of his section while Smith operated as a freelancer, pursuing what he thought to be most useful to the army. The task Smith set went beyond intelligence. He would influence the army to adopt some of the best of German innovations regarding organization and tactics as it expanded from fewer than 200,000 men in 1939 to well over 8 million men in May 1945.

The vast and rapid expansion of the U.S. Army was accompanied by reorganization both at the top and in the formations in the field. Marshall streamlined his General Staff for rapid decision making in Washington, and the divisions that would do the fighting were reduced in size and reconfigured to take advantage of new ideas and means of incorporating motorization, mechanization, and other technological innovations. The challenge in synchronizing the mobilization and training of a mass of citizen soldiers and, at the same time, arming and equipping them was enormous. The army's recent experience with leading, organizing, and housing the young men of the Civilian Conservation Corps proved useful, but mobilization of material was further complicated by policy decisions that would require the construction of staggering numbers of ships, aircraft, weapons, and a long list of general supplies to be procured and transported both to American troops and to newly acquired allies.

Smith's advice was welcomed by other sections of the General Staff as Hitler's Wehrmacht defeated the highly regarded Polish army in a matter of weeks. Soldiers and laymen around the world asked how that was possible. Smith's American colleagues were fully aware that he had observed and reported all aspects of the German military expansion from the Treaty-limited army of 100,000 and the attendant innovations in tactics, organization, and armament whose synchronization was revealed beginning in 1939. Departing from his usual professional modesty, Smith writes, "Indeed, I believe that in these early months of the European war, I contributed more than my fair share to the shape of our new American army."[2]

It would have been surprising had his peers and comrades from the small U.S. Army of the 1920s and 1930s not solicited the views on Germany of the fellow among them generally regarded as the German expert. Smith's activity was not limited to the G-2. In fact, as then-Major Albert Wedemeyer in the War Plans Division prepared "a broad plan for the full mobilization of U.S. resources, human and material, in the event of war," later known as the Victory Program, he said he relied heavily "upon the shrewd and informed assessments of Truman Smith."[3] Historian Charles E. Kirkpatrick emphasizes precisely that point: "Like Marshall, Wedemeyer had absolute faith in Smith's judgment about the Germans, and the War Plans Division merged Smith's intelligence reports into periodic strategic assessments as the basis for further planning."[4]

We shall see that Smith was indeed an outstanding strategic thinker. During his first "retirement"—from which he was recalled by Marshall after the bombs fell on Pearl Harbor—he was a syndicated military columnist who wrote under the pen name Strategicus.

Wedemeyer expressed his gratitude for Smith's contributions to his professional development and his help with the Victory Plan. He also regretted the price Smith paid for his friendship with Charles Lindbergh when Lindbergh went public, challenged the interventionists, and alienated President Franklin Roosevelt and his supporters.[5]

Percy Black, Smith's principal assistant in Berlin who succeeded him as military attaché there in April, was ordered back to the War Department in November 1939. Black was a very valuable asset. He had continued the first-rate reporting from Berlin before he accompanied the German army in its invasion and stunning defeat of Poland. And he provided a detailed account of the performance of that army in combat.

A G-2 Information Digest of military attaché reports from Germany shortly after Black had succeeded Smith has these entries from June 1939: "[Hitler's] almost uncanny faculty of seizing the most opportune moment for daring action [is striking.] . . . Germany is rapidly approaching the point where she will feel strong enough to enforce her will militarily, if unable to achieve results otherwise."

Black and Smith were in complete agreement about Hitler's psychological and military readiness for war.[6]

The real test of an army is performance in war. Black was able to confirm the soundness and validity of Smith's prewar thinking, analyses, and accurate reporting—and his own—as the Wehrmacht passed its test in Poland with very high marks. A "Special Bulletin" on the Polish campaign stated, "The principal lesson which the German Army learned from the war in Poland was that its organization, armament, and tactical doctrine were correct." It continued, emphasizing the "balanced field army with a balanced organization and balanced armament executing a plan under almost perfect leadership."[7] Also, "German tactical doctrine and training stress the responsibility for individual leadership and initiative of subordinate commanders . . . subordinate troop leaders accomplish tactical missions with a minimum of interference from higher commanders. Written orders in the division are rare. It was to this tactical doctrine and training that the extraordinary speed of the attack can largely be attributed."[8]

But the German victory in Poland was neither a cheap one nor—as was widely believed at the time and after—entirely a matter of Panzer formations and tactical air support defeating a second-rate Polish Army. German casualties were 10,000 killed in action, 30,000 wounded, and 3,000 missing in "three weeks of war and eight days of actual fighting, as officially published" by German authorities. It was not a walkover. The Poles fought like hell!

Of the fifty German divisions identified in combat, ten were mechanized, four were motorized, three were mountain, and thirty-three were infantry divisions, foot infantry. (There were also four fully motorized SS regiments). Black's bulletin makes a point to describe the "remarkable marching ability and superb physical condition of the German soldier . . . 72 kilometers in three days and 50 kilometers a day for another three days." The Germans used all of the mechanized and motorized formations available, giving the impression to uninformed observers that the entire German Army was mechanized and motorized. "Mechanized and motorized units were employed on cavalry missions, both by exploiting the breakthrough and by attacks around the flanks of the Polish Armies to gain their rear, disrupt their communications, prevent their taking up delaying positions and so cut off their retreat to their final defensive line." The Germans' stunning success was popularly attributed exclusively to the backfield. Black points out, however, that "like the backfield of a football team, it was the Air Corps and the mechanized troops which received the publicity, but like the line, it was the German infantry which bore the brunt of the attack."[9]

Swift German success in Western Europe in the spring of 1940 further magnified the idea of the Blitzkrieg as a kind of magic enabled by mechanized formations and well-coordinated tactical air support. That is still the most common perception of the campaigns in Poland in 1939 and in France in 1940. But Percy Black and Truman Smith made it clear to colleagues in MID and on the army staff that a *balanced* German force was a better explanation for German success. It consisted mostly of tough infantry, horses pulling guns and wagons for logistical support, and initiative among German leaders at all levels. Mechanized and motorized formations were intelligently employed, but the force was balanced. Foot infantry and superior troop leadership played a key, but less visible, part in victory. Inspiration was visible in doctrine, weapons, force development, and tactics, but the perspiration and determination of junior leaders and the German infantry soldier deserve much credit for the campaign.

The close association and mutual respect of Smith and Black facilitated the rather unusual evolution of their professional relationship, as Black became chief of the German Intelligence Section, nominally Smith's boss. But making Smith "special G-2 consultant and German specialist" finessed possible awkwardness. Smith deftly touches on this point when he writes, "I remember no single serious disagreement between us in those long years. Just as in Berlin previously, I admired Black's generous character, his unselfishness, and his intelligence abilities." They worked together through 1945, with breaks in their association when Black was serving in North Africa and England.[10]

A state of war existed between Germany, on the one side, and Britain and France, on the other, from early September 1939, but the belligerents conducted no major offensive until the spring of 1940. That period of war without close combat was called "the Phony War" and "the Sitzkrieg," despite the fact that there was some bombing and sinking of Allied ships by German submarines. Then, the German thrust into Norway and Denmark in April 1940 was followed by even more dramatic events as the Wehrmacht rolled over the Netherlands, Belgium, and France in May and June. The British retreated and ignominiously evacuated troops minus heavy equipment at Dunkirk, France fell in June, and the Battle of Britain began in August.

When the German offensive in France commenced on 10 May, Black and Smith predicted that "the French army would not be able to withstand Hitler's highly mechanized forces, its Panzers, Stukas, and bombers." Smith wrote, "Our estimate proved correct, though the disintegration of the French army proceeded more quickly than either Black or I thought likely."[11] That ranks high in any list of understatements. The French Army that had defended France for more than four years in the last war folded in weeks.

In the small circle of American General Staff professionals, Smith enjoyed great credibility. But despite his impressive credentials, he was in for a rough patch. Ironically, his very expertise in matters German—particularly his assessment of the German army and the Luftwaffe—was misrepresented and used to characterize him as pro-Nazi. His diabetes was managed by diet and insulin injections; the assault on his integrity was not so easily deflected. Despite his continued adherence to the code of public neutrality in domestic party politics, his friendship with Lindbergh enmeshed him in the acrimonious struggle regarding U.S. policy as the European Powers were fighting the first two years of World War II.

Anne Morrow Lindbergh was correct in asserting that Pearl Harbor erased from national memory the violent extremes of opinion for and against American involvement in the war, despite a considerable specialist literature on the subject. In her book *War Within and Without,* she wrote: "Today [in the late 1970s], hardly anyone gives much thought to what was once called 'the Great Debate' over the question: Should we or should we not enter World War Two? The general conclusion today is that we waged a just war against evil forces and that we won."[12]

But Anne Lindbergh could not forget the active political part played by her husband in the America First Committee in 1940 and 1941, which caused a firestorm. The America First experience was painful to Anne and to Kay and damaged the reputations of both Charles and Truman while contributing to the polarization of American politics.

Charles Lindbergh was a complicated person. He was courageous, charismatic, and perhaps brilliant in some ways, as has been suggested earlier, but he suffered enormous blind spots. Detailed analysis of his personality is best left to competent medical authority and his biographers. However, the historian can report without reservation that he was curious, intelligent, courageous, and hardheaded. Those characteristics were what made him the admired Lone Eagle. He was widely respected as an aviation pioneer, absolutely current in the state of aviation industries around the world, and familiar with the generation of aircraft with which belligerents began World War II. But when he dipped his paddle into political waters, his stubborn self-righteousness cost him his once-universal popularity. Sharply alert to technological nuances, he was tone deaf as a political and social actor.

In April 1939, Lindbergh returned to the United States. He and his family had resided for two and one-half years in France and Britain and had also visited other places, the Soviet Union and Germany among them. It was not at all unusual that General Henry (Hap) Arnold, the senior American aviation officer then and during World War II, contacted Lindbergh immediately upon his return to get his views on European, particularly German, aviation. Anne Lindbergh reports that Arnold sent a radiogram received by Charles "while still on the boat" approaching the United States.[13] After their face-to-face conversation, Arnold pressed Lindbergh "to go on active duty, to make a study of and attempt to increase the efficiency of American [aeronautical] research organizations."[14]

It is puzzling that Arnold made no reference to the thorough Lindbergh-Smith reporting on the Luftwaffe from 1936 onward. It is unlikely that it was an oversight. One must assume that he hadn't read the reports from Berlin. In any event, Lindbergh accepted the invitation to active duty as an army officer.

Anne later wrote, "Since his work required constant traveling over the country on inspection trips, with Washington as his home base, we considered moving to the Capital for the summer, but finally decided to rent a house on Long Island, not far from an airfield, from which he could take off on his trips." That is what Lindbergh did until he gave his first speech against American involvement in the European war on 15 September 1939. He consulted General Arnold about the speech in advance. Arnold did not object to the speech, but he "suggested" that Lindbergh should return to civilian status if he became involved in antiwar activity. It was simply bad form for a serving officer to criticize the policy of his commander in chief.[15]

It is part of being human that impels an expert in one field to share his views on subjects related to, but not strictly in, his or her field. Lindbergh's undeniable technical expertise and knowledge of foreign air forces did not prepare him for the mudslinging that characterized American public debate of policy immediately after the German invasion of Poland.

Determined to keep the United States out of the European war, he used his fame, influence at home and abroad, international experience, and aviation expertise to campaign in the America First effort to maintain American neutrality. Convinced that the time had passed for France and Britain to stop Germany's resurgence, Lindbergh believed it was a mistake for Britain and France to go to war with Germany in 1939, when Germany was once again the most powerful state in Europe. He believed that the train had left the station, and that it would be folly compounded for America to intervene in a Europe once more engaged in fratricide.

In fact, when confronted with a stark either-or choice between German or Soviet domination of Europe, Lindbergh preferred the Germans. Indeed, if that choice had to be made, both Smiths also preferred the Germans. But before it actually came to that, the Smiths and Charles Lindbergh could hope that Hitler, perhaps like Bismarck—who, at the conclusion of the three successful wars of German unification focused on consolidating his gains and acting as an "honest broker"—would moderate his behavior after his initial successes.

Acceptance of German domination in Europe in 1939, 1940, and 1941 was a matter of Realpolitik, not necessarily pro-Nazism. Germany was on the march and seemingly unstoppable; better the Germans than the Bolsheviks. In any event, it was best for America to stay out of yet another of so many European wars.

Sensitive Anne was a very different case. Her stance tended to be more philosophical than political. She wrote in 1980, "I was deeply absorbed by my studies in history, literature, and writing [at Smith College, 1924–1928.] . . . The Nazi era was still in the future, and I had yet to learn that there were worse things than war." Her thirteen books, including *The Flower and the Nettle,* covering her years in England and France, and *War Within and Without,* covering the period 1939–1944, both of which contain her diary entries and letters, reveal the soul of a poet forced to accept the fact that while we walk with our heads in the clouds, our feet must often tread through muck. The poet was also a wife and mother living in an existential time and place.

On Friday, 15 September 1939, the day that the publicity-averse Lindbergh made his first national radio broadcast, Truman visited to buck up his friends. Anne writes that Smith "comes in looking very tall and terribly thin, a ghost of himself in Berlin; but it is very good to see him. I feel warmed by it." Fulton Lewis, a well-known radio commentator and journalist covering "national affairs," is also present and has lunch and dinner with the Lindberghs. Anne is very nervous. "I sit and think and pray people will understand. . . . They can't know how *hard* it is for him to give it [the speech], how *hard* to say how much he loves France and how much I do. Oh, how *can* they understand?" (Italics in original.)

Anne then quotes from her husband's speech in order to capture the essence of his position and that of the America First movement. That speech will provoke a rash of articles and letters on both sides of the debate. Lindbergh called the war in Europe "an age-old struggle between the nations of Europe. . . . Our safety does not lie in fighting European wars. It lies in our own internal strength, in the character of the American people and of American institutions. . . . If Europe is prostrated again by war . . . then the greatest hope for our Western Civilization lies in America. By staying out of war ourselves, we may even bring peace to Europe more quickly. Let us look to our own defenses and to our own character."[16]

In succeeding speeches over the next two years Lindbergh's halo was further tarnished by his own prose. (Even in the quiet of library archives some seventy years after the speeches were delivered, they are provocative.) The response they got in the tense war-or-peace atmosphere of 1939–1941 was volatile. Despite Anne's attempts to soften and modify some of his language, Charles insisted upon what he regarded as the objective honesty of the technician. Insensitive to nuance readily apparent to his wife, he didn't seem to understand this simple fact of life: a man will never embrace the bearer of news that informs the listener that his wife is ugly—even if that is true.

In his Des Moines speech on 11 September 1941, he said: "The three most important groups who have been pressing this country toward war are the British, the Jewish, and the Roosevelt Administration. Behind these groups, but of lesser importance, are a number of capitalists, anglophiles, and intellectuals." One is tempted to chide him for omitting the Salvation Army and the Boy Scouts of America from his list of warmongers. Anne warned him. "Headlines will flame 'Lindbergh attacks Jews.' He will be branded anti-Semitic, Nazi, Fuhrer-seeking, etc. *I can hardly bear it. For he is a moderate.*" (Italics in original.) Of course she was right. After the event, she wrote, "He is universally condemned by all moderates."[17]

The passion he evoked is seen in a few samples from hundreds of handwritten and typed letters, many on hotel stationery, and telegrams sent from all over America to President Roosevelt from 1939 to 1942. Some supported Lindbergh, but most were expressions of anger close to hate, opposing him.[18]

They began with Lindbergh's compliance with General Arnold's request that he assess the state of the American aviation industry. That earned him this unedited reaction in a 19 April 1939 handwritten letter from Fayetteville, Arkansas, here quoted in full:

> His Excellency, The President of the United States:
> Dear Mr. President!
>
> The thinking people of the United States must be, and are, amazed over Lindbergh's appointment as Adviser to the United States Government.
>
> Here's a man with a distinctly German name and most undoubtedly filled with German ideas, and who has most recently accepted a German decoration, called in for consultation with the American Government!! What foolishness!!! Particularly as the fact holds good—that once a German always a German!!
>
> The name of Secretary Woodring is associated with the appointment to Lindbergh. If this is really so—then Mr. Woodring ought to be dismissed from the Cabinet.
>
> This German American (Lindbergh) is the one who is largely responsible for the Munich fiasco through his falling in—with German propaganda in notifying us and the world that German might and strength are incomparable—that Russia was a weakling nation—that Britain and France were no match for Germany and Italy. I know Germany—the Germanies only too well—they

> are using Lindbergh! I conclude by saying—watch Mr. Lindbergh!—for let me reiterate—once a German always a German. And I mean Lindbergh . . .
>
> s/ [unreadable first letter] S. Simpson Atmore

There were as many underlined words as exclamation points. Lindbergh's ancestral roots were to be found in Sweden, not Germany. But underlined words and a profusion of exclamation points have been known to defeat facts—and rational discourse.

The following two telegrams to the president, also quoted in full, are (mercifully) brief.

> 14 October 1939. Americans wish pseudo-American Lindbergh returned to Germany with his decorations. Nathaniel Moss Salley
>
> 4 August 1940. After listening to Lindbergh's speech this afternoon, as a foreign born citizen adopted by America, if he is not in a concentration camp in seventy two hours, I will denounce [probably *renounce* was intended] my citizenship. J P Hayes

And an 11 September 1941 handwritten letter, this one—except for the word "radio"—in the language of Chaucer: "Tonight I feel if I could smash the radio crush him, I would do it. In his speach he never have a wrong word to say about the brutles tirant of Adolph Hitler, his speach stink worse and a dead fich, and I hope when the war is over he will get 12 bullets in his body, like the rest of the Quislings." Sara Orre Pederson of San Francisco, the letter writer, adds, "P.S. This came from my heart, would like to hear from you."

Two letters on *New York Mirror* letterhead pages confirm Smith's reference to Walter Winchell's personal attacks, both signed by Rose Bigman for Walter Winchell. The first, dated 8 July 1940, is to Miss LeHand at the White House. "Mr. Winchell asked me to send the attached to you for the President's attention." The attachment reads in full: "Information relayed to me by eminent war correspondents now in the U.S. is that Major Truman Smith, USA, is Col. Lindbergh's host while Lindbergh visits Washington. That Lindy lives at Smith's home there. When the Lindberghs came to Berlin it was Major Smith, then a military attaché in Berlin, who found a house they liked. These newspaper aces allege Smith is an adviser on the Lindbergh speeches made recently on the air. They are not sure if Smith is still attached to U.S. Military Intelligence. Smith allegedly a terrific pro-Nazi."

The second letter, signed by the same Rose Bigman for Walter Winchell and dated 8 May 1941, was a cover letter for a package of several responses to a Winchell column in the *Mirror,* mostly in support of his attack on Smith. The lead to the Winchell column was "Portrait of a Ham" and compared Lindbergh to "a faded actor" trying to get back in the limelight after scoring "one terrific hit." "Lindbergh lost his big audience, so he's playing to the cheers of the Bundists and other riff-raff." Winchell revels in Roosevelt's decision to accept Lindbergh's resignation of his commission saying, "Our army air corps doesn't want the flying Colonel."

A response to Winchell from the Tampas brothers of Valdosta, Ga., on 1 May 1941 is clear. "After twelve years we have changed the name of our restaurant from Lindbergh Restaurant to Roosevelt Restaurant. We read your column."

Another, from Emma Toores to the president, dated 29 April 1941: "So glad that Lindbergh has resigned, Send him to Germany where he belongs."

But Lindbergh continued to be a hero to many Americans. His supporters tended to be more moderate (and less quotable). They asserted Lindbergh's right to disagree and to speak out and referred to his expertise. "The only man who knows the score in this country is Charles Lindbergh," wrote one. And his "calm logic" was admired.

The pro-Lindbergh people were not entirely bloodless. K. M. Edwards sent a pointed two-liner to the president on 24 April 1941: "Why don't you resign instead of Colonel Lindbergh and give us a chance to protect ourselves."

Smith never denied his friendship and respect for Lindbergh, nor his friend's stubbornness. "There was not one word of truth in their charge," wrote Smith, that he or anyone else was Lindbergh's ghost writer. "To be sure," he continued, "I had seen Lindbergh several times since my return from Germany. No human being, however, as I knew well, could influence Lindbergh on any matter, let alone write his speeches. A Lindbergh ghostwriter on any subject never existed at any time in his past and never will exist in the future. In speech writing as in flying, Charles Lindbergh was a 'lone wolf.'" Smith added that Justice Felix Frankfurter and Secretary of the Interior Harold Ickes "had suggested to the president that I be court-martialed," presumably for associating with Lindbergh.[19]

Smith was not court-martialed. According to him, General Marshall warned the president that a trial would acquit him, estrange the administration and the army, and possibly make Smith an American Dreyfus. But the press attacks continued. At one point Colonel E. Warner McCabe, the G-2 of the army, told Smith that Marshall wanted him out of Washington "until the political heat cooled." No leave was necessary. Smith was to keep McCabe informed of his whereabouts. The Smiths left town.

Smith could not recall exactly how long he and Kay were in "exile." They drove to Fort Benning to spend a week or two with Al and Dade Wedemeyer, half expecting to be recalled to Washington for a court-martial. That visit was followed by a leisurely drive via Savannah and Charleston back to Washington. Smith was informed by Colonel Frank McCarthy, Marshall's aide, that Bernard Baruch, at Marshall's request, went to Roosevelt "and begged him to end the press attacks" on Smith. The press attacks ceased.[20]

Anne Lindbergh also recalled the exile in her 29 June 1940 diary entry, noting that Smith "was shunted off temporarily 'till the storm blew over,' to Fort Benning." She says, "Morgenthau *asked that he be removed!*"(her emphasis), adding that Smith offered to resign, but Marshall "would not hear of it."[21]

The press was only part of Smith's problem. He believed that his reporting on Germany and his friendship with Lindbergh had alienated the interventionists, New Dealers, and government insiders who were determined to get rid of him. In September 1940, he was summoned to Colonel McCabe's office and asked if he had attended a certain cocktail party on a certain day in July 1939. An unnamed person had reported that a Truman Smith, in the presence of witnesses, had said, "President Roosevelt was paralyzed from the neck up." In fact, Smith was in Walter Reed Hospital at the time and not at the cocktail party. It is unclear if this was a case of mistaken identity or a deliberate effort to blemish Smith's reputation. Smith was in for about six weeks of "suspense and intense worry" before the issue was resolved. Finally, Secretary of War Henry L. Stimson summoned Smith to his office, where a stranger, upon seeing Smith, said, "Oh, this is not the officer who made the remarks about the president. I seem to have been falsely informed as to his identity. I desire to express my apologies to Colonel Smith."

Smith, writing in 1964 about the incident, said, "I feel grateful to this day to Mr. Stimson" for what amounted to acquittal. "My troubles ceased for good and all. . . . Never again was there any recurrence of the difficulties I encountered between August and Christmas 1940."[22]

Smith was particularly pleased that Marshall, in a letter of 28 May 1955 to Smith, congratulated him for the way he conducted himself in the summer of 1940, saying, "another thing which quite properly you do not touch on was the bitter resentment and the serious attacks made upon you because you recited the facts of the German buildup of military power. All these things are an inevitable part of democracy and the consequent political reaction." Smith said he was as proud of his coolness under political fire as he was of his coolness under German fire in the Meuse-Argonne in 1918.[23]

These firsthand accounts from the letters, diaries, journals, and memoirs of both Smiths and both Lindberghs convey their feelings of personal stress as well as a sense of immediacy. Historians can place the individual dramas in context. Geoffrey S. Smith, a scholar of American politics in the interwar period, puts what Anne Lindbergh called the Great Debate in perspective. He writes, "Isolationism was a respectful term in the 1920s and early 1930s, but, as America drew closer to actual war it became an epithet."[24]

The German invasion of Poland in September 1939, the Soviet attack on Finland in December of that year, and the German defeat of France and domination of Western Europe in the spring of 1940 "hit the American people with the force of a jackhammer." Presidential aide Robert Sherwood called the close Anglo-American relationship before the United States entered the war a "common-law alliance."[25] And historian William L. Langer called his book about the clashes between German submarines and American shipping, including warships of the U.S. Navy, *The Undeclared War, 1940–1941*.[26] Finally, after vanquishing Wendell Willkie in 1940 and winning his third term as president, FDR announced that his country would become an "arsenal of democracy," thus ending the debate about lend-lease and neutrality laws, and effectively abandoning neutrality.

Adding to the unpopularity of the isolationists was the fact that several extremist movements robbed isolationism and nonintervention of their respectability. Unfortunately for the Lindberghs and Smiths, they and the America First Committee were lumped together with appeasers, anti-Semites, pro-Germans, anti–New Dealers, and assorted crazies of the Right. Prominent among them was the Reverend Charles E. Coughlin, a Catholic priest whose rhetoric and expert use of radio amplified his voice and message in his rabid attacks on FDR, Jews, and interventionists. William Pelley, an Asheville, North Carolina, journalist turned superpatriot, led a nativist Silver Legion that promised to "use guns, not votes, here in America" to resolve political issues. "Semitic internationalism," "trade union dupes," and "the New Deal crackpot in Washington" were among these right-wing extremists' favored targets.[27] Fritz Kuhn was führer of the German-American Bund, which drew thousands to Madison Square Garden in New York City as the Garden was transformed to imitate a Nazi Party Day in Nuremberg.

Events conspired against Lindbergh. By the time the America First Committee became well known, the Axis threat had stimulated interventionist sentiment. And perhaps worse, he was further burdened by the enthusiastic support of nationalistic extremists. "In fairness," Geoffrey Smith writes, "Lindbergh did nothing to encourage the yahoos; yet he did nothing to repudiate them either."[28] He sums up: "Citizens who for the previous decade had either ridiculed or feared Coughlin, Pelley, and the Bundists, now fastened their attention on the flier . . . noninterventionists were everywhere on the defensive, explaining that they were not Nazis."[29] And it wasn't just the yahoos who hurt the once universally respected Lindbergh. FDR took notice of his activities at a press conference on 25 April 1941. Days later, in a letter to the president on 28 April 1941, Lindbergh "resigned his rank as colonel in the US Air Corps Reserve."[30]

And this kind of public mocking had to hurt:

Lindy used to be a hero;
Now his stock is down to zero.
Badly has he got in Dutch—
Just because he talked too much.[31]

His wife had warned him, but apparently Charles Lindbergh never understood that cool logic does not always make one a winner in debating the emotionally laden policies of war and peace.

In July 1941, Smith was again ordered before an army "retiring board." The order had nothing to do with Lindbergh. Marshall personally told Smith why he was being retired. Marshall had been weeding out officers who, in his opinion, could not handle the demands of modern war, among them "many inefficient National Guard officers who had been taken in 1939 and 1940 into federal service." One of these Guard generals had learned of Smith's continuing service despite his diabetes and protested to General Marshall that he was unfairly discriminating between Regular and Guard officers. Marshall "stated flatly to me that now that my case was in the open, he could no longer oppose the Medical Corps." He was, after all, violating an army regulation that required Smith's medical retirement. Marshall asked Smith to stay on as a civilian in the same position after retirement. Smith declined. "We were not then involved in war, and I felt I had still time in life to start a new career."[32]

On 10 September 1941, a retirement board recommended Smith's immediate retirement. Allowing him time to wrap up business and to take the leave due him, his effective date of retirement was 31 January 1942. His "retirement" would be brief.

17

Smith as "Strategicus"

> There were very few military reporters or columnists in the American press. Therefore, I and Paul Palmer . . . decided to establish a weekly military column.
>
> —Smith's reaction to forced medical retirement

Retirement meant that Truman and Kay were no longer nomads subject to relocation on receipt of orders from duly constituted military authority. They showed no hesitation in selecting their place of permanent residence. Like pigeons coming home to roost, on 1 September 1941 they settled on four acres on Greenfield Hill in Fairfield, Connecticut. The Smiths had been New Englanders from colonial days and for over a century Connecticut Yankees. They were home. Nearby New York City beckoned. Kay's roots were there, and so was their social network. "Northeastern establishment" was not a glib cliché. Both Kay and Truman were born to that establishment and remained connected to it for their entire lives. They defined it.

Truman and his sister had inherited their mother's house in nearby Stamford, but there was a fly in that ointment. His sister would neither agree to rent it nor allow Truman to buy her share. Kay was rather testy about that, refusing to live there on any conditional basis. Between the lines in her memoir, here and elsewhere, one could see that Kay was less than enchanted by her sister-in-law. The issue had a simple solution: the Fairfield house became their permanent residence.[1]

Residence established, Truman, forty-eight years of age and vigorous despite diabetes, next sought gratifying work. He found it in writing a military column.

The speed at which so many outlets were found for his column in 1941 is quite remarkable. He praised his collaborator, Paul Palmer, a former editor of *Reader's Digest* and "as fine an editor as any in the country," adding, "I had much military knowledge. Together we were a strong team." Smith did the writing; Palmer got the copy published.

They chose the pen name "Strategicus" for Smith and were off and running. They knew there was an unsatisfied craving in the American public to understand what invasions and bombings in faraway places meant to the United States. By 1 December 1941, the Strategicus column was appearing in some sixty newspapers and magazines, among them the *Boston Herald*, the *Cincinnati Enquirer*, and the professional naval and military officers' "hometown newspaper," the *Army and Navy Journal*. "Week by week," Smith recalled, "we were obtaining new subscribers for our column."[2]

Smith's career as a military columnist was as brief as it was successful. Before George Marshall recalled Smith to active duty after the Pearl Harbor attack, he produced a body of work that showcased his skill as a strategist. Sensing that he was on borrowed time as an active duty soldier since 1939, he and Palmer at some point had discussed a concept for the Strategicus articles. From mid-1941 to February 1942, Smith produced a score of think pieces on current operations and their strategic implications. The number of articles and the details they contained suggest that they were the product of someone who had thought long and hard about the subjects and was current in knowledge of the geopolitical situation. Smith's professional training and clear writing enabled him to put newspaper headlines of current military operations into a strategic context as he wrote for both the general reader and the professional military man. Energy, currency, and background partially explain the number and quality of the articles he wrote, each requiring detailed knowledge of quite varied topics. Interaction with General Staff colleagues specializing in all staff functions and all regions of the world was extremely useful to Smith, both as a columnist and later, when he returned to the staff as a G-2 analyst and briefer.

While at the Army War College in 1932–1933, Smith had added industrial mobilization to his professional knowledge base. That expertise, so useful in his Berlin reporting of Wehrmacht expansion, was most useful as his own army modernized for war. His training and experience came together as if designed for the purpose of strategic analysis and not a consequence of bad luck called diabetes. Examination of the published and unpublished Strategicus articles reveals the thought process of a good mind and a focused professional. What he wrote as Strategicus was more or less what he had mulled about as a General Staff officer.

The *Army and Navy Journal* announced in its 1 November 1941 issue: "The *Army and Navy Journal* presents herewith the first article by a contributor new to our column—'Strategicus.' The author's analytical skill and informed background are better shown in the article itself than could be done by a description of his qualifications. We commend it to your reading. Subsequent articles by 'Strategicus' will appear in future issues of the *Army and Navy Journal*."[3]

This first published article was on 1 November 1941, entitled "What May America Expect from Russia?" In June 1941 the battle of Britain had subsided and Germany invaded Russia. As Smith wrote, the Germans were enjoying a series of spectacular victories. His article analyzes the relative strength of the German and the Russian forces, their industrial capacity, and the possibility of Japanese intervention. It concludes that Anglo-American supplies must arrive in sufficient numbers for 50 or 75 Russian divisions, plus tanks and aircraft in yet larger quantities, if Russia was to survive. "Truly, supplies to Russia are a key issue of the 1942 campaign year. Can America and England deliver these supplies?"

The 15 November 1941 issue of the same publication contained a follow-up article: "Supplies for Russia." Here Strategicus wrote, "This article will confine itself to an analysis of the available routes by which Anglo-American supplies can be sent to Russia." Smith then examines the trade-offs in each of three routes, making it clear that getting the materials there will determine "the fate of the Soviet armies." Writing a month before Pearl Harbor was attacked, he noted regarding his first route that Vladivostok may be cut by the Japanese. As for the second route, he pointed out that Archangel would ice over in winter, limiting its usefulness as a port of entry. Murmansk, an ice-free port, is an option, but the Germans and Finns might make that option untenable. Third, overland transportation from the Persian Gulf to Russia (Smith persists in referencing "Russia" rather than "the Soviet Union") would be difficult and might be delayed until late 1942 or even 1943, due to the lack of roads in the region sufficient to handle the required traffic. He points out that supplying aircraft was not a problem, since they could fly to Alaska and then, by bounds, to wherever in Russia they were needed.

"Much Ado about Turkey" was the lead for the 29 November 1941 column in the *Army and Navy Journal*. Britain, Germany, and

Russia were all courting Turkey. Turkish neutrality favors Germany, since Turkey denies British access to the Black Sea with supplies and troops for Russia. Turkey could be "a fortress" for either the Axis or the Allies, defending British Egypt or the German Balkans. All factors considered, Smith concludes that it is in Turkey's national interest to maintain its neutrality.

"Wanted: More Mountain Troops" appeared in the 20 December 1941 issue of the *Army and Navy Journal.* "Mountain troops" in Smith's time means "light infantry" in later military usage. He describes infantry formations suitable for combat in mountains, in the jungle, and in the Arctic, in the process reviewing Austrian, French, and Italian combat experience in the Alps in World War I and the recent German use of mountain troops in Norway, Greece, and Albania. Asserting that the bulk of the U.S. Army will be armored, mechanized, or motorized, Smith recommends that "15% of all our divisions should be organized with pack transportation," light infantry with animal transport capable of fighting in terrain unsuitable for armor or mechanized infantry. This recalls his experience in Hawaii, where he demonstrated that tough infantry conducted a successful attack through "impassable terrain."

The public life of Strategicus was abbreviated by events that occurred in December of 1941. The last of Smith's four articles is separated from the first three by 7 December 1941, when the Japanese attacked Pearl Harbor. The United States declared war on Japan on 8 December. Germany and Italy declared war on the United States on 11 December. Soon thereafter Marshall called, and Smith returned to active duty in G-2.

But these four published articles represent only a portion of Smith's writing as Strategicus. A number of undated articles had been drafted and were in various stages of readiness for publication. Some were later published. Others exist as typewritten drafts that were not published, either because the author returned to active military duty, or because they were overcome by events. For example, some unpublished drafts connected the fate of Moscow to the fate of Singapore, as Smith thought through the likelihood of war between Russia and Japan in 1941–1942. He returned to that issue in several other places. In all cases, the draft articles show a sophisticated mind and purposeful professional at work as the world was turning upside down and he explains what events mean to the United States. The sheer number of articles is noteworthy. So is the degree to which Smith got it about right in 1941 and early 1942. It took decades for many scholars to get it as right.

He also got some of it wrong.

He wrote several pieces for a series under the general heading "Inside This War." One was "The Battle of South Russia." A note from the McClure Newspaper Syndicate in New York at the top of the page says, "Mailed 2 Dec. 1941. For Release Subject to Specific Telegraphic Permission." This note and similar notes on other draft articles tell us that McClure had a "string" on the article. That is, the newspapers had Smith's copy ready for the press, but the "go" for publication had to be triggered by a telegram from the McClure Syndicate at the last minute, based on actual events. In other words, publishing the article when actions on the ground immediately before planned publication could make McClure, the newspapers carrying the column, and Smith look foolish and cost them credibility was something to be avoided. It would not be to anyone's credit to publish a column saying a city would be successfully defended if the headlines on the front page announced that that city had just fallen to the enemy.

In "The Battle of South Russia" Smith addresses the German operational choice at the time: Would the Germans head for the Caucasus or for the Volga? After analysis, he concludes that they would go for the Volga and be successful in getting to Stalingrad. He points out that for modern mechanized forces, "the frozen roads of winter are more passable than the muddy morasses which in the spring pass for roads in this part of the Ukraine." He adds that deep snow is unusual until February. The Germans chose to go to Stalingrad, did so, and fought well, but a little over a year later, the remnants of the surrounded German Sixth Army died or surrendered there.

Smith also noted that the German Army Group "is a most heterogeneous force, containing important contingents from half a dozen different nations. . . . In all ages it has ever been a difficult task, militarily and politically, to lead in battle such a composite force." He is suggesting here that when hard pressed, not all of Germany's friends would fight as well as Germans.

Another Inside This War article, "Can Russia Defeat Germany?" was marked "Mailed 31 December 1941, For Release 3 January [1942]." (Smith was called by Marshall a few days after the attack on Pearl Harbor and was back for duty in Washington on 2 February 1942. Apparently this draft article was killed.) His lead sentence is, "Germany will win the battle of Russia—unless a miracle happens." His concluding sentences are, "If Josef Stalin can hold off Hitler's hordes the position of the Allies will be immeasurably strengthened everywhere on the globe. But if the Nazi war-machine smashes through, the day of final Allied victory may be indefinitely postponed." The miracle happened.

At the time of Smith's writing, there were reports of local victories by Soviet troops before Moscow, possibly a turn in the tide. But Smith believed that the Russians were not strong enough to sustain a major counteroffensive. He went on to say that a Soviet disaster is inevitable in 1942 unless the Allies draw off German strength by an invasion of Western Europe, or unless supplies from the United States reach the Russians in sufficiently large quantities to increase the number of their divisions. He was right about the Russians' inability to sustain a major counteroffensive, but the Russians were able to tough it out and survive that first winter without either a second front in Western Europe or massive amounts of U.S. supplies. Neither was going to happen *at that time.* Winston Churchill had already ruled out a 1942 invasion of Western Europe, and the United States would be too busy mobilizing and arming itself—and keeping the Brits in the war—to get desperately needed supplies to Russia immediately. Smith was wrong in his estimate of the situation. The tenacity of Russian soldiers and the readiness of their leaders to spend the lives of their soldiers made him wrong.

But, he was not alone in expecting German victory in Russia. The early capture of hundreds of thousands of Soviet troops by the Germans and the massive destruction of Soviet matériel in 1941 caused many analysts, professional and amateur, to doubt that Russia could survive. But survive it did.

There was an understandable emotional reaction and a public clamor in the United States to avenge Pearl Harbor, Wake, and Guam and to punish Japan. Instead of sending planes, tanks, and guns to Britain, Libya, and Russia, and requiring U.S. soldiers, sailors, and marines to "fight with sheer grit," many Americans believed that the United States should simply arm itself and fight the Japanese. The general public was unaware that in the event of war with both Germany and Japan, U.S. strategy was already decided: defeat "Germany First," then Japan. That would have seemed odd to laymen: after all, it was Japan, not Germany, that had attacked American territory in a "sneak attack."[4]

Writing during a period of uninterrupted Japanese and German martial successes as America sang "Let's Remember Pearl Harbor," Smith understood the strategic priorities: "To keep a realistic view we must realize that the one most important sector in this world at war—both to the Allies and to the Axis—is now the Moscow front. Here is where the fate of Europe will be decided." And so it was. The "miracle of the Marne" in an earlier war was matched by the miracle before Moscow.

Calm analysis of dramatic events and their strategic significance—as they were unfolding—was Smith's strength. It is one thing to write history decades after events, when passions have cooled and documentary evidence becomes available, and quite another to declaim on them as they unfold in an atmosphere of confusion and passion. Smith remained the dispassionate analyst.

In another Inside This War column, "Singapore Must Be Held," released by McClure for publication on 13 December 1941, Smith turned to Asia and the Pacific, saying that military facts had to be understood "by every American." First, "Jap" (it didn't take long for the Japanese to become Japs) attacks on Guam, Wake, Midway, Borneo, China, the Philippines, and a dozen other points on a ten-thousand-mile front were made primarily to veil the main attack upon Singapore. He advised that all available American air strength be sent to the Malay Peninsula. "Singapore is the *sine qua non,* the crossroads of victory, the place at which we win or we perish." He linked two theaters of war, calling the battles for Moscow and Singapore keys to victory or defeat.

In a fifteen-page draft typescript called "Russia in the Far East," Smith laid out the implications of a statement made by Maxim Litvinov, the Soviet ambassador to Washington, after the declarations of war by the United States, Germany, and Italy. Russia, said the ambassador, "would confine her military efforts to the struggle with Germany, remaining at peace with Japan, but that, nevertheless, Japan was a member of the Axis and hence an enemy." Smith edited and rewrote the draft, changing the title to, "Will Russia Declare War on Japan," as another in his Inside This War series. The rewrite is marked "For Release Dec. 27, 28 [1941]." He proceeded from the Litvinov statement to illustrate the Japanese and Russian shared dilemmas of a two-front war. Litvinov's intention "to confuse the issue and thus keep Japan uncertain as to the ultimate intentions of the Soviets," Smith wrote, "succeeded only too well in its purpose. It confused everybody."

Smith unravels the knot. Japan will not initiate war with Russia until Singapore, Manila, and the Dutch East Indies are secured. The Japanese would be overextended if they attempted both efforts at the same time. Likewise, Russia will not take on Japan while fighting desperately against the Germans. That would exceed Russia's capabilities. But in the spring, if the Japanese succeeded in the Pacific, Russia and Japan would likely be at war. The keys are Moscow and Singapore. Russia needs to hold Moscow. The best bet for the Americans and the British is to "retard" the Japanese in the Malay Peninsula and in the Philippines.

In fact, Moscow survived, and the Japanese were victorious in the Malay Peninsula and in the Philippines. Most significantly, a smashing defeat at the hands of the Americans at Midway in June 1942 ruled out any ambitious Japanese campaign on the Asian mainland. The Russians had their hands full fighting Germans; the Japanese had their hands full fighting the Americans. Russia did not intervene in the Far East until August 1945 to share the fruits of victory, only after the Americans had effectively defeated Japan.

On 3 January 1942, the *Army and Navy Journal* published "Strategic Situation in the Pacific," another calm assessment by Strategicus.[5] Post–Pearl Harbor war fever was intense as the United States found itself almost overnight at war with Japan, Germany, and Italy. Volunteers flocked to recruiting stations to "join up" to the sound of "Praise the Lord and Pass the Ammunition." Hollywood responded in 1942 with *Casablanca, Days of Wrath,* and *Mrs. Miniver,* the latter a drama of wartime British sacrifice, which won Academy Awards for Best Picture, Best Director, and Best Actress (Greer Garson). Irving Berlin's *This Is the Army* appeared on Broadway. War fever surpassed the naive "Over There" cheerleading of 1917–1918, and nothing like it has been seen since in the United States, with the possible exception of the passionate public reaction to the destruction of the World Trade Center in New York City in 2001.

Strategicus turned to the Pacific once more for bad news, but he reminded his readers that despite early Japanese successes in the Pacific and in Asia, time was on the side of the Allies. We should not lose sight of the big picture, he wrote: British and American superiority in manpower and industrial capacity will win in the long run.

The loss of the battleships at Pearl Harbor and the impending loss of Manila, no matter how much "a blow to American pride," are setbacks that will be made up. In fact, he pointed out, the Allies have North America and "the Australian Indian Ocean base area," while the Japanese forces are overextended and divided in three ways: in Manchuria and Korea; in China; and in Malaysia and Philippine Islands.

Smith was more perspicacious regarding Japanese strategy than were the Japanese. He anticipated Japanese-German coordination in a great offensive that would bring down Russia: "It is almost certain that large-scale Russo-Japanese hostilities will begin in April or May [1942], and that this extension of the Asiatic battle front will materially reduce Japanese pressure on Singapore and Manila." That did not happen, but it was a wiser course of action than the one pursued by the Japanese and the Germans. Had the Germans and Japanese cooperated and coordinated war plans and their execution just half as well as the United States and Britain coordinated theirs, the outcome of the Second World War might have been very different. Smith believed that knocking Russia out of the war would have given Germany hegemony in Europe and allowed the Japanese to pick up all the pieces they desired in East Asia, both on the mainland and in the resource-rich European colonies—later. The first step was to defeat Russia.

Without the enormous demands for German resources on the Russian front, opening a front in Western Europe might never have been undertaken. Britain, Canada, and the United States would have paid a very high price to establish a beachhead in the west without the enormous German effort required to fight on the Russian front. Even with the Russians gaining the upper hand and doing most of the bloody fighting for the entire period from 1941 to 1945, the Allies took almost a year and heavy losses to get from Normandy to the heart of Germany. And it was the Red Army that got to Berlin first.

Japanese and German strategic blunders were monumental. The Axis countries' failure to coordinate their efforts produced disastrous results for their people. By taking on the United States in the Pacific, the Japanese effectively chose national suicide. Historian Samuel Eliot Morison put it bluntly: "The decision, for a man of Yamamoto's intelligence, was strange, for as strategy it was not only wrong but disastrous."[6]

The Germans, after failing to knock Britain out of the war in

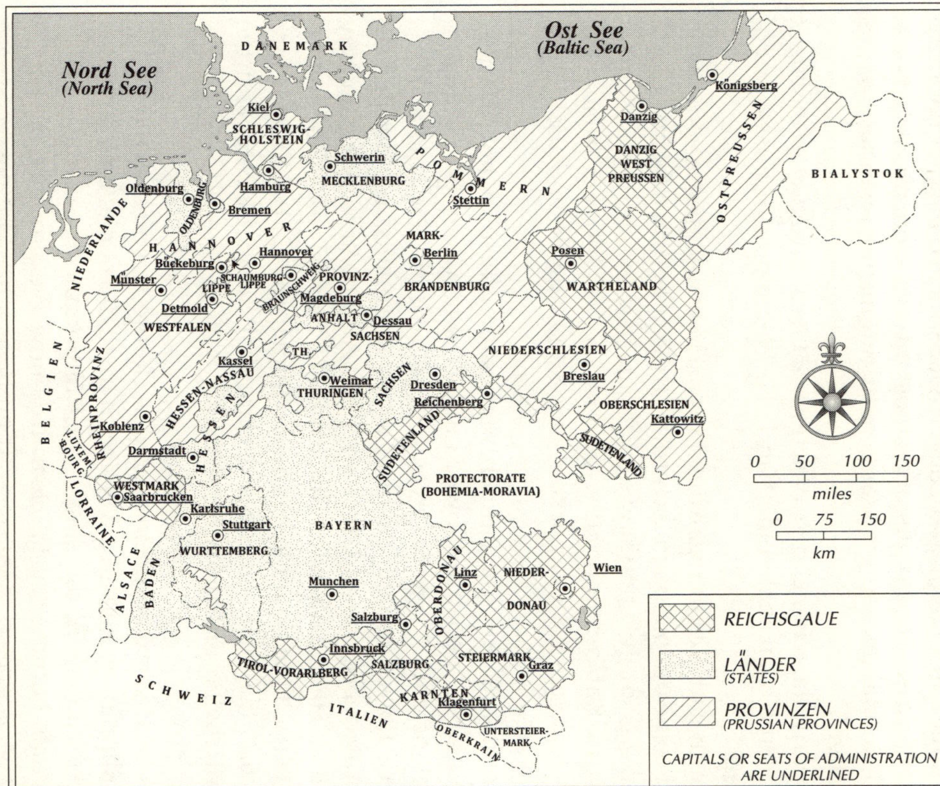

Austria and much of middle Europe is included in Greater Germany, 1943. (Handbook for Unit Commanders, Germany, Supreme Headquarters Allied Expeditionary, 15 September 1944.)

the summer and fall of 1940, nevertheless turned east with Operation Barbarossa, "one of history's most misbegotten, mistakenly executed campaigns," in the words of distinguished historian Dennis Showalter.[7]

Clearly, the wiser course of action for Germany and Japan would have been a coordinated blow in 1941–1942 to knock Russia out of the war.

Smith had it right regarding Japan. He was less sure about who would come out on top in the brutal struggle between Germans and Russians, a struggle that saw some of the nastiest protracted combat in history. But certainly he was right about the German-Japanese failure to cooperate in knockout blows to bring down Russia early in the war.

Smith's geopolitical acumen, interest in industrial mobilization, and military experience allowed him to range widely, providing important insights into force development not limited to land warfare. His "Air Power and the Pacific War" is an undated typescript that, once edited, became an article entitled "Air Power Is Our New Key to Victory Hence Waste of Time to Build Battleships." (The manuscript carried the notation "Mailed 8 January 1942/For Release January 10.") His first sentences declare that theory, debate, and the Billy Mitchell brouhaha were settled.

> As U.S. Army bombers roared back into the offensive over Philippine waters this week with three direct hits on a Japanese battleship, the single most important fact of the war to date became crystal clear. It is now the province of the plane. *Air power is sea power.* [Emphasis added.] If we recognize this fact and act upon it, we have in our own hands the key to winning the war, for we are the one people who can muster air power so overwhelming that no force on earth can stop us. An extraordinary revolution in naval warfare has taken place before our very eyes. The mighty battleship is outmoded, a washed up weapon of the past. The future belongs to the combat plane.
>
> One short month of war in the Pacific has witnessed a destruction of war vessels on a scale never before equaled in all naval history. More capital ships have been lost than at Jutland. . . . A greater total tonnage has been sunk than at Trafalgar. And the revolution in warfare is revealed when we

> realize that all these mighty fortresses of the deep have been sunk, not by other heavy surface craft, but from the thin air.

The prose sparkles, matching his logic.

The toll: "*The Prince of Wales,* pride of England's Navy, and the huge battle-cruiser *Repulse.* A Jap battleship of the Kongo class, and the 29,000-ton *Haruna.* At Pearl Harbor, our own *Arizona* and *Oklahoma.*" He also highlights German success in Norway, British torpedo planes against an Italian cruiser in the Mediterranean Sea, and German seizure of Crete as examples of air power successes against sea power.

He concludes, "It is not time for the American people to draw up a balance sheet to tabulate gains and losses . . . [but to focus on] how best to utilize for victory our enormous manufacturing potential" by producing aircraft and merchant tonnage, not battleships. "Sea control of Asiatic waters can be won only by the airplane. First our airplanes will have to destroy the Japanese surface fleet and furnish the bulk of the protection for our convoys carrying our soldiers to the Far East." Therefore, build aircraft carriers, cruisers, destroyers, submarines, and merchantmen, not battleships. "The instruments of sea-power are torpedo planes, bombers, and fighter planes."

An account by a Japanese Zero pilot and ace, Saburo Sakai, describes his war in the skies over the Pacific and validates Smith's appreciation of American advantage. American aviation simply overwhelmed the Japanese in quantity and quality of aircraft and the constantly improving skills of American aviators. Sakai was flying the same aircraft in 1945 that he had flown in 1941, while the Americans routinely replaced older models with new ones with the latest technology. The Japanese air arsenal simply wore out.[8]

Historian Edward J. Drea's closing sentence in his excellent monograph on Japanese-Russian combat in the summer of 1939 gets to the essence of the Japanese dilemma. Japanese doctrine relied upon morale, fighting spirit, and courageous leadership to compensate for the relative lack of matériel compared to the Soviets or the Americans. Drea writes, "As infantry they were excellent, but as soldiers fighting a modern war they were an anachronism, as the Pacific War would ultimately demonstrate."[9]

It was with regret that Smith had to abandon his work with Paul Palmer and the McClure Syndicate. Shortly after the Japanese attack on Pearl Harbor, Marshall asked Smith to return to his former job in G-2. By 2 February 1942, Smith was back at his old desk in G-2. His return to active duty in Washington would necessarily end the Strategicus articles. "The McClure people behaved well," he noted. "Although they had spent much money in promoting our column and were just beginning to reap profits from it, they released Palmer and me from our contracts. The column thereupon ceased, and Palmer returned to the *Reader's Digest*."[10]

Several of the unpublished pieces show why George Marshall so valued Smith and wanted his analysis and briefings. For example, in considering military actions in North Africa, Smith reminds his readers that outcomes in the Russian theater have strategic priority: in a piece entitled "The Battle of North Africa" (no date, typescript, 14 pp.) Smith notes that the fighting there has relegated American interest "in the more important Russian theater" to the background. He stresses the importance of the lines of communication and concludes that despite the proximity of the Axis to the battle area, British superiority in the Mediterranean gives them the advantage. Malta is the key. "Until, therefore, this fortress shall have been captured by the Axis, Egypt may rest assured that no German or Italian troops will ever enter from the West the valley of the Nile." The message: Don't be distracted by North Africa.

Another piece, "North Africa" (no date, typescript, 7 pp.) says, "Mobility has been restored to war and with mobility have also returned the importance of the personality and skill of the general." The British had not distinguished themselves, but "the leader of the Axis army, on the other hand, General Erwin Rommel, is a soldier who has again and again proven himself an able battle commander." Soldiers and historians would write admiringly of Rommel later, but Smith and enlightened professional soldiers recognized his skills as they were being applied.

"Sea Power Versus Air Power in the Mediterranean" (no date, typescript, 10 pp.) is a highly speculative tour of the strategic horizon, which Smith drafted sometime before September 1939. "General war," he writes, is in the future. His first sentences frame "this unsolved riddle of warfare" in the title. Recent events had not provided an answer. "Neither China nor Abyssinia had air forces to resist their invaders. In Spain, the air forces on both sides were small." He concludes that the two sides intending to dominate the Mediterranean Sea, Italy and Britain, are hedging their bets, building both warships and airfields, "so whichever way the cat jumps, their nation will not be placed in too disadvantaged a position." Smith's early rumination and speculation here are interesting, since his post–Pearl Harbor articles give clear advantage to airpower based upon the evidence of combat from 1939 into 1942.

"The Relief of General Field Marshal von Brauchitsch and the Situation on the Russian Front" (no date, typescript, 15 pp.) was not published, but Smith used much of it in "Can Russia Defeat Germany?" a piece that was intended for publication on 31 December 1941. Hitler assumed direct command of the army and, asserted Strategicus, made von Brauchitsch the scapegoat for Hitler's strategic errors. At the time of writing, both Russia and Germany were claiming success on the Russian front. The Wehrmacht was at the gates of Moscow; the Red Army had had some local tactical successes; the outcome could not be predicted. But one thing was certain: "The Moscow front is still today, as it has always been, the critical theater of war. . . . A great Russian victory may well be impending. However, this victory is still to be won."

In "The Battle of Leningrad" (no date, typescript, 7 pp.) Smith compares that fight to the encirclement of Vicksburg in the American Civil War in the summer of 1863. While investing the city of three and a half-million inhabitants and 250,000 troops, it was also necessary for the Germans to ward off enemy forces to the rear and on the flanks.

Smith's ruminations about the place of airpower in Allied strategy are balanced. "The idea that Germany can be conquered by an Anglo-American all-out bombing attack is an extremely appealing one," wrote Strategicus in "Can Hitler Be Licked by All-Out Bombing of Germany?" (no date, typescript, 16 pp.). If the answer were yes, that would spare the need for sending ground forces to Europe, a very happy solution, though one "based on the assumption that Great Britain and the United States can out build Germany."

Victory through air power promised war on the cheap. Smith, as we have seen, was a believer in air power, but he recognized its limitations. Writing after the Battle of Britain and after some British bombing on the Continent, but before the massive deployment of U.S. air forces to England and their employment over the Continent, Smith concluded that Germany could not be defeated by air power alone. Considering the later debate about the cost-effectiveness of the massive bombing campaign against Germany, Smith's observations before that campaign was undertaken provide an appreciation of what had happened by 1942.

He asserted that fighters cost about one-tenth or one-twentieth the price of bombers and "can ascend into the stratosphere and shoot down even the heaviest bombers of the Flying Fortress type." Even with the most optimistic assumptions, the United States and Britain "would have to be prepared to accept fifteen times the casualties of the enemy." (Bomber crews comprised up to ten men; a single pilot flew most fighters.) Both the Battle of Britain and British attacks on Germany showed the fighter to be superior to the bomber at all altitudes. "The fighter plane had made itself the monarch of the air."

But, he continued, Anglo-American fighters lack sufficient range to accompany bombers to "Germany proper." The Germans, flying escort fighters much shorter distances out of airfields in "a semi-circle around England . . . from Brest, through Belgium, Holland, Northern Germany, and Denmark to the far northern Norwegian fields at Trondheim" nevertheless took intolerable losses and terminated their daylight offensive.

Smith cites these figures in his undated and unpublished draft (without providing his sources): in August 1940, 400 fighters accompanied 275 German bombers; in mid-September 1940, 600 fighters to 125 bombers; in late September 1940, 1,000 fighters to 150 bombers. The result of British bombing efforts confirmed those figures. "Indeed, on one occasion England lost thirty-nine bombers on a single raid into Germany." One hundred and twenty-five airmen were killed in action or in POW camps. Smith somehow worked out a cost for this action: 8 million dollars. The RAF concluded that daylight bombing of industrial objectives did not pay. "The defensive fighter plane," Smith wrote, "has become ruler of Europe's daylight skies."

He also notes that downed fighter pilots and some of the damaged aircraft could fight again. Downed attacking pilots who survived, however, found themselves in prisoner of war camps.

The Germans turned to night bombing, pulverizing Coventry with 450 bombers, attacking London with 700 bombers, and raiding other industrial cities. Night bombing was less accurate, but it was safer for the bombing crews. Then British night-fighters "equipped with locators" took to the air with some success.

Smith writes that a "telephone net" allowed coordinated and concentrated British defense. It is likely that at the time of his writing, Smith was unaware of early British use of radar, which was a closely guarded secret and a major contributor to British success, later shared with the American allies.

Considering how events played out later, Smith's conclusions are provocative. "We shall have to discard the bombing plane as a weapon by which Germany can without assistance by other arms be forced into submission. The defense fighter plane now rules the air. . . . Unless inventive genius discovers ways to overcome fighter plane defense, daylight bombing of cities will not become an important feature of air war."

The facts are that the United States accepted the extremely high cost of daylight bombing of Germany without fighter escort (all the way to the target), while the British bombed at night. Despite what he knew and had reported while in Berlin, Smith—in this draft of "Can Hitler Be Licked by All-Out Bombing of Germany?"—does not describe the effectiveness of German antiaircraft cannons fired from the ground. Fortunately for American bomber crews, "inventive genius" in the form of the P-51 Mustang later provided fighter cover to bombers at extreme range. That was, however, well after the time in which Smith was attempting to answer the question of whether airpower alone could defeat Germany. He concluded that the employment of "other arms" was necessary to close with and destroy the German Army and so defeat Germany.

Smith shines as a strategist and writer in addressing the opening of a second front for the Germans to deal with, the Russian front being the first. "The Truth about an AEF" is an undated typescript of 53 pages. His phrase "so long as Japan's attitude is unfriendly" puts the piece before 7 December 1941; reference to the Germans' frustration at their inability to cross the "twenty-mile water barrier" puts it after June 1940. Smith dismisses "facile talk . . . about sending another American Expeditionary Force across the Atlantic" and sets forth, "plainly and concisely, the fundamental facts in the case." He answers these questions: Where could an American Expeditionary Force be landed? How big a force is required? How strong would be the force opposing the landing? How many ships would be needed? How much matériel—planes, tanks, guns, ammunition, etc.—would be required? Finally, what would be the chances of eventual success?

He dismisses a peripheral strategy as nibbling at the edges. *"Hitler's armies can be beaten only on the continent of Europe where they now stand—and not in Iceland, nor Madagascar, nor at Dakar."* (Emphasis in original.)

Then he gets to specifics. "In 1917 the American army was disembarked in secure and efficient ports. Today there exists not a single bridgehead on the European continent within which an A.E.F. could land in security." England is, obviously, an island. "This geographical factor has been dramatically brought home to us in recent months by the vain effort of the Germans to cross the twenty-mile water-barrier of the English Channel." Getting an American army to England would be just the first step. The "crux of all military difficulties confronting an A.E.F. [is that] no matter to what part of the world it might be initially transported, sooner or later it would have to carry out *in Europe itself* that most difficult of all military operations—a landing on a hostile shore" (emphasis in original).

He then considers five alternate landing sites: the Middle East, Morocco, Portugal, northern Norway, and the French Channel Coast, analyzing each in detail. Here are his main points summarized.

He dismisses the Middle East option as the main American military effort on the following basis. Although it would be possible to get into the Persian Gulf, even with the Japanese naval threat in the Pacific and Indian Oceans, it would be difficult to get out on land due to the lack of roads and rail transport. And even if they were successful in Egypt, for example, the Allies would find themselves a long way from Berlin. Getting into the Caucasus makes no sense for the same reasons that fighting westward from the Balkans or northward in Italy makes no sense: terrain favors the defender, and, in either case, it is a long slog to Germany. Furthermore, if the Allies alienate Turkey, they could well face another belligerent. So Smith dismisses the Middle East option as the locus of the main American military effort.

Turning to North Africa he asks: if we land in Morocco, would we be required to fight Vichy France? Would Spain fight and/or invite German and Italian troops into Spain and close the Straits of Gibraltar? "Once the initial cheap success had been obtained," he writes, then what? Again, it is a long way to either Berlin or Egypt. What do we do with the assets in Morocco?

He further opines: if Portugal is entered, either by force or by permission, "an immediate Spanish-Axis attack against Portugal would be certain to follow as soon as an AEF commenced to land." The Axis would have a two-to-one superiority within thirty days, and their advantage would grow. This choice "would be an inexcusable blunder."

He next considers a lodgment in the north of Norway. That is possible, Smith thinks, but he asks, then what? Going south would be extremely difficult. "A few aircraft and infantry battalions succeeded in inflicting a decisive repulse upon the British." German strength has increased. Swedish reaction is unknown. In brief, geographic and military considerations "speak strongly in favor of a prospective AEF keeping as far away from Norway as possible."[11]

Smith then makes the case for a cross-Channel operation. England is the only place providing a secure base for a necessarily large expeditionary force, a place with massive cargo handling capability and "airfields close so fighters attain air mastery." An amphibious operation against a defended coast is difficult and must be *big*! "No petty expedition could hope to defeat the German army on terrain perfectly adopted for defense." Smith concludes that all five areas considered for invasion "found one fact common to all—sooner or later an AEF would have to confront the German army holding permanent fortifications behind a broad water-barrier." He lists those barriers: the English Channel, the Straits of Gibraltar, the Kattegat, the Straits of Sicily, and the Bosporus.

He declares that Germany has 8 million soldiers, and that 5 million of them would be available to resist an American offensive, "once Germany has succeeded in crushing Russia." This statement earned him the following penciled note from a reader, possibly his editor Paul Palmer: "Your paper seems to [unreadable word] premise that Russia is out—yet you mention here sending more equipment [to Russia]." Smith was not alone in his uncertainty regarding Russia's survival. The early months of the war had produced an almost unbroken series of German victories. Writing in the period June 1940 to December 1941, Russian resilience was yet to be determined.

Fully aware of the difficulties, Smith proceeds to estimate how many British and American troops would be required for contingencies and responsibilities around the world. The British contribution for the cross-Channel operation, he figures, would be one million men. The American contribution for the AEF, plus some 200,000 for the "newly acquired island possessions in the Atlantic and Caribbean and older Pacific possessions," plus one million men for possible war with Japan, plus "depot troops and anti-aircraft defense units," plus replacements of casualties leads Smith to this conclusion: *"It is, therefore possible to see the size of the army needed at a minimum of 12,500,000 and a maximum of 15,500,000 men."* (Emphasis in original.) He also estimated the requirements for tanks (72,000), aircraft (72,000), and merchant shipping (8 million tons). It would take three to four years "to complete the necessary preparations."

In fact, the army of May 1945 had approximately 8.2 million men. Albert Wedemeyer's August 1941 estimate for total army was 8,795,658, of which 2,050,000 were air force.[12]

It is not clear why Smith's minimum figure is about 3.5 million greater than Wedemeyer's estimate in his Victory Plan. One suspects that Smith safe-sided his estimate as he planned for possible defeat of Russia, thereby enabling the Germans to dedicate all their forces to defeat the Allied cross-Channel landing. His estimate of the time required to raise, equip, train, and deploy the cross-Channel force, three or four years, would have the force in England and ready to go in 1944. Not a bad estimate!

In any event, he dismisses "facile talk" and hope of cheap victory through airpower alone or nibbling at the edges. Smith also predicts by-products, not all of them good. Among them is "the vast economic transformation which would be necessitated in our country by the raising, training, equipping, transportation and support of an army of more than twelve million men." (He adds a footnote to his narrative at this point that promises an article on the subject of economics in a forthcoming issue; such a piece, however, was not found among his draft articles.)

Smith continues, "One of the results would be to send millions of women into the factories. The equipment and supply of those troops would automatically necessitate the stoppage of all luxury and comfort goods such as automobiles, radios, etc." And ominously, "What effect the transformation to a purely military economy would have on our political system—whether democracy could survive here—is, again, not within the province of this writer to remark."

The magnitude of the numbers took Smith beyond his attempt to debunk silly talk by armchair generals, as the world seemed to be going to hell in a handbasket in 1940–1941. His military estimate is sound as a basis for military planning. And he was right as well about women entering the workforce, the rationing of luxury goods, and the notion that economic realities have social and political consequences that might outlast the period of war. That alarmed him.

His concern for the health of American democracy during transformation to a military economy for World War II is prescient in anticipating similar concerns expressed by his famous contemporary, Dwight D. Eisenhower, twenty years later. On 17 January 1961, Eisenhower delivered his famous "military-industrial complex" speech. (Others would later identify the emergence of "the national security state" as a residue of World War II and the Cold War.) It is this broad-gauged thinking that caused Albert Wedemeyer to say that, but for his diabetes, Smith might have been as influential as Eisenhower in wartime leadership and perhaps later.

Smith was conservative in temperament and outlook. Working in civil affairs in 1919–1920, witnessing revolutionary Germany in 1920–1924, experiencing the New Deal after 1933, living in Hitler's Germany of 1935–1939, and finding himself in the midst of the America First versus interventionists controversy in 1939–1941 added up to a practical study in government. Anti-Bolshevik, anti-Hitler, and dubious about Roosevelt and strong central government, Smith saw the need for wartime national transformation. At the same time he feared the potential for long-term and permanent accretion of governmental power and possible social dislocation in the United States.[13]

These sketches of Smith's geopolitical thinking and work as a columnist make it clear why George Marshall wished to make every effort to keep Smith on active duty and at his elbow in Washington. In fact, when at one point Marshall had reason to believe that President Roosevelt intended to send him to England to do the job that Eisenhower later did—lead the Allies in the field in the invasion of Europe—Smith was told that he would accompany Marshall as his chief of intelligence, even if Smith had to work from a hospital. That was not to be. In the end, the president said that he slept better with Marshall in Washington. Apparently Marshall slept better with Smith in the Pentagon. (See appendix F as an example of his clear and concise analyses.)

18

Wartime Washington

> We were now at war. Although retired, I regarded myself still as an army officer. To put on the uniform once again now seemed to be my duty.
>
> —Truman Smith, on being returned to active duty

> There is very little chance for an individual to stand out in General Staff work. . . . Committee work is the rule. Staff papers are prepared not by individuals but by groups.
>
> —Smith, on the anonymity of staff work

It is inconceivable that Truman Smith could have chosen to sit on the sideline as friends and comrades from twenty-six years of military service marched off to the great crusade, many to serve with distinction. One imagines the visceral reaction of the professional soldier and combat veteran in the charged atmosphere of the days after the bombing of Pearl Harbor, so close to Schofield Barracks, where Kay and Truman had so recently enjoyed the pleasures of peace in a tropical paradise. In addition to the adrenaline rush accompanying the declarations of war, Smith knew that his professional training and experience made him a valuable national asset, not least for his understanding of Germany and his strategic skills. He and his cohort of Regulars were the bedrock upon which a mass of amateurs had to be transformed if the war were to be won. That's why many middle-grade American officers of early 1942 would become the famous generals and admirals of World War II. Many more would serve as unknown staff officers. Smith knew that; so did Marshall.

It was equally unthinkable that George Marshall, the army's chief of staff, could have overlooked Smith, one of his Fort Benning men, at a time of national emergency. Keeping Smith on active duty from 1939 to 1941 in violation of army regulations was extraordinary behavior by Marshall, the very paragon of rectitude. So was protecting him from powerful political enemies—friends of the president—when the spotlight directed at Charles Lindbergh caught Smith in its glare. Clearly, Marshall believed Smith to be worth a great deal of trouble even before the United States was at war. (See appendix C.)

Nevertheless, it is striking that Marshall found time to *personally* telephone Smith, as the latter wrote in his memoirs, "a few days subsequent to the catastrophe of Pearl Harbor." One can only imagine the flood of issues rushing through Marshall's mind in the immediate wake of that tremendous shock. The battleship fleet of the United States was effectively lost; the Pacific was a Japanese lake; the invasion of Hawaii loomed as a possibility; the security of the American West Coast was endangered; reinforcing the American garrison in the Philippine Islands risked throwing limited resources at a lost cause; Britain had been knocked about and Russia was in a death struggle with the German Army, promising no help from those quarters; what the president intended to do had to be determined or sensed. Someone was accountable for the Pearl Harbor debacle. And Marshall had to make personnel decisions to get the right men to key staff positions to think through complex issues and to command the millions of civilians to be trained, armed, equipped, deployed, and employed in faraway places. All of that and more was on his plate when Marshall thought of Smith.

Smith's Strategicus column was highly successful. Readership was growing week by week when, shortly after the Japanese attack, Smith's telephone rang in his living room in Connecticut. George Marshall was on the line. "In his usual formal and cold tone," Smith recalled, "he asked me to return to my former position in G-2." Aware of Smith's poor health and his writing career, Marshall said that he would not order him to active duty if that were contrary to his wishes. Smith's response was immediate and affirmative. He was a soldier. He had not wanted to leave the army or Washington. "However, I requested the general to defer my orders until my wife could locate an apartment in Washington." Marshall assented.[1]

Smith regretted abandoning his work with Paul Palmer—he was very good at it—and appreciated the understanding of the McClure syndicate, which, although just beginning to make a profit from their investment in the Strategicus venture, released Smith and Palmer from their contract.

Finding a place to live in wartime Washington was no small

matter. The national capital was being transformed from sleepy southern town to hyperactive city as the United States by degrees accepted world leadership and the attendant responsibilities. Housing was in short supply as bureaucrats, businessmen, soldiers, secretaries, journalists, and foreign officials streamed into Washington to join what was called "the war effort." It was fortuitous that Kay and Truman Smith knew their way around town, having lived there when Truman attended the Army War College, and that they were socially well connected. They found a suitable apartment, and Truman went to work.[2]

"On February 1 [1942]," Smith wrote, "I was back at my former desk in the old Munitions building, though soon thereafter we moved into the new Pentagon building south of the Potomac River. There began three-and-one-quarter years of war service in the Intelligence Division of the General Staff of the army. On February 1, I received the rank of a full colonel in the National Army."[3]

While their manner of describing their wartime Washington years differs, the Smiths' separate memoirs are complementary. Truman and Kay agreed on those things that mattered to each of them: the importance of their daughter, loyalty to one another and their country, interpretation of events and conditions in Europe, domestic politics, and social values. Smith's professional reputation and respect as a person of integrity were as important to Kay as they were to Truman. She was unreserved in her affection, respect, and support of her husband and would be protective of his legacy. He treated her as his equal, partner, and confidant. He was discreet in his writing because he knew that what he set down might one day become public, as it has. But one may safely assume that the views Kay reveals so openly also reflect Truman's views. Her memoir is a frank and valuable insight into attitudes shared, but not necessarily pronounced in his writings.

Smith accepted his modest status as a staff officer more gracefully than Kay resigned herself to being just another army wife and not the belle of the ball she had been in Berlin and in other assignments. He remarked that in Berlin he had been quite autonomous, deciding where and when he would go and what he would do and report to Washington. Moreover, he stood out—literally—because he was tall, because he was well connected to key Germans, and because in the military community in Berlin he *was* the United States of America. In Washington in 1942, by contrast, he had no illusions of stardom. He knew it was his duty as a General Staff officer to function as "an anonymous cog in a machine."[4]

He showed no resentment as peers and former subordinates won headlines, stars, and battle command. Omar Bradley got five stars. So did William F. Halsey, who was a student at the Naval War College when Smith was a student at the Army War College. Several of the younger men whom Smith mentored while they attended the Kriegsakademie in Berlin went on to flag rank. But he was still Truman Smith, widely respected for who he was, not for the badges of rank. He would do his job.

Kay had a more difficult time in adjusting to the new reality. Her feeling that she and Truman deserved better emerges from between the lines in her memoir, sometimes quite pointedly. Her constant name-dropping and evident sense of entitlement suggest that she believed that somehow they had been cheated from enjoying in full their due. That attitude, usually subdued, was particularly evident in the period of decompression upon their return from Germany to Washington in 1939, a period she called "a low point in our lives."[5]

At that time, they were facing the possibly abrupt end of Truman's military career due to his diabetes, press attacks for their anti-FDR and pro-Lindbergh views, and, as Kay confesses in her unpublished memoir, her physical condition associated with female "change of life" issues. Her tone changes in the 1942–1945 period. As Truman settles into his routine on the General Staff, Kay accepts life as it comes at them—with a diminishing number of prickly observations. But she is quick to point out that the Smiths continued to be well connected. For example, she notes that the secretary of war asked Truman to ask Charles Lindbergh if he was interested in becoming secretary of air, a position that did not exist at that time. Lindbergh declined.[6]

Relegated to the second team and assisting Mrs. Marshall pour tea at a reception for Latin American military attachés and their wives, Kay recalls, "I had been so often on the opposite side of the present lines," that is, as queen bee. "Suddenly General Marshall sat down beside me. . . . I said something banal. Shortly he left. It was unpardonably stupid of me, but General Marshall had a way of freezing one's blood."[7]

Some twenty-five years after the event, as she wrote her memoirs, Kay was still regretting her failure at an audition of little consequence to anyone—but Kay. She could never figure out Marshall, which probably really means that she could never figure out a way to manage him.

Her intellectual curiosity never diminished. At a social event in the company of Loy Anderson, former chargé d'affaires in Moscow, Kay asked him if the recently published *Darkness at Noon,* Arthur Koestler's novel of the Moscow trials conducted while the Smiths were in Berlin, was an accurate picture of Stalin's purge of potential Soviet competitors. Among other insights, the book shows how confinement, interrogation, and feelings of guilt at one's heresy in doubting the absolute wisdom or authority of the Party resulted in numerous public confessions. Confession condemned the sinner to execution, an execution that numerous heretics—to the shock of Western observers at the trials—accepted as just. Anderson replied, "I sat in that court every day of the trials. When I read that book I could smell that room."[8]

That is memorable reporting by a veteran diplomat, and it shows Kay's lifelong and genuine intellectual curiosity. She read serious books, from Keynes to Koestler, and asked incisive questions. Recall that as a very young lady in Coblenz she recommended Keynes's *Economic Consequences of the Peace* (1919) to her mother. But direct contact with intellectual luminaries risks disappointment, as Kay found out when she met H. L. Mencken.

Paul Palmer arranged for Kay to meet Mencken for lunch one day in a small Italian restaurant in Baltimore. She was "most anxious to meet him." He was, Kay wrote, "a brilliant writer, sharp, biting . . . as a political writer unsurpassed." He also shared her view that Roosevelt was driving the nation to war under pressure from the British and Jews. Alas, at the lunch she learned that sometimes "it is better to admire at a distance than to meet the object of one's admiration." She found Mencken physically unattractive. In addition, he was generally disagreeable, "his language was foul . . . I returned home much saddened."[9] William Manchester, a great admirer, saw similar things in Mencken, as he entitled his biography of the man *Disturber of the Peace.*

The convictions Kay shared with Truman and Lindbergh regarding nonintervention in the war in Europe—before the attack on Pearl Harbor—put her at odds with an old friend from Coblenz days, Sir Neville Butler, then British ambassador. Any British subject, certainly Her Majesty's man in Washington, wanted and expected the unreserved support of the American allies from "the last war" in confronting the Hun once again—most certainly support from an old friend. Kay's friendship with Butler was strained in that period before the United States was at war. (There was no question that U.S. intervention meant siding with Britain.)

The same noninterventionist views, not surprisingly, cemented Truman's friendship with General von Boetticher, the German military attaché in Washington. That relationship made him an excellent source of intelligence for Truman Smith—and Smith an excellent source for Boetticher—right up to the declaration of war by Germany on the United States on 11 December 1941. Certainly Kay's identification with American national interest took precedence over personal relationships, even old and special friendships. Happily, national interest and friendship coincided in the case of Boetticher, a most interesting man.

The friendship went back to Smith's first tour in Germany. Kay told historian Alfred M. Beck that a German officer took offense at something Truman said at a meeting in 1921 and challenged him to a duel. According to Kay, Boetticher smoothed over the misunderstanding, saving embarrassment, injury, or worse. The friendship was renewed when Smith represented Fort Benning and Marshall on the trip to Germany in the summer of 1931 and visited the artillery school commanded by Boetticher. While Smith was a student at the Army War College (1932–33), in Washington, Boetticher was accredited as the German military attaché, a post he held from 1933 to 1941, when Germany and the United States went to war. (Boetticher was ordered to Washington six weeks before Hitler took power in 1933.) Smith was in contact with him as a student in 1933 and as a staff officer from 1939 to 1941.

Boetticher, well informed about the American Civil War and a great admirer of Robert E. Lee, met and corresponded with historian Douglas Southall Freeman. Ambassador William E. Dodd, who was not kindly disposed to the military attachés on his own staff, found Boetticher "interesting in his discussion of American military history" and more knowledgeable about the American Civil War than any "American attaché here [in Berlin] knows about German war history." General Ira Eaker, later commander of the Eighth Air Force and air force chief of staff, remembered taking Boetticher up in an army aircraft for aerial tours of Civil War battlefields. In brief, Boetticher knew and liked America and Americans.[10]

And he thoroughly appreciated the latent strength of the United

States. After a visit to the 1935 Pine Camp, New York, maneuver conducted to test the mobilization plan, he wrote in his report of 2 October 1935 (when the total strength of the U.S. Army was approximately 140,000): "In time of great political tension, the little recognized work of the Army in peacetime will move to the fore. In a surprisingly short time the United States will undergo a very strong mobilization on land and in the air. They will become a united nation, which on the basis of its riches in men and material is capable of all manner of deployments of great strength."[11]

Boetticher was as well connected, informed, and exhaustive in his reporting from Washington as Truman was in Berlin. The similarity is striking. Each understood and had great respect and even affection for the host country even as their reporting prepared their home countries for bloody conflict with the other. Through it all, Smith and Boetticher extended personal courtesies to one another from the 1920s into the 1960s. According to historian Beck, "Boetticher sent home elaborate recommendations on Smith as his long-time friend once Smith had accepted the job [in Berlin] and had arrived in Washington for briefings before going to the German capital."[12]

Boetticher describes the quid pro quo system that governed his work as attaché. He lobbied his government to approve Major Percy Black's request to allow an American military field team to study the war at first hand, pointing out that he had been given almost unlimited access to the American military. Black accompanied German troops into Poland in September 1939 and reported his findings in written reports and in person upon his return to the United States shortly thereafter.

During the period of acrimonious wrangling between isolationists and interventionists, while anti-Nazism was widespread in the country, Boetticher's access to the American military sources continued uninterrupted, even after the German invasion of Poland in 1939, the swift German victories in Western Europe in 1940, and during the Battle of Britain that followed. As Beck wrote:

> For a full year, from August 1940 to August 1941, Boetticher supplied the War Department with detailed reports on German air operations, aircraft strengths, and bomb damage assessments. . . . Luftwaffe cables reached the German attaché in a steady stream. Each of them summarized opera-

> tions of one or two days at a time, giving the targeted cities, individual installations hit, and meteorological conditions affecting the operations. Also important from Boetticher's point of view was the accurate count of German planes lost or damaged and German claims of English planes destroyed. He took the cables to the War Department as he received them, and Truman Smith abstracted them himself, producing a thick file entitled, "Digest of Telegrams Sent by the Air Ministry in Berlin to the German Military Attaché in Washington."[13]

Beck writes that Boetticher was so respected for veracity among American officers that the bundles he carried in and out of the Munitions Building were exempted from security searches. Among them were cables that enabled the U.S. Army General Staff to depict a balanced account of the air war being fought by the RAF and the Luftwaffe. This was particularly useful to the Americans, since Colonel Raymond E. Lee, the American military attaché in London, was considered "a thorough Anglophile" who had lost objectivity and was inclined to pass on only good news from London. After May 19, 1940, Churchill furnished daily war situation dispatches to the White House through the British Embassy, but the British were intent on minimizing losses and damage. The balanced appreciation made possible by weighing the German cables and the British dispatches by the American G-2 enhanced both the reputation of the G-2 on the General Staff and Smith's personal value to Marshall as a key staff officer.[14]

The utility of the Boetticher-Smith friendship to Germany and the United States—and in this case to Britain as well—is illustrated by the manner in which Boetticher floated the proposal of a German-British bombing pause for Christmas in 1940. Berlin authorized the German Embassy in Washington to approach the British via the Americans. The German ambassador had Boetticher bring the German announcement to the General Staff. To Boetticher, that meant to Smith. He called on Smith at home. Finding him out, he left a personal note saying that he had important news for Smith. And he left a white Christmas tree! After confirming the substance of the communication with Boetticher, Smith notified his boss, the G-2, and in due course a bombing pause followed.[15] Well-connected, anonymous contacts serve a useful purpose. (See appendix D.)

Patrician status—with its attendant social connections and friendships that translated to political clout—mattered very much to Kay Smith. They colored her interpretations of events, some significant, some frivolous. For example, she believed that columnist Drew Pearson ceased attacking Smith as a noninterventionist when informed that he and Truman had been in an upper-class boys' camp together. She also notes with satisfaction that Marshall had Smith meet Bernard Baruch, who then went to the president to tell him to stop the attacks on Smith in order to avoid an American Dreyfus case.[16]

References to the Roosevelts consistently bring out Kay's sharp claws. "In spite of various make work programs, WPA, CCC (copied from the Nazi's Labor Corps incidentally)," she wrote, "nothing availed [to get the country out of the depression]." She also refers to "the race problem, which Mrs. Roosevelt was stirring up." Kay apparently believed that it should not have been stirred up, that it was better left undisturbed. But she was just warming up in the 1939–1942 period. She gives full vent to her spleen at some news in April 1945:

> A knock at the door. I opened it. In blew Connie Brown [Constantine Brown of the *Washington Evening Star*]. His eyes popping out of his head, sparking, and his face one large beaming smile. He said never a word but hugged me violently. Rushed to Truman. Embraced him. Threw his arms high in the air in exultation. Whirled around and flew out the door leaving us speechless. Truman and I looked at each other and burst into roars of delighted laughter. We knew only one thing could have given him such fierce delight! The evil man was dead![17]

Kay did not mellow with the passage of time, at least not when the subject was Franklin D. Roosevelt. "Writing in this year of 1974," she says in her memoir, "I know how right we were to hate him so bitterly. There is no ill foreign or domestic that cannot be traced back directly to his policies. Our decline, our degeneracy stems from that man and his power mad, greedy wife who stooped to gather money as the President's wife by advertising over the airwaves for Emerson Radios and Sweetheart Soap. Her children setting an example of drunkenness, divorce and bad manners. The White House reached depths of ill conduct not attained even by Jack Kennedy."[18] Harry Truman is spared because, one presumes, Kay didn't apply her high northeastern standards to the simple folk of America's Midwest. But the Kennedys are added to the Roosevelts as patrician traitors to their class.

Consistent with the style and content of their respective memoirs, Kay covers the 1939–1945 period in 125 personality-driven pages. Fair enough: she was a private person writing for her own pleasure. Truman covers the same period in a dozen pages with considerably less drama, fewer ad hominem attacks, and more focus on the essential elements of information. He began writing his memoirs, he said, to bring the Smith family chronicle up to date, but the reader strongly suspects that he was looking over his shoulder at posterity even then. Despite his early remarks to the contrary, in the twilight of his life Smith consciously added data historians would find useful, knowing that sooner or later they would take note.

The improvements made during his wartime service did not change Smith's mind about G-2 being the "least regarded section of the General Staff." He had been unimpressed with his consultations and briefings there in 1935, before assuming his duties in Berlin. Once on station, he found it necessary to return to Washington at his own expense to confront his boss in person with the accuracy and significance of what he was observing and reporting from Berlin. Despite the expansion and reorganization of G-2—he points out that it expanded every month during the war, was reorganized once or twice each year between 1942 and 1945, and grew to "some two to three thousand" people assigned—its purported increase in efficiency, said Smith, "never seemed to me to increase proportionately to the expansion of personnel."[19] Part of the problem was that his four bosses during the war—Sherman Miles, Raymond E. Lee, George V. Strong, and Clayton Bissell, all major generals about whom he had some kind words, and one of whom (Lee) was a friend—did not succeed "in raising the prestige of the Military Intelligence Division, either within the General Staff or in the army at large to a level equivalent to that of its British or German counterparts."[20]

It was Smith's opinion that none of these individuals gained the confidence of General Marshall. Smith thought Strong was the most capable, "but it also seemed to me that he enjoyed the confidence of the chief of staff least of all." (Smith does not say so, but that is probably why Marshall, had he assumed command in Europe, would have brought Smith along as his key intelligence officer, not one of those G-2 generals.)

Kay was less detached in her analysis. She called Miles "a bit stupid" and "a petty crook."[21]

Smith was one of three officers who presented eight-minute oral briefings of enemy operations in Europe at the chief of staff's daily conferences, which were held, Smith wrote, "whenever Marshall was in Washington." The conference took place at 0800 hours. First came the European intelligence officer briefing, followed by the European Operations Division briefing on current friendly operations. Then both of those officers would leave, and their Pacific counterparts would present their intelligence and operations briefings. The audience usually included the War Department chiefs: Secretary Stimson, Under Secretary John McCloy, and Generals Brehon B. Somervell (supply), John E. Hull (operations), and H. H. Arnold (air). But the briefing was essentially for Marshall's benefit.

Smith shared the presentation of German current intelligence summary with Percy Black and Harvey Smith of the G-2's German Section—for good reason. Smith arose at 0200 hours and spent from 0300 to 0800 examining and digesting the message traffic that had arrived in the Pentagon in the previous twenty-four hours. The challenge, and Smith's great skill, was to reduce a mass of information to an eight-minute presentation. Smith wrote that this included coaching "our soldier-artists [in] preparation of the maps and charts I was to use in my presentation." Smith said that Marshall "had the memory of an elephant." He was a demanding chief who would raise pertinent questions from information provided in earlier briefings.

In the first two war years, Smith also presented summaries of army operations in the Navy Department War Room. "I remember Secretary [Frank] Knox, Under Secretary [James] Forrestal, and Admiral [Ernest] King being present at some of my presentations." Later, and less frequently, he gave similar summaries to the generals of the Air Corps in their new Air War Room.[22] Smith was very high profile to a very small audience.

Smith was surprised in the late summer of 1943 to be ordered by his boss, General Strong, the G-2, to report to Walter Reed for a special physical examination. Upon asking Strong for the reason, Smith was told that Marshall was about to leave for England to command the army being assembled to invade Europe. Marshall had informed Strong that Smith would accompany him as a special intelligence consultant. (See appendix F.)

Smith complied with the order. The medical board stated unequivocally then, in the summer of 1943, as it had in 1939, that Smith was unfit for overseas service. But Marshall held to his decision. He was prepared to have Smith live in an army hospital in England while working in army headquarters, just as he had earlier lived at Walter Reed Hospital while working in the G-2 Section of the General Staff. In the end, of course, General Dwight D. Eisenhower would command those assembling troops, not Marshall. Smith's calm reflection years after this event indicated his great respect for Marshall and his pride in being held in such high regard by the man he admired more than any other. "I have always felt," Smith wrote, "that Marshall's insistence to have me with him in Europe amounted to the greatest single compliment I ever received in my life."[23]

The long hours of intense concentration on matters affecting millions, Smith later confessed, wore him down. In the winter of 1943–1944, the especially heavy workload as the United States anticipated the coming landings in Normandy took its toll. He noted the soaring of his blood sugar and felt that he was not "pulling [his] weight in G-2 or even earning [his] army pay." He made a written request to be returned to retirement in Fairfield. The then G-2, Major General Bissell, said that he did not have the authority to approve or disapprove the request. General Marshall had reserved the right to himself to make all decisions affecting Smith.

Marshall summoned Smith to his office to inform him "in very firm tones," Smith recalled, "that he would not permit me to return to retirement." Marshall then lightened up "in one of his rare and curious smiles." He gave Smith an unlimited sick leave and placed an aircraft at his disposal, to go where he liked—"here again he smiled"—and Kay was to accompany him as his nurse! This is a side of Marshall that few have seen or reported. It is striking that in all that was written and is known about the man, the observation that he was a cold fish is one of the few negative remarks one sees. In this case at least, the cold fish smiled.

Kay and Truman wanted to go to Africa or Mexico, but they were advised that foreign travel would not be permitted. So, Smith wrote, "my wife and I decided on a rest cure in New Mexico. . . .

I fell during this vacation rather in love with the West. I returned again and again in the years after the war."

The rest worked wonders. He felt much better. The pressure felt by the G-2 shop in Washington also diminished as Eisenhower and Mark Clark organized and built up their intelligence staffs in theater. This meant that much of the work that Smith and his colleagues had previously performed in Washington was now being done in Europe. Smith and his colleagues in Washington began to feel that the War Department Intelligence was "just a secondary cog in the huge intelligence transmission belt."[24]

Smith's war was winding down.

A story that surfaced during the presidential campaign of 1944 began the rehabilitation of Smith's public reputation (and Lindbergh's), which would eventually lead to Smith's decision to run in the Republican primary in 1946 for the U.S. Congress.

On 24 October 1944, Representative Albert Engel, a Republican from Michigan, issued a news release accusing the administration of ignoring the 1937 Smith-Lindbergh report from Berlin on Germany's vastly increasing airpower. The intent of the press release was to hurt FDR's bid for a fourth term in the White House, but it had the unintended consequence of beginning the restoration of the reputation of both Smith and Lindbergh after the pillorying of both by the press several years earlier. Chiles Coleman of the United Press picked up the story, and it was printed in the *Chicago Daily Tribune* on 26 October 1944. Among the inaccuracies in the article was the assertion that Smith was "brought home by his commander in chief and placed on the shelf," without reference to Smith's illness. On 2 February 1945, the *Baltimore Sun* fleshed out the story in a piece by Paul W. Ward with the lead "Colonel Smith Is Vindicated." On 5 March 1945 *The Progressive* carried an expanded version of the story, which was picked up by the Associated Press on 12 March of the same year. Smith was once again becoming a familiar name to the reading public, most significantly in his home state. The *Bridgeport Telegram* on 1 October 1946 reported that a Smith speech, "U.S. Air Strength Insufficient," was attended by Lindbergh and Igor Sikorsky.

Lindbergh's image also improved as stories about his wartime service emerged and were published into the 1950s and 1960s. For example, General George C. Kenney, USAF (Retired) described Lindbergh's role in the Pacific in the *Bridgeport Telegram* on 27 August 1957. His lead sentence: "In February 1954, President Eisenhower commissioned Charles Augustus Lindbergh a brigadier general in the United States Air Force."

Smith's name also surfaced in a favorable way in several leaked media reports of wartime incidents. For example, Smith and Percy Black had concluded in the autumn of 1944 that the Germans were still capable of conducting a major counteroffensive in Europe. In the normal course of their duties in G-2, they reported their estimate of enemy capabilities. General Marshall generally made a point not to interfere unnecessarily in field commanders' business. He felt that by that time Eisenhower had the staff and means in theater to make his own estimate and response without meddling from Washington. When the Battle of the Bulge followed, a leak intended to expose a presumed *faux pas* by FDR and civilian leadership was published, but Smith's reputation was enhanced as a consequence. John O'Donnell of the *New York Daily News* wrote an article that made Smith and Black look as though they had predicted Hitler's last great offensive and were ignored. And on 30 January 1945 Smith's sister's hometown newspaper, the *Stamford Advocate,* published a story on the award of the Distinguished Service Medal by General Marshall to Smith in the presence of the secretary of war.

That award, the Silver Star from 1918, his reporting from Berlin in the Hitler time, and his wartime service in G-2 became a permanent part of Smith's vita, to be trotted out whenever his name was printed in newspapers. So at the very time that Smith returned home to Connecticut on sick leave before retirement, his star was rising. His family tree was filled with elected public officials; his grandfather and namesake had been a U.S. senator from Connecticut; the time seemed propitious in 1946 for another country squire, another Truman Smith, to go to Congress.

On 19 January 1945, Smith received an unexpected honor. General Frank McCarthy, General Marshall's aide, told Smith to get to Marshall's office right away and to bring with him anyone he wished. Secretary of War Stimson was about to award him the Distinguished Service Medal. There was no time to get Kay to the ceremony. Marshall was in his flying togs and within the hour was to leave for Yalta in President Roosevelt's plane. General Bissell, Percy Black, and a few friends hastily rounded up went to Marshall's office, where the general read the citation aloud, emphasizing Smith's performance in Berlin and on the War Department Staff. The secretary pinned on the DSM. Smith was enormously pleased and completely surprised. He learned later that Marshall had personally edited and written the citation in his own hand, a fact that Smith treasured.

Some four weeks after Germany's surrender, in June 1945 Smith decided that it was time to retire and was pleased to receive yet another favor from Marshall. Noting that Smith would not get full retirement pay until he had completed thirty years of military service in June 1946, Marshall placed him on extended sick leave in Fairfield until that date. Smith's carefully chosen words in his memoir are unambiguous: "This was the last of many favors I received between 1928 and 1945 from the hands of George Catlett Marshall. He was in my opinion one of America's great soldiers and the most capable chief of staff that ever presided over the War Department General Staff."[25]

Smith concludes his 1964 memoir with a comment that appears self-serving to one unaware that it simply repeats the thrust of what he had been saying about the Bolsheviks and Russia during his tours in Coblenz immediately after the Great War, in Berlin in the early 1920s, again at the end of the 1930s, and during the acrimonious 1939–1941 debates in the United States about American intervention in the European war: "It was already clear to me that, however determined the administration was in April 1945 to wipe out the German army, not too many years would elapse before the threat from Russia would become so serious that we would be forced to resurrect the very army we were now determined to destroy. I therefore came to feel that if I withdrew now from all connection with German affairs and disappeared from Washington, I might someday find myself in a position when once again I could play a constructive role in German military matters."

Smith would not live to read it, but historian Harold C. Deutsch was highly complimentary in his review of the *Handbook on German Military Forces,* a 1945 War Department Technical Manual that was reissued by Louisiana State University Press in 1990. Deutsch agrees with Stephen Ambrose, who wrote the introduction to the new edition. Ambrose is unstinting in his praise. He calls it "the authoritative work on the German Army, 1939–1945," adding, "No other army in history has ever known its enemy so well as the American army knew the German army when the Americans crossed the Rhine River and began their final offensive." He says it is "indis-

Truman Smith and Adolf von Schell, together again in 1963 (with Grafin von Broich in Lieutenant General von Broich's apartment) during the Smiths' visit to Germany. The two men shared a friendship with George C. Marshall, which began in 1930 at Fort Benning. (Courtesy of Katharine Smith Coley and family.)

pensable" for scholars of the war. His assessment of the scholarship and the writing is glowing. He makes a point of describing the "frequent sprightliness" of the prose, saying that such is not generally characteristic of government publications. "I can see no reason to restrain my enthusiasm," he writes. Finally, he gives credit to Truman Smith for the *Handbook* in a manner that takes us full circle, back to Colonel Hunt giving credit to Smith for the Hunt Report on civil affairs during the American occupation of Germany after the Great War.[26]

One finds Smith's hand in several other wartime government

publications. (The three cited here are in the possession of the current author.) The first is *German Military Training,* Special Series no. 3, prepared by the Military Intelligence Service, War Department, 17 September 1942. The informed reader of this publication can picture Smith consulting his reporting from 1935 to 1939, discussing the work with Percy Black, and thinking back to his Fort Benning days with Marshall and Adolf von Schell as he drafted this 106-page publication.

Then there is *German Guns, Brief Notes and Range Tables for Allied Gunners,* SHAEF/16327/2A/GCT, Allied Expeditionary Force, July 1944. It begins, "This book is designed to assist Allied Gunners should they require to fire captured equipment in an emergency." Drawings of the weapons, range tables, conversion tables, and technical information regarding guns and ammunition are provided. Again, one can picture Smith going to his reports and those written by the American Kriegsakademie students who spent time with German units under Smith's supervision from 1935 to 1939.

A third is *Handbook for Unit Commanders (Germany),* published by the Supreme Headquarters of the Allied Expeditionary Force, 15 September 1944. Its purpose was to assist commanders "during the period of the occupation of Germany." Chapter 1 is entitled "Occupation of Germany after World War I." This part of the text must have caused Smith to recall his yearning for Kay, and then their honeymoon on the Rhine as they began their long association with Germany and their deep affection for the people and the country.

Smith did see a 13 June 1945 letter from Bernard M. Baruch to General Marshall. Baruch wrote Marshall that "in the last few days" he had been going over some of Smith's reporting from Berlin, noting how timely his warnings about Germany were and "what little attention we paid to them." Baruch fails to understand "the prejudice" against "a man of character, outstanding ability and with unquestioned devotion to his country." He also wonders why Smith "had not received the promotion he so richly deserves" and hopes he will receive recognition for his great service. Moreover, as America faces the postwar period, Baruch says that Smith "would be a most valuable man." Baruch sent a copy of this letter to Smith.[27]

Smith was retired officially in the grade of lieutenant colonel on

12 June 1946, but an act of Congress granted him the retired rank and pay of a colonel, the highest temporary grade he had during the war. This final retirement came thirty years after he had been sworn into federal service and departed with the 12th New York National Guard regiment from New Jersey to the Rio Grande.

19

The Road to German Rearmament

The move to Greenfield Hill was to begin for me a new life.
—Truman Smith, 1945

I think the present outlook for the world is scarcely better than it was in 1939.
—Truman Smith, letter to Hans Speidel, 8 March 1946

The Smiths' 1945–1946 transition from active duty to retirement—again—was bridged by a year of sick leave at home in Connecticut. General Marshall's appreciation of Truman's decade of outstanding performance of duty in Berlin and Washington accounts for the unusually long leave. Marshall was fully aware that debilitating illness had brought Smith to the brink of exhaustion more than once during the war. He also respected the dignity Smith had demonstrated during the unfair 1939–1941 attacks on his integrity. Perhaps the long sick leave was unspoken compensation for the fact that Marshall was unable to get Smith a star. As a practical matter, Smith would not be entitled to full retirement benefits until he had thirty years of service in 1946. (See appendix J.)

By mid-June 1945, Kay and Truman were settled in their home in Connecticut, this time permanently. During the period of his assignment in G-2 from 1942 to 1945, after Marshall's telephone call brought him back to Washington, the Smiths maintained two households. Kay was grateful to Andrew and Anna Marie Arendt, Germans who had been in the United States for many years. The Arendts took care of the house in Fairfield as well as Tauila, the family dog, while the Smiths were in Washington.[1] Andrew, the gardener and handyman, and Anna, cook and housekeeper, were held in high regard by their employers, not least for making the return to their permanent residence painless. (Enemies might have made political hay at the Smiths' expense had the national origin of their domestic staff been made public during the period of the America First brouhaha, but that did not happen.)

One of Kay's memoir entries made retirement sound like a German fairy tale: "In June we left Washington, our many friends of Army days, our happy Army life. We returned to Fairfield to make a new life, a quiet life, one no longer at the vortex of world affairs, but a happy one revolving around our dear daughter, her work, her marriage, her husband and then her two children, our dear granddaughters."[2] She omits only the coda: And they lived happily ever after.

Good husband, father, and grandfather though he was, Truman was not quite ready to limit his activities to tending roses and playing Papa Bear—and never would be. He plunged into this new phase of life with the intensity that characterized his entire professional life, renewing German friendships and connections, engaging in elective politics, responding to calls for his geopolitical and military expertise, serving on blue ribbon committees, debating on radio, writing about public affairs, and indulging his passion for travel. Ivy League, Regular Army, and northeastern establishment credentials gave him access to elites in and out of government and, hence, to insider information. His well-established roots and personal charm—"breeding" was still in the vocabulary of elites—enhanced his considerable speaking and writing skills. And he was a loyal friend. Fortunately, although he did not write much for publication while in retirement, he was a prolific—and very careful—letter writer.

He never really retired.

Smith's major activities from 1945 to his death in 1970 fell into three broad categories. The first, unsurprisingly, was his continued interest in Germany. Initially, he supported old friends in devastated postwar Germany with basic needs, like food. That effort segued into keeping abreast of evolving political and military events there. In the 1950s, he would play an important role in Germany's rearmament. His second major activity was engagement in domestic politics. Given his family history and his convictions, that was not at all unusual. He was conservative, well connected, fearful of FDR big government becoming permanent, and deeply concerned about America turning leftward. The way he came to a run for Congress illustrates how life is as much a matter of luck as planning. And, as

Old friends meet in an apartment in New York in 1963. From left: Guido Brunner, Paul Thompson, Hans Speidel, and Truman Smith. Speidel and Smith reestablished contact in letters even before World War II ended. Smith acted as midwife and Speidel led the Bundeswehr when Germany rearmed in the mid-1950s. (Courtesy of Katharine Smith Coley and family.)

Kay noted, personal matters, particularly family and travel, gave both of them great pleasure.

As early as April 1945, while the war in Europe was still on, Smith received a letter from German General Dr. Hans Speidel, whom he had known in Berlin and with whom he shared interests in history, the military, and current events on both sides of the Atlantic. Speidel had been implicated in the 20 July 1944 attempt to kill Hitler and was lucky to be alive. He had been arrested by the Gestapo on Himmler's orders on 7 September 1944, and was liberated in 1945 by French troops whose senior commanders knew him from prewar years, when he had served as German assistant military attaché in Paris and again as a senior German officer in Paris during the war. Significantly, the French considered him a good and decent man.

As the victors attempted to sort out "good Germans" from "bad Germans" during the military occupation and de-Nazification period of a Germany then in ruins, for the Americans Speidel was a convenient and happy find. He was a politically clean senior leader, qualified and young enough to lead when Germany rearmed a decade later. Smith's familiarity with German soldiers and his contacts in elite American circles would become particularly relevant as the German Federal Armed Forces—the Bundeswehr—were reestablished and integrated into the North Atlantic Treaty Organization's military defense system. Smith would be perfectly positioned to vet senior German military leadership, including Speidel. Some German friends of his youth were now postwar elder statesmen, and his American military and civilian peers held positions of great influence and responsibility. Speidel's good reputation in France would be particularly important as the French were most reluctant to consider German rearmament in the 1950s.

Smith's exchange of letters with Speidel, beginning in April 1945 and ending only two weeks before Smith's death in 1970, were later copied and sent to Kay Smith along with a handwritten note from Speidel's daughter.[3] The letters, always cordial but at first somewhat at arm's length, as one might expect from gentlemen of status born in the late nineteenth century, became more intimate as time went on: "Dear Speidel" of 1945 became "Dear Hans" by 1950. Almost all of the letters are a mix of matters personal and professional, the sense of which was captured in Smith's first letter to Speidel of 15 April 1945. He inquired about Hitler's order to cross the Caucasus, Speidel's brother, Speidel's opinion of certain German generals, how food packages might be sent to Speidel, Kurt Hesse, Adolf von Schell, Walter Warlimont, Rabe von Pappenheim, "and my other old friends." He concluded with questions of strategy before sending personal greetings from Kay and himself to Speidel and his wife.

In a letter dated 8 March 1946, Smith expressed regret at lives lost, referred to the "war criminal matter," mentioned testimonials he had written for old German friends, and wondered about Hitler's 1942 decision to attack in the direction of Stalingrad rather than Moscow. He referred to "this era of war" being just half over after thirty-two years, sent personal wishes to Mrs. Speidel, and concluded gloomily, "I think the present outlook for the world is scarcely better than it was in 1939."

This letter is representative of the Smith–Speidel correspondence, ranging as it does from the personal to the professional and philosophic. Smith's pessimistic tone is consistent with his long-held views regarding Bolshevism abroad and the increasing power of central government at home. But it ran counter to a generally self-congratulatory and celebratory popular mood among his countrymen in the decade after World War II. Americans had put depression and war behind them. Ahead were unmatched and unprecedented global power, wealth, influence, and a long binge of consumerism. Americans fled the city tenements for Levittowns and suburbia and drove powerful automobiles with baroque tail fins resembling those of a rocket from a Flash Gordon comic strip. Madison Avenue advertising became as famous and ubiquitous as Wall Street finance. Hollywood and Coca-Cola reigned. The United Nations, with headquarters in New York City, would fix international problems and improve on the failed League of Nations. America was ready to let the good times roll; Smith was glum.

He had reservations about the Nuremberg trials of war criminals. He believed that some semblance of justice could and should be served, but he doubted that the climate of Hitler's Germany could be fully comprehended by anyone who had not lived in the Nazi time in Germany. Asked to do so, he made a sworn statement to investigators about his 1935–1939 observations in Germany, doing his best to provide a sense of that time and place, a feel for the dynamism of the period. This statement was neither an indictment nor a testimonial for specific individuals. That would come later, when German rearmament was being considered. Smith was not an apologist for Germany's Hitler period.

Succeeding letters of Smith to Speidel over the years continued to address a mix of practical matters and broad geopolitical ruminations: sending food packages, locating old friends, questioning Nazi World War II strategic decisions, and understanding contemporary political and military issues. Asked to address "Nazi War Planning" to a National War College audience on 23 January 1948, Smith sought Speidel's thoughts in a 5 December 1947 letter, and Speidel complied. Smith thanked Speidel in a letter dated 1 February 1948, saying it was of "enormous" value in preparing the lecture.

Smith changed the title of his presentation typescript to "Nazi Strategy." After addressing the subject, he concluded by returning to a long-held personal concern. To be efficient in war, Smith said, control of all elements of national strength is necessary, "a fully straight-jacketed economy and even iron political controls. . . . Let us be very careful, however, that we, like Hitler, do not step over that undefinable [*sic*] line where the cheerful support of the people changes into mere sullen compliance with orders. If that should happen with us, half of our nation's peculiar strength—its enthusiasm—would vanish in a jiffy. It did in Germany."

He emphasized this point by raising pertinent questions. Is our strategy too far-reaching? Is our strength too low? Is the calculated risk we are taking too great?

His final sentence is seemingly a statement of the obvious: "Strategy and strength *must* under all circumstances be in balance" (emphasis in original). But the recently concluded war had demonstrated that neither of the major disturbers of the peace—Germany and Japan—had had the strength to achieve the objectives they had set for themselves. They had overreached. That defines failed strategy.[4]

Another aspect of national security continued to trouble Smith: that freedom was being risked in the name of security in postwar America. That concern echoes what he had written in his Strategicus articles early in the war, particularly the conclusion of the article addressing the magnitude of the Allied effort that would be necessary to conduct the cross-Channel assault in 1944. Total mobilization of national power for war, he speculated, might be addictive and lead to what Eisenhower later called the military-industrial complex and others called the garrison state. He was concerned with trends that threatened the very essence of the United States. Experience with Bolshevism and Fascism—and, Smith would add, Roosevelt's New Deal—convinced him that powerful central government threatened individual freedom and diminished acceptance of individual responsibility.

In the same 5 December 1947 letter to Speidel, Smith addressed Charles de Gaulle's notion of a federated Europe, sought Speidel's views, and then arranged for Anne Lindbergh to meet and interview Speidel for articles about Europe she was preparing for *Reader's Digest.* These tours of the horizon continued in his correspondence, as does his service as a kind of matchmaker of German and American elites.

Friends were located and food packages were sent. Smith was personally attentive to various food shortages in Germany over time and the specific requirements and preferences of his friends. Once satisfied that their basic needs were being addressed, his attention turned increasingly to contemporary European issues and American politics. In an 8 March 1948 letter to Speidel, Smith wrote, "Nothing but a miracle can now save [President] Truman. [Thomas]

Dewey or [Senator Arthur H.] Vandenberg will be the Republican nominee."

In a letter of 14 April 1948, he asked Speidel for "a military estimate of American and Soviet military potentialities as seen by top notch German General Staff Officers (you are of course one) for the perusal of Senator Taft and Mr. Herbert Hoover." It was apparent to Smith that revival of European civilization required the acceptance of Germany as a partner. Stalin had rejected the Marshall Plan. The line between East and West was drawn. The clear need was to stop punishing Germany and bring her into the fold of the liberal democratic West. But the time was not yet quite ripe for public advocacy of such a policy.

Smith sent several American friends intending to visit Germany to meet Speidel in order to get his insights and a European perspective. Lieutenant General Albert Wedemeyer, then chief of operations of the U.S. Army, in response to Smith's proposal, planned to visit Speidel while in Europe. However, Wedemeyer was sidetracked. A crisis in Berlin arose from the Russian blockade of that city in 1948 and the American response: the airlift to feed Berliners and to keep them warm.

At the onset of the crisis, Smith asked Speidel to estimate Russian strengths and weaknesses. Letters of 19 June 1948 and 3 July 1948 anticipated Wedemeyer's meeting with Speidel, but Wedemeyer's 16 August 1948 letter to Smith expressed regret that Wedemeyer had not been able to meet Smith's German friend, explaining that his "time in Germany had to be devoted *exclusively* to the Berlin airlift" (emphasis in original).

Smith kept abreast of European affairs via Speidel, who sent European newspaper clippings and commentary. Smith reciprocated with news from America. In a 3 September 1948 letter, Smith wrote that he was a delegate to the Republican Connecticut state convention and spent "every other week in Washington in connection with the work of the Hoover Commission. My work is connected with the structure of the National Military Establishment." He added, "Dewey's victory seems about as certain as anything can be." (But Smith was mistaken. Harry Truman was reelected. Smith was not alone in his incorrect prediction. A widely circulated photo showed a grinning Truman on the day after the election holding a newspaper to the camera with a bold upper-case headline announcing, DEWEY WINS!)

In a letter of 21 June 1950, Smith told Speidel that he passed a Speidel memorandum (subject not mentioned, but presumably an appreciation of the political-military situation in Europe) to Wedemeyer, who found it "magnificent." Smith also reported "deeply appreciative notes from [General] Omar Bradley, [General] Joe Collins, Mr. Herbert Hoover and [John] Foster Dulles." In the same letter, Smith called Allen Dulles and Hanson Baldwin, the military correspondent for the *New York Times,* "my friends." Smith continued to regard Germany as an essential part of Europe and a counterweight to the Soviet Union and Speidel as a man trusted by the French.

French suspicion of Germany in the aftermath of the most recent war, and with memories of previous wars, was hardly unexpected. But General Lucius D. Clay put the contemporary situation in clear terms in late 1947: "We must have the courage to proceed quickly with the establishment of a government for western Germany. . . . 42 million Germans in the British and American zones represent today the strongest outpost against Communist penetration that exists anywhere."[5]

The likelihood of America and Russia becoming superpowers had been famously anticipated by Alexis de Tocqueville, who wrote in 1835 that the two would one day "hold in [their] hands the destinies of half the world." An interesting reference to the place of Germany in the Russian-American competition was provided by Adolf Hitler in April 1945: "And it is equally certain that both these Powers will sooner or later find it desirable to seek the support of the sole surviving great nation in Europe, the German people."[6]

That is precisely what Smith was doing. He makes no specific reference to Korea in connection with German rearmament, but others did. Author Robert McGeehan, in his book *The German Rearmament Question,* points out that "the outbreak of the Korean War was the specific stimulus for the decision to strengthen the security of the NATO area by adding German troops. It was widely thought that aggression in the Far East signaled the possibility of a similar Communist move against a militarily feeble Western Europe." American secretary of state Dean Acheson "abruptly stated a unilateral US decision in 1950," but at that time neither the French nor the Germans were ready to accept a remilitarized Federal Republic. As the *New York Times* of 5 November 1950 put it, "The French aversion to arming the Germans appears to be matched only by the German aversion to being rearmed." German newspaper polls reported that

The Federal Republic of Germany, post-1949. (Press and Information Office of the FRG, May 1980.)

67 percent were opposed to participation in Western defense or service in any army.[7]

U.S. Army strength was 554,030 in 1948, down from over 8 million in 1945. NATO obligations accepted by the United States in 1949 required raising and filling the Seventh U.S. Army in Europe. The onset of the Korean War in 1950 required filling the undermanned Eighth U.S. Army in the Far East. From 1951 to 1954 U.S. Army strength was about 1.5 million. Uncle Sam desired help, specifically German help, in Europe. One scholar of German-American military cooperation in the period 1950–1960 put it succinctly: "German rearmament remained the sine qua non of American defense policy in Europe."[8] But another scholar of the period noted that because rearmament was "the primary question in West German domestic politics of the early 1950s . . . it took six years of wearisome negotiations to get the West Germans into uniform [in 1956]."[9]

On 5 May 1955, the Allied Commission abrogated the Occupation Statute. The Western Powers would be represented in Bonn by ambassadors; the Federal Republic of Germany had become a member of the club. On 7 June 1955, the office called Dienststelle Blank became the Ministry of Defense, and Theodore Blank was named defense minister.

The "wearisome" process concluded in 1955, but 1956 was not devoid of humor. Seeking a name for the armed forces—Reichswehr or Wehrmacht, used in the Hitler time, simply wouldn't do—one candidate was "Die Gesamtstreitkraefte der Bundesrepublick Deutschland." But, it was correctly asserted by a clever commentator, "Germany's new allies would never get it right."[10] (It was hard enough that in Germany visitors had to go to the Fremdenverkhersbuero for travel information!) Thankfully, the name "Bundeswehr" came into formal use with the passage of the Soldiers' Law in March 1956. An acceptable name was found, but Germans were unenthusiastic about rearmament. One veteran of the early Bundeswehr said of the experience, "Lepers in the middle ages probably had it better."[11]

Smith was deeply involved in Germany's rearmament. With the passage of time, the Smith-Speidel friendship deepened and came to include the wives and children of the old soldiers. The correspondence described thus far had begun as a private matter. It is not easy to ascertain the relative weight of friendship and compassion, on the one hand, and Smith's geopolitical appreciation, particularly his

Ruth Speidel, wife of German general Hans Speidel, with Kay and Truman Smith in the backyard of their Fairfield, Connecticut, home in 1963. The relationship between the two families became personal and reached into the next generation. (Courtesy of Katharine Smith Coley and family.)

long-standing antipathy regarding Communism and the possibility of it overwhelming Western civilization, on the other. His personal feelings and his professional estimate of the situation coexisted. There is no question that he was favorably disposed to Germany at several levels.

Smith showed Speidel's letters to selected American friends, several still in office, among them Wedemeyer and the army G-2, informing Speidel when he did so. When the United States came to favor a rearmed Germany, Smith's role became official, as is shown in this heavy-handed letter of 18 May 1955 from Major General Robert A. Schow, G-2, to Colonel Smith. Stamped TOP SECRET (since declassified), it began,

> With reference to your forthcoming trip, the following is the mission assigned to you:
>
> 1. Convince the leaders of the new German army that it is to their, our, and the West's interest to play ball with us and

> to recognize the United States as the leader of the Democratic Forces of the world, as well as to subordinate their national interests for the time being.

There is no pretense of equality, no bow to German sovereignty. Germany had few friends. Uncle Sam was issuing marching orders. It is not a diplomatic note; it is a directive.

The rest of the letter continues to address issues with a similar lack of subtlety. The German army should assume responsibility for all German military intelligence. "Dispatch at once to the German Embassy in Washington that German officer who will be named military attaché. Establish an office for German intelligence liaison with the G-2 of the US Army in Germany . . . no top-flight generals should be named whose past history will provoke a Jewish storm of anger in the US . . . get German officers to our schools pronto, in time for the term commencing in the Autumn of 1955." Mentor the U.S. attaché designate in Bonn and introduce him to the right Germans. "For the time being at least, USAREUR [the United States Army, Europe] should be kept out of this operation. It should be sufficient that they be informed of your mission, and instructed to lay off, other than to provide whatever administrative or logistic support that you might require."

Finally, almost as an afterthought, Smith is asked to bring back a German wish list. Language matters. "The mission assigned to you" makes Smith's involvement official.

He made the trip to Germany, did what he was told to do, and corresponded with key German players to determine just what needed to be done to field a German army in 1955. Among those with whom Smith conferred were Speidel, Gerhard Graf von Schwerin, Guenther Blumentritt, and Kurt Hesse. Smith relayed questions from the U.S. General Staff, mostly from G-2, and raised issues that were on his mind. The responses, in German, were provided to the G-2, where they were translated into English. The original and an English translation were then returned to Smith.[12]

Smith also corresponded with other Germans on a purely personal basis to assist them in their physical needs and to share memories of happier times the way old friends do. Adolf von Schell and Rabe von Pappenheim, for example, fit into that category. So does Friedrich von Boetticher. Smith also called Field Marshall Walter von Reichenau, General Colonel Walter Warlimont, and Horst von

Mellenthin "friends." Smith, as the Germans do, makes a sharp distinction between friends and acquaintances.

In a 1 December 1947 letter from American Lieutenant General C. R. Huebner, Smith learned that the former German military attaché in Washington, his old friend von Boetticher, is well in Bielefeld, in the British Zone of Occupation. Von Boetticher's youngest daughter married a British major, and his wife applied through the U.S. Consul in Bremen to emigrate to the United States to make her home with another daughter in Rochester, New York. Huebner writes: "I have asked that he be given some kind of employment in writing in order to keep his mind busy, and he has indicated that he might do so." In a follow-up 4 June 1949 letter, Huebner writes that von Boetticher is well. Clearly German-American friendship was thriving in the von Boetticher family. Several of Smith's American military friends in Germany kept him posted on personal as well as professional issues regarding his German friends.

Professionally relevant was Smith's influence with those whose views and actions mattered in shaping the new German army. In a letter of 23 September 1955, Wedemeyer informed Smith, "I am highly complimented that Hans Speidel would want me to be an adviser on his staff," but he declined, saying, "I do not share your optimism concerning the future of the German Army. Psychologically, the Germans were affected by the program of de-Nazification and de-nationalization of our officials in post-war Germany . . . destroying self-respect and national respect." Eight years later, after his final visit to Germany in 1963, Smith would come to share that view. (See appendix H.)

Although the biggest external obstacle to German rearmament was France, Wedemeyer was correct in noting that a very wide and deep antimilitary attitude had taken root in Germany. Memories of the loss of life and destructiveness of the recent war were fresh, and by the mid-1950s it had been ten years since citizens had seen German soldiers in German streets. Many, perhaps most, Germans were as opposed as their neighbors to the prospect of Germans in uniform in the 1950s. More than a half-century later Germans remain ambivalent about their army. In any event, the issue of acceptance of a new German Army had to be addressed as Germany's rearmament and membership in NATO were being considered.

Antipathy regarding all things martial at the time was captured in a slogan popular among German youth: *Ohne mich.* Loosely translated: "You can have your damned army, but *without me.*" Authorities attempted to counter this widespread attitude by establishing the Federal Forces' School for Leadership from Within (Schule der Bundeswehr fuer Innnere Fuehrung). The idea was to explain to the soldier why he serves; to leaders how citizen soldiers of a democracy are to be led; and to society just what the military is and what it does. One of the components of highly regarded German combat skills in the past was discipline: *Kadaver Gehorsamkeit,* corpse-like obedience by the individual soldier to orders. At its best, *Innere Führung* is education for modern leadership. Skeptics, however, among them some Wehrmacht veterans, considered it public relations claptrap.[13]

The new German army would not be an all-volunteer force like the Reichswehr after World War I. Conscription would put citizens in uniform. The period of service for German conscripts has varied over the years, usually from twelve to eighteen months. But recruitment of longer-service soldiers remained a major problem. *Beruf Soldaten,* regulars, served for a full career up to age fifty-two or sixty, depending on grade. Another category of longer-service military was *Soldaten auf Zeit,* soldiers who served under contract for up to twelve or fifteen years. From the beginning provision was made for those who objected to military service as a matter of conscience. Many German young men refused to serve on that basis then, and in the decades that followed.

Officers and NCOs who had served in the Wehrmacht were carefully screened before acceptance into the Bundeswehr, a process that was as imperfect as de-Nazification in general. That is, rabid Nazis were rather easily identified, as were those who spoke out against Hitler and his followers—if they had survived the war. But there was a very large gray area. And, as has been observed earlier and cannot be overstated, talk about resistance to dictators is cheap. Most people in most places most of the time go along to get along. The process of sorting out the "good Germans" was exceedingly difficult, whether the screening was conducted by Germans or Americans.

American Colonel (later Lieutenant General) John A. Heintges described the selection and training of soldiers for the new German army. He did so with unique insights. He was chief, Army Section, Military Advisory Assistance Group, Germany (MAAG) from 1954 to 1957. Born in Coblenz in 1912, his German infantryman father was killed in action in 1915. Young Heintges arrived in the United States in 1920; his widowed mother married an American infantry officer in 1921; he attended the United States Military Academy at West Point and graduated in 1936. He had an excellent war record in fighting Germans in World War II. After the war he attended Heidelberg University (1946–1947) and taught German at West Point (1947–1951). Of his 1954 assignment he recalled: "I was sent over there to write the German Army Training Plan. I was told by the Chief of Staff and the Secretary of Army that this was the Army's number one project, because we wanted the West German Army established and organized as quickly as possible to take its place in the defense of Western Europe. . . . I had quite a time convincing those old German experts that, by golly, they were not going to get their way this time. They were going to do it our way." Asked how the Germans themselves reacted to the new Bundeswehr, he said, "Initially there was a lot of trouble and opposition."[14]

In response to a specific expression of concern by the U.S. Army chief of staff about recruitment of German soldiers, Heintges raised that issue with Kurt Bransteller, a former Wehrmacht major general then acting as a senior personnel officer—and a tennis partner of Heintges. Bransteller showed Heintges a building filled with file cabinets, saying that the Bundeswehr had 368,000 volunteers. However, some 30 percent were former Nazis and were therefore not acceptable. Another 14 percent were Wehrmacht veterans too old to serve. That left 56 percent of the volunteers available for consideration. Heintges commented, "Boy, oh boy, were they screened!"[15]

Federal Border Guards, armed mobile police subordinate to the Interior Ministry in Germany (as they were in similar organizations in other European nations), were a source of recruitment of longer-serving or professional officers and NCOs. Anticipating rearmament, the Federal Border Guards more or less stockpiled men who would be the future junior leaders in the Bundeswehr. Clearly, the top military leadership had to be as clean as a whistle: demonstrably not Nazis. The establishment of each of these categories of personnel—and many other issues, such as the question of discipline in a conscript army serving a democracy and the pace at which the total armed forces should be built to 500,000 men, most of them in a twelve-division army—was exhaustively researched and vigorously debated.

Smith was literally in the middle of these discussions. He, his army, and his German colleagues were keenly aware that as the twig is bent, so grows the tree. They knew that what they were doing was consequential. They were shaping Europe for an unknown future. Smith believed he was helping to shape the successor of the kaiser's army, the Reichswehr of the Weimar Republic and Hitler's Wehrmacht. He had known German armies both as a friend and as an enemy. Now he was acting as midwife at the birth of the Bundeswehr.

Some recent scholarship purports that German military leaders duped the United States, whitewashing the sins of the Wehrmacht in World War II. Historians Ronald M. Smelser and Edward J. Davies II write that "the Germans, through a network of former high Wehrmacht officers and Bundeswehr officers who had served in World War II, created in the minds of the American military, then journalists and popular writers, an interpretation of World War II in the East disturbingly similar to that projected by [the Germans]." Imperatives of the Cold War caused the United States to accept a German-sanitized version of what happened on the Eastern Front. The Germans used the U.S. and NATO need for German troops to make a distinction between the "good" soldiers and the "bad" Nazis. In brief, "The Cold War blinded the Americans to crimes committed by the German military." Eisenhower, Ridgway, Adenauer, and others bought into what Smelser and Davies call *The Myth of the Eastern Front.* The whitewash was so effective that, as Smelser and Davies state at the conclusion of their book, "The 'good German' seems to be destined for an eternal life."[16]

Thoughtful observers, dubious about trusting Germany, asked if the leopard could change its spots. But Smith was among those who saw rearmament as a pragmatic solution to a simple geopolitical reality: West Germany was a key part of a NATO bulwark designed to protect European civilization from the Soviets. That is the way he saw Europe in 1918; and that is the way he saw it after World War II. And he doubted that Europe was better off in 1945 than in 1939.

Smith visited Germany for the last time in 1963 and wrote an excellent and comprehensive analysis of what he found there. He also wrote an objective appreciation of the quality of the Bundeswehr, in which he expressed admiration of its material resources but disappointment in Germans' refusal to accept their new army.

20

Politics, Travel, and Writing

> Colonel Smith Is Vindicated.
>
> —Headline, *Baltimore Sun*, 2 February 1945

> I expect to read any day now in the *New York Times* that Mr. Ferdinand Mayer and Col. Truman Smith, prominent Rightists, have contributed to stirring up the hate and violence which played the key role in bringing about the recent assassination of our President.
>
> —Truman Smith, letter to Ferdinand Mayer, December 1963

Smith had some creative notions about the U.S. Army's personnel policies, at least one of which came to fruition in part due to his friendship with Clare Boothe Luce. Both Smiths knew and liked Luce from Berlin and Washington days, and Kay enjoyed telling amusing stories about the attractive woman who would be a journalist-playwright-congresswoman-ambassador in the course of her life. She was also the wife of *Time* magazine publisher Henry Luce. Kay once remarked of her good friend that she had a woman's body and a man's mind, and knew how to use both.

In an 18 September 1944 letter, as a member of Congress serving on its Military Affairs Committee, Luce thanked Smith, who was also her constituent, for "suggestions on making the regular army more effective." She said she awaited a memorandum from him, "and when I get it will draft it into legislation at the earliest possible moment."[1]

Smith had proposed that members of Polish units that had participated in Allied campaigns in the war in Europe should be settled in the United States. Luce's Joint Resolution of the House of Representatives on 19 February 1945 said, in part, that "upon the cessation of hostilities in Europe, with their wives and children, all officers and enlisted men and others who have served with the Polish Armed Forces in French, British and American theatres of war" will be admitted to the United States. Smith wanted to do right by the Polish fighters and their families whose homeland was dominated by the Soviets after the war and who were displaced persons. But, having experienced the drastic reduction in the size of the U.S. Army after World War I from millions to about 140,000 for most of the interwar period, Smith was also concerned with how much his army would be reduced in the aftermath of World War II. The conscription law was allowed to expire but was then renewed when voluntary enlistments were insufficient to man the force. Various plans for universal military service were surfaced and discussed, but none was made law. Smith, in his proposal to Luce, was promoting a kind of foreign legion. His initiative would be modified, but eventually an approximation of what he wanted would be realized.

Five years later, on 2 June 1950, Luce sent a "Dear Truman" letter from the Waldorf-Astoria saying, "Here's a copy of that Bill, you remember, which we introduced in 1945." She signed off, "love to you and Kay, affectionately, Clare." That bill had evolved into a program granting American citizenship to qualified young men—most of them formally identified as displaced persons adrift in a broken postwar Europe—after five years of honorable service in the U.S. Army. Many were from Middle and Eastern Europe and found themselves in Germany after the war for a variety of reasons.[2]

Luce chose not to run for reelection in 1946, when she resumed writing plays. Smith ran for her office, but he was defeated in the Republican primary by John Davis Lodge, who went on to win Connecticut's 4th congressional district seat. Smith and Lodge enjoyed an amicable relationship, and Smith gave both Luce and Representative Lodge credit for pursuing the 1950 displaced persons legislation, the seed for which he had planted in 1944.[3]

Smith's daughter, Kätchen, a Smith graduate of 1943, later worked briefly for Congressman Lodge, which suggests the absence of any lingering resentment from the 1946 primary contest on the part of either man. Kätchen had earlier worked as a reporter for the *Washington Times Herald* and would later work for the United Nations in New York before marrying and settling in Middletown, Connecticut.

Smith, like most Regular Army officers of his vintage, had

Smith with his daughter. Kätchen was a *Washington Times Herald* reporter, then worked for Congressman John Davis Lodge and later for the United Nations. She married Bill Coley, son of Truman's Yale friend Brad Coley, in 1950. Bill and Kätchen raised two daughters, Kitty and Lissy. Bill became a professor of English at Wesleyan University; Kätchen was active in civic affairs. (Courtesy of Katharine Smith Coley and family.)

not spoken out regarding party politics while in uniform, but his private writings and Kay's letters and memoir leave no doubt regarding their political orientation. They were conservatives, very displeased with FDR and Harry Truman and uncomfortable with centrist Republicans.

How Smith came to run for public office in 1946 was outlined earlier. At least two attempts by President Roosevelt's political enemies to undermine FDR's campaign for another term as president worked to Smith's advantage. One was a favorable press release in October 1944 regarding the Smith-Lindbergh Luftwaffe reporting from Berlin before the war. The other was a Smith-Black report of German capability to conduct a counteroffensive in the winter of 1944–1945. The intent was to hurt FDR, but in so doing the writers made Smith, Black, and Lindbergh look good.

Smith took his primary defeat gracefully and continued to support the conservative wing of the Republican Party by speaking and by making monetary contributions to various campaigns. Senator Joseph McCarthy, for one, expressed thanks to Smith "for your financial support" in a signed letter dated 29 November 1952. In addition to his voluminous correspondence with German and American military luminaries, Smith's personal papers include correspondence with H. L. Mencken, Herbert Hoover, Bernard Baruch, Mrs. Douglas MacArthur, and others, comprising a veritable Who's Who in America.

In a letter, followed by a redundant telegram to Smith, both dated 14 May 1948, Herbert Hoover wrote, "You may be aware that I have been appointed chairman of the recently created Commission on Organization of the Executive Branch of the Government . . . in my opinion the most formidable attempt to improve the whole federal executive structure. . . . It would be a great service to the country and a great satisfaction to this commission if you would consent to become a member of this military advisory committee." Of course Smith consented and served. At his core, that's what Truman Smith was about: service to the United States.

The Hoover-Smith relationship became personal. Kay in her memoir referred to frequent dinners at the Waldorf with Hoover, and among Smith's correspondence the former president addressed letters to "My dear Truman" (7 August 1954) and "My dear friend" (8 May 1958).

Smith's exchange of letters with sophisticated, conservative, and retired diplomat Ferdinand Mayer reveals his political bias. The former counselor of the embassy in Berlin, and an eyewitness to the Goering-Lindbergh medal incident (his account was precisely the same as Smith's), was a lifelong friend, trusted confidant, and kindred soul. Friendship permitted the indiscretion found in their private correspondence.

In a 1 May 1957 letter to Smith, Mayer included Eisenhower and "modern Republicanism," along with New Dealers and Fair Dealers, as unfortunates unable to comprehend the constant verities of the human condition. Understanding that condition, they imply, is a birthright of conservatives perched on Mount Olympus, or at least on Mount Washington.

Smith reported in a letter to Mayer of 28 May 1960 that he had attended a lunch in the home of John Davis Lodge at which Lodge informed his guests that he was organizing a list of "Ambassadors for Nixon." Smith suggested to Mayer that he might add his name to that list. But, said Smith, perhaps Mayer preferred Reagan, as Smith did. "In my heart," he wrote, "I prefer Reagan, but am at present supporting Nixon out loud. I do not think that Nixon is the man to save the country. I do think however Nixon has the best chance to be nominated in Miami and the best chance to defeat Humphrey (or possibly though not likely) Kennedy in November. . . . Nixon's delegates would never (except for a handful) shift to Rockefeller—but rather to Reagan."

Smith speculated on 23 October 1961 about the conservative student revolt on campuses, concluding that it was relatively strong at Princeton, Yale, and Williams, but "a big fat zero" at Wesleyan (where his son-in-law, the son of old Yale friend Brad Coley, was a professor specializing in eighteenth-century English literature). The student revolt later in the 1960s would become quite a bit more than a big fat zero—and it was not conservative!

In a letter of 18 December 1963, Mayer refers to "an orgy of emotionalism" following the assassination of President John F. Kennedy. "If I ever had any doubts about it, I am convinced now that so-called liberals need psychoanalysis badly. They are 'sick.' . . . The more I think of it, the more I believe we conservatives should stand on principles rather than on personalities. I am all for [Barry] Goldwater [the Republican candidate in 1964]. . . . Before 1932 it didn't matter particularly whether you were a Democrat or a Republican, but today it matters basically whether you are for socialism or for the American way of life."

Smith turned to a personal matter in a December 1963 letter [day not indicated] to Mayer that indicates the Smiths' comfortable financial status. He informed Mayer that Kay sold a painting that had been "discarded" in the cellar for eighteen years, since the death of her mother. "She nearly suffered a coronary during the [auction] proceedings but recovered when it brought $14,000." (The starting salary of a high school teacher in Connecticut at the time was about $5,000 a year.)

In the same letter, Smith wrote, "I expect to read any day now in the *New York Times* that Mr. Ferdinand Mayer and Col. Truman Smith, prominent Rightists, have contributed to stirring up the hate and violence which played the key role in bringing about the recent assassination of our President." (Smith and Mayer in their letters were routinely critical of the *Times* and the *Washington Post*.) Smith concluded, "The Democratic dominated board of aldermen of Milford [Connecticut] has requested President Johnson to rename Long Island Sound Kennedy Sound. It is reported that the action of the board was in compliance with a request of the widow." One may safely assume that Truman and Mayer would be pleased that the waters of Long Island Sound—not Kennedy Sound—continue to wash the shores of Smith's beloved Connecticut to this day.

Shortly before the assassination of President John F. Kennedy, Smith made his last trip to Germany. Though he originally intended the trip to be entirely personal, he apparently could not resist the impulse once more to survey and analyze contemporary Germany. His observations were a lucid estimate of Germany's much-diminished place among nations. That estimate was followed by a careful evaluation of the military worth of the Bundeswehr, an estimate that he shared with trusted friends and several officials in high places.

But before turning to Smith's valedictory trip to Germany, it bears mentioning that both Smiths were inveterate travelers, constantly curious about the human condition, and always prepared for new adventures in faraway places with strange-sounding names. And they left a paper trail of their adventures in the form of memoir entries and letters, some of which were later published.

Their discovery of New Mexico was a consequence of Truman's poor health. Near exhaustion in the winter of 1943–1944, when he felt that he "couldn't pull his weight in G-2" and asked to be retired, he was sent by Marshall, with Kay as his nurse, on unlimited sick leave, with an aircraft at their disposal. Three weeks in New Mexico restored Smith's morale, and probably his health. And there was a lasting bonus: "I fell during this vacation rather in love with the West," he wrote. "I returned there again and again in the years after the war."[4]

Kay reacted in the same way to her introduction to the American West. She was fascinated by Holy Week ceremonies, which struck her as more medieval Spain than twentieth-century North America. She read the history of the West and wondered at the natural beauty found there. "Thus began the first of our visits to the Land of Enchantment," she wrote. "A great love of this country seized us from which we shall never be free, thank God!" She added that they introduced their daughter, as well as Kätchen's husband and children, "to the glorious land which they love as much as we."[5] One of Kay's

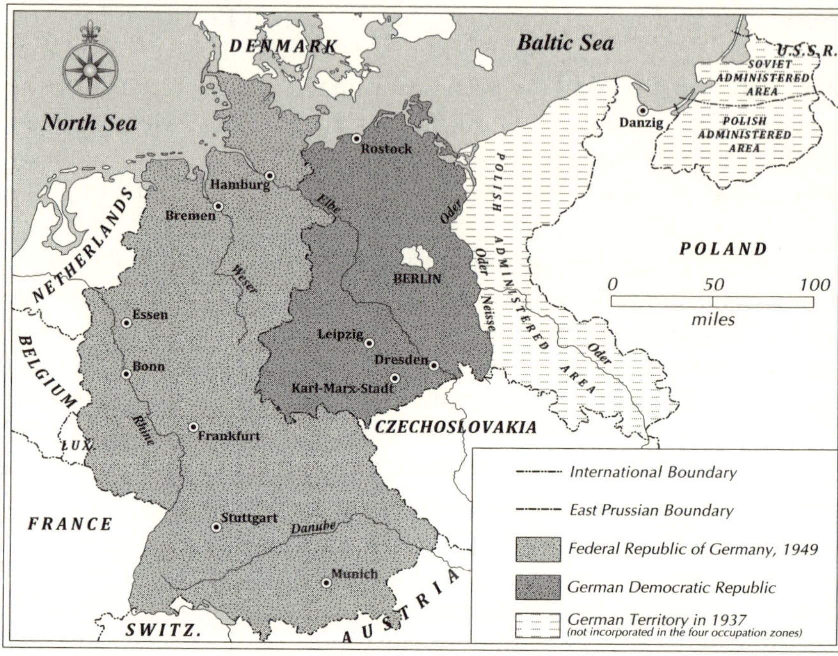

Prewar and postwar Germany. (U.S. Army Handbook for Germany, Department of the Army Pamphlet no. 550-29, June 1960.)

granddaughters settled in Texas and the other in Utah, suggesting that she did not exaggerate the attraction of the Southwest to the Smith–Coley clan.[6]

On a cruise in the Caribbean, Kay and Truman made a friend of Phoebe H. Gilkyson of Pennsylvania, editor of the *Phoenixville Daily Republican*. Precisely how they became acquainted is not revealed—Truman probably impressed the editor, as he had military colleagues and superiors, with his keen observations, logical analysis, and communication skills—but the result was that Gilkyson eventually published three articles written by Truman: "Jamaica's Brown Men Have British Training" (21 July 1961); "A Trained Observer Comments upon Haiti" (24 July 1961); and "Porto Rico Is Showplace of the Caribbean" (26 July 1961).

While loafing on a beach in the Caribbean, Smith had seen and heard two young men speaking German. That stirred his critical juices to compare the British-influenced Jamaica, the American-influenced Puerto Rico, and Haiti, the "Black Republic," independent since 1798. His conclusions are not the point. The point is that he could never not analyze! He brings the same skills to this self-generated tongue-in-cheek task that he brought to his Strategicus articles, adding a dose of humor: how the local bartender makes his Planter's Punches matters more than who is Germany's chancellor or France's president. "Such is the fate of a once intelligent being, gone wrong in the tropics," wrote Smith.[7]

Truman's description of the Smith family vacation in 1962 begins with a note saying that it was based on a letter to Lieutenant General Rabe von Pappenheim. It is a warm and humorous account of an idyllic five-week family holiday at the "Elkhorn" dude ranch, some eighty miles from Bozeman, Montana. Truman, Kay, Kätchen, Bill, Lissy (age ten), and Kitty (age six) enjoyed what "seemed to me more like Paradise than any spot I had ever stayed at before." All agreed that it was "the most relaxing and entertaining vacation we had ever experienced."[8]

The following year, 1963, found Truman and Kay on a five-day visit to the ancient Mayan temple city of Tikal, the centerpiece of a three-week vacation in Guatemala. The Smiths had been helpful in 1955 in establishing the University of Pennsylvania's project to explore, excavate, and restore the temple city. In a nine-page essay, "Jungling as a Winter Sport," Truman, with characteristic wit and interest in the subject at hand, describes "the digs."[9]

There is less humor in Truman's 30 March 1964 account entitled "1964 Latin America Cruise." During this trip, he fell, injuring a knee, which caused him to be immobile; and he got dysentery, "causing my diabetes to kick up a fuss." He also reported some unpleasant observations. "The Canal Zone was in a state of siege," he noted. In Quito, "the poverty all about one was shocking." The sheer numbers of people, many begging, evoked this reaction from Truman: "If I had my way, I would devote every penny of our aid money to establishing birth control clinics." Kay agreed.[10]

On 13 September 1965, Truman and Kay "took off for a three-week jaunt to Spain and Portugal." They had visited neither country before, nor did they speak the languages. However, letters of introduction to the Spanish editor of *Reader's Digest,* as well as to an American businessman in Madrid, resulted in access. As usual, the Smiths stayed at first-class hotels in Spain and Portugal and passed judgment on them and the food. Smith's account of this trip, a piece he called "Not Much Rain in Spain," is the most superficial of his travel writings.[11] It concludes:

> Espana: Si!
> Portugal: Non!

Smith's writings were carefully organized, and his prose was near perfect, even in letters and notes apparently not intended for publication. His Strategicus articles indicate that after his retirement from active duty, he might have chosen to continue writing on military affairs for a newspaper or journal. It is evident that he took time to write well, and that he was proud of his writing. But he didn't publish much and claimed credit for less.

In an appendix to his memoir, "Facts of Life," which he labeled "Writings by Truman Smith Now in His Library at 1235 Mine Hill Road, Fairfield, Connecticut," he lists just seven of his "writings"—five published pieces and two manuscripts. The published five are:

Introduction to the English edition of *Invasion* by Hans Speidel, 1953;
Foreword to *Hitler's Defeat in Russia* by W. Anders of the Free Polish Army, 1953;
"Infamous Record of Soviet Espionage," *Reader's Digest,* August 1960;
"Stalingrad or Bust," *Infantry Journal,* August 1946;
"The German General Staff Abdicates," *Infantry Journal,* January 1946.

The two manuscripts are:

"Air Intelligence Activities," Office of the Military Attaché, American Embassy, Berlin, Germany, August 1935–April 1939. With Special Reference to the Service of Colonel Charles A. Lindbergh, Air Corps (Res.).
"Hitler and the National Socialists," Notebook and Report of Captain Truman Smith, Infantry, U.S. Army, Assistant Military Attaché, Berlin, Germany, describing a visit to Munich from November 16th to November 22nd 1922.

The omission of other of his important published and unpublished writings is puzzling. Smith's initial modest intent for his memoir was simply to add the latest chapter to the Smith family chronicle. It was written for the family. But, upon reflection, he realized that Dame Fortune had placed him in the middle of major historical events that needed to be recorded for scholars. Therefore, he added an "Estimate of Lindbergh's Services to the Office of the Military Attaché, Berlin, July 1936–January 1939" to be absolutely clear that not only was Smith's reporting from Berlin about the Luftwaffe accurate, but the lion's share of credit belonged to Lindbergh. Second, he added his response in a sworn statement to the Nuremberg Trials investigators in a manner intended to capture not only facts but also what it was like to live in Hitler's Germany. But neither "Facts of Life" nor the sworn statement are on his short list of writings. The "Special Reference" to Lindbergh is.

Also, Smith edited the Hunt Report ("Report on Civil Government of the Army") and was the major contributor to it. That published document was resurrected and served as a textbook by the school of military government at Charlottesville, Virginia, during World War II as the United States prepared once again for an occupation of Germany by American forces (see chapter 4). But it is not on his short list.

Four of Smith's Strategicus articles were published in the *Army and Navy Journal,* and several more existed in typescript when he returned to active duty after the telephone call from Marshall in 1941. They are the very models of calm and lucid strategic analysis as his world was turned upside down (see chapter 17). But they did not make it to his list.

When Robert Hessen assembled and edited Truman's "unpublished autobiographical writings" from the Archives of the Hoover Institution in the volume *Berlin Alert,* he included the important documents Smith listed as "manuscripts": the "Air Intelligence Activities," 1935–1939; and the notebook of November 1922. (The notebook entry for 20 November is the one that describes Smith's meeting with Hitler at Georgen Strasse 42, Munich, and summarizes the views Hitler "expounded" to Smith.)

But Hessen also included in *Berlin Alert* three pieces that Smith did not put on his short list of seven writings: "The Facts of Life" (1964); "Conditions in Bavaria" (1922); and "The German Fascisti" (1924). One wonders why Smith failed to list them for posterity at a time when he seemed to be tidying up his affairs. The piece on Bavaria is a brilliant political piece that analyzes evolving events in the south of Germany in the early days of Weimar. The German Fascists article is prescient in projecting realistic possibilities in Germany's future and in comparing Mussolini's movement to similar stirrings in Germany.

One surmises that Smith did not list his three newspaper articles about his vacation travel and adventures in the Caribbean—the pieces that were published in the *Phoenixville Daily Republican* on 21, 24, and 26 July 1961—nor the description of the Montana vacation, because he regarded them as being personal, or perhaps frivolous. But he also published an evaluation of the Bundeswehr in the *Daily Republican* in six articles between 13 April and 19 June 1964. These were decidedly not frivolous, as we shall see in the next chapter. But for some reason Smith chose not to put them on his short list of writings.[12]

21

Retrospective and a Graceful Exit

> Of the many officers I met before and during World War II, few impressed me as being more destined for challenging responsibilities and signal success than Truman Smith.
>
> —A. C. Wedemeyer, 1984

> I would now be surprised if I ever saw Europe again.
>
> —Truman Smith, in letters to Hans Speidel and Rabe von Pappenheim two weeks before he died in 1970

Germany remained a magnet to Truman Smith to the end of his life. He returned with Kay to meet with old friends in September and October 1963, the best time of year to be in that part of the world, as he knew. Then-and-now comparisons were unavoidable as they toured the land they knew so well. Memories abounded: honeymoon on the Rhine; the loss of a child; the Germanies of Weimar and Hitler; close observation of Germany as an enemy during the war; and, in the 1950s, Truman's liaison between American and German leadership as rearmament was contemplated and then carried out in a divided Germany. The 1963 visit would be the last time they saw Germany.

His detailed account of his observations is found in three letters to his daughter, Katchen, in 1963. These are letters in name only. They are actually a comprehensive report in three parts dated 25 September (seven pages), 4 October (eight pages), and 19 October (eight pages), tightly written, carefully edited, single-spaced typescripts. They effectively comprise an estimate that might have been called, had it been official, An Appreciation of the State of the Federal Republic of Germany in 1963. Ferdinand Mayer, that fellow old Germany hand and confidant, upon reading them called the letters an unofficial "white paper." In his letter to Smith dated 7 January 1964, Mayer wrote: "Words fail to tell you how much I appreciated your sending me a copy of the letter to Katchen, and I am at a loss to say how greatly interested I was in its reading."[1]

In another letter Truman catches himself guiltily reverting to his strong suit, analysis. He notes that he went to Munich to enjoy the city and friends there. "I did not expect nor desire to return to my military-political past," he writes. "Yet, that is exactly what happened." He boldly concludes, "Germany is today sort of an American colony." (In his letters Smith's references to "Germany" are always to the Federal Republic, that is, West Germany, as though the German Democratic Republic, East Germany, did not exist.)

In his first letter to Katchen, written from a hotel in Wiesbaden, Smith says he must be careful not to generalize too extensively, "in view of our limited travel. This first letter, therefore, contains mere impressions, not conclusions. The latter will come later, probably in a concluding letter from Munich."

But he does generalize on "a mixture of the eternal and a brand new Germany." He is impressed by the dense automobile traffic and ubiquitous construction. He remarks on a variety of subjects: finance, agriculture, banking, *Gastarbeiter* (guest worker) presence, the free market, socialism, working women. The economic miracle that had taken place in West Germany since about 1955 unleashed the explosion of energy Smith noted in 1963.

In his 4 October letter, written in Heidelberg, he focuses on West Germany's economic recovery, concluding that "all my German friends agree that the German factory worker and farmer have never before possessed such a large share of the national wealth, and that this share tends to increase a bit each year." Given his lifelong opposition to socialism, Smith's impressions of the West German economy since the end of the war required him to square a circle. He declared that the central control of everything by the occupying powers in the desperate immediate postwar years was a necessity. However, he adds, from the financial stabilization of 1949–1950, "the new Germany has turned its back on Socialistic theories and embraced Erhard's 'Free Market' economy." (Ludwig Erhard was Konrad Adenauer's economics minister from 1949 to 1961 and was himself federal chancellor from 1963 to 1966.)

Smith credited co-determination (*Mitbestimmung)* by capital and labor with allowing industry to prosper as labor got what it regarded as its fair share in wages and benefits. Regarding the Welfare State, he said, "in the dreadful half decade which followed the 1945 debacle, it was felt that every individual needed the protection of the government. Now, Bonn is trying desperately to reduce its welfare budget." His view was that in extremity, government could and should act. In normal circumstances, the free market economy should determine outcomes.

As a student of German history, Smith knew that many of the social benefits introduced by the New Deal in the United States in the 1930s under Roosevelt had been granted to Germans in the 1880s under Bismarck and Kaiser Wilhelm I. They were granted because of pressure from the Left, particularly from the SPD, the Social Democratic Party, which grew in strength before the Great War. Assassination attempts on Kaiser Wilhelm I, one severely wounding him, also encouraged political leadership to address the social ills that accompanied industrialization and urbanization. In any event, medical, old age, and unemployment benefits were regarded as a birthright in Germany and in much of Europe long before 1963. Putting the social welfare genie back in the bottle was more easily said than done. Moreover, both laymen and economists can—and do—debate what Smith called "normal circumstances." But Smith's stance in 1963 is consistent with his long-held convictions regarding socialism.

He concluded this letter to Kätchen by flatly stating that America should adopt Erhard's Free Market economy "and send the brigades of University economics professors now running our economy from Washington back to their classrooms. I firmly believe that if the New Frontier would adopt such measures, our unemployment would vanish just as Germany's have, and that, simultaneously, we would witness new factories rising up all over the American landscape."

Smith's third letter, written in Munich, a city he considered "the pleasantest in Germany," began with personal recollections of Erich Ludendorff's funeral, which Smith had attended there in 1935, "and to the dilapidated apartment house at 42 Georgen Street in which I talked politics with Hitler for hours at a time, way back in 1922." He then segued to "some general conclusions as to Germany's strengths and weaknesses eighteen years after her debacle."

Because "German men between thirty and forty five years old lie in war graves scattered from one end of Europe to the other," he noted, the traditional *Kinder, Kirche, Küche* (children, church, kitchen) role of German woman had changed to that of the career girl, often unmarried, who joined the postwar workforce out of need—because of the country's shortage of labor. This transformation took place without much of the fanfare that accompanied the feminist movement in the United States.

Turning to the place of West Germany in the international pecking order, Smith observed that whether Adenauer, Erhard, "or even the Socialist mayor of Berlin, Willi Brandt," were chancellor, Germany was unable to set an independent diplomatic course. The reality in Europe meant that West Germany was identified with the western democracies. To prevent further losses to Russia, to restore German unity, and to snuggle in the bosom of Europa, West Germany was required to dance to the tune played by Washington for the foreseeable future. Moreover, "both the German government and the German people wish it that way."

He took apparent satisfaction in noting that "nothing indicates more clearly the success of German Free Enterprise capitalism than the fact that the once so doctrinaire Marxist German Socialists have recently swallowed it, bag and baggage." Here again, Smith obviously meant *West* Germany. Marxism was alive—and unwell—in *East* Germany as he wrote.

But Smith overstates the case. First, the Social Democratic Party (SPD) would take strong exception to being called Marxist. The evolutionary SPD expected to win at the ballot box, not in revolution on the barricades. As historian Peter Gay put it, "Discussion, vote-getting, parliamentarianism—rather than terrorism, violence, revolution—constitute the arsenal of the democratic Socialist."[2]

Second, "mixed economy" more accurately describes the German economy, then and now. The Germans did not swallow free enterprise capitalism, bag and baggage. Third, although Smith didn't mention it, as he toured Germany political campaigning at the federal level was being conducted there. It resulted in a coalition government formed on 18 October 1963 with the Christian Democratic Union (CDU); its sister party in Bavaria, the Christian Social Union (CSU); and the Free Democratic Party (FDP). That campaign, and the Right-Center government that resulted, with an SPD opposition, no doubt influenced Smith's opinion of contemporary German domestic politics. However, just three years later, in December 1966, a Grand Coalition of the two major parties, the CDU/CSU and the SPD, was formed, with Willi Brandt as Foreign Minister. Then, in 1969, Brandt became federal chancellor in an SPD-FDP coalition government. Much as Truman wanted to bury the Socialists, the SPD was alive and well in Germany as a major party.[3]

Smith closed his three-letter assessment with these words: "I regard the Germany of 1963 as industrially powerful, financially rich and prosperous, socially well adjusted and militarily and diplomatically impotent."

Upon his return to the United States, after taking time to think about what he had observed, Smith could not resist writing a detailed analysis of the German army. Several letters exchanged by Smith and Mayer from 1964 to 1966 addressed Smith's 15 December 1963 document entitled "Estimate of the Combat Value of the German Army." That seven-page single-spaced typescript was sent to friends and to influential Americans. It shows Smith at his best as a military analyst and reporter. The sense of it is contained in the first two paragraphs.

> The German army of 1963 is unworthy to stand comparison with any German army of the past two centuries. It is inferior, in all respects, to the United States Seventh Army now garrisoned in South Germany.
>
> The weakness of the new German army—the Bundesheer [the Federal Army, as distinguished from the Bundeswehr, the Federal Armed Forces]—is due primarily to its psychological isolation from the nation. It is neither respected nor cherished by the Bonn government and parliament, nor by the German people. This has been the case ever since the resurrection of the German armed forces in 1955. The army was then an alien, unassimilated element, and today it is looked upon merely as an auxiliary American force. People begrudge the large amounts of money they must pay for it in taxes and the fact that their sons must serve in it for eighteen months. For the rest, they feel little concern or interest.

Smith summed up his assessment as follows: "Where money can do the job, the Bundesheer is good. Indeed, its equipment in all categories is excellent. However, in the intangibles where money is helpless, such as in creating and inculcating pride in the individual soldier, esprit de corps in units, willingness of all ranks to sacrifice themselves for country and people, the army is poor."

Both Smith and Mayer expressed regret for this unhappy state of affairs, but it was objectively true. In his letters, Mayer admired Smith's analysis, agreed with his conclusions, and told him that "so overwhelming today is the German realization of the power of the United States" that Washington can and must "compel Bonn to undertake army reform." (The use of "compel" by a career diplomat to describe a peacetime relationship between sovereign states strongly indicates Mayer's view that the Cold War was indeed a life-and-death contest with no holds barred.) The two old Germany hands understood just what the West expected of the Bundeswehr: that it be strong enough to stop the Red Army, but not strong enough to invade Luxembourg. The United States emphasized the former, European NATO the latter.[4]

Shifting to American politics in his letter of 1 May 1964, Mayer lamented that for much of the past thirty years "prosperous people have been trying to destroy and to replace [American government] by a patriarchal tyranny called Socialism which will level down everybody to nobody." Mayer informed Smith that he had given "a very large contribution" to Barry Goldwater, the Republican candidate for the presidency. "This is about our last chance, Truman, and I think we had better 'invest' as much in it as we can for the sake of our children and grandchildren if nothing else."

The Smith-Mayer correspondence often returned to comparisons of contemporary Germany to the country they knew in the Hitler years and to shared memories of that time. In his letter of 29 October 1969, a year before Smith's death, Mayer wrote, "And, Truman, what amazing days those were when we worked together in Berlin in the middle 1930s. I often think how fortunate we were to have been in the middle of things there at that particularly crucial time. And, if I may say so, how very fortunate I was to have your so valuable support and friendship in the difficult job given to me by the Department."

Smith knew the end was near when he was released after a stay in the hospital in 1970. He wrote identical letters to two dear German friends, both dated 15 September 1970, differing only in salutations and closing paragraphs, in which he added personal notes to people by name. One letter was to Hans Speidel, the other to Rabe von Pappenheim.

Smith told them that he was out of the hospital and "under Kay's tender nursing care at home." While not getting worse, he reported that he was generally weak and "doubtful that I am recovering. . . . I would now be surprised if I ever saw Europe again." The naval tradition of piping an officer ashore at the end of his service comes to mind: this was clearly Smith's good-bye.

Nevertheless, true to form and like an old fire horse responding to the alarm, he turned quickly from his health to his favorite subject: a tour of the political horizon. He disapproved of newly elected Chancellor Brandt's Ostpolitik, approved of Defense Minister Helmut Schmidt (also SPD and later chancellor), commented on Bundeswehr reforms, and turned to the war in Indochina. He remarked that his army friends told him that General William Westmoreland is "a man of stalwart character, [but] he is far from being the brightest officer in the Army." He touched lightly on contemporary leaders and current issues: General Creighton Abrams, Senator J. William Fulbright, Senator George McGovern, Cambodia, Korea, the race issue in America (particularly "sharp repercussions in our Army"), the press, Germany, Richard M. Nixon. He concluded the Pappenheim letter with "love to Hildegarde" and the letter to Speidel with "love to Ruth."

He died two weeks later, on 3 October 1970.

How does one sum up such a life?

It would be poetic, but facile, to suggst that an aspirational motto—Duty, Honor, Country—fixed Smith's course as he navigated through a life that began at West Point in 1893. Life is too complex to be explained by mottos, however noble, however true.

One begins on firmer ground with what might have been. Some 75 percent of Smith's contemporaries who attended the Army War College in the period 1933–1940 would serve as generals. (That is probably one reason to explain why so many American generals were relieved in combat in the war that came. Making 75 percent of promising lieutenant colonels generals almost overnight was necessary as the army grew from thousands to millions, but it is likely that the army made a lot of mistakes in elevating so many so quickly.) Eisenhower, Patton, Bradley, Halsey, Nimitz, and others were successful and became wartime leaders whose names are still recognized by literate people, if by fewer and fewer with each passing year.

Smith might have been in this first tier but was not. Despite universal respect and admiration from his peers, he is lodged in the second or third tier of military personalities of World War II, either entirely unknown or a footnote to that history. There are many Smiths in our telephone books, many generals among them. If Truman Smith is remembered at all, it is probably for his association with Charles Lindbergh, rather than for his timely and accurate reporting on Germany from Berlin on the eve of war. Still, we know that George Marshall valued Smith's staff work in Washington, so much so that he saw to it that the disabled Smith was kept readily available to him throughout the war years, and in regular contact. That was a point of honor to Smith, and it tells us much about him.

Smith's friend and colleague Ferdinand Mayer properly reflected on how fortunate he and Smith were "to have been in the middle of things there at that particularly crucial time." He believed that service in Berlin in the Hitler period was the high point of both his career and Smith's.

In addition to being in the middle of things at a crucial time and performing well as a brave fighting soldier, a graceful representative of his country, and a military intellectual, Smith is also among the last of a type. He was an American aristocrat comfortable in every way among Europeans of that class, with its style and values not

Rick Eiserman took these three photos in Fairfield in June 1992. The photo on the opposite page shows a portrait of Edmund (center, high) and, immediately below it, a depiction of the combat action in the Philippines that killed him. The above photo includes portraits of Kätchen, Truman, granddaughters, and other family photos, as well as personal awards and citations. (Courtesy of Rick Eiserman.)

unlike those of Truman and Kay's American social circle in Greenport, New York City, and New England. Kay's reaction to social life in Coblenz, Cologne, and Mainz, and later in Berlin, Paris, and London, was to remark almost in passing on the similarity that made it so effortless for her to glide from the Hudson to the Rhine and back to Long Island Sound. Manners, social grace, personal cultivation, and easy conversation in several languages characterized that elite and privileged circle on both sides of the Atlantic.

Truman personified the American version of the Old World nobleman or the ideal English gentleman. The resemblance was more than superficial, although his physical presence and graceful speech did give him a gravitas noted by Americans and Europeans. A less visible but genuine sense of noblesse oblige animated him. He derived fulfillment and professional satisfaction from a life of service and from his marriage. He was blessed in having precisely the temperament and skills that enabled him to serve his country while thoroughly enjoying his work.

He was also blessed in having in Kay a wife, partner, and confidant who could keep up with him, support him, and provide him with a sensitive social antenna. In their time between assignments to Germany, where she played starring roles, by degrees she willingly subordinated herself to duty as she absorbed the army way of life and what was good for the service and her country. Her written reflections on Forts Hamilton and Benning and her pride in Truman's command of infantry soldiers who performed well illustrate how she evolved from being a privileged girl to a loyal partner in service. Perhaps most admirable is the absence of boasting as her life blended accomplished wife, mother, and responsible representative of her country seamlessly. Her recovery from severe injuries while at Fort Benning shows that she was a tough and determined woman.

Reflecting on the Smiths' era, one recalls a scene from the film *La Grande Illusion* (1937) in which the two central characters, both aristocrats, chat easily over a dinner for two; one is a French prisoner of war and guest, the other his German captor and host. It is the time of the Great War. They refer pleasurably to shared prewar memories of mutual aristocratic friends from all parts of Europe by Christian or pet names without regard to nationality—races at Ascot, a birthday party in Paris, a funeral in Berlin, a ball in Vienna. One of the diners observes that that part of Western civilization is gone, ended by the Great War still being fought. The mob, sometimes called the Nation, has taken over. Their aristocratic class henceforth will count for little of substance. The other diner nods in agreement. Confirming this observation, the Nazis banned the showing of this film during their occupation of France.

Similarly, Barbara Tuchman, in the elegant first paragraph of her book *The Guns of August,* captures perfectly the sunset of that world as the nobility and royalty of seventy nations assembled for the funeral of Edward VII on a May morning in 1910. "In scarlet and blue and green and purple, three by three the sovereigns rode through the palace gates, with plumed helmets, gold braid, crimson sashes, and jeweled orders flashing in the sun." In striking contrast, the Europe that emerged eight years later was, in the words historian Raymond Sontag used for the title of his book, *A Broken World.*

Smith was a part of that world that died. He witnessed the Nazis brushing aside the Junkers, the German landed aristocracy and king's friends that had provided the state its military and civilian leaders. He saw the Atlees displacing the Churchills as the great English manor houses increasingly became commercial tourist stops. He feared the trend in his country toward domination by new money and the masses as "the Establishment"—his club—became a term of derision in his country in the last decade of his life. The office of secretary of state, long the preserve of Dean Acheson, John Foster Dulles, and other members of Smith's club, would be occupied by men born in Middle Europe, by women, a black man, and a black woman. America had changed. The American version of aristocracy probably died with Smith sometime around 1970.

Historian Rick Eiserman interviewed Kay Smith on 22 June 1992. He spent most of a day with her in Greenfield Hill, where she had resided since 1945. She was gracious, witty, keenly alert, and still living her patrician lifestyle with a full-time servant. Her sense of humor and capacity for self-deprecation was alive and well. Eiserman sent flowers after the interview. She thanked him and sent a "better" photo than the close-up he had earlier given her. The improvement had to do with both the lovely garden setting of the long-shot photo and, more to the point, the greater distance at which the "better" one was taken—better, Kay impishly implied, to obscure her abundant facial wrinkles. A second interview was planned, but Kay died before Eiserman could return to Connecticut.

Rick Eiserman interviewed Kay in June 1992. He took and sent the indoor photo to her. In return, she sent him a garden photo *(opposite page)* with this tongue-in-cheek comment: "Dear Colonel Eiserman, This may be a better picture than the one you took because it is further away! . . . am looking forward to your next visit." She died before he could return. (Courtesy of Rick Eiserman.)

There is little that is new or surprising in Kay's interview with Eiserman, including her continued amazing vitality; but much was confirmed. Not unexpectedly, she was still protective of Truman's reputation, never missing an opportunity to influence the interviewer with a positive spin that she probably considered truth. Truth has various versions; some versions are influenced by loyalty.

Kay recalled details—for example, how Truman recruited artilleryman Percy Black, with whom he had gotten on so well in Hawaii, to be his assistant in Berlin. She noted that Black did "an excellent job" there and later, but Kay regretted that Mrs. Black neither learned German nor interacted well with others on the diplomatic circuit—a blot in her copybook. That was Kay's impression in the 1930s. It hadn't changed in 1992.

Al Wedemeyer got high marks, and so did Dade, his wife. Truman had told Dade at their first meeting in Berlin, "Young lady, I don't want to hear another word of English out of you as long as you are here. Speak German and talk to everybody you can." Apparently she did just that. She was Old Army and knew vey well that a commander's expression of a wish was an order! Dade's father was Lieutenant General Stanley D. Embick, whom the Smiths had met in Berlin and with whom they socialized in Washington during the war. The Smiths and the Wedemeyers were, of course, lifelong friends.

Discussing Berlin days, interviewer Eiserman alluded to the difficulty in separating politics from military matters. Kay pounced. She made it clear that Truman had nothing to do with the Nazi party. She stated forcefully, "He did not have any social relations—*I would like you to put that down* [emphasis added]—any social relations whatsoever with anything of the party or the people of the party. Our social relations were entirely with the Army and the Air Corps."

She mentions Adolf von Schell in this connection and their relationship at Fort Benning and in Berlin, presumably because he was politically clean. That line of thought somehow caused her to recall that at the Nuremberg party rally in 1935, she and Truman were free to "wander around." That changed in the annual rallies they attended in the following years, when the Nazis more tightly controlled them.

Of course it was impossible to function as an American Embassy official in Nazi Germany without contact with Nazis. But Kay's extreme sensitivity to politics reflected her recollection of the personally trying period when Truman's friendship with Charles Lindbergh—both of whom were labeled Nazis—became painfully public during the acrimonious debates between America First proponents and interventionists.[5]

In her interview, Kay confirmed what we know from Truman's correspondence, that he had vetted German military leaders for the top jobs in the Bundeswehr in the mid-1950s as Germany rearmed. She particularly enjoyed returning to the Rhineland that she knew so well and loved, and the opportunity to visit German friends then and once more in 1963, confirming the central place of Germany in her life and in her husband's.

It is unfortunate that Eiserman did not get back to Kay in time for a promised follow-up interview. But it is time to end her story, and to end this account of Truman Smith's life and times.[6]

Katharine Alling Hollister Smith's obituary appeared in the *Fairfield Citizen* on 29 July 1992. She was ninety-four. Following a brisk summary of her education and life, the obituary states, "She was an activist in political and environmental causes." As recently as 1989, "she led 450,000 people and appeared on television in a pro-choice march on Washington." Somehow it is not surprising to read that at the age of ninety-one, Kay was active and leading.

The notice says that she was survived by her daughter, Katharine T. S. Coley (their Katchen) of Middletown; and granddaughters Katharine L. Coley of Austin, Texas, and Dr. Phyllis M. Coley of Salt Lake City, Utah. A memorial service was conducted at Trinity Episcopal Church, Southport, Connecticut. (See appendix K.)

Truman and Kay Smith lived their lives well. Their firsthand observations and reporting of great events succeed in humanizing and personalizing abstractions as well as old headlines, while filling in some blank spots. Names, dates, and events are put in a human context. Their story began as a romance in correspondence, then captured the feel of fairy-tale Germany on the Rhine and revolutionary Berlin in the aftermath of the Great War. They brought mature judgment to what they reported on Hitler's Germany before the catastrophe of World War II. Caught up in domestic mud-slinging before America's entry into war, Truman emerges with reputation intact to be of use to the man he admires most, George C. Marshall, in war. Engaged in domestic politics as the tide runs against his position and his class, Smith performs his last mission well, serving as a bridge between his country and Germany as Germany rearms. To the very end of his life he was an astute analyst, a lucid writer, a responsible and decent man of integrity who added a noteworthy chapter to his family's distinguished history.

His sense of realism and his appreciation of clear prose make these words from the Book of Common Prayer particularly appropriate.

> The busy world is hushed,
> The fever of life is over,
> And our work done.

He died a friend of Germany and an American patriot.

Appendix A

Losses in Smith's 4th Infantry, October 1918

American time in combat in the Great War was brief, intense, and costly; infantry paid the price—as usual. The following table shows clearly the losses Smith's 4th Infantry incurred in October 1918. (*Source:* 3d Infantry Division, American Battle Monuments Commission, U.S. Government Printing Office, 1944, p. 98.)

Strength of 3d Division[a]							
Units	**May 31**	**June 30**	**July 31**	**Aug. 31**	**Sept. 30**	**Oct. 31**	**Nov. 30**
4th Inf	3,597	3,490	2,499	3,624	3,662	1,843	3,515
7th Inf	3,161	2,843	2,587	3,772	3,672	2,263	3,323
30th Inf	3,361	3,345	3,700	3,561	3,549	2,132	3,217
38th Inf	3,225	3,202	3,649	3,770	3,756	1,879	3,273
7th MG Bn	361	395	384	381	385	306	369
8th MG Bn	719	742	614	707	780	569	673
9th MG Bn	633	709	522	757	763	729	751
Total Inf and MG[b]	**15,137**	**14,785**	**14,003**	**16,614**	**16,615**	**9,766**	**15,166**
10th FA	1,184	1,400	1,553	1,317	1,459	1,397	1,479
18th FA	1,503	1,569	1,648	1,501	1,633	1,535	1,673
76th FA	1,330	1,437	1,487	1,271	1,402	1,358	1,473
Total FA[c]	**4,139**	**4,589**	**4,936**	**4,339**	**4,717**	**4,507**	**4,850**
6th Engrs	1,492	1,593	1,248	1,699	1,688	1,282	1,458
Others	3,395	3,525	3,771	3,884	4,694	4,353	4,013
Total	**24,163**	**24,492**	**23,958**	**26,536**	**27,714**	**19,908**	**25,487**

a. Present with the units of the division; does not include absentees.
b. Includes both infantry brigade headquarters.
c. Includes field artillery brigade headquarters and the 3d Trench-Mortar Battery.

Appendix B

Smith to His Sister on the Death of His Daughter, 1923

The Smiths were living in Germany when their firstborn child, Alling, died at the age of two. Smith sent this radiogram to his sister, Charlotte, with the news. The baby was cremated and the ashes were buried in Connecticut. Kay was determined to have another child and did, in 1924.

RADIOGRAM
WORLD WIDE WIRELESS
RADIO CORPORATION OF AMERICA

Send the following Radiogram "VIA RCA" subject to terms on back hereof, which are hereby agreed to

INY A 9IO AM I4 RADD VIA RCA
BERLIN JUNE 17 1923
CHARLOTTE SMITH
SHIP POINT STAMFORD

ALLING DIED SATURDAY AFTERNOON CREMATING SENDING ASHES HOME

TRUMAN

Appendix C

Marshall on Smith's Berlin Reporting and Dignity

George Marshall sent the following handwritten letter to Smith just prior to the latter's departure for Germany in 1955. Smith had been asked to comment on Lindbergh and reporting on the Luftwaffe from Berlin in the 1930s; he sent a copy to Marshall.

GENERAL G. C. MARSHALL
DODONA MANOR
LEESBURG, VIRGINIA

Saturday May 28–55

Dear Smith:

Your letter of yesterday and the Report reached me at noon today. As you take off by air Thursday I write immediately and read the suggested chapters of the Report. The last is intensely interesting and I think in style, arrangement and English excellent. I have no other comments.

The State Department's apparent withholding of your first Report and Ambassador Kennedy's cable is not understandable. Elegant language, form and protocol always seem more important than simple facts.

Then another thing which, quite properly, you do not touch on, was the bitter resentment and the serious attacks on you because you recited the facts of the German build up of military power. All these things are an inevitable part of democracy and the consequent political reactions.

I'm glad you are going over. Give my best wishes to von Schell and his Lady. I would like to have seen him when I was traveling in Germany but in my position it did not seem wise.

Wish our best to Mrs. Smith and you.

Faithfully yours,
[signature of George C. Marshall]

I am mailing the Report back to you.

Appendix D

The German-British Bombing Pause, Christmas 1940

When Smith received a letter from his friend, German Military Attaché Friedrich von Boetticher, he immediately contacted General Miles, G-2, by phone and followed up with the following letter and attachment. The personal dimension matters in diplomacy, as in all human activities.

December 27, 1940

MEMORANDUM TO GENERAL MILES,
ASSISTANT CHIEF OF STAFF, G-2:

The attached letter was delivered to me at my house on Christmas Eve between the hours of 4:00 and 5:00 P.M., at a time when I was not at home. Accompanying the letter were some flowers.

Upon arrival at my house, I saw the note attached to the flowers and that the envelope was marked to read, "Urgent. Please Open." I recognized at once that the letter contained an informal notification of a German intention and that it was intended by General Von Boetticher that I pass it on immediately to higher authority. I, therefore, telephoned you at once.

Through my knowledge of German methods of doing business, it is my impression that this form of transmission was chosen for the following reasons:

(1) The question of air bombardment, or no bombardment, of English cities during the holidays was a purely Air Force matter. It was not intended that formal notification be given Britain through diplomatic channels. It was intended that the matter should remain one between Air Force and Air Force; therefore, a method of transmission was selected by General Von Boetticher which passed through the Army of the United States and not through the State Department.

(2) It is, furthermore, my definite impression that they did not wish to embody this statement in any formal note of any sort and

that this personal method of conveyance was selected rather than a formal notification to the War Department, probably because they did not wish to go on record in any such formal way.

(3) I spoke to General Von Boetticher yesterday during his visit to the War Department, told him my action in the matter, and he stated that it was exactly what he hoped I would do.

TRUMAN SMITH,
Lieutenant Colonel, Infantry.

TS/laf
Enc.—2:
Original Letter
Translation.

• • •

TRANSLATION

Christmas Eve, 1940.

Dear Friend:
I desire to extend the most cordial Christmas greetings to you, Mrs. Smith, and your daughter, Katharine.

I have just received the information from the Air Ministry in Berlin that the German Air Force will carry out no attacks on English cities from the afternoon of December 24th until the early morning of the 27th; hence, on all three festival days. During this period, retaliatory attacks will only take place in case the Royal Air Force, during this period, itself attacks cities.

In friendship,
F. VON BOETTICHER.

Appendix E

Marshall on Smith's Assessment of the Balkans, 1943

Smith's advice to Marshall went well beyond estimates regarding Germany.

WDCSA/000.24 (20 Oct 43)

20 October 1943

MEMORANDUM FOR GENERAL HANDY:

Colonel Truman Smith in talking to me about the Balkans said that really the most important thing now was to make some effort to compose, at least temporarily, the differences between the various guerrilla bands; that it was probable rather than merely possible, that they would neutralize each other. On the other hand if for a moment at least they would strive together, along with the supplies that probably now can be given them by plane and by boat, great things might be achieved to embarrass the Germans on their Mediterranean front.

I commented that apparently we needed another Lawrence of Arabia and he thought that was exactly the point; some man to go in there in the effort to influence these people for the time being. Offhand I proposed that we might send General Donovan. He has been there before and was supposedly partially responsible at least for the Yugoslavs entering the war against the Germans. You may remember that he left Yugoslavia just as the campaign began. I don't believe he can do us any harm and being a fearless and aggressive character he might do some good.

I spoke of this to Admiral Leahy and he thought it was a fine idea and that we should go ahead and do it. I added that it would certainly have to be coordinated with the British, that we must not send somebody in there without even telling them. He called me up a little while ago to say that the President was in favor of sending Donovan in and that he saw no necessity for informing the British.

I explained again to Admiral Leahy that we could not do it

that way and he agreed. It is now up to me to prepare a message either for Dill from the U.S. Chiefs of Staff to be transmitted to London for quick acquiescence, or for the President to the Prime Minister.

Have some of your bloodhounds take a flyer at this this afternoon.

G.C.M.

• • •

20 October 1943

MEMORANDUM FOR GENERAL MARSHALL:

Attached is a draft of a proposed message from the President to the Prime Minister. The only hope of getting action at once is to go to the top.

The guerrillas are fighting each other in the Balkans. Also, as I understand it, the situation in this area is further complicated by rivalries and competition between our O.S.S., the British S.O.E., and similar Russian agencies. You know that the Russians are extremely touchy on any question affecting the Balkans and feel that they should have the say. It will be difficult enough to get our efforts and those of the British united. It probably will be impossible if we attempt to bring the Russians into the picture.

Another factor is the possibility of a major United States involvement in the Balkans if we take the lead in guerrilla activities there. If General Donovan's activities were successful, it would have an enormous popular appeal and we might be subjected to pressure from our own people to move forces into the Balkans. This is exactly what the Prime Minister has wanted right along.

All the activities in support of the guerrillas are handled from the Middle East. The Chiefs of Staff yesterday took action to get Eisenhower to help. If Donovan goes, both the Middle East and Eisenhower should be instructed to support him.

I suggest that you submit the attached draft to the President through Admiral Leahy. If the President agrees to send it, then furnish a copy to the British Mission here.

THOS. T. HANDY,
Major General,
Assistant Chief of Staff.

To Admiral Leahy:

Attached is a proposed message re Donovan

• • •

20 October 43

Draft of Message
President to Prime Minister

The chaotic condition developing in the Balkans causes me concern. I am sure you are also worried. In both Yugoslavia and Greece the guerrilla forces appear to be engaged largely in fighting each other and not the Germans. If these forces could be united and directed toward a common end they would be very effective. In the present confused condition the only hope I see for immediate favorable action is the presence of a "Lawrence of Arabia." The only man I can think of now who might have a chance of success is Donovan. I do not believe he can do any harm and being a fearless and aggressive character he might do much good. He was there before and is given some credit for the Yugoslavs entering the war against the Germans. If we decide to send him in all agencies of ours now working in the Balkans should be placed under his direction and the resources we put into this effort should be at his disposal. I understand that your General Gubbins is now in the Middle East. Donovan could consult with him en route.

I feel this is an urgent matter. If you are inclined to agree to my idea I will discuss the possibilities with Donovan at once.

Appendix F

Smith on the Situation in Europe, May 1944

On 19 May 1944 Smith wrote this memo to General Clayton Bissell on the strategic situation the Allies faced just prior to D-Day. Smith's estimate reminds us that General Eisenhower had prepared two press releases: one for failure and one for success.

WAR DEPARTMENT
War Department General Staff
Military Intelligence Division G-2
Washington

19 May 1944

MEMORANDUM FOR GENERAL BISSELL:
Subject: Personal estimate of Colonel Truman Smith as to general strategic situation in Europe.

I consider that Germany faces the coming 1944 campaign on the strategic defensive in all areas.

The German High Command intends two main defensive efforts—on the Channel Coast and in Galicia. Elsewhere it will give ground if strongly pressed, especially in Italy and in the vast area from the Baltic to the Pripet Swamps.

France.

I consider the German defenses, both in material and personnel, along the Channel Coast as *very strong*. Our invasion will be met at the beaches and no foot of ground abandoned voluntarily. The Germans will not hesitate to commit the full power of their Air Force to break up or disrupt our initial assault both at the invasion ports and on the beaches. I consider their chances of preventing an impregnable Allied beachhead being established on the Channel Coast as about 45%. If our great air superiority and capability of large-scale air landings did not enter the picture, I would estimate the German chances of a successful defense at better than 70%.

At any rate, the Allied margin of success is uncomfortably

small and the miscarriage of any important detail of the plan would shift the odds of success definitely in the German favor.

In view of the general strategic situation, which is highly unfavorable for Germany, notably in Russia, the invasion should be carried through despite undoubted risks and even the possibility of disaster.

Italy.

Until a decision has been reached both along the Channel and in Galicia, no large reinforcing units, except in dire need, will be sent by Germany into Italy. Kesselring will give ground in Italy as [unreadable]. If pressed by the Allies, Rome will be abandoned and retirement slowly effected to the line Pisa—Rimini.

Balkans.

Germany will seek to maintain her present positions, without transferring to this area any important reserves.

Russia.

If Germany is attacked in strength in Galicia, or in fact anywhere south of the Pripet, she will be forced to accept decisive battle.

If Germany is attacked in strength north of the Pripet, she will fight delaying battles similar to those of 1943 back to the Niemen. If the fighting reaches the latter river, she will be forced to accept decisive battle just as she must do now in Galicia.

A detailed consideration of the German situation and a review of CIC 56/2, 13 May 1944, is attached.

/s/ Truman Smith
TRUMAN SMITH
Colonel, General Staff

4 encls.
Tabs A, B, C, and D.

Appendix G

Marshall Saves a German General

In 1959, upon hearing of the death of George C. Marshall, Smith's colleague and friend Adolf von Schell wrote a brief piece recalling the humanity of the man. The long and bitter war did not diminish affection and respect. (Translated from the original German.)

GENERAL MARSHALL SAVES A GERMAN GENERAL

For over a year I had been transferred from prison camp to prison camp after I had been arrested by the British in 1946. At first, through repeated efforts, I found out that I was accused of murder—murder in Poland. I did not take this matter seriously because I had never been in Poland and I had never had anything to do with Poles. Now, however, in the summer of 1947, it appeared that the British were prepared to deliver me to the Poles inasmuch as they were not able to clarify my case. Now the matter became serious. To fall into the hands of the Poles in those years meant to fall into the hands of those who were still filled with feelings of passion and hatred, and at least meant an uncertain fate, long prison sentences, or perhaps something even worse, whether one was guilty or not.

The Yugoslav guards in the camp gave me a letter from the outside. American friends were aware of my situation and they had written to General Marshall who was then Secretary of State.

I had met him in 1930. I was then a Captain in the German General Staff serving in the United States. I went to the Infantry School at Fort Benning where Lt. Colonel Marshall was the Assistant Commandant. I learned to recognize in him an outstanding General. We spent many hours discussing together military questions and problems. In 1937 I was again in the United States and I saw him for the last time. After I left he sent me his picture.

Now, however, in 1947, ten years had gone by; ten terrible years filled with war and hate. Because General Marshall now occupied one of the most responsible positions in the world, he could perhaps not find time to concern himself with the fate of an imprisoned German general. He had no way of knowing how I had developed. Perhaps I had really become a murderer. Certainly it would have been simpler for him to put this small matter aside and do nothing about it. But this was not General Marshall. Only a short time passed and I was free.

What had happened? This I only found out later when General Marshall himself wrote to me. He had informed the British that he had known me for a long time and he would vouch for me unless there was a concrete case proved against me.

Now General Marshall is dead. The great men and the newspapers of the world praise him as a general and as a statesman. I want the whole world to know this small story. It shows better than long speeches what this man was really like. His noble character and his outstanding thoughtfulness was such that long and terrible years of war could not destroy a personal friendship. You will understand that I am proud to have known such a man. The world may mourn him as a general and as a statesman. I mourn him as a human being and a friend.

Appendix H

Smith on the German Army, 1963

Smith wrote this estimate of the combat value of the German Army, the Bundesheer. He was clearly disappointed that the Bundeswehr did not measure up to the kaiser's army, the Reichswehr, or the Wehrmacht that he knew so well as friend and foe.

December 15, 1963

ESTIMATE OF THE COMBAT VALUE OF THE GERMAN ARMY

The German army of 1963 is unworthy to stand comparison with any German army of the past two centuries. It is inferior, in all respects, to the United States Seventh Army now garrisoned in South Germany.

The weakness of the new German army—the Bundesheer—is due primarily to its psychological isolation from the nation. It is neither respected nor cherished by the Bonn government and parliament, nor by the German people. This has been the case ever since the resurrection of the German armed forces in 1955. The army was then an alien, unassimiliated element, and today it is looked upon merely as an auxiliary American force. People begrudge the large amounts of money they must pay for it in taxes and the fact that their sons must serve in it for eighteen months. For the rest, they feel little concern or interest.

This national indifference to the defense forces, occasionally even assuming tones of hostility, displays itself occasionally in parliament and frequently in the press, television and radio. It has produced profound repercussions in the army which, one soon discovers, is filled with discouraged officers, indifferent, prideless, sloppy soldiers and units without proper discipline or *esprit de corps*. Discipline is well below the level of the American army of that of any other world power.

I have seen little of the new German airforce and nothing whatsoever of the Navy. I have been told, however, by competent American and German observers that these two arms are more efficient and possess better morale than the army.

With few exceptions, active officers are keenly aware of the army's many weaknesses. They complain of lack of understanding and support in cabinet, parliament and press.

Retired officers express, almost unanimously, amazement, shock and distress at the sloppy appearance and lack of discipline of non-commissioned officers, soldiers and units. In some cases these criticisms were of a violent nature. In other instances, retired officers, coming from families which had given officers to the army for generations, expressed the hope that their sons would not seek commissions.

The formation of the Bendesheer began in 1955, just ten years after Germany went down in May, 1945, to catastrophic defeat. From the disaster, the German people emerged, not only with anti-Hitler and anti-Nazi feelings, but with anti-army feelings as well. Living in poverty and hunger in their ruined cities, they blamed the generals for much of their misery. This anti-army feeling was reinforced by skillful anti-militaristic propaganda emanating from the occupying armies, propaganda that was successful and left deep psychological scars which persist today.

Thus, the Bundesheer was born amongst conflicting pressures. NATO desired a stronger, conventional force and the Bonn government, fearing the Soviet and anxious to do what Washington desired, was prepared to comply. On the other hand, the German people feared a rebirth of Prussian mililtarism. The solution adopted was to compromise these conflicting pressures.

An armed force, 500,000 strong, was to be built up over a term of years, but it was to be a "democratic" armed force. It is the interpretation which Germany gave to the term "democratic," which contains the germ of the present army's weakness. Every trace of Prussian militarism, the Bonn parliament felt, needed to be abolished so that the German people and the Western allies would not be alarmed. The ensuing purge took strange forms.

The authority and prestige of the officer corps was reduced deliberately. Both are today far less than that prevailing in other armies. Disciplinary power was taken away from the army and lodged in special civilian courts. Discipline was to be "relaxed," not "Prussian." Soldiers were to be regarded primarily as citizens, secondarily as soldiers. Only a minimum degree of discipline was to be insisted on. Soldiers were to be commanded as little as possible. Their reason was to be appealed to.

This attitude toward discipline constituted a swing from one extreme to another. Whereas "Prussian" discipline erred in severity and rigidity, the existing discipline of the Bundesheer errs in leniency and slackness. Consequently, it does not give the present day soldier pride in his calling. These departures from military custom amounted to throwing overboard the lessons of past and recent military history that discipline, soldierly pride and unit *esprit de corps* are as necessary to the army of a democracy as they are to the army of a king, Fascist dictator or Communist boss. Neither the Russian, French, British, or American armies have discipline of the German "relaxed" sort. In all four of these armies the officers have authority and prestige and the soldiers are proud, patriotic and disciplined.

The new Bundesheer, in 1963, is eight years old. Let us make a detailed survey of its positive achievements, its deficiencies and its prospects.

Strength and Organization

As of autumn, 1963, the army has attained a strength slightly in excess of 225,000 officers and men: 125,000 less than its eventual goal. The defense budget has reached a height of about 15 billion marks.

The army possesses twelve divisions, of which one exists only in embryo. The other eleven are still incomplete, ranging from 80% to 90% of full strength. These eleven divisions have been assigned to NATO. The Bundesheer possesses few corps and army troops, and almost no supply formations. The rate of expansion of the army since 1955 has been very gradual. There seems to be no urge in Bonn to speed up this rate.

Army and Equipment

The Bundesheer is exceptionally well equipped. Tanks, armed personnel carriers, artillery, helicopters and much special equipment is of American manufacture. A few items have come from Britain and France. The automotive equipment and small arms are German. Bonn plans to design and manufacture its own tanks within a few years. There is no intention in Germany to build its own artillery and missiles. Bonn has promised its Western allies that it will not seek to construct atomic bombs. The equipment of the Bundesheer appears to be only slightly inferior to that of the

Russian and American armies, but better than that of the French and English divisions now stationed in Germany.

The Officer Corps

The officer corps of the Bundesheer suffices in number and quality. A small group of able generals have directed the rearmament, and commanded the troop units since 1955. The majority of the veteran officers, which form the bulk of the officer corps and fill the grades from Colonel to Captain, are of average quality, overage for the ranks they now hold. The new army was not able to use many of the ables[t] officers of Hitler's army, a large proportion of whom had by 1955 found lucrative positions in industry; others had become physically unfit or were found to have had Nazi sympathies. The young lieutenants, commissioned since 1955, are idealistic, patriotic and impassioned soldiers. They have received a fine basic military education in the cadet schools. They constitute Germany's best hope for a fine army in the future.

Non-Commissioned Officers and Technicians

These two classes together number 90,000. Their quantity is insufficient, their quality inadequate. Neither the pay given them nor the security promised them after they leave the army is sufficient to attract to the service, or retain therein, the type of men the Bundesheer needs. Since 1955, the army has had to wage an unending and losing war with industry for these indispensible elements of a modern army. The present non-commissioned officers all too often lack the character, education and self-assurance to discipline their soldiers in the usual manner. On occasion, they have resorted to their fists, when conscripts proved recalcitrant, a form of discipline almost unknown in German armies of the past. The "fist discipline" has been frequently aired in the press and has served to make the army in general and the non-commissioned officer corps in particular, unpopular with the German people. The quality of both non-commissioned officers and technicians is well below that prevailing in the British and American armies.

Conscripts

The conscripts in the Bundesheer number about 135,000. These serve eighteen months with the colors, then pass into the reserve. Four times yearly, groups of conscripts enter the army.

Theoretically, almost every young German reaching the age of eighteen is obligated to do military service. In practice, almost everyone who has enough intelligence to enter high school is able to defer service indefinitely. In consequence, the conscripts entering the army come largely from the least intelligent and least educated portion of the German people. This negative method of selecting recruits has had catastrophic effects on the quality of the army. The small number of better-educated conscripts are, perforce, assigned to staffs, radar, communications and artillery formations. The tanks, the mechanized infantry and the pioneers, the true fighting elements of the army, take the leftovers.

There are other unhappy consequences of this failure to conscript the more intelligent and better-educated young men. The level of both the non-commissioned officer corps and of the technicians is lowered, as it is from the ranks of the conscripts that most of these classes are recruited.

The conscripts now being called up for service do not appear to measure up physically with the soldiers of other NATO armies. They were born and brought up in the war and early post-war years, when nourishment was inadequate. The German elementary schools seem not to have made any effort to remedy the physical defects of their pupils. When the Bundesheer receives them, it has no spare time to build up their strength and endurance.

The German soldiers are well behaved by any standard. There is little drunkenness. They commit few serious crimes. Their conduct in France, Britain and America, where a good deal of their training is carried out, has received many commendations.

Technical Training and Maintenance of Equipment

Neither is satisfactory. In no other fields of military training is the inadequacy of the corps of non-commissioned officers and technicians, or the low level of intelligence, the indifference and the lack of discipline of the conscripts more evident. A far higher percentage of valuable equipment is constantly out of order and in the repair shops in the Bundesheer than is the case in the American Seventh Army.

Field Training

The Bundesheer displays its best side in unit combat exercises and large-scale maneuvers. German armies have ever excelled in field training. Also their military schools have always been very good. The Bundesheer places more emphasis on field training than do the French and British. The young German conscripts appear to enjoy this part of their service. The results achieved, however, do not equal those of our Seventh Army, except in the isolated instance of German parachute formations. These latter would be classified as elite units in any army.

Supply

The reserve supplies of the Bundesheer are inadequate in quantity. Few supply formations exist at the present time. American officers do not believe that supply units can be established after the outbreak of war. They also feel that Bonn places inadequate emphasis on the difficult problems of supply in this atomic era.

Summing up, it seems fair to say that where money can do the job, the Bundesheer is good. Indeed, its equipment in all categories is excellent. However, in the intangibles where money is helpless, such as in creating and inculcating pride in the individual soldier, *esprit de corps* in units, willingness of all ranks to sacrifice themselves for country and people, the army is poor.

There are many valid explanations and excuses for the present defects of the Bundesheer. In particular, the attempt of the West German Republic to try to reform its past rigid methods of military discipline and to adopt new ones more suitable for postwar age, is to be commended, even if the results have been harmful. Nevertheless, explanations and excuses do not alter the overall picture. The present Bundesheer in 1963, is weak, and does not add to NATO that strength proportionate to its numbers.

I consider the future outlook for the Bundesheer as bleak. There are dangerous shoals ahead. In the face of the prevalent mood of cabinet, parliament, press, television and radio to find fault and criticize the army, the officer corps is revealing a tendency to withdraw within itself, and to regard its own nation and people as hostile. If this mood continues for long, the Bundesheer is all too apt to become a state within the state, as are the armies of many Latin American and Asian countries. Carried to extremes, this army mood could some day endanger the stability of West German Republic. Nothing can be more dangerous for a democracy than the development of a deep gulf between the army on the one hand and the people and state from which the Army springs, on the other. The seeds of such a development are visible in Germany today.

If the NATO armies are to be made strong enough to check a Soviet onslaught without immediate recourse to atomic weapons, then the serious deficiencies of the numerically strongest army of NATO, the Bundesheer, must be rectified.

The prestige and authority of its officer corps must be restored.

Discipline must be tightened, and court-martial power restored to the army. That level of appearance and discipline striven for should be comparable to that at which prevails in the American Seventh Army.

Higher pay and post-service security must be given non-commissioned officers and technicians.

The conscription laws must be so revised and administrative application of the law so rigidly enforced that the conscripts called to the colors represent a fair cross section of the German people, not merely its least intelligent and educated portion.

I do not believe that Bonn, by itself, can carry out these indispensible reforms. The anti-army feeling in the German people is still too great, and its indifference to problems of the Bundesheer too widespread. There is also deep and instinctive fear in Bonn governmental circles that a tightening of army discipline will awake fears among their allies that Prussian militarism is being reborn.

The impulse to induce or compel Bonn to remedy the defects in its army can come only from the United States.

If the quality of the German army, for one reason or another, cannot be raised to a much higher level than it possesses today, the United States ought to reconsider its whole strategy in Europe. However, since 1955, so many positive and commendable achievements are to the credit of the new German army, that once the decision is made in Bonn to carry out the necessary reforms, results would become apparent almost immediately.

It is immaterial whether Washington's pressure to induce or compel Bonn to undertake army reform comes directly from the State and Defense Departments acting jointly, or indirectly from NATO. Whichever method is adopted, Bonn can be expected to comply, so overwhelming today is the German realization of the power of the United States.

Appendix I

Smith's Letter to Brigitta von Schell, 1967

On hearing of the death of his old friend, Adolf von Schell, in October 1967, Smith wrote the following letter to his widow. The friendship of "Marshall's Men" began in Fort Benning

October 14, 1967

Dear Brigitta;

The black boardered envelope, postmarked "Heidelberg" told me without opening it of the catastrophe which had occurred. I had not dreamed that Adolf would soon depart this life. No word had reached me that he was even in poor health. To be sure, his letter to me, written a month or so ago, and letting me know of the tragic death of his Hanover son was itself a grim, melancholy letter. I took this letter from my file and re-read it. In retrospect, this letter seems to contain a premonition of his own approaching death; that his life was scarcely worthwhile any longer.

I have always looked on Adolf von Schell as one of my closer friends, one of the dozen trusted comrades who stood by me in good and bad times. Ours was not a causal friendship.

I first encountered Adolph at Fort Benning, Georgia. (Whether it was in 1929 or 1930 I can no longer remember.) I think that I was the first American officer to greet him at Benning, and Kay and I were the first to entertain him in our home. Adolf had come to Georgia as one of a group of German American officers who studied for a year in the other nation's military schools. It was, in view of what subsequently occurred, a rather curious arrangement.

For that subsequent happy year, we had numerous joyous days together. We rode many days each week. Sometimes we galloped through the Georgian pinewood, chasing fox and wildcats. Sometimes we rode on paper chases. More often we picniced in large groups. Occasionally we motored off on excursions to neighboring towns. One such trip I remember distinctly. It was to Albany, Georgia to locate and photograph a legendary, huge, 14 foot alligator, who was reported as liking to bask on a sandbank in the local river which I think was the Appalachicola. We were successful. I am sure that you will find the resulting photograph somewhere in one of Adolf's scrapbooks or files. I too had never seen an alligator before outside a zoo. We both were very excited.

From his first week in Fort Benning, Colonel George C. Marshall, later our famous Chief of Staff took to the young German Captain. Marshall both liked and admired Adolf. At this time, Marshall was trying to revolutionize the school system of the American army. He felt that our training methods were ultra-formalized. Adolf, after a month or so at Fort Benning thought so too. Schell had very strong ideas of his own as to how tactical training of young officers ought to be conducted. Marshall liked those ideas. So Marshall asked our War Department in Washington to ask Berlin to leave von Schell at Fort Benning a further year. Both Washington and Berlin acceded to Marshall's request and so, Adolf stayed on with us for another twelve months.

I think this second year at Benning was one of the happiest of Adolf's life. America was no longer strange to him. He felt at home with us. The Marshall–von Shell relationship became still closer. Between them was mutual admiration. In a score of ways, Adolf helped the development of the American Infantry school and assisted Marshall especially in revolutionizing the teaching of tactics.

Meanwhile the Kay, Elena, Adolf and Truman foursome continued. Eventually even Elena took to horseback riding, although I sense, with some fear and reluctance. However, she loved, as everyone did, the riding picnics.

For Kay and I these Benning years loom in our memories as among the happiest of our lives. I suspect that they did also in Adolf's memory. As one grows older, he tries to forget the tragedies of the Hitler years, the savageness of the second world war, and the misery of Germany's post war years. So all of us try to forget the age of the holocaust and tend to relive in our memories those far happier pre-war years.

I shall miss being with Adolf when we come once again to Germany this coming summer. Far too many of my close German friends have gone. A few still remain. Sometimes I wonder whether in my case it is not too tragic to cross the ocean again.

Adolf, my friend gave me an understanding, a loyalty and a devotion which I have encountered only very rarely in my life. I am now of an age when I can no longer find a new friend of Adolf's character and understanding.

Adolf von Schell was of course a great soldier, though an unfortunate one. Better than that, he was a great man.

I thank you, Brigitta for making the last two decades of his life, such happy years for him. Kay and I took to you immediately in 1955, when we met you in Gehrden. We liked you still better when we spent such happy hours with you in your charming Heidelberg apartment.

Far away in America, Kay and I can do little but extend our sympathies. How we regret that we could not honor Adolf on September 19th at the Gehrden ceremony.

May God bless Brigitta, Adolf, Joachin, the grandchildren, and your three daughters, all of whom helped to make Adolf von Schell so happy in his last years.

Appendix J

Smith to Marshall on Smith's Retirement

The following letter, which Smith wrote to George Marshall on the occasion of Smith's retirement from the army, is a reflection of the mutual respect and personal feelings each had for the other. Smith was right about history overlooking Marshall's human touch. Although much admired, he is generally described as a rather cold fish.

WAR DEPARTMENT
OFFICE OF THE CHIEF OF STAFF
MILITARY INTELLIGENCE DIVISION
WASHINGTON, D.C.

28 June 1945

Dear General:

I have been debating several days whether I should try to see you to say goodbye or whether I should attempt to place on paper what is in my heart.

I have decided to write rather than to try to express my thoughts orally, in the belief that, face to face, one never says what one has planned to say.

I leave the Army with deep gratification for its loyalty to me. Often loyalty in the service is one-sided, from subordinate to superior. In my case the reverse has been true.

Rightly or wrongly, I feel that I owe this feeling of loyalty to the Army to you personally.

You stood by me in the very trying days of 1940. Without your loyalty at that time, I do not know where I would be today.

I owe my DSM largely to you.

In recent weeks, I have received further evidence of your loyalty and kindness, which means a great deal to both me and my family.

That your conduct of the military operations has been

superb, no subordinate doubts. It would be foolish or futile for an individual to say anything. The success speaks for itself.

History will probably overlook your "human touch." Some day I shall speak my piece in this regard.

Sincerely,
[signature of Truman Smith]

General George C. Marshall
Chief of Staff
Room 3 E 921
Pentagon Building
Washington 25, D. C.

Appendix K

Obituary, Katharine Alling Hollister Smith

The following obituary appeared in the *Fairfield (Connecticut) Citizen* on 29 July 1992. Kay continued to be very active until she took her last breath.

KATHARINE ALLING HOLLISTER SMITH

Katharine Alling Hollister Smith, 94, died Friday.

The widow of Col. Truman Smith, she lived in Greenfield Hill since the end of World War II. The daughter of G. Trowbridge Hollister and Rosemary Alling Hanks, she grew up in Greenport, N.Y., and New York City, where she graduated from Miss Spence's School. During World War I, she served with the American Red Cross on the troop ships docked in New York, and she was one of the first women to enter Germany at the end of the war. She remained in Germany for five years with her husband while he served first in the Army of Occupation and later as assistant military attaché. When he was appointed military attaché, they returned to Germany in 1935. During the War, they lived in Washington, D.C., where he headed the German section of military intelligence. She was an activist in political and environmental causes. In 1989, she led 450,000 people and appeared on television in a pro-choice march in Washington. She was a former member of the New York Colony Club and the Washington Army and Navy Club, a member of the Fairfield Hunt Club and the Mayflower Society, and a past president of The Garden Club of Fairfield.

She is survived by her daughter, Katharine T. S. Coley of Middletown; her granddaughters, Katharine L. Coley of Austin, Texas, and Dr. Phyllis M. Coley of Salt Lake City, Utah; and a grandson-in-law, Dr. Thomas Kursar of Salt Lake City.

A memorial service will take place August 28 at 11 a.m. at Trinity Episcopal Church, Southport.

Memorial contributions may be made to the Army Distaff Hall, a residence for Army widows, 6200 Oregon Avenue, N.W.,

Washington, D.C. 20015, or to the Garden Club of America, Tropical Botany Scholarship Committee, 598 Madison Avenue, New York, N.Y. 10022.

A Note on Sources

Berlin Alert, Robert Hessen's collection of Truman Smith's writings, is an excellent source. It provides a good selection of Smith's writings throughout his life and is easily accessible to the general reader. Hessen deleted "purely personal" passages from what he intended to be a documentary record. His book is drawn from writings and documents found in the Truman Smith Papers, Hoover Institution Archives, Stanford University, Stanford, California. The twenty-one-page inventory of Smith's papers there is clear and comprehensive. Materials were acquired in 1969, with increments added in 1974, 1978, 1979, 1980, 1981, 1993, and as recently as 2010.

The biographer strives to capture as much of the truth as possible, including some background noise, unguarded commentary, and spontaneous remarks that are honest rather than discreet: in brief, the purely personal. The point is to paint a complete portrait of a man in the context of his time.

In addition to the Truman Smith Papers at the Hoover Institution Archives, research in the archives at the U.S. Army Military History Institute (MHI) at Carlisle Barracks, Pennsylvania, the Yale University Library in New Haven, Connecticut, and the Franklin D. Roosevelt Presidential Library and Museum in Hyde Park, New York, yielded further useful information, as did documents from the National Archives and Records Administration.

I am particularly grateful to fellow historian Rick Eiserman, who collected several boxes of research materials for his planned dissertation on Truman Smith and gave them to me when personal and professional considerations caused him to discontinue the project. He also gave me the audiotape and transcription of his interview with Kay Smith, conducted shortly before she died in 1992.

The foundation of this work is two memoirs: Truman Smith's "The Facts of Life" and Katharine Alling Hollister Smith's "My Life." Truman, a masterful writer, records events clearly and concisely. Kay, also a good writer, is colorful and expansive. Both are fun to read, so much so that the killjoy historian must constantly remind himself that he is reading just one version of the truth. Both memoirs can be found in the Truman Smith Papers, Hoover Institution Archives. "The Facts of Life" is also in MHI, Truman Smith

Papers. "My Life" is also in the Personal Papers of Katharine A. H. Smith, OCMH Collection, MHI. To avoid confusion, references to "My Life" in the endnotes are to the copy in the Truman Smith Papers in the Hoover Institution Archives. The boxes containing Kay's work are as follows:

- Box 4: "My Life, 1904–1914"
- Box 5: "My Life, 1916–1923"
- Box 5: Diary, 1916–1919
- Box 5: "My Life, 1924–1925"
- Box 6: "My Life, August 1935–April 1939"
- Box 6: "My Life, 1939–1946"

Scholars finding the MHI in Carlisle, Pennsylvania, convenient will find the whole of "My Life" in MHI, OCMH Collection, Personal Papers of Katharine A. H. Smith.

Memoirists are tempted to gild the lily, to enhance or protect reputation. Therefore, I have consulted other sources for both context and alternative versions of the truth.

Kay outlived her husband by twenty-two years and did some editing as she considered the disposition of her papers and his after his death in 1970. The biographer must assume that loyalty to the reputation of a respected and beloved life companion influenced her recollection of events in her unpublished memoir and in her selection and editing of Truman's papers.

Both the published version and the unpublished typescript of Truman's "Facts of Life" are stark, as befits reporting style. For example, he describes the eventful 1935–1939 Berlin years in just two pages in *Berlin Alert* (29–31). The entire published version of his "Facts of Life" is just 39 pages long (*Berlin Alert*, 3–42); the typescript is 154 pages, double spaced. Kay, by comparison, took 136 typed pages of her "My Life" to cover a single year, 1935 to 1936, their first year back in Berlin, and 286 pages to cover August 1935 to April 1939.

In 1964, at the age of seventy-one, with attendant intimations of mortality probably influencing him, Truman added several documents and letters that made his memoir, originally intended for the family, more than just another chapter in the Smith family chronicle. He wrote, "Most of these [documents] are of interest solely to historical students of the period. Others are of a technical nature and scarcely likely to interest my family. Yet, in some form or another, a record ought to be left of this important chapter of my life" ("Facts" typescript, 77). Conscious that he had witnessed and acted in events leading to global war, he felt an obligation to flesh out his memoir. The resulting 1964 document was for posterity. Truman did his best to get his facts right. Kay, by contrast, recorded her personal impressions of people and events in an uninhibited manner, sometimes repeating colorful stories that are hearsay—witty, charming, and excellent background material.

The existence of two versions of Smith's memoir can cause confusion regarding pagination, but his inclusion of material from his files in 1964 was deliberate and purposeful. It was important to him to provide a first-person précis of his 1935–1939 Berlin reporting. Even more important to Smith was making historians and biographers fully aware of Charles A. Lindbergh's great contribution to Smith's intelligence collecting and reporting on the Luftwaffe. I refer to the 1964 unpublished version of Truman's memoir as "'Facts' typescript" to distinguish it from simply "Facts," the published version included in Hessen's collection *Berlin Alert*. I cite Hessen's published volume in my narrative wherever possible, because it is more readily available to the reader than the archival materials.

Biographers and historians will be grateful for Smith's unpublished typescript, which includes personal and other details that Smith wanted for the record, reminding us that he trained in history and was a skilled reporter. The 1964 addenda include:

- a list of his writings;
- a list of the books in which he is mentioned or quoted;
- correspondence, not all of which deals with his Berlin days;
- a summary of his 1935–1939 Air Intelligence reporting (which appears in full in published form in *Berlin Alert*); and, most particularly,
- his unpublished sworn statement made in 1945 for the Nuremberg Trials.

Smith called the Nuremberg statement "the most complete account of the official phase of my life in Berlin . . . a sworn statement I prepared in 1945 in Fairfield for the use of the War Crimes Commission." (That sworn statement is contained in the Typescript, 79–91.) He notes that his 1945 sworn statement "was written six to ten years after the events described. It made use however of a large number of contemporary documents still in my Fairfield files. My memory of these events was far fresher in 1945 than it is in 1964" ("Facts" typescript, 78).

He describes as "perhaps the most important [document] of all, 'Air Intelligence Activities, Office of the Military Attaché, Berlin, with special reference to the services of Colonel Charles Lindbergh.'" He wrote, "It was written and bound as a manuscript in 1953. The original is in the Yale University Library. Copies are also in the Army Historical Section, in the Air Force Library, in the library of Colonel Lindbergh and in my own. Only one portion from Air Intelligence Activities has been included in this memoir, and that because of its constant re-publication." (The portion that he includes in the "Facts" typescript is on pages 93–98; for the published version, see *Berlin Alert*, 75–166.)

At the time Smith was asked to make the sworn statement in 1945, he was assigned to G-2, War Department General Staff, in Washington, but was on extended sick leave at his home, 1880 Hillside Avenue, Fairfield, Connecticut. Weakened by diabetes and exhausted, Smith had attempted to retire as the war in Europe wound down in 1945, but George Marshall personally intervened to keep him on active duty. Marshall slept better with Smith in Washington. He also knew that Smith would not be entitled to full retirement benefits until 1946, when he would have thirty years of military service. This was Marshall's practical way of thanking Smith for his valued contributions from 1935 to 1945, for his service while ill in Washington, and for his earlier reporting from Berlin that proved so useful during American mobilization and war with Germany. It was also an unspoken way to compensate Smith for the stars he never got. Smith, for his part, admired Marshall more than any other man.

Smith's service did not end in 1946. Because he had many close connections to highly placed Americans and Germans, he was in a position to serve as the midwife of the Bundeswehr when the Federal Republic of Germany rearmed in the mid-1950s. His correspondence from this period of his life, available at the Hoover Institution, is particularly useful in telling this part of his story.

Finally, I am grateful for the interview granted by Katchen Coley, the daughter of Truman and Kay, and for the exchange of emails with her and her daughters, Phyllis (Lissi) and Katharine (Kitty) Coley—the granddaughters of Truman and Kay—in 2011 and 2012, as I was gathering information and photographs for this book.

Notes

1. Patrician Heritage

1. Henceforth "Facts." Unless indicated otherwise, citations from "Facts" are found in Truman Smith, *Berlin Alert*, ed. Hessen, 3–42. "'Facts' typescript" is a longer, unpublished version of the memoir, with addenda and amendments found in Truman Smith Papers, Box 2, Hoover Institution Archives, Stanford University, Stanford, CA (hereafter cited as TSP, box [no.], HI). See also "A Note on Sources" for more details on the Hoover Institution (not to be confused with the Herbert Hoover Presidential Library, West Branch, Iowa).

2. Truman Smith Papers, Box 1, "Edmund Dickinson Smith, 1857–1900," United States Army Military History Institute, Carlisle Barracks, Carlisle, Pennsylvania (hereafter MHI).

3. Ibid. Smith's typescript includes sources found in the National Archives; the diary of fellow officer William P. Evans; a long eyewitness account in a letter written by Benjamin Foulois, Corporal, G Company, 19th U.S.I., to Truman's mother; an official report to the Adjutant-General by Neil A. Campbell, Second Lieutenant, 19th Infantry, Company G, dated 6 February 1900; General Orders No. 16, 19th Infantry, 8 February 1900, announcing the death of Captain Edmund D. Smith; a letter of sympathy from the acting commander of the 19th to Truman's mother dated 8 February 1900; and an extract from the citation awarding the Medal of Honor to Private Louis Gideon.

4. Ibid. The description is in the Foulois letter to Truman's mother from Cebu. Truman's early writings are in Box 4. For more on Foulois and the early days of military aviation, see also Arnold, *Global Mission*. For context, see also Linn, *The Philippine War, 1899–1902*.

5. "Dear Shant Claus" and "Winter" are in Box 4, Photo Albums, Truman Smith Papers, MHI.

6. "Facts," in *Berlin Alert*, 7–9, summarizes Smith's years at Yale and his early military service.

7. See TSP, Box 15, HI, for the 1916 Mexican border letters, TS to Katharine. Kay wrote a foreword of two pages to put the twelve letters in context.

2. Over There

1. "Facts," in *Berlin Alert*, 10.

2. "My Life," TSP, Box 4, HI. Subsequent citations to "My Life" are

from the copy in TSP, HI. See the Note on Sources for details on boxes containing the various portions of "My Life" as well as Kay's diary, which spans the years 1916–1919.

3. "Facts," in *Berlin Alert*, 11.

4. See Barnett, *The Swordbearers*, Part IV, "Full Circle," for an excellent account of the last phase of the war. See C. S. Forester's novel *The General* for a sense of how close Ludendorff came to breaking through the British lines. Lawrence, *Fighting Soldier*, is a good firsthand account of the short but intense American infantry experience at the very end of the war.

5. TSP, Box 16, HI. I have copies of 124; others may have been expunged or lost. Unless otherwise noted, all quotations from Smith's letters in this chapter are from this source.

6. *History of the Third Division United States Army in the World War for the Period December 1, 1917 to January 1, 1919*, Andernach-on-the-Rhine, 1 February 1919. Copy in MHI. See also American Battle Monuments Commission, *3d Division—Summary of Operations*.

7. American Battle Monuments Commission, *3d Division—Summary of Operations*, 98.

8. See *History of the Third Division United States Army in the World War* and American Battle Monuments Commission, *3d Division—Summary of Operations*.

9. American Battle Monuments Commission, *3d Division—Summary of Operations*, 98. See ibid., 96 for a further breakout of W (wounds not mortal), DW (died of wounds), and K (killed in action). It is interesting to note that there is no Missing category.

10. "Sectors" is the term Smith uses. In American Battle Monuments Commission, *3d Division—Summary of Operations*, 92, the term "Provisional Battalions" is used. The 4th Infantry placed all of its companies into two Provisional Battalions. Truman Smith commanded one of them.

11. "Facts," in *Berlin Alert*, 14.

12. Ibid.

13. Ibid., 15.

14. The memo following up the recommendation for promotion is dated 2 January 1919 and is signed by G. A. Herbst, Colonel, 4th Infantry. It is found with the 5 November 1918 letter Truman wrote to Kay from the hospital.

15. See "Facts" typescript, in TSP, Box 2, HI, for attachments: (1) General Orders no. 22, 8 July 1919, S/Robert L. Howze, Major General, U.S. Army, Commanding; (2) Officer's Record Book, Remarks, 16 April 1920, S/Fred W. Sladen, Colonel, then commanding the 4th Infantry. He had been a brigadier general commanding the 5th Infantry Bri-

gade, 3d Division, during the period for which Smith is cited in glowing words.

16. "Facts," in *Berlin Alert*, 14.

3. Deutschland and Yearning

1. *American Military History*, 403.

2. TSP, Box 16, HI. Unless otherwise indicated, all quotations from Smith's letters in this chapter are from this source.

3. Manchester, *The Last Lion*, 655.

4. It should be noted in passing that Smith's kind words about President Wilson are the only such words about a Democrat found by this diligent and sometimes perspicacious researcher. Smith was a Taft Republican when he became active in politics in 1946.

4. Civil Affairs and Romance on the Rhine

1. *American Military History*, 406–7.

2. The Will Rogers remark is cited in Keith Nelson, *Victors Divided*, 257. Kay Smith's comment is from her diary, 19 September 1919. See TSP, Box 5, HI.

3. "Facts," in *Berlin Alert*, 15, and letter to Kay, 4 May 1919.

4. "Facts," in *Berlin Alert*, 15–16. Smith directs readers to the Hunt Report in the Yale University Library and the National Archives. Another copy is at MHI. See also Irving L. Hunt, "Some Principles of Military Government," a lecture delivered at the Army War College, 28 February 1933, AWC Curricular Archives 1932–1933, G-1 Course, File 391-A-7.

5. Page citations in this chapter, unless otherwise noted, are to Kay's memoir, "My Life," a 418-page typescript covering the period 1916–1946 (TSP, Box 5, HI, contains her diary; Boxes 4, 5, and 6 contain "My Life").

5. Berlin, Munich, and Hitler in Weimar Germany

1. Gerard, *My Four Years in Germany*, 270–71. Gerard had assumed his duties in Berlin in 1913.

2. John F. Votaw, "United States Military Attachés, 1885–1919" (PhD diss., Temple University, 1991), 198.

3. Ibid., 210. For the evolution of MID, see also "The MID and How It Works," Leroy W. Yarborough Papers, Box 2, MHI, which includes notes and publications on the MID's organization, function, and regulations.

4. Edward Davis Papers, 1915–1929, MHI. Davis's typescript memoir, "Military Attaché," is organized by books. Book 9 is "Secret Service in the Netherlands, 1918"; Book 10 is "In Berlin after Armistice, 1919–1921," 425.

5. "My Life," 292.

6. Ibid., 256.

7. It is the usual practice of governments to maintain an office to both assist and keep an eye on foreign military officers accredited to the host country. That office, part of the war or defense department of the host country, is called, for example, the Attaché Referat (in Germany) or the Foreign Liaison Office (in the United States).

8. Ibid., 230.

9. Pages 46–49 in "Facts" typescript and 16–18 in the published "Facts" in *Berlin Alert*. See also "Hitler and the National Socialists," *Berlin Alert*, 43–61, and especially Smith's notebook, 48–61. His notes from the Hitler interview are on 60–61.

10. "Facts," in *Berlin Alert*, 16. This source, rather than the typescript found in MHI, is used here and below because it is more available to readers. Smith rewrote his memoir in 1964, saying that the original was for family. The revision includes material he thought of value to historians and other scholars. Some of the friendships he refers to here were maintained until his death in 1970.

11. Ibid., 16, 17. See also *Global Mission* for references to Foulois and the early days of American military aviation.

12. Smith's "Introductory Remarks, 1960" to "Hitler and the National Socialists" in *Berlin Alert*, 43–47. Three stand-alone parts follow. The first is "Notebook of Captain Truman Smith, Infantry, U.S. Army, Assistant Attaché, Berlin, Germany, November 1922," 48–61; the second is "Conditions in Bavaria: The National Socialist Labor Party Service Report, 1922," 62–66; the third is "The German 'Fascisti,' 1924," 67–74.

13. *Berlin Alert*, 43.

14. Ibid., 48. Murphy was later political advisor to Dwight D. Eisenhower in World War II and author of *Diplomat among Warriors.*

15. Ibid., 46. See also Murphy, *Diplomat among Warriors,* 24–28. Murphy, who was American consular officer in Munich (1921–1925) and well connected to Bavarian officials and the American community there, believed that inflation "did more than any other single factor to make Hitlerism possible" (38).

16. *Berlin Alert,* 60, 46.

17. Ibid., 61.

18. Ibid., 47.

19. Ibid., 66.

20. Their second child, another daughter, was born in New York City and was interviewed by Henry Gole on 26 September 2011.

21. *Berlin Alert*, 67.

22. Ibid..

23. Ibid., 67–68.

24. Ibid., 68.

25. Ibid., 69.

26. Ibid., 70.

27. Ibid., 72.

28. Ibid., 72–73.

29. Ibid., 73–74.

30. Ibid., 74.

31. "Facts," in *Berlin Alert*, 18.

32. "My Life," 294.

33. Ibid., 264.

34. Ibid., 254.

35. Allen, *The Rhineland Occupation*, 192; see also chap. 16, "The Separatist Movement," 186–202.

36. Craig, *Germany, 1866–1945*, 431–32. For a summary of events from 1918 to 1920, see ibid., 396–433. For an account closer in time to the events, see Lutz, *The German Revolution, 1918–1919* (published in 1922.)

37. Quoted in Halperin, *Germany Tried Democracy*, 175.

38. "Facts," 18. Kay and her daughter Kätchen were both named Katharine. Truman and Kay's granddaughter was also named Katharine; she became known as Kitty.

6. Years of Preparation

1. "Facts," in *Berlin Alert*, 18.

2. "My Life," 4. TSP, Box 5, HI.

3. Ibid., 3.

4. Ibid., 6.

5. Ibid., 8.

6. "Facts" typescript, 50–51.

7. "My Life," 14.

8. "Facts," in *Berlin Alert*, 18.

9. Ibid., 19.

10. "My Life," 15.

11. "Facts" typescript, 52–53; "Facts," in *Berlin Alert*, 19.

12. "My Life," 19–20.

13. Ibid., 18.

14. Ibid., 29–31. See also "Facts," in *Berlin Alert*, 19–20. Truman's one-paragraph account omits the yarns about alcohol.

15. "My Life," 48. Of course, in 1929 "straight" did not have quite the meaning later attached to it; nor, for that matter, did "gay."

16. Ibid., 36.

17. "Facts," in *Berlin Alert,* 20.

18. Ibid.

19. Ibid., 21.

7. Marshall's Men

1. *Education of a General, 1880–1939; Ordeal and Hope, 1939–1942; Organizer of Victory, 1943–1945;* and *Statesman, 1945–1959* (New York: Viking Press, 1963–1986). See also Mark Stoler's *George C. Marshall, Soldier-Statesman of the American Century,* a one-volume account of the emergence of the United States as a world power and Marshall's career, which paralleled this rise to power. Stoler's bibliographic essay is particularly comprehensive.

2. Pogue, *Education of a General,* 123.

3. Ibid., citing Lt. Beebe, 127.

4. Ibid., 130.

5. "Facts," in *Berlin Alert,* 21, 22–25; and Pogue, *Education of a General,* 247–267. See also *The Stilwell Papers,* ed. White, for a sampling of Stilwell's direct and often indelicate prose.

6. Pogue, *Education of a General,* 270.

7. Marshall quoted in ibid., 259.

8. Ibid., 248.

9. "My Life," 23.

10. Pogue, *Education of a General,* 260.

11. Ibid., 249, citing a letter from Marshall to Stuart Heintzelman, 4 December 1933.

12. Quoted in ibid., 250. Italics added.

13. Ibid., 251, Marshall letter to Heintzelman, 18 December 1933. Italics added.

14. Ibid. Italics in original.

15. "Facts," in *Berlin Alert,* 22.

16. Hewes, *From Root to McNamara,* chapters 2 and 3, 57–120, describes in detail the Marshall reorganization of the War Department General Staff.

17. "Facts," in *Berlin Alert,* 21.

18. The total strength of the Regular Army in the period 1923–1935 was around 135,000; the commissioned officer strength was around 12,000. See Kreidberg and Henry, *History of Military Mobilization in the United States Army, 1775–1945,* Table 51, 379.

19. "Facts," in *Berlin Alert,* 21.

20. Ibid.

21. Leslie Anders's book *Gentle Knight* is an excellent biography of

Harding. See also James Campbell's *Ghost Mountain Boys* for a description of infantry combat about as nasty as it gets. Both authors contend that Harding's relief from division command by MacArthur was unjustified.

22. Pogue, *Education of a General,* 255. See also the unpublished addenda to Smith's "Facts of Life" in which Smith writes that Pogue furnished him extracts from a transcript of a tape recording made by Marshall on 14 February 1957, in which Marshall makes favorable remarks about Smith's reporting on "the small force [the Reichswehr] that was in itself literally an officer corps and was being trained as if all of them were to be officers." "Facts," typescript, 152–53.

23. "Facts," in *Berlin Alert,* 23.

24. The Leroy W. Yarborough Papers, Box 9, MHI, contains a typescript of the history.

25. See Deutsch, *Hitler and His Generals,* chapter 4, "The Eclipse of Blomberg."

26. "Facts," in *Berlin Alert,* 24.

27. Foreword to Schell, *Battle Leadership.*

28. "My Life," 70.

29. Ibid., 68, 62.

30. Ibid., 68.

31. See *Infantry in Battle,* 2nd ed., 16–19.

32. See Corum, *The Roots of Blitzkrieg.* Corum's description of Reichswehr doctrine is excellent, and how the Reichswehr arrived at its tactical methods is relevant to what Marshall wanted in tactical training.

8. Army War College and Command

1. "Facts," in *Berlin Alert,* 24. See also Pappas, *Prudens Futuri;* and Ball, *Of Responsible Command.*

2. Gole, *The Road to Rainbow,* appendixes G and H, 170–80.

3. Curricula Archives: 395-5B, Course of the AWC, 1932–1933, G-2 #14, 12-20-32, MHI.

4. Curricula Archives: 395-4A, WP Group 4A, 4-14-33, MHI.

5. Curricula Archives: 394-8, G-4 #15, Committee 8, 11-22-32, MHI.

6. Curricula Archives: 393-1, G-3 #6, MHI.

7. Curricula Archives: 391-3, G-1 #10, Committee 3, MHI.

8. Curricula Archives: 389-5B, Analysis #11, Committee 3, reported to class 25 January 1933, MHI. The Finns fought the Soviet Union alone in the Winter War, November 1939 to March 1940. Later, the Finns fought the Soviet Union at the side of the Germans in the Continuation War.

9. Curricula Archives: 398-10A, Analysis 23A, Committee 2A, MHI.

10. Curricula Archives: 392-5A, Course of the AWC, 1932–1933, G-2, MHI. Supplement to No. 1 to Rpt. of Comm. No. 5.

11. Curricula Archives: 397-73, Course at AWC, 1932–1933, "Germany and Hitler," prepared by Major Truman Smith, Infantry, 29 April 1933, MHI.

12. Curricula Archives: 392-5A, Supplement no. 1 to Rpt. of Comm. no. 5.

13. Ibid., 45, 46.

14. See, for example, Gole, *General William E. DePuy,* 33, 151–52, 280. DePuy admired and imitated German suppression tactics in Europe and in Vietnam.

15. See Lunde, *Hitler's Preemptive War,* for many examples of German decisiveness at the tactical, operational, and strategic levels.

16. Curricula Archives: 392-5A, Supplement no. 1 to Rpt. of Comm. no. 5, Q&A.

17. Ibid.

18. Ibid.

19. Curricula Archives: 393-1, G-3 #6, Joint and Army Strategic War Plans (German, French, and British Pre-WWI Planning and Our Present Planning and Plans), reported to the class on 23 September 1932, MHI. The quotations between here and note 20 are all from these reports.

20. Curricula Archives: 397-73, "Germany and Hitler," prepared by Smith, 29 April 1933. Unless otherwise specified, all information and quotations below are from this paper, his ISM.

21. Craig, *Germany, 1866–1945,* 588.

22. "My Life," 85–87.

23. "Facts," in *Berlin Alert,* 25–29.

24. "My Life," 89–130.

25. Ibid., 113.

26. "Facts," in *Berlin Alert,* 26.

27. "My Life," 89.

28. Ibid., 91–92.

29. Ibid., 101, 108–10, 112. Kay's memory betrays her. The CV-41 *Midway* was constructed during the war.

30. Ibid., 121. Colonel Barnett was not "in command of G-2." He headed a section of G-2. BG Alfred T. Smith was G-2 from 3 January 1931 to 2 January 1935. BG Harry E. Knight succeeded him.

31. "Facts," in *Berlin Alert,* 27.

32. "My Life," 129–30.

9. Hitler Takes Power

1. Luvaas, *Dear Miss Em,* 12.

2. Ibid., 30–32. It took the Australians and Americans almost four months to dislodge the Japanese from Buna, New Guinea.

3. "Facts," in *Berlin Alert,* 28.

4. Army War College Curricular Archives 132-18, "An Address by Colonel Jacob W. S. Wuest, A.C., to Officers of the War Department on May 10, 1935 Relative to Conditions in Germany," 1–6, MHI.

5. Craig, *Germany, 1866–1945*, 683–84.

6. "Facts," in *Berlin Alert*, 27–28, 30–32.

7. Gole, *The Road to Rainbow*, 124, and Appendix G for AWC Graduates, 1934–1940, by name, year, and highest rank attained. For 1933, see Directory of U.S. Army War College Graduates, available in paper and CD from alumni@awc.carlisle.army.mil and www.usawcalumassoc.pa.net.

8. Croft quoted in "Facts," in *Berlin Alert*, 27.

9. Langer, *Encyclopedia of World History*, 1125–32, provides a précis of major events in the periods discussed here.

10. Craig, *Germany, 1866–1945*, covers the period of Smith's Berlin tour admirably. See also Craig's *Politics of the Prussian Army*, 342–503; and *War, Politics, and Diplomacy*, especially the three essays on 194–247.

11. Craig, *Germany, 1866–1945*, 568.

10. Hitler's Germany

1. For Smith's "German Fascisti" article, see *Berlin Alert*, 67–74.

2. Quoted in Bullock, *Hitler*, 261.

3. Hitler quoted in Meyer, *The Long Generation*, 244.

4. Craig, *Germany, 1866–1945*, 582.

5. Bullock, *Hitler*, 272.

6. Ibid., 283.

7. Craig, *Germany, 1866–1945*, 589.

8. Ibid., 590.

9. Ibid., 547, quoting the translation by Ralph Manheim.

10. Obersturmführer Georg Zeidler, 30 August 1934, cited in Remak, *The Nazi Years*, 26.

11. Fest, *Hitler*, 411. See Book 5, "Seizure of Power," and Book 6, "The Years of Preparation" (for war), 387–604, for Fest's thorough account of Hitler in the 1930s.

12. Lubrich, *Travels in the Reich, 1933–1945*, 27.

13. Craig, *Germany, 1866–1945*, 674.

14. Bullock, *Hitler*, chapter 6, 312–71. The quotation is on 320.

15. Fest, *Hitler*, 507.

16. Craig, *Germany, 1866–1945*, 649. Chapter 17 is a marvelous précis of cultural decline in Hitler's Germany.

17. Lewin, *Hitler's Mistakes*, 53–54; and Craig, *Germany, 1866–1945*, 661.

18. "Facts," in *Berlin Alert*, 28–29.

19. Craig, *Germany, 1866–1945*, 685.
20. Ibid., 690, citing Andre Beaufre.
21. Ibid., 691.
22. Fest, *Hitler*, 497.
23. Weinberg, *The Foreign Policy of Hitler's Germany: Diplomatic Revolution in Europe, 1933–36*, x.
24. Weinberg, *The Foreign Policy of Hitler's Germany: Starting World War II, 1937–1939*, preface and xi.

11. Kay, Germany, and Ambassador Dodd

1. "My Life, August 1935–April 1939," TSP, Box 6, HI.
2. "My Life," 1.
3. Ibid., 13.
4. See Ahamed, *Lords of Finance*, 481–83.
5. "My Life," 8.
6. Ibid., 83.
7. Ibid., 57. There is no need here or elsewhere to correct Kay's misuse of the genitive case or other small abuses of German grammar, or her English, for that matter.
8. Ibid., 22.
9. Ibid., 23.
10. Ibid., 24.
11. Ibid., 27.
12. Ibid., 24–25.
13. Ibid., 26.
14. Martha Dodd, *Through Embassy Eyes*, 63–65. See also Larson, *In the Garden of the Beasts*. Larson's book focuses on Ambassador Dodd and his daughter Martha in the year beginning July 1933 and ending June 1934, a year before the Smiths began their second tour in Berlin.
15. "My Life," 26.
16. Ibid., 30.
17. Ibid., 32.
18. Ibid., 33.
19. Ibid., 33–34.
20. Ibid., 35.
21. Ibid., 36–37. Johnson (b. 1906) was chairman of the Museum of Modern Art's architecture department, collaborated with Mies van der Rohe on the Seagram Building in New York City, and produced other major architectural works.
22. Ibid., 38.
23. Ibid.
24. Ibid., 37–39.

25. Ibid., 3–4.

26. Ibid., 5.

27. William E. Dodd Jr. and Martha Dodd, eds., *Ambassador Dodd's Diary, 1933–1938,* entry 20 September 1938, 446.

28. "My Life," 2–3. See Larson, *In the Garden of the Beasts,* for more details regarding Martha Dodd.

29. Shirer, *Twentieth-Century Journey,* vol. 2, *The Nightmare Years,* 183–184. Shirer called Martha Dodd "the vivacious young daughter of the American ambassador," without amplification (127).

30. Lubrich, *Travels in the Reich,* 91.

31. See Craig and Gilbert, eds., *The Diplomats, 1919–1939,* vol. 2, *The Thirties;* chapter 14, Franklin L. Ford, "Three Observers in Berlin: Rumbold, Dodd, and Francois-Poncet," esp. 447–60, puts Dodd in perspective. See also Martha Dodd, *Through Embassy Eyes,* and William E. Dodd Jr. and Martha Dodd, *Ambassador Dodd's Diary.* Dodd's last diary entry in Germany is dated 26 December 1937. He adds an entry dated 20 September 1938 in which he says he did not keep a daily account since he left Berlin. He reports the death of his wife from a heart attack on 28 May 1938 in their home in Round Hill, Virginia (444–46).

32. Charles A. Beard in his introduction to William E. Dodd Jr. and Martha Dodd, *Ambassador Dodd's Diary,* ix–xii. It may seem odd to the general reader that an American scholar went to Leipzig to write about Jefferson. But in 1900 American graduate programs were new, while German universities were enormously prestigious, not least for "scientific history." See also Ford, "Three Observers in Berlin," n. 31.

33. Ford, "Three Observers in Berlin," 449–50.

34. William E. Dodd Jr. and Martha Dodd, *Ambassador Dodd's Diary.*

35. Ford, "Three Observers in Berlin," 452–55.

36. William E. Dodd Jr. and Martha Dodd, *Ambassador Dodd's Diary.*

37. "Air Intelligence Activities," in *Berlin Alert,* 79.

38. Transcript and tape of interview, Katharine Smith with Rick Eiserman, 22 June 1992, in author's possession.

39. "My Life," 84–86.

40. Ibid., 88–89.

12. Hitler Arms, Smith Reports

1. TSP, Box 2, HI: "Facts" typescript, 80. Pages 77–105 of the 155-page typescript contain the new material Smith added that would be of interest to scholars. Pages 79–91 are from his 1945 sworn statement made for the War Crimes Commission. His 1 November 1937 estimate of the German Air Force is on page 93–98. Subsequent citations to page numbers in this source are given in this chapter in parentheses in the text.

2. For the Marshall-Smith correspondence, see Marshall, *The Papers of George Catlett Marshall*, vol. 1, *The Soldierly Spirit, December 1880–June 1939*, 479, 482–84, 670. See also Pogue, *George C. Marshall: Education of a General*, 317–49. The succeeding two Pogue volumes cover the period 1939–1945. For Marshall's reorganization of the General Staff, see Hewes, *From Root to McNamara*, 57–103.

3. Hjalmar Schacht was a financier who served as head of the Reichsbank under both the Republic and Hitler, and was Minister of Economy. He was later sent to a concentration camp for his alleged part in a plot against Hitler's life. After the war, he was tried and acquitted by the tribunal at Nuremberg.

4. See Wilson, *Diplomat between Wars*. Wilson was an experienced diplomat as well as being an interesting man. He wrote, for example, that "the Catholic Church had then and possibly has now [Wilson was writing in 1941] the best information service in Europe" (27) and that "economic distress from 1930 to 1933 was probably as potent a factor as policy in bringing the Germany we see today" (102); and he found it almost touching that the Germans were unable to understand how the outside world hated them after the Great War.

5. Smith is incorrect in stating that Oshima was executed. In fact he was convicted, sentenced to life imprisonment, paroled in 1955, and died of natural causes in 1975.

13. Smith's Trojan Horse

1. Smith, *Berlin Alert*, 75. See ibid., 75–166, for "Air Intelligence Activities, Office of the Military Attaché, American Embassy, Berlin, Germany, August 1935–April 1939." The "General Estimate as of November 1, 1937" (114–18) is the intelligence coup made possible by Smith's use of Lindbergh to penetrate the Luftwaffe.

2. Ibid., 77.

3. Ibid., 76.

4. Ibid., 79.

5. Ibid., 76.

6. Arnold, *Global Mission*, 188–89.

7. *Berlin Alert*, 84.

8. Ibid., 87.

9. Kay Smith, "My Life," 89. TSP, Box 6, HI.

10. Ibid., 90–91.

11. *Berlin Alert*, 87.

12. The letter and Lindbergh's response are found in ibid., 89–90 and 91–92.

13. Ibid., 92–94.

14. Quoted in ibid., 95.

15. The German designation of the aircraft was Bf-109. Later models, such as the ME 262, carried the "ME" designation. However, Smith used "ME 109" in his report.

16. *Berlin Alert*, 99.

17. Ibid., 100–102.

18. Smith credits Udet "with shooting down over ninety enemy airplanes, the highest number of any pilot on either side." Historian Roger Cirillo, however, credits Udet with sixty-two confirmed kills, and von Richthofen with eighty (personal communication, 2012).

19. *Berlin Alert*, 104.

20. Ibid., 105–11.

21. See "Air Intelligence Activities," Report no. 15540, in ibid., 113–27. Smith later published it in *Air Power*, April 1963, and included it in his 1964 "Facts" typescript.

22. *Berlin Alert*, 118–19.

14. The Lindbergh-Smith Friendship

1. "Facts," in *Berlin Alert*, 29. Long Barn belonged to Harold Nicolson and Vita Sackville-West. He was a diplomat and author, she a poet and novelist; both were members of the Bloomsbury Group. Nicolson met Lindbergh while doing research to write the biography of Dwight Morrow, Anne's father. See *Portrait of a Marriage* (1973) by Harold and Vita's son Nigel Nicolson.

2. "Facts," in *Berlin Alert*, 29.

3. Ibid., 30.

4. "My Life," 91.

5. Ibid., 97.

6. Ibid., 94.

7. Ibid., 95.

8. Ibid., 96.

9. Ibid., 97.

10. Ibid., 98.

11. Ibid., 98–99. Anne Morrow Lindbergh describes the same scene in *The Flower and the Nettle*, her diaries and letters for 1936–1939 (98).

12. "My Life," 100.

13. Ibid., 101.

14. Lochner, *What about Germany?*, 31 (autobahn); 99, 100, and 106 (Hitler); and 62 (Schacht). Lochner's remark about Hitler addressing even a single interviewer as though addressing masses is echoed by a former follower, Otto Strasser, in *Flight from Terror*, who wrote, "It would have been easier for him to harangue, sway and persuade ten

thousand listeners than to carry on a logical discussion with one or two intelligent men" (32).

15. "My Life," 102.

16. Arnold, *Global Mission,* 187–89.

17. "My Life," 104.

18. Ibid., 105.

19. See Arnold, *Global Mission,* 280n15. See also Lee, *London Journal,* 410–11. Lee's widow gave Kay a copy of her husband's book, with this inscription: "To Kay Smith, who will understand, in loving remembrance of two gentlemen. S/Jeanette, Dec. 6, 1971." Lee did not like Lindbergh's noninterventionist views and distrusted him.

20. "My Life," 106.

21. A. Lindbergh, *Flower and the Nettle,* 185–87.

22. Ibid., 440.

15. Hitler Is Ready

1. A. Lindbergh, *Flower and the Nettle,* 234, 187.

2. Kay Smith, "My Life," 230. TSP, Box 6, HI.

3. "Facts," in *Berlin Alert,* 30.

4. Ibid., 30–31. See also letters between Smith and Marshall in Marshall, *The Papers of George Catlett Marshall,* vol. 1, *The Soldierly Spirit, December 1880–June 1939,* Marshall 16 December 1935 re: *Infantrie im Kampf,* 479; Smith 2 January 1936 re: changes in the German Army, 482–84; Marshall 8 December 1938 re: von Schell, Smith's next assignment after Berlin, and German air personnel. Marshall said in the last letter above, "I had G-2 ask the questions for me while I was head of War Plans Division."

5. "My Life," 204–5.

6. Ibid., 208. Kay gets it right. For a detailed and scholarly treatment, see Deutsch, *Hitler and His Generals.*

7. See Craig and Gilbert, *The Diplomats, 1919–1939,* 427, specifically Craig's essay on the Foreign Office, 406–436. See also Craig, *Germany 1866–1945,* for a succinct account of Hitler taking control of the instruments of power in Germany, 571–601.

8. "My Life," 213.

9. T. Taylor, *Munich,* 978.

10. "Air Intelligence Activities," in Smith, *Berlin Alert,* 75–166; quotation on 127.

11. See ibid., 129–38, for the top men in German aviation met by Lindbergh, Vanaman, and Smith.

12. Ibid., 138.

13. "My Life," 203. See also Wilson, *Diplomat between Wars.* Wilson

served in Berlin before the Great War, after the war during the Weimar Republic, and during the Hitler time. He was in Berne during World War I and in Paris for the peacemaking efforts immediately after the war.

14. Smith, *Berlin Alert,* 127.

15. Ibid., 127–28.

16. Ibid., 131–33.

17. Ibid., 133.

18. Ibid., 134. In "My Life," 235, Kay referred to "the fatal dinner."

19. Craig, *Germany, 1866–1945,* 631, citing Albert Speer's remark on 10 November 1938. See also Shirer, *The Rise and Fall of the Third Reich,* 430–33, for excerpts from the war trials in Nuremberg regarding responsibility and American reaction.

20. *Berlin Alert,* 134. Hessen, the editor of *Berlin Alert,* notes on p. 43 that Smith followed the custom common in military circles of referring to himself in the third person, either by name or title. William L. Shirer, unaware of Wilson's purpose in bringing Lindbergh and Goering together, called Lindbergh insensitive and ignorant "of what was going on in the world," joining a growing chorus of critics who vilified the aviator in the following years. Shirer, *Twentieth-Century Journey,* vol. 2, *The Nightmare Years, 1930–1940,* 238.

21. "My Life," 239, 245.

22. Lindbergh, letter to Smith, 31 May 1955, in Smith, *Berlin Alert,* 134.

23. Shirer, *The Rise and Fall of the Third Reich,* 433.

24. "My Life," 246. See Lipstadt, *Beyond Belief,* for a thorough account of how the story of Jewish persecution was told and how it was largely ignored. In a nutshell, "negative assessments of German life did not dispel the doubts of those who had not personally witnessed these developments" (37).

25. *Berlin Alert,* 134.

26. A. Lindbergh, *Flower and the Nettle,* 429.

27. "My Life," 251.

28. Ibid., 253.

29. C. Lindbergh, *Wartime Journals,* 143.

30. "My Life," 213–14.

31. Ibid., 220.

32. Ibid., 215.

33. A. Lindbergh, *Flower and the Nettle,* xxv, 84, 85, 95, 90, 93, 430, and 433.

34. Quoted in Berg, *Lindbergh,* 374–75.

16. Welcome Home

1. Smith's account of his diabetes and Marshall's intervention is most readily available in "Facts," in *Berlin Alert,* 30–32.

2. Ibid., 32.

3. Quoted in *Berlin Alert,* viii. See also Wedemeyer, *Wedemeyer Reports!* 39–41, 60–63.

4. Kirkpatrick, *An Unknown Future and a Doubtful Present,* 65–66, 71.

5. See Wedemeyer, *Wedemeyer on War and Peace,* 1–9, for Wedemeyer's Kriegsakademie experience and Smith's mentoring, 10–13, for the rationale for the Victory Plan.

6. MHI. AWC Curricula Archives Records Section, 236-D Germany, G-2 to P-3. Box 2, G-2 Information Digest, Military Attaché Reports, Germany, IG nos. 6300–6545; vol. 26, 26–27.

7. Ibid., Box 2. See Special Bulletin No. 3, 1 February 1940, "The German Campaign in Poland, 1 September–5 October 1939," a 61-page narrative with two maps, one an operational sketch of 1–16 September 1939, 53 and 52. See also an AY 1940 AWC lecture by Black on the Polish campaign in the AWC Curricula Archives.

8. Ibid., 55.

9. Ibid., 59.

10. "Facts," in *Berlin Alert,* 32.

11. Ibid., 32–33.

12. A. Lindbergh, *War Within and Without,* xvii.

13. Ibid., xvi–xvii.

14. C. Lindbergh, *Wartime Journals,* 184.

15. A. Lindbergh, *War Within and Without,* xvii.

16. Ibid., 56–57.

17. Ibid., 220–25.

18. The following letters and telegrams are all from the Franklin D. Roosevelt Library, Charles A. Lindbergh, OF 92, Box 1, folders 1933–41 and 1941.

19. "Facts," in *Berlin Alert,* 33.

20. Ibid., 34. Smith seems to have confused McCabe (G-2 from 1 July 1937 to 29 February 1940) and BG Sherman Miles (G-2 from 30 April 1940 to 31 January 1942).

21. A. Lindbergh, *War Within and Without,* 121. See also C. Lindbergh, *Wartime Journals,* 352.

22. "Facts," in *Berlin Alert,* 35. See above, n. 20. Miles, not McCabe, was G-2 at that time.

23. Ibid., 36.

24. G. Smith, *To Save a Nation,* 9. See also Duffy, *Lindbergh vs. Roosevelt,* which is decidedly pro-Lindbergh.

25. G. Smith, *To Save a Nation,* 169.

26. Langer, *The Undeclared War.* See also Doenecke, *From Isolation to War.*

27. G. Smith, *To Save a Nation,* 142; *New York Times,* 27 May 1938.

28. G. Smith, *To Save a Nation,* 178.

29. Ibid., 180.

30. Ibid., 176n58.

31. Ibid., 177. Smith's daughter, Katchen, emphasized how much it hurt her and her parents, then and later, to have her father, who had worked himself to near-exhaustion in Berlin, called a Nazi. Interview with Gole, 26 September 2011. See also Mosley, *Lindbergh.* Mosley points out that elected officials favoring isolation were defeated at the polls. "The isolationists had backed the wrong horse, and when you do that, you lose" (339). The Lindberghs bought a house in Darien, Connecticut, near the Smiths. Truman later encouraged Lindbergh to write a book about the Cold War, showing that his 1940–1941 prophecies were coming true. The British Empire *was* disintegrating, the Soviets *did* control half of Europe, U.S. presence *was* required to protect the other half, and "alien hordes were still knocking on Western Civilization's gate . . . America was in greater danger than ever before" (341).

32. "Facts," in *Berlin Alert,* 36.

17. Smith as "Strategicus"

1. Kay Smith, "My Life: The War Years, 1939–1946," 2 (TSP, Box 6, HI). This impression was confirmed in an interview by the author with the Smiths' daughter, Katchen, on 26 Sepember 2011. Katchen inherited the Stamford house when her aunt died.

2. "Facts," in *Berlin Alert,* 36–37. In the course of my research, I found that H. C. O'Neill (1879–1953), author of the book *The War for World Power* (1940), also used "Strategicus" as a pen name. Another use of Strategicus was found in *The Pakistan Army till 1965* by Agha Humayun Amin; see www.wodldcat.org/Pakistan-army-mi11965/ocic/45493199. In addition, there is a strategic consulting firm with that name: www.strategicus.ro/echipa_en.html.

3. TSP, Boxes 11 and 12, HI.

4. See Gole, *The Road to Rainbow,* for the evolution of American one-on-one Color Plans (48–78) to coalition-versus-coalition warfare plans, later called Rainbow (117–21).

5. TSP, Boxes 11 and 12, HI. Also available at MHI. Microfilm, Reel 44. *Army and Navy Journal,* 6 September 1941–29 August 1942.

6. Morison, *The Two-Ocean War,* 40.

7. In Showalter's review of *Operation Barbarossa and Germany's Defeat in the East* by David Stahel: *Journal of Military History* 74, no. 4 (October 2010): 1318–20.

8. Sakai, *Samurai!* The small corps of well-trained pilots was so reduced that Sakai flew missions after he lost one eye.

9. Drea, *Nomanhan,* 90.
10. "Facts," in *Berlin Alert,* 37.
11. Norway proved to be a large and constant drain on German resources. "At times, nearly a half-million men from the armed forces were tied up in Norway" (Lunde, *Hitler's Pre-Emptive War,* 550).
12. Kirkpatrick, *An Unknown Future and a Doubtful Present,* 101n41.
13. Thomas, *Ike's Bluff,* 3–4. He addresses precisely the dangers of the military-industrial complex and the national security state, a sophisticated treatment of guns versus butter.

18. Wartime Washington

1. "Facts," in *Berlin Alert,* 36–37.
2. See Brinkley, *Washington Goes to War,* for a well-told eyewitness account of the city's transformation. The "suitable apartment" was at 2800 Wooley Road.
3. "Facts," in *Berlin Alert,* 36–37. Smith is making a distinction here between the Regular Army list and non-Regulars—Reservists and National Guardsmen of the National Army—a distinction that mattered to Regulars.
4. Ibid., 37.
5. Kay Smith, "My Life," 28. TSP, Box 6, HI.
6. Ibid., 24.
7. Ibid., 15.
8. Ibid., 21.
9. Ibid. In the introduction to his biography of Mencken, Manchester describes a lunch he had with Mencken in 1947, during which Mencken referred to "Roosevelt's War" (xiii).
10. Beck, "Hitler's Ambivalent Attaché" (PhD diss., Georgetown University, 1977), duel, 48–49; Lee and Freeman, 121–22; Eaker, 122 and n. 65. (Beck's dissertation was published in 2005 under the same title, but page references here and below are from the dissertation.)
11. Ibid., 163 and n. 72.
12. Ibid., 184.
13. Ibid., 277 and n. 15.
14. Ibid., 278–79.
15. Ibid., 290 and n. 42.
16. Kay Smith, "My Life," 29.
17. Ibid., 33.
18. Ibid., 124–25.
19. "Facts," in *Berlin Alert,* 31–42.
20. Ibid., 38.
21. "My Life," 47.

22. "Facts," in *Berlin Alert*, 39.
23. Ibid., 40.
24. Ibid., 40–41.
25. Ibid., 42.
26. A note from Deutsch to Rick Eiserman, postmarked 16 April 1990, accompanied the Deutsch review and a typescript of the Ambrose introduction. All are in the possession of the current writer. In an interview conducted by Eiserman on 29 March 1990, Deutsch, who had been in Germany to interview German generals from World War I, described several direct contacts with Ambassador William Dodd and Truman Smith in 1935–1936 in the American Embassy.
27. Rick Eiserman provided me with a photocopy of Baruch's 13 June 1945 letter.

19. The Road to German Rearmament

1. Kay Smith, "My Life," 41. TSP, Box 6, HI.
2. Ibid., 125. Daughter Katchen, in a 26 September 2011 interview with Gole, suggested that there was a period during which Truman suffered "depression"; but, she said, the birth of his granddaughters snapped him out of it. He was a doting father and grandfather, noting with great pride the physical and mental growth of Katharine (Kitty) and Phyllis (Lissy).
3. The note is dated 30 December 1989. The correspondence cited in this chapter, unless otherwise indicated, can be found in TSP, HI. (The inventory of the Truman Smith Papers identifies correspondence by box and folder.)
4. TSP, Box 12, HI.
5. Gaddis, *We Now Know*, 119.
6. Ibid., 1.
7. McGeehan, *The German Rearmament Question*, xi, 68, 69.
8. Birtle, *Rearming the Phoenix*, 19.
9. Large, *Germans to the Front*, 1–2.
10. Ibid., 243.
11. Ibid., 245.
12. TSP, HI (see note 3 above). German letters to Smith, about the time of German rearmament, include, among others: Blumentritt, 2 September 1955, 17 October 1955, and 7 December 1955; Hesse, 4 November 1955; Schwerin, 5 December 1955 and 25 January 1956; Speidel, 3 May 1955 and 8 December 1955. American letters to Smith include: John J. McCloy, 1 and 29 November 1954. Letters from G-2 to Smith in this period are dated 8 April 1955, 18 May 1955, 14 September 1955, 3 January 1956, and 16 March 1956.

13. See Gole, "Leadership from Within," 83–89.

14. MHI, John A. Heintges Papers, OH, 472–73.

15. Ibid., 481.

16. Smelser and Davies, *The Myth of the Eastern Front,* 3. See also Trauschweitzer, *The Cold War U.S. Army,* which argues that the buildup of German forces was critical to the forward defense posture of the Alliance (45, 100–101). See also W. Nelson, *Germany Rearmed,* written in a popular style by a person who knew Germany well and was optimistic about its future.

20. Politics, Travel, and Writing

1. Unless indicated otherwise, the correspondence referenced in this chapter is found in TSP, HI.

2. The current writer served in the 10th Special Forces Group in Germany in the mid-1960s and estimates that some 10 percent to 15 percent of the group's men were "Lodge Act" soldiers. See note 3 below. See also Partial Text of Truman Smith's Broadcast on Station WEVD Foreign Affairs Round Table, Friday March [unreadable], 1948—10: 00 to 10:30 PM, Smith Papers, Hoover Institution. Smith's lead sentence reads: "In my opinion the United States should organize a Foreign Legion at once." The source of personnel would be the Displaced Persons Camps in Europe and other territories under American control in Europe and Asia. Smith again proposed the creation of a foreign legion during a debate with Socialist leader Norman Thomas on WEVD, New York [date obscured, 1948 or 1949].

3. See Carafano, "Mobilizing Europe's Stateless," for various schemes in the post–World War II period to use displaced persons in the U.S. Army. Senator Henry Cabot Lodge of Massachusetts was the driving force behind what became known as the Lodge Act—Public Law 597, "An act to provide for the enlistment of aliens in the Regular Army," 2d Session, 81st Congress, passed on 30 June 1950. Smith credited Luce and her successor, Congressman John Davis Lodge of Connecticut (not to be confused with the Massachusetts senator) with the legislation cited in the text. See also Mayer to Smith letter, 8 December 1967: Mayer refers to Smith's suggestion to raise a division of Ghurkas and the creation of an Asian-American "Special Asian force."

4. "Facts," in *Berlin Alert,* 40–41.

5. Kay Smith, "My Life," 102, 122, 123. TSP, Box 6, HI. Kay wrote twenty-one pages to describe the first New Mexico visit; Truman did it in a paragraph.

6. In the summer of 2011, I exchanged emails with Katchen Coley in Middletown, Connecticut, and her daughters Katharine (Kitty) in Texas and Phyllis (Lissy) in Utah, in order to obtain family photos.

7. "Notes on a Lazy Winter," TSP, Box 12, HI.

8. "A Summer at a Montana Dude Ranch," TSP, Box 12, HI.

9. "Jungling as a Winter Sport," TSP, Box 12, HI. Phyllis (Lissy) Coley had just returned from two months at a field camp in French Guiana when she responded (positively!) by email on 5 August 2011 to my request for photos of her mother and grandparents. Clearly, one Smith-Coley is still digging.

10. "Latin America Cruise," TSP, Box 12, HI. Perhaps related to the Smiths' wholehearted support of birth control is a story that Katchen reported, with amusement, of how surprised young people were to see Kay, then over ninety years old, not only vigorously participating in a women's rights demonstration in Washington, but leading it! Gole interview with Katchen, 26 September 2011.

11. "Not Much Rain in Spain," TSP, Box 12, HI.

12. Smith's six articles on the Bundeswehr appeared on 13 April, 27 April, 4 May, 15 May, 5 June, and 19 June 1964. They were originally three letters from Truman to Katchen described in chapter 21.

21. Retrospective and a Graceful Exit

1. The documents and correspondence cited in the narrative in this chapter by date, unless otherwise indicated, are found in TSP, HI.

2. Gay, *The Dilemma of Democratic Socialism*, 7.

3. Grosser, *Germany in Our Time* (first published as *Deutschlandbilanz*, Munich: Carl Hauser Verlag, 1970), "Federal Cabinets, 1949–69," 170–173.

4. I spent over ten years between 1961 and 1985 in Germany, four of them as the assistant army attaché in Bonn (1973–1977). Smith's report was right on the mark: the Bundeswehr was very well armed and equipped, but most Germans and Germany's neighbors regarded it as a necessary evil. After World War II and into the twenty-first century, Europe—perhaps above all Germany—seems to have decided, "We ain't gonna war no more." On 1 July 2011, the Bundeswehr established the all-volunteer force after fifty-four years of conscription. See Koltermann, "Citizen in Uniform."

5. Twenty years after the Eiserman interview with Kay, on 26 September 2011 the Smiths' daughter, Katchen, emphasized to me how painful it was for her and for her parents when Truman was slandered, particularly since his dedication to duty had cost him his health. Katchen is an elegant lady. The apple did not fall far from the tree.

6. Historian Rick Eiserman gave me the twenty-page transcription, an audiocassette tape, and photographs taken 22 June 1992. They will be given to the Military History Institute upon completion of this work.

Selected Bibliography

Books

Ahamed, Liaquat. *Lords of Finance: The Bankers Who Broke the World.* New York: Penguin, 2009.

Allen, Henry T. *The Rhineland Occupation.* Indianapolis: Bobbs-Merrill Co., 1927.

Allen, William Sheridan. *The Nazi Seizure of Power: The Experience of a Single German Town, 1930–1935.* New York: Franklin Watts, 1973.

American Battle Monuments Commission. *3rd Division—Summary of Operations in the World War.* Washington, D.C.: U.S. Government Printing Office, 1944.

American Military History. Army Historical Series. Washington, D.C.: Center of Military History, U.S. Army, 1989.

Anders, Leslie. *Gentle Knight: The Life and Times of Major General Edwin Forrest Harding.* Kent, Ohio: Kent State University Press, 1985.

Armstrong, Hamilton Fish. *Peace and Counterpeace: From Wilson to Hitler; Memoirs of Hamilton Fish Armstrong.* New York: Harper and Row, 1971.

Arnold, H. H. *Global Mission.* New York: Harper and Brothers, 1949.

Ball, Harry P. *Of Responsible Command: A History of the U.S. Army War College.* Rev. ed. Carlisle Barracks, Pa.: Alumni Association of the United States Army War College, 1994.

Barnett, Correlli. *The Swordbearers: Supreme Command in the First World War.* New York: William Morrow and Co., 1964.

Beck, Alfred M. *Hitler's Ambivalent Attaché: Lt. Gen. Friedrich von Boetticher in America, 1933–1941.* Washington, D.C.: Potomac Books, 2005.

Bekker, Cajus. *The Luftwaffe War Diaries.* Translated and edited by Frank Ziegler. New York: Ballantine Books, 1969.

Bendersky, Joseph W. *The "Jewish Threat": Anti-Semitic Politics of the U.S. Army.* New York: Basic Books, 2000.

Berg, A. Scott. *Lindbergh.* New York: G. P. Putnam's Sons, 1998.

Berghahn, V. R. *Modern Germany: Society, Economy, and Politics in the Twentieth Century.* Cambridge: Cambridge University Press, 1982.

Bidwell, Bruce W. *History of the Military Intelligence Divsion, Department of the Army General Staff, 1775–1941.* Frederick, Md.: University Publications of America, 1986.

Birtle, A. J. *Rearming the Phoenix: U.S. Military Assistance to the Federal Republic of Germany, 1950–1960.* New York: Garland, 1991.

Bloch, Marc. *Memoirs of War, 1914–1915.* Translated by Carole Fink. Ithaca, N.Y.: Cornell University Press, 1980.

Boyd, Carl. *The Extraordinary Envoy: General Hiroshi Oshima and Diplomacy in the Third Reich, 1934–1939.* Washington, D.C.: University Press of America, 1980.

Bracher, Karl Dietrich. *The German Dictatorship: The Origins, Structure, and Effects of National Socialism.* New York: Praeger Publishers, 1970.

Brinkley, David. *Washington Goes to War.* New York: Knopf, 1988.

Bullock, Alan. *Hitler: A Study in Tyranny.* Completely rev. ed. New York: Harper Torchbooks, 1964.

Campbell, James. *The Ghost Mountain Boys.* New York: Crown, 2007.

Carr, Edward Hallett. *German-Soviet Relations between the Two World Wars, 1919–1939.* New York: Harper Torchbooks, 1966.

Carr, William. *Arms, Autarky, and Aggression: A Study in German Foreign Policy, 1933–1939.* New York: W. W. Norton and Co., 1973.

———. *A History of Germany, 1815–1945.* 2nd ed. New York: St. Martin's Press, 1979.

Carsten, F. L. *The Reichswehr and Politics: 1918–1933.* Berkeley: University of California Press, 1973.

Cole, Wayne S. *America First: The Battle against Intervention, 1940–1941.* Madison: University of Wisconsin Press, 1953.

———. *Charles Lindbergh and the Battle against American Intervention in World War II.* New York: Harcourt Brace Jovanovich, 1974.

Conze, Werner. *The Shaping of the German Nation: A Historical Analysis.* New York: St. Martin's Press, 1979.

Corum, James S. *The Roots of Blitzkrieg: Hans von Seeckt and German Military Reform.* Lawrence: University Press of Kansas, 1992.

Craig, Gordon A. *From Bismarck to Adenauer: Aspects of German Statecraft.* Rev. ed. New York: Harper Torchbooks, 1965.

———. *The Germans.* New York: G. P. Putnam's Sons, 1982.

———. *Germany, 1866–1945.* Oxford: Oxford University Press, 1978.

———. *NATO and the New German Army.* Policy Memorandum no. 8. Princeton, N.J.: Center of International Studies, Princeton University, 1955.

———. *The Politics of the Prussian Army, 1640–1945.* New York: Oxford University Press, 1964.

———. *War, Politics, and Diplomacy: Selected Essays.* New York: Frederick A. Praeger, 1966.

Craig, Gordon A., and Felix Gilbert, eds. *The Diplomats, 1919–1939.* Vol. 2: *The Thirties.* New York: Atheneum, 1967.

Dahrendorf, Ralf. *Society and Democracy in Germany.* Garden City, N.Y.: Doubleday and Co., 1967.

Davidson, Eugene. *The Making of Adolf Hitler.* New York: Macmillan, 1977.

Dehio, Ludwig. *Germany and World Politics in the Twentieth Century.* New York: W. W. Norton and Co., 1959.

Deist, Wilhelm. *The Wehrmacht and German Rearmament*. Toronto: University of Toronto Press, 1981.

Deutsch, Harold C. *The Conspiracy against Hitler in the Twilight War*. Minneapolis: University of Minnesota Press, 1968.

———. *Hitler and His Generals: The Hidden Crisis, January–June 1938*. Minneapolis: University of Minnesota Press, 1974.

Dodd, Martha. *Through Embassy Eyes*. New York: Garden City Publishing Co., 1940.

Dodd, William E., Jr., and Martha Dodd, eds. *Ambassador Dodd's Diary, 1933–1938*. New York: Harcourt, Brace and Co., 1941.

Doenecke, Justus D., and John E. Wilz. *From Isolation to War, 1931–1941*. Wheeling, Ill.: Harlan Davidson, 2003.

Drea, Edward J. *Nomanhan: Japanese-Soviet Tactical Combat, 1939*. Leavenworth Papers no. 2. Fort Leavenworth, Kans.: Combat Studies Institute, U.S. Command and General Staff College, 1981.

Duffy, James P. *Lindbergh vs. Roosevelt: The Rivalry That Divided America*. Washington, D.C.: Regnery Publishing, 2010.

Easton, Laird McLeod. *The Red Count: The Life and Times of Harry Kessler*. Berkeley: University of California Press, 2002.

Ehlers, Robert S. *Targeting the Third Reich: Air Intelligence and the Allied Bombing Campaigns*. Lawrence: University Press of Kansas, 2009.

Evans, Richard J. *The Coming of the Third Reich*. New York: Penguin Books, 2005.

Eyck, Erich. *A History of the Weimar Republic*. New York: John Wiley and Sons, 1963.

Fest, Joachim C. *The Face of the Third Reich: Portraits of the Nazi Leadership*. New York: Pantheon Books, 1970.

———. *Hitler*. New York: Harcourt Brace Jovanovich, 1974.

Forester, C. S. *The General*. Boston: Little, Brown, 1936.

Friedrich, Otto. *Before the Deluge: A Portrait of Berlin in the 1920s*. New York: Harper and Row, 1972.

Gaddis, John Lewis. *We Now Know: Rethinking Cold War History*. Oxford: Oxford University Press, 1998.

Gatzke, Hans W. *Germany and the United States: A "Special Relationship"?* Cambridge, Mass.: Harvard University Press, 1980.

———. *Stresemann and the Rearmament of Germany*. New York: W. W. Norton and Co., 1969.

Gay, Peter. *The Dilemma of Democratic Socialism*. New York: Collier Books, 1962.

Gerard, James W. *My Four Years in Germany*. New York: Grosset and Dunlap, 1917.

Gole, Henry G. *General William E. DePuy: Preparing the Army for Modern War*. Lexington: University Press of Kentucky, 2008.

———. *The Road to Rainbow: Army Planning for Global War, 1934–1940.* Annapolis, Md.: Naval Institute Press, 2003.

Graves, Robert, and Alan Hodge. *The Long Week-End: A Social History of Great Britain*, 1918–1939. New York: W. W. Norton and Co., 1963.

Grosser, Alfred. *Germany in Our Time: A Political History of the Postwar Years.* Harmondsworth, U.K.: Penguin Books, 1970.

Grunberger, Richard. *The 12-Year Reich: A Social History of Nazi Germany, 1933–1945.* New York: Ballantine Books, 1972.

Halperin, S. William. *Germany Tried Democracy: A Political History of the Reich from 1918 to 1933.* New York: W. W. Norton and Co., 1965.

Handbook on German Military Forces. Baton Rouge: Louisiana State University Press, 1990.

Hanfstaengl, Ernst. *Unheard Witness.* Philadelphia: J. B. Lippincott Co., 1957.

Hardach, Karl. *The Political Economy of Germany in the Twentieth Century.* Berkeley: University of California Press, 1980.

Hemenway, Frederic Vinton. *History of the Third Division United States Army in the World War for the Period Demember 1, 1917 to January 1, 1919.* [Cologne: Printed by M. Dumont Schauberg], 1919.

Henderson, Nevile. *Failure of a Mission.* New York: G. P. Putnam's Sons, 1940.

Hersh, Burton. *The Old Boys: The American Elite and the Origins of the CIA.* New York: Scribners, 1992.

Herwig, Holger H. *Politics of Frustration: The United States in German Naval Planning, 1889–1941.* Boston: Little, Brown, 1976.

Hewes, James, Jr. *From Root to McNamara: Army Organization and Administration, 1900–1963.* Special Studies Series. Washington, D.C.: U.S. Army Center of Military History, 1975.

Hoffman, Peter. *The History of the German Resistance, 1933–1945.* Cambridge, Mass.: MIT Press, 1977.

Holborn, Hajo. *A History of Modern Germany, 1840–1945.* New York: Alfred A. Knopf, 1969.

———. *The Political Collapse of Europe.* New York: Alfred A. Knopf, 1951.

Homze, Edward L. *Arming the Luftwaffe: The Reich Air Ministry and the German Aircraft Industry, 1919–39.* Lincoln: University of Nebraska Press, 1976.

Ickes, Harold L. *The Secret Diary of Harold L. Ickes.* Vol. 1, *The First Thousand Days, 1933–1936.* New York: Simon and Schuster, 1953–1954.

Infantry in Battle. 2nd ed. Washington, D.C.: The Infantry Journal, 1939. Reprinted by the USACGSC. [First edition, 1934.]

Irving, David. *The War Path: Hitler's Germany, 1933–1945.* New York: The Viking Press, 1978.

Jäckel, Eberhard. *Hitler's World View: A Blueprint for Power.* Cambridge, Mass.: Harvard University Press, 1981.

Kaufmann, William W., ed. *Military Policy and National Security.* Princeton, N.J.: Princeton University Press, 1956.

Kershaw, Ian. *Hitler, 1889–1936: Hubris.* New York: W. W. Norton, 1998.

Kirkpatrick, Charles E. *An Unknown Future and a Doubtful Present: Writing the Victory Plan of 1941.* Washington, D.C.: Center of Military History, United States Army, 1990.

Kitchen, Martin. *A Military History of Germany: From the Eighteenth Century to the Present Day.* London: Weidenfeld and Nicolson, 1975.

Klein, Burton H. *Germany's Economic Preparations for War.* Cambridge, Mass.: Harvard University Press, 1959.

Knorr, Klaus, ed. *NATO and American Security.* Princeton, N.J.: Princeton University Press, 1959.

Kochan, Lionel. *The Struggle for Germany, 1914–1945.* New York: Harper Torchbooks, 1963.

Kreidberg, Marvin A., and Merton G. Henry. *History of Military Mobilization in the United States Army, 1775–1945.* Department of the Army Pamphlet no. 20–212. Washington, D.C.: Department of the Army, 1955.

Langer, William L., ed. *An Encyclopedia of World History.* Boston: Houghton Mifflin, 1980.

———. *The Undeclared War, 1940–1941.* New York: Harper, 1953.

Large, David Clay. *Germans to the Front: West German Rearmament in the Adenauer Era.* Chapel Hill: University of North Carolina Press, 1996.

Larrabee, Eric. *Commander in Chief: Franklin Delano Roosevelt, His Lieutenants, and Their War.* New York: Harper and Row, 1987.

Larson, Erik. *In the Garden of Beasts: Love, Terror, and an American Family in Hitler's Berlin.* New York: Crown, 2011.

Lawrence, Joseph Douglas. *Fighting Soldier: The AEF in 1918.* Boulder: Colorado Associated University Press, 1985.

Lee, Raymond E. *The London Journal of General Raymond E. Lee, 1940–1941.* Edited by James Leutze, with a foreword by Dean Acheson. Boston: Little, Brown, 1971.

Leiser, Erwin. *Nazi Cinema.* New York: Collier Books, 1975.

Lewin, Ronald. *Hitler's Mistakes.* New York: William Morrow and Co., 1984.

Lindbergh, Anne Morrow. *The Flower and the Nettle: Diaries and Letters of Anne Morrow Lindbergh, 1936–1939.* New York: Harcourt Brace and Co., 1976.

———. *War Within and Without: Diaries and Letters of Anne Morrow Lindbergh, 1939–1944.* New York: Harcourt Brace and Co., 1995.

Lindbergh, Charles A. *The Wartime Journals of Charles A. Lindbergh.* New York: Harcourt, Brace, Jovanovich, 1970.

Linn, Brian McAllister. *The Philippine War, 1899–1902.* Lawrence: University Press of Kansas, 2000.

Lipstadt, Deborah E. *Beyond Belief: The American Press and the Coming of the Holocaust, 1933–1945.* New York: Free Press, 1986.

Lochner, Louis P., ed. *The Goebbels Diaries.* New York: Popular Library, 1948.

———. *Herbert Hoover and Germany.* New York: Macmillan, 1960.

———. *What about Germany?* New York: Dodd, Mead, 1942.

Lubrich, Oliver, ed. *Travels in the Reich, 1933–1945: Foreign Authors Report from Germany.* Chicago: University of Chicago Press, 2010.

Lunde, Henrik O. *Hitler's Preemptive War: The Battle for Norway, 1940.* Philadelphia: Casement, 2008.

Lutz, Ralph Haswell. *The German Revolution, 1918–1919.* Stanford, Calif.: Stanford University Press, 1922.

Luvaas, Jay, ed. *Dear Miss Em: General Eichelberger's War in the Pacific, 1942–1945.* Westport, Conn.: Greenwood Press, 1972.

Mahnken, Thomas G. *Uncovering Ways of War: U.S. Intelligence and Foreign Military Innovation, 1918–1941.* Ithaca, N.Y.: Cornell University Press, 2002.

Manchester, William. *Disturber of the Peace: The Life of H. L. Mencken.* Amherst: University of Massachusetts Press, 1986.

———. *The Last Lion: Winston Spencer Churchill, Alone, 1932–1940.* Boston: Little, Brown and Co., 1988.

Mann, Golo. *The History of Germany since 1789.* New York: Frederick A. Praeger, 1968.

Mantoux, Etienne. *The Carthaginian Peace: Or, the Economic Consequences of Mr. Keynes.* [Pittsburgh]: University of Pittsburgh Press, 1952.

Marshall, George C. *Memoirs of My Services in the World War: 1917–1918.* Boston: Houghton Mifflin Co., 1976.

———. *The Papers of George Catlett Marshall.* Edited by Larry I. Bland. Vol. 1, *The Soldierly Spirit, December 1880–June 1939.* Baltimore: Johns Hopkins University Press, 1981.

———. *The Papers of George Catlett Marshall.* Edited by Larry I. Bland. Vol. 2, *We Cannot Delay, July 1, 1939–December 6, 1941.* Baltimore: Johns Hopkins University Press, 1986.

Mau, Hermann, and Helmut Krausnick. *German History, 1933–1945: An Assessment by German Historians.* London: Oswald Wolff, 1971.

May, Ernest R. *Knowing One's Enemies: Intelligence Assessment before the Two World Wars.* Princeton: Princeton University Press, 1984.

McGeehan, Robert. *The German Rearmament Question: American Diplomacy and European Defense after World War II.* Urbana: University of Illinois Press, 1971.

Mellenthin, F. W. von. *Panzer Battles: A Study of the Employment of Armor in the Second World War.* New York: Ballantine Books, 1971.

Meyer, Henry Cord, ed. *The Long Generation: Germany from Empire to Ruin, 1913–1945.* New York: Walker, [1973].

Moose, George L. *Nazi Culture: Intellectual, Cultural, and Social Life in the Third Reich.* New York: Grosset and Dunlap, 1968.

Morison, Samuel Eliot. *The Two-Ocean War: A Short History of the United States Navy in the Second World War.* Boston: Little, Brown and Co., 1963.

Mosley, Leonard. *Lindbergh: A Biography.* Garden City, N.Y.: Doubleday and Co., 1976.

Mott, T. Bentley. *Twenty Years as Military Attaché.* New York: Oxford University Press, 1937.

Mowrer, Edgar Ansel. *Germany Puts the Clock Back.* Rev. ed. Middlesex, U.K.: Penguin Books, 1939.

———. *Triumph and Turmoil: A Personal History of Our Time.* New York: Weybright and Talley, 1968.

Murphy, Robert. *Diplomat among Warriors.* New York: Pyramid Books, 1965.

Muth, Jorg. *Command Culture: Officer Education in the U.S. Army and the German Armed Forces, 1901–1940, and the Consequences for World War II.* Denton: University of North Texas Press, 2011.

Nagorski, Andrew. *Hitlerland: American Eyewitnesses to the Nazi Rise to Power.* New York: Simon and Schuster, 2012.

Nelson, Keith L. *Victors Divided: America and the Allies in Germany, 1918–1923.* Berkeley: University of California Press, 1975.

Nelson, Walter Henry. *Germany Rearmed.* New York: Simon and Schuster, 1972.

Nicholls, A. J. *Weimar and the Rise of Hitler.* 2nd ed. New York: St. Martin's Press, 1979.

Nicolson, Nigel, ed. *Harold Nicolson: Diaries and Letters, 1930–1939.* New York: Atheneum, 1966.

———. *Portrait of a Marriage.* New York: Atheneum, 1973.

Olson, Lynne. *Those Angry Days: Roosevelt, Lindbergh, and America's First Fight over World War II, 1939–1941.* New York: Random House, 2013.

Pappas, George S. *Prudens Futuri: The U.S. Army War College, 1901–1967.* Carlisle Barracks, Pa.: Alumni Association of the U.S. Army War College, 1967.

Peukert, Detlev J. K. *Inside Nazi Germany: Conformity, Opposition, and Racism in Everyday Life.* New Haven: Yale University Press, 1987.

Plotkin, Abraham. *An American in Hitler's Berlin: Abraham Plotkin's Diary.* Urbana: University of Illinois Press, 2009.

Pogue, Forrest C. *George C. Marshall: Education of a General, 1880–1939.* New York: Viking Press, 1963.

———. *George C. Marshall: Ordeal and Hope, 1939–1942.* New York: Viking Press, 1965.

———. *George C. Marshall: Organizer of Victory, 1943–1945.* New York: Viking Press, 1973.

———. *George C. Marshall: Statesman, 1945–1959.* New York: Viking Press, 1986.

Presseisen, Ernst, L. *Germany and Japan: A Study in Totalitarian Diplomacy, 1933–1941.* New York: Howard Fertig, 1969.

Remak, Joachim, ed. *The Nazi Years: A Documentary History.* Englewood Cliffs, N.J.: Prentice-Hall, 1969.

Rich, Norman. *Hitler's War Aims: Ideology, the Nazi State, and the Course of Expansion.* New York: W. W. Norton and Co., 1973.

Ross, Steven T., ed. *American War Plans, 1919–1941.* New York: Garland, 1992.

Ross, Walter Sanford. *The Last Hero: Charles A. Lindbergh.* New York: Harper and Row, 1967.

Rupieper, Hermann-Josef. *Der besetzte Verbündete: die Amerikanische Deutschlandpolitik 1949–1955.* Opladen: Westdeutscher Verlag, 1991.

———. *The Cuno Government and Reparations, 1922–1923: Politics and Economics.* The Hague: Martinus Hijhoff, 1979.

Sakai, Saburo. *Samurai!* Annapolis, Md.: Naval Institute Press, 1991.

Schell, Adolf von. *A Theoretical Study of State Control.* Koenigstein: Historical Division, European Command, 1949.

———. *Battle Leadership: Some Personal Experiences of a Junior officer of the German Army with Observations on Battle Tactics and the Psychological Reactions of Troops in Campaign.* Fort Benning–Columbus, Ga.: Benning Herald, 1933. Reprinted by the Marine Corps Association, Quantico, Va., 1982.

———. *Kampf gegen Panzerwagen.* Oldenburg, i.O.: G. Stalling, 1936. English translation typescript, *Anti-tank Operations* [Fort Leavenworth, Kans.?], 1936.

Schifferle, Peter J. *America's School for War: Fort Leavenworth, Officer Education, and Victory in World War II.* Lawrence: University Press of Kansas, 2010.

Schoenbaum, David. *Hitler's Social Revolution: Class and Status in Nazi Germany, 1933–1939.* New York: Doubleday and Co., 1967.

Shartle, Samuel G. *Spa, Versailles, Munich: An Account of the Armistice Commission.* Philadelphia: Dorrance and Co., 1941.

Shirer, William L. *The Rise and Fall of the Third Reich: A History of Nazi Germany.* New York: Simon and Schuster, 1960.

———. *Twentieth-Century Journey: A Memoir of a Life and the Times.* Vol. 2, *The Nightmare Years, 1930–1940.* Boston: Little, Brown and Co., 1984.

Simpson, Amos E. *Hjalmar Schacht in Perspective.* The Hague: Mouton, 1969.

Smelser, Ronald, and Edward J. Davies II. *The Myth of the Eastern Front.* Cambridge: Cambridge University Press, 2008.

Smith, Geoffrey S. *To Save a Nation: American Countersubversives, the New Deal, and the Coming of World War II.* New York: Basic Books, 1973.

Smith, Howard K. *Last Train from Berlin*. New York: A. A. Knopf, 1942.

Smith, Truman. *Berlin Alert: The Memoirs and Reports of Truman Smith*. Edited and with an introduction by Robert Hessen. Stanford, Calif.: Hoover Institution Press, Stanford University, 1984.

Sontag, Raymond J. *A Broken World, 1919–1939*. New York: Harper and Row, 1972.

Speer, Albert. *Inside the Third Reich: Memoirs*. New York: Macmillan, 1970.

Speidel, Hans. *Invasion 1944: Rommel and the Normandy Campaign*. Chicago: Regnery, 1950.

Spiller, Roger J., ed. *Combined Arms in Battle since 1939*. Fort Leavenworth, Kans.: U.S. Army Command and General Staff College Press, 1992.

Stachura, Peter D. *Nazi Youth in the Weimar Republic*. Santa Barbara, Calif.: Clio Books, 1975.

Stilwell, Joseph Warren. *The Stilwell Papers*. Arranged and edited by Theodore H. White. New York: W. Sloane Associates, 1948.

Stoler, Mark A. *George C. Marshall, Soldier-Statesman of the American Century*. Boston: Twayne Publishers, 1989.

Strasser, Otto, and Michael Stern. *Flight from Terror*. New York: Robert M. McBride and Co., 1943.

Taylor, A. J. P. *The Course of German History: A Survey of the Development of Germany since 1815*. New York: Capricorn Books, 1962.

Taylor, Telford. *The March of Conquest: The German Victories in Western Europe, 1940*. New York: Simon and Schuster, 1958.

———. *Munich: The Price of Peace*. Garden City, N.Y.: Doubleday and Co., 1979.

Thomas, Evan. *Ike's Bluff: President Eisenhower's Secret Battle to Save the World*. New York: Little, Brown, and Co., 2012.

Toland, John. *Adolf Hitler*. 2 vols. Garden City, N.Y.: Doubleday and Co., 1976.

Trauschweizer, Ingo. *The Cold War U.S. Army: Building Deterrence for Limited War*. Lawrence: University Press of Kansas, 2008.

Tuchman, Barbara. *The Guns of August*. New York: Macmillan, 1962.

Turner, Henry Ashby, Jr. *German Big Business and the Rise of Hitler*. New York: Oxford University Press, 1985.

———, ed. *Nazism and the Third Reich*. [New York]: Quadrangle Books, 1972.

United States. Army. American Forces in Germany, 1918–1923. *American Military Government of Occupied Germany, 1918–1920: Report of the Officer in Charge of Civil Affairs, Third Army and American Forces in Germany*. 4 March 1920. [Also known as the Hunt Report.] Reprint, Washington, D.C.: U.S. Government Printing Office, 1943.

United States. War Department. *United States Military Intelligence* [*1917–1927*]. New York: Garland, 1978–1979.

Waite, Robert G. L., ed. *Hitler and Nazi Germany.* New York: Holt, Rinehart and Winston, 1965.

Wallace, Max. *The American Axis: Henry Ford, Charles Lindbergh, and the Rise of the Third Reich.* New York: St. Martin's Press, 2003.

Weber, Eugen. *Varieties of Fascism: Doctrine of Revolution in the Twentieth Century.* Princeton, N.J.: D. Van Nostrand, 1964.

Wedemeyer, Albert C. *Wedemeyer on War and Peace.* Edited with an introduction by Keith E. Eiler. Stanford, Calif.: Hoover Institution Press, Stanford University, 1987.

———. *Wedemeyer Reports!* New York: Henry Holt and Co., 1958.

Weinberg, Gerhard L. *The Foreign Policy of Hitler's Germany: Diplomatic Revolution in Europe, 1933–36.* Chicago: University of Chicago Press, 1970.

———. *The Foreign Policy of Hitler's Germany: Starting World War II, 1937–1939.* Chicago: University of Chicago Press, 1980.

Wilson, Hugh R. *Diplomat between Wars.* New York: Longmans, Green and Co., 1941.

Winks, Robin W. *Cloak and Gown: Scholars in the Secret War, 1939–1961.* New York: William Morrow and Co., 1987.

Wohl, Robert. *The Generation of 1914.* Cambridge, Mass.: Harvard University Press, 1979.

Zuckmayer, Carl. *Second Wind.* New York: Doubleday, Doran and Co., 1940.

Articles

Allen, C. B. " The Day FDR Tried to Bribe Lindbergh." *Pathway,* November 1970, 7–8.

———. "The Facts about Lindbergh." *Saturday Evening Post,* 28 December 1940, 12.

Campbell, Kenneth J. "Truman Smith: American Military Attache." *Intelligencer,* October 1998, 16–17.

Carafano, James Jay. "Mobilizing Europe's Stateless: America's Plan for a Cold War Army." *Journal of Cold War Studies* 1.2 (1999): 61–85.

Glantz, Mary. "An Officer and a Diplomat? The Ambiguous Position of Philip R. Faymonville and United States–Soviet Relations, 1941–1943." *Journal of Military History,* January 2008: 141–77.

Gole, Henry G. "Leadership from Within." *Military Review,* February 1973: 83–89.

Koltermann, Jens O. "Citizen in Uniform: Democratic Germany and the Changing Bundeswehr." *Parameters* 42.2 (Summer 2012): 108–26.

Rupieper, Herman J. "American Ambassador in Germany, 1922–1925." *International History Review,* October 1979: 490–508.

Schell, Adolf von. "Battle Field Psychology." *Illinois Guardsman,* June 1940: 1–13, 18.

———."The Battle of Villers." *Cavalry Journal,* January–February 1935: 48.

———. "A Typical Fight in Open Warfare." *Infantry Journal,* July–August 1931: 345.

———. "A Young Company Commander in a Rapidly Changing Situation." *Illinois Guardsman,* March 1940: 15–17.

Showalter, Dennis. Review of *Operation Barbarossa and Germany's Defeat in the East* by David Stahel. *Journal of Military History* 74, no. 4 (October 2010): 1318–20.

Smith, Truman. "The German General Staff Abdicates." *Coast Artillery Journal,* January–February 1946: 8–13.

———. "The Infamous Record of Soviet Espionage." *Reader's Digest,* August 1960: 36–42.

———. "Much Ado about Turkey." *Army and Navy Journal,* 29 November 1941: 358.

———. "Strategic Situation in the Pacific." *Army and Navy Journal,* 3 January 1942: 483.

———. "Supplies for Russia." *Army and Navy Journal,* 15 November 1941: 302.

———. "Wanted: More Mountain Troops." *Army and Navy Journal,* 20 December 1941: 446.

———. "What May America Expect from Russia?" *Army and Navy Journal,* 1 November 1941: 229.

Dissertations and Theses

Beck, Alfred M. "Hitler's Ambivalent Attaché: Lt. Gen. Friedrich von Boetticher in America, 1933–41." PhD diss., Georgetown University, 1977.

Hall, Karin W. "Truman Smith, United States Military Attaché: An Examination of His Career." Master's thesis, San Jose State University, 1992.

Koch, Scott Alan. "Watching the Rhine: U.S. Army Military Attaché Reports and the Resurgence of the German Army, 1933–1941." PhD diss., Duke University, 1990.

Trauschweizer, Ingo Wolfgang. "Creating Deterrence for Limited War: The U.S. Army and the Defense of West Germany, 1953–1982." PhD diss., University of Maryland, College Park, 2006.

Votaw, John F. "United States Military Attachés, 1885–1919." PhD diss., Temple University, 1991.

Handbooks

German Guns: Brief Notes and Range Tables for Allied Gunners. SHAEF/16527/2A/GCT/ARTY. London: Supreme Headquarters, Allied Expeditionary Force, July 1944.

German Military Training. Special Series no. 3. Washington, D.C.: War Department, Military Intelligence Service, 17 September 1942.

Handbook for Unit Commanders (Germany). Supreme Headquarters, Allied Expenditionary Force, 15 September 1944.

Handbook on German Military Forces. U.S. War Department and Supreme Headquarters Allied Expeditionary Force, with an introduction by Stephen E. Ambrose. Baton Rouge: Louisiana State University Press, 1990. [Republication of War Department Technical Manual TM-E 30–451, same title, dated 15 March 1945.]

Archives

Hoover Institution Archives, Stanford University, Stanford, California

Truman Smith Papers: correspondence, memoranda, reports, clippings, speeches, remarks, testimony, postcards, debates, reviews, articles (typescript and published), writings, newspaper columns, photographs, army service (commendations, decorations, orders, personnel file, retirement benefits), memoirs (Truman and Katharine A. H. Smith), intelligence reports, diary of Katharine. Electronic access: http://www.oac.cdib.org/findaid/ark:/13030/tf2h4n98v1.

George C. Marshall Foundation, Lexington, Virginia

Marshall correspondence with Truman Smith
Marshall correspondence with Forrest C. Pogue

United States Army Military History Institute, Carlisle Barracks, Carlisle, Pennsylvania

Papers and Oral Histories

Truman Smith. OCMH Collection includes his memoir, "Facts of Life," and wife Katharine Smith's memoir, "My Life"
Willis D. Crittenberger
Edward Davis
John A. Heintges
William C. Koenig
Sidney P. Spalding

Leroy W. Yarborough
Ivan D. Yeaton
United States Army War College Curricular Archives
World War I Survey, Veterans' Survey

Franklin D. Roosevelt Presidential Library and Museum, Hyde Park, New York

Lindbergh, Charles A., OF 92, Box 1, 1933–41, and Box 2, 1941–44 contain letters and telegrams to FDR regarding Lindbergh speaking against United States intervention in the European war in the period 1939 to 1941. Electronic access: http://www.fdrlibrary.marist.edu/archives/askthearchivist.html.

Yale University, Sterling Library, New Haven, Connecticut

Truman Smith Papers, Manuscripts and Archives, Guide to the Truman Smith Reports Collection, MS 405. Overview, Biographical sketch, Description of the Papers, Inventory. Gift of Truman Smith in 1957 and 1961. (The Truman Smith Papers are located in the Hoover Institution, Stanford University.)

Box 1: "Hitler and the National Socialists: Notebook and Report of Captain Truman Smith, Infantry, U.S. Army, Assistant Military Attache, Berlin, Germany, Describing a Visit to Munich from 15 to 22 November 1922" (notebook and typed transcript), Post 1924.

Reel 1: "Air Intelligence Activities, Office of the Military Attache, American Embassy, Berlin, Germany, August 1935–April 1939, with Special Reference to the Services of Colonel Charles A. Lindbergh, Ari Corps (Res.)" (typescript), 1954–1956.

Paul Palmer Papers, Gp. no. 387, Series 1, Box No. 1.

Interviews

Harold C. Deutsch with Rick Eiserman, 29 March 1990.
Katharine (Kay) Hollister Smith with Rick Eiserman, 22 June 1992.
Katharine (Kätchen) Smith Coley with Henry Gole, 26 September 2011.

Index